Astrology and Spiritual Awakening

Greg Bogart

First Edition Copyright 1994 by Greg Bogart
Published by Dawn Mountain Press

Second Edition Copyright 2014 by Greg Bogart
Published by American Federation of Astrologers

Portions of this book previously appeared in *The Mountain Astrologer, NCGR Journal, Aspects,* and *Considerations*.

No part of this book may be reproduced or transcribed in any form or by any means, electronic or mechanical, including photocopying or recording or by any information storage and retrieval system without written permission from the author and publisher, except in the case of brief quotations embodied in critical reviews and articles. Requests and inquiries may be mailed to: American Federation of Astrologers, Inc., 6535 S. Rural Road, Tempe, AZ 85283.

ISBN-10: 0-86690-651-7
ISBN-13: 978-0-86690-651-7

Cover Artwork: *Zodiac Time Space Continuum* by Patricia M. Bowers
www.patriciambowers.com

Cover Design: Jack Cipolla

Published by:
American Federation of Astrologers, Inc.
6535 S. Rural Road
Tempe, AZ 85283
www.astrologers.com

Printed in the United States of America

What Others Are Saying About Astrology and Spiritual Awakening

This valuable book explores the essential purpose of astrology: To serve as a beacon that can illuminate our individual road to enlightenment. I highly recommend this book to astrologers, psychologists, and other fellow travelers on the Path.—Dennis Harness, Ph.D., Director, Institute of Vedic Astrology

Brilliantly summarizes a transpersonal approach to astrology.—Stephanie Austin, review in *The Mountain Astrologer*

A ground-breaking book. All students will profit from reading an astrologer whose insights are backed up by thorough research and balanced judgment.—Tim Lyons, Review in *Planet Earth Magazine*

Such terms as 'personal growth' and 'transformation' are often just nice, fuzzy buzzwords behind which resides very little but more nice, fuzzy words. But as Bogart uses them, there's neither fuzz nor buzz, as he tells the reader exactly what he means by them. . . . Exceptionally straightforward. Well-done, fascinating, and highly recommended reading.—Ken Irving, review in *American Astrology*

Using dozens of examples, Greg Bogart provides a cosmic framework for understanding the crises, turning points, and challenges on the spiritual path of clients and of well-known personages. With writing that burns brightly, this cultural creative details these fascinating lives and, by book's end, as if by magic, leaves the reader warm in the glow of embers of understanding. This work is a transformative gift of the Spirit gently delivered via a therapist and astrologer devoted to Service.—Brad Kochunas, M.A., author of *The Astrological Imagination: Where Psyche and Cosmos Meet*

This is a spiritual self-help book. It teaches those who love astrology how to see their charts as a map for their spiritual path. It's also a good book for learning basic astrology. Greg conveys to the reader a wealth of valuable and precious information.—Arlan Wise, Organization of Professional Astrologers

If you're an astrologer who would like to more effectively guide yourself and your clients on a path of spiritual transformation, this greatly expanded edition of Dr. Bogart's book is the only one you'll need. The author's personal experiences as a long-time practitioner of meditation and yoga inform every page. I especially love the insights he offers on the growth potentials of Uranus, Neptune, and Pluto transits as seen through the lens of transpersonal astrology. This is a profound handbook for using astrology as an evolutionary tool in the 21st century.—Kate Sholly, *The Mountain Astrologer*

Books by Greg Bogart

In the Company of Sages

Planets in Therapy

Dreamwork and Self-Healing

Astrology and Meditation: The Fearless Contemplation of Change

Nine Stages of Spiritual Apprenticeship

Therapeutic Astrology

Finding Your Life's Calling

Acknowledgements

I'd like to thank Chakrapani Ullal, one of the world's great living astrologers, who has offered me so much encouragement since we first met in Bombay in 1978.

I thank Dane Rudhyar for corresponding with me for several years and inviting me to meet him in 1985, the last year of his life.

I'm grateful for the wisdom and generosity of my astrology teacher, Andres Takra, who taught me the craft during a nine month apprenticeship in Boulder, Colorado, during the 1981 Jupiter-Saturn conjunction in Libra.

Nancy Carleton, Jim Tucker, and Paul Hoffman deserve special thanks for their assistance in launching this book's first edition; I couldn't have completed this without them. I thank Kris Riske and the American Federation of Astrologers for their kind invitation to publish a new edition of this work. A bow of gratitude to Patricia Bowers for her radiant artwork. And I warmly thank Kate Sholly for her skillful editorial assistance; I value her wisdom and discernment. I also acknowledge Brad Kochunas for his suggestions and comments on the text.

I'm grateful to my beloved friends, mentors, and allies: Sid Aaronson, Rick Amaro, Stephanie Austin, Lynn Bell, Agneta Boorstein, Ken Bowser, Margaret Cahill, Nick Campion, Cathy Coleman, Robert Corre, Kitty Dahl, Maru Dana, Sangye Drolma, Robert Forte, Jennifer Freed, Nur Richard Gale, Rob Gellman, Margaret Gray, Ray Grasse, Dennis Harness, Dan Johnson, Alexandra Karacostas, John Damian Kennedy, David Kesten, Michael Lutin, A. T. Mann, Neil Marbell, Colleen Mauro, Michael Mayer, Michael Meyer, Nicki Michaels, Charles Mintz, Bob Mulligan, Gregory Nalbandian, Laura Nalbandian, Yvonne Paglia, Claude Palmer, Glenn Perry, Kim Phelps, Steve Pincus, Robert Powell, Leyla Rael Rudhyar, Jozef Slanda, Barbara Somerfield, Elizabeth Spring, Marcia Starck, Ena Stanley, Georgia Stathis, Richard Tarnas, Kay Taylor, Jonathan Tenney, Tem Tarriktar, Linea Van Horn, Stuart Walker, Barbara Morgan Winkler, and Arlan Wise. Thank you one and all.

I would like to offer special thanks to Shelley Jordan, a friend for more than thirty years who has been an ocean of encouragement; to Richard Cook, who, in a spirit of service and generosity, allowed me to conduct classes at his Sunrise Bookshop; and to my wife, Diana Syverud, the bright Sun in my life, the star I'm steering by.

Contents

Foreword	xi
Preface	xiii

Part I: Astrology and Spiritual Awakening

Astrology: A Language of Change	3
The Planets	3
Signs of the Zodiac	4
The Astrological Houses	7
Cycles	9
Interplanetary Aspects	10
Aspects of the Natal Sun	11
Transits	15
Progressions	19
Lunar Cycles, Aspects, and Transits	21
Saturn and the Practical Business of Life	24
Prediction, Destiny, and the Symbolic Attitude	25
The Influence of C. G. Jung on Modern Astrology	26
The Archetype of Time, and the Birth Chart as Archetype	28
Finding a Spiritual Path: The Twelve Yogas of the Zodiac	31
The Twelve Yogas of the Zodiac: A Model for Spiritual Development	32
Aries/Mars/First House: Prana: The Yoga of Identity, Vitality, Will, and Self-Assertion	35
Taurus/Venus/Second House: Karma: The Yoga of Action and Reward, Money, and Enjoyment of the Body	43
Gemini/Mercury/Third House: Mantra: The Yoga of Mind, Thought, and Speech	47
Cancer/Moon/Fourth House: Mama: The Yoga of Emotional Attachment, Caring, and Family	50
Leo/Sun/Fifth House: Ananda: The Yoga of Self-Expression, Creativity, and Joy	54

Virgo/Mercury/Sixth House: Viveka: The Yoga of Health, Discipline, and Apprenticeship	59
Libra/Venus/Seventh House: Bhakti: The Yoga of Love, Cooperation, and Relationship	62
Scorpio/Mars/Pluto/Eighth House: Shakti: The Yoga of Power, Sexuality, and Regeneration	69
Sagittarius/Jupiter/Ninth House: Jnana: The Yoga of Knowledge, Truth, and Philosophy	77
Capricorn/Saturn/Tenth House: Dharma: The Yoga of Mastery Through Accomplishment	84
Aquarius/Uranus/Eleventh House: Sangha: The Yoga of Groups, Community, and Organizations	88
Pisces/Neptune/Twelfth House: Moksa: The Yoga of Tranquility and Self-Realization	92

Part II: Transpersonal Astrology and the Path of Transformation

From Predictive to Humanistic Astrology — 105
   The Four Levels of Astrological Interpretation — 105
   The Ancient Attitude of Dread Toward the Planets — 110
   Humanistic Astrology — 111
   The Astrology of Meaning: Cyclical Awareness and Life Interpretation — 117
   A Humanistic Approach to a Saturn Transit — 118
   Example of a Transit to Natal Moon — 121

The Transpersonal Level of Chart Interpretation — 125
   Psychosynthesis, Meditation, Visualization, and the Act of Will — 128
   A Call to Transformation in Early Adulthood — 132
   An Astrology of Crisis and Transformation — 134
   A Turbulent Spiritual Metamorphosis — 136
   Outer Planet Rites of Passage — 140
   Uranus — 141
   Neptune — 147
   Neptune and Holotropic Consciousness — 149
   The Downside of Neptune — 149

Delusion or the Dawning of Enlightenment	150
Methods for Expansion: Meditation, Yoga, Pranayama	152
Neptune and Surrender	153
Pluto	155
Two Meditations on Death	157
Pluto: The Dynamic Ground and Regeneration in spirit	162

The Six Shaktis — 165

Para Shakti: Physical and Emotional Purification	167
Jnana Shakti: The Power of Knowledge and Eonic Wisdom	169
Ichcha Shakti: The Power of the Will	170
Maitrika Shakti: The Modes of Creative Activity	171
Kriya Shakti: Action Transformed Through Visualization	172
Kundalini Shakti, Self-Consecration, and Transpersonal Activity	174
From Karma to Dharma	176

Part III: Astrological Biographies of Spiritual Teachers

An Astrological Biography of Meher Baba — 181

An Astrological Biography of Bhagwan Rajneesh (Osho) — 193

An Astrological Biography of Mircea Eliade — 199

An Astrological Biography of Swami Muktananda — 213

An Astrological Biography of Sri Kriyananda — 233

An Astrological Biography of Rabindranath Tagore — 243

An Astrological Biography of Ram Dass — 265

Writing Your Astrobiography — 277

References — 281

Foreword

Astrology has been in a state of transition ever since the 1936 publication of Dane Rudhyar's seminal work, *The Astrology of Personality*. Dane Rudhyar could be called the Copernicus of astrology. Like Copernicus, who stated that the Sun was in the center of the solar system, Rudhyar observed that it was the individual, not the planets, that control the astrological birth chart. His perspective radically challenged the ancient claims that astrology could predict the future, and that there were "good" birth charts and "bad" birth charts. Gradually, as a result of Rudhyar's innovation, astrology has been extricating itself from its eons-old association with fortune-telling. Particularly during the astrological renaissance of the past three decades, astrology has been releasing more and more the idea of predestination from its group of essential assumptions, replacing this with concepts of holism, humanism, and depth psychology.

In recent years, the focus in the astrological literature has shifted from a judgemental, predictive style to one that's more psychologically and philosophically mature and realistic. Thus, the birth chart is increasingly employed as a valuable tool for self-improvement, insight, and personal transformation. Among those who stand at the forefront of this trend is Dr. Greg Bogart, an impeccable role model for the New Astrologer. His years of extensive study, training, and discipline are evident in this especially creative, innovative, and insightful work.

In *Astrology and Spiritual Awakening*, Greg Bogart has taken astrological biography—the blending of astrology, psychology, and biographical studies—to new levels of excellence. Using profoundly perceptive biographies of spiritual teachers, Greg demonstrates chart analysis with a high degree of technical and psychological sophistication. His dramatic, story-telling method of recounting the stories of their lives while examining their birth charts is both entertaining and inspiring. The book is also full of fascinating case examples written with a rare depth of insight.

This book exemplifies the philosophy that life isn't predestined and that an individual can use astrology to take control of his or her life and development. Greg uses his expertise and personal experience in spiritual and yogic traditions to suggest practices that we may choose as appropriate ways of catalyzing our personal evolution.

It is a pleasure for me to recommend *Astrology and Spiritual Awakening*, one of the most clearly written and practical works on astrology I've ever seen, a book that will enrich any reader's understanding of astrology.

Shelley Jordan, M.A., Madison, Wisconsin

Preface

This book is for those who seek a deeper understanding of how astrology illuminates the process of spiritual growth and awakening. Its goal is to help you follow the path of astrological self-study to discover your unique spiritual path. My fundamental premise is that the process of transformation spoken of by humanity's great spiritual traditions is a structured process, the nature of which can be clearly discerned through study of the birth chart. Moreover, in an era when many sources of spiritual and moral authority have come into question, the stellar art provides an invaluable means of guiding ourselves through our own initiatory processes.

Originally derived from classes and workshops I conducted between 1986 and 1992, this book is presented in three parts, each self-contained, yet each exploring from different perspectives the theme of astrology and spiritual awakening. Part I discusses how to utilize the birth chart to find a spiritual path. Part II explores humanistic and transpersonal approaches to chart interpretation. Part III illustrates these practical and theoretical principles through a series of astro-biographical studies. It's my hope that you'll use the material presented in each section to study and work with your own chart.

Chapter 1 describes some basic astrological principles as a place to begin our discussion. While no substitute for a comprehensive introductory text, this material will hopefully make this book accessible even to readers who are fairly new to the subject.

Chapter 2 describes how the twelve zodiacal signs and houses of the birth chart represent twelve dimensions of the process of self-transformation. Studying this chapter's numerous examples will help you discern the form of spiritual practice that's most appropriate to your natal chart, and to the transits and progressions operative during a particular period.

Chapters 3, 4, and 5 examine theoretical foundations and dynamic applications of humanistic and transpersonal astrology, first developed by Dane Rudhyar. My intention isn't to present a complete survey of Rudhyar's work, a task Leyla Rael admirably fulfilled in her book, *The Essential Rudhyar*. Instead I focus on a few of his core ideas that I find particularly relevant to contemporary practitioners. As Rudhyar was devoted to the principle of creativity, I have chosen to freely amplify his teachings as a springboard for my own formulations.

In Chapters 3, 4, and 5, several examples illustrate how an enlightened astrology can guide us through periods of crisis and awakening. We'll contemplate the initiations catalyzed by Uranus, Neptune, and Pluto, the trans-Saturnian planets. In Chapter 5, I discuss how astrologers can integrate spiritual teachings and practices that intensify the process of transformation. As an example of this, I show how the yogic philosophy of Kashmir Shaivism can be applied in transpersonal chart interpretation and spiritual counseling.

Chapters 6–12 feature *astrological biographies* of seven renowned spiritual teachers, each of whom confronted in varying ways the quest for enlightenment and the challenges of transpersonal living. These astrobiographies examine various tests, crises, and turning points in relation to their natal charts. It's important to note that these studies aren't definitive biographical sketches but *life interpretations*. They're intended to be entertaining and practical illustrations of the insights astrology can provide into the process of human transformation.

This series of biographies was presented in lectures during my first Saturn Return, which was many years ago. I chose to study these individuals because their lives resonated with my personal interests in mysticism, yoga, and contemplative practices. At the time, several decades ago, when I gave these talks I was most interested in men's lives and the psychology of men because I was learning things that helped me work out issues in my own development as a young man. Unfortunately I never did a comparable series of lengthy astrobiographies of women. To balance this, I've added profiles of female luminaries such as Ammachi, Pema Chodron, and Byron Katie. I also refer the reader to Lois Rodden's *Profiles of Women*.(1)

Also, while it may seem redundant to explore the lives of seven people connected with the spiritual traditions of India, the contrasts in their personalities and life-histories should be evident. Their lives illustrate greatly varying paths: service to the poor (Meher Baba); kundalini yoga (Muktananda); psychedelics, love, service, and devotion (Ram Dass); intellectual inquiry, religious studies, and enlivening tantric sexual yoga (Eliade); forming spiritual communities (Rajneesh, Kriyananda); and the path of creativity and committed social activism (Tagore).

The goal of these biographical studies is threefold. First, they provide detailed examples of basic astrological methods such as transits and secondary progressions. This is a good way to refine our chart interpretion skills. My approach is in keeping with Rudhyar's statement that students of astrology should devote themselves to:

> [no less than] a few years of concentrated study not only of the elements of the language of astrology per se, but even more, of well-known people's birth-charts, progressions, and transits in connection with their detailed year-by-year biographies—the only way of intelligently studying the intricacies of actually applying and using astrology.(2)

Secondly, in-depth astrological biographies enable us to understand the coherent pattern of the lives of the individuals studied, showing that each event in life can be a necessary and significant phase of transformation. These studies illustrate Rudhyar's concept of *eonic consciousness*, the awareness of how all events are moments within larger cycles.

Thirdly, study of these "famous lives" illuminates our own processes of spiritual growth and metamorphosis, and can inspire our own efforts on the path of awakening. These astrological biographies can teach us lessons that help us navigate the turbulent waters of our own spiritual journeys more wisely and courageously. While studying these lives we have the opportunity to reflect upon how we might respond to similar placements of natal planets, or analogous transits and progressions. Our own struggles and strivings come into perspective, and we begin to better understand our own multi-dimensional transformations.

My purpose in presenting these biographies is to suggest how we can each activate our distinctive birth potentials and evolve spiritually. Each of these famous individuals passed through struggles and tests similar to those that you and I experience. Their quests didn't lead them directly into transcendent realms of divine light, but straight into the heart of many highly charged, emotionally turbulent dimensions of human life: concerns about money and sexuality, ostracism by the family, confusing visions, fear of becoming insane, difficult relationships with mentors, and questions about how to actualize a spiritual vocation in the world. Their biographies demonstrate that spiritual life is a battle with numerous material, psychological, and relational obstacles, complexities, and uncertainties. It's my hope that these astrological portraits will also serve as examples of the luminous victory that's possible.

Part I

Astrology and Spiritual Awakening

ASTROLOGY IS THE YOGA OF TIME. It's a form of sacred knowledge that teaches us to live consciously as embodied beings in a temporal world. Study of the birth chart enables us to find our next step in evolution, whether this means going to school and choosing an occupation, forming a relationship, healing ourselves emotionally or physically, building a business, focused social activism, or developing a meditation practice. Astrology is a reliable guide through life's changes, a means of sanctifying earthly existence and fulfilling its challenges with courage, clarity, and joy.

This book describes how astrology can be utilized to understand the stages and facets of the spiritual path, the process of awakening to a more encompassing reality or consciousness—God, Atman, Buddha Mind, the pure Light. Toward this end, we'll discuss the theory and practice of humanistic and transpersonal astrology and study examples of people undergoing deep psycho-spiritual transformations. Before embarking on our journey, let's survey some basic astrological information that will serve as a shared language and a foundation for understanding the material that follows.

Chapter 1

Astrology: A Language of Change

ASTROLOGY STUDIES THE EVER-CHANGING PATTERN OF THE PLANETS AND STARS in relation to human experience. Astrologers examine planetary positions at the moment of a person's birth in order to discern themes, characteristics, and interests that may be emphasized over the course of that person's life. Dane Rudhyar taught that the birth chart is a *seed pattern*, a set of *celestial instructions* revealing what an individual potentially can become and the kinds of experience and actions that may be necessary to fulfill one's life purpose.(3)

The astrological birth chart can be viewed as a roadmap provided by the Creator. This roadmap provides individualized guidance through life's changes and challenges—the sharp turns, steep climbs, and occasional plateaus that all of us experience. To understand your birth chart, it's important to grasp the meaning of five basic factors: planets, signs, houses, cycles, and aspects. We'll examine each of these topics, as well as transits and progressions, two methods astrologers use to determine the timing of events and experiences.

The Planets

The planets represent various facets of the personality: Sun is the symbol of identity, our conscious sense of self, the quality of our self-expression and self-emanation. Moon represents feelings, moods, and needs, our emotional life. Mercury signifies our speech, thinking, verbal, cognitive, and communication skills. Venus signifies the expression of love, affection, our social style and way of relating with others. Venus also symbolizes beauty and describes what we find desirable and attractive. Mars symbolizes self-assertion, instincts, drives, and vitality; it's the symbol of the will, the vital energy that fuels activity and achievement. Mars signifies how we express anger, desires, and sexual drives. Sun, Moon, Mercury, Venus, and Mars are called the *personal planets*.

Jupiter and Saturn are the *social planets*. Jupiter represents our capacity for planning and aspiration, our urge for expansion, conceptual understanding, adventure, and social participation. Saturn represents the urge to stabilize our lives through focused, sustained effort. It symbolizes the maturity and hard work needed to meet the pressures of material existence and to actualize the goals and aspirations of Jupiter. Saturn represents the desire for security and tangible accomplishment, social adaptation, conformity to tradition, and our ability to function within social institutions and defined occupations.

Uranus, Neptune, and Pluto are called the *transpersonal planets*. Physically, they're outside the orbit of Saturn and symbolically operate beyond the laws of Saturn, defined by family, tradition, and cultural institutions. These planets disrupt and transform the structures developed by Saturn. Uranus impacts our lives through rebellion, defiance, unconventional behavior, scientific pursuits, becoming excited about discoveries and innovations, politics and social change, and undergoing major changes of attitude or direction. Neptune awakens us to subtle, etheric, nonmaterial realms, and incites an urge for expansion of consciousness, transcendence, religion or spirituality, and development of intuitive or psychic capacities. In some cases Neptune represents a tendency toward helplessness, victim mentality, avoidance, and escapist behaviors. Pluto transforms through catharsis, detoxification, purging and letting go, and through surfacing and elimination of impurities such as hatred, greed, resentment, or jealousy.

Signs of the Zodiac

Each planet is placed in a sign, which shows the quality of energy with which the planet expresses itself. The signs are divisions of the ecliptic, the path of the Sun's apparent motion around the Earth. This is from Earth's perspective; in actuality, Earth orbits around the Sun. Imagine the ecliptic as a band of light surrounding Earth with twelve colors, with each color representing one of the twelve zodiacal signs. Now visualize a planet such as Mars passing through red, blue, green, yellow, orange, purple, or black zones. Mars will express itself with a particular modality, quality, or style depending on which sign it's placed in at a given time. Signs modify and give thematic coloration to each planet. Signs also symbolize the cyclic passage of the seasons, with Aries, Cancer, Libra, and Capricorn corresponding respectively to the beginning of Spring, Summer, Autumn, and Winter (in the northern hemisphere).

Most people know their Sun sign and a few popular phrases describing qualities associated with that sign. For example, Taureans are said to be stubborn, Leo natives to be vain, proud, and theatrical, and so forth. However, the zodiacal signs are better understood as a sequence of symbols representing twelve phases of the cycle of evolution. Let me briefly describe the story described by the zodiac.

Imagine a formless, vast ocean of potentialities in which no distinct entities exist, a condition of expansiveness, emptiness, and nothingness. This is the evolutionary phase called **Pisces**. It's an oceanic condition that's shrouded in mist, uncertainty, and peace. It's the state of quiescence that precedes creation.

Then, a distinct individual form or organism begins to crystalize and seeks to become autonomous and to distinguish itself from the collective, the undifferentiated ocean of potentiality symbolized by Pisces. This is the **Aries** phase of *emergence* of individual identity. Considered the first zodiacal sign in Western astrology, Aries represents Spring, the birth of individual consciousness. Here one experiences a surge of physical strength and instinctual energy, emboldening our personal will, drives, motivation, and impulses to act.

As we learn to stand on our own and become autonomous, we gain the capacity to procure food, shelter, and physical ease of being. This is the **Taurus** phase of *substantiation* of personality. Taurus is the phase of embodiment and productive, pragmatic activities supporting biological growth and material comfort and sustainment. In this phase of unhurried sensory experience, we develop grounded awareness of the physical world and intelligence about money, purchases, and ownership.

In the phase of **Gemini**, we experience curiosity to explore our surroundings, to investigate and name the many objects, people, and events we perceive. This is the phase of *extension* of personality outward into the environment. In Gemini, linguistic ability emerges, enabling us to communicate and to acquire and exchange information.

In the zodiacal phase of **Cancer**, we tire of roaming in search of new experiences and seek to put down roots in a particular location. We feel the instinct to nest, to establish a home, a sense of family, a safe environment, and focus our attention on some limited area of activity. Thus Cancer is the phase of *orientation* and emotional development. We evolve the capacity to feel, to care, to develop emotional attachments with other people, and to establish a home, dwelling, office, an atmosphere, a personal space.

Leo is the phase of fun, play, taking risks, self-expression, and creativity, the *externalization* of the self. Leo is the moment to experience joy, celebrate life and our capacities, and express our love and individual talents with dignity, pride, self-respect, dramatic flair, and a sense of fun. In Leo, we want to feel seen, mirrored, validated, and witnessed.

In the next phase, **Virgo**, we develop self-reflectiveness, analyze ourselves, recognize our imperfections, and strive for self-betterment. Sometimes in Virgo we feel dissatisfied, anxious, or self-critical. Virgo is the phase of *purification* and self-betterment through discipline or technique, training, employment, or apprenticeship. Personal crises may catalyze adjustments of our habits, skills, or attitudes.

The first six signs, Aries through Virgo describe the process of *individualization*, the development of individual potentials. The second six signs emphasize *social integration* of the individual. In **Libra**, we want to know others, to interact. We perceive others as attractive and seek to love, share, cooperate, and relate harmoniously and congenially. Libra is the phase of *interaction* and the path of relationships and friendships.

Next, a new stage is reached when two individuals attempt to live and work together and to find a social purpose for their relationship. In the life-cycle phase of **Scorpio**, the energies of relationship become intense and productive as two individuals attempt to work toward some common end. Emotional, sexual, and shared financial commitments create new challenges, because as two people try to cooperate and work together, conflicts of will and differences of opinion inevitably arise. In Scorpio we experience the dynamics of power, anger, control, mistrust, jealousy, resentment, dominance, hostility, and aggression that arise in many deep and committed human interactions. Scorpio represents the *regeneration* we may experience as a consequence of interpersonal crisis and the adjustments that all relationships require. The regeneration may also stem from traumatic events or a brush with death.

In **Sagittarius**, we seek wisdom and understanding through a more developed intellectual life. This is the phase of *comprehension* or *conceptualization*; we're concerned with defining our beliefs, formulating theories, and reflecting on moral or philosophical doctrines that can guide our lives and give meaning to events. Sagittarius is the phase of learning, education, travel, pilgrimmage, and expanding our intellectual and cultural horizons.

In **Capricorn**, we apply the concepts and guiding principles defined in Sagittarius within the realm of social institutions and occupations. The predominant concern is to find our place within the social hierarchy. This is the stage of ambition, attempts to advance, achieve, to gain respect and stature. In Capricorn we strive for success; it's the phase of *accomplishment* and *incarnation* of our ideals.

In **Aquarius**, we look beyond personal ambitions and achievements, recognizing ourselves as part of a collective, a member of a society at a particular moment of time and history. We're interested in furthering the welfare of the group, society as a whole, and envisioning new ideals and goals for the future. To pursue these ideals and goals, it's important to join together with other like-minded people in groups, political parties, communities, collectives, cooperatives. This is the pinnacle of the process of social integration, just as Leo is the pinnacle of *individualization*. Here we broaden our awareness beyond personal concerns to social issues. This is the phase of *participation*, and involvement in activities promoting innovation, social change, or scientific discovery.

Finally, returning to **Pisces**, the evolutionary process leads beyond even socially focused activity and identification with a group and toward union with the source of all life: God, Spirit, the infinite, the wholeness of existence. Pisces is the phase of *self-transcendence*, openness of being, and feeling our oneness with the great ocean from which our individual existence emerges. At times Pisces signifies loss of individual control and experiences of powerlessness, helplessness, or victimization. Pisces can also be the phase of enlightenment through merging into consciousness, Spirit, the source and ground consciousness that encompasses all manifest and unmanifest realms.

In later chapters we'll examine many examples illustrating interpretation of planets in zodiacal signs. There are numerous books available that systematically explore this topic.(4)

The Astrological Houses

Each planet is placed a zodiacal sign and also in a house of the birth chart. Houses are regions of the chart representing the space surrounding us at the moment of birth. Using the exact date, place, and time of birth, astrologers determine the position of the degree and sign rising on the Eastern horizon (the Ascendant), the point setting on the Western horizon (the Descendant), the point directly overhead at the birth moment (the Midheaven or MC), and the point directly below, opposite the MC (the Nadir or IC). (See Figure 1 on page 8.)

These four angles define four quadrants of the sky, which are then subdivided into twelve divisions of the sky that define the astrological houses. The houses represent specific situations and fields of life, and encompass the full spectrum of human experience. Each of the twelve houses has some correspondence with one of the twelve signs. For example, in the tenth house one deals with situations and concerns related to those that are the focus of the tenth sign, Capricorn. The houses are realms of significant human concerns:

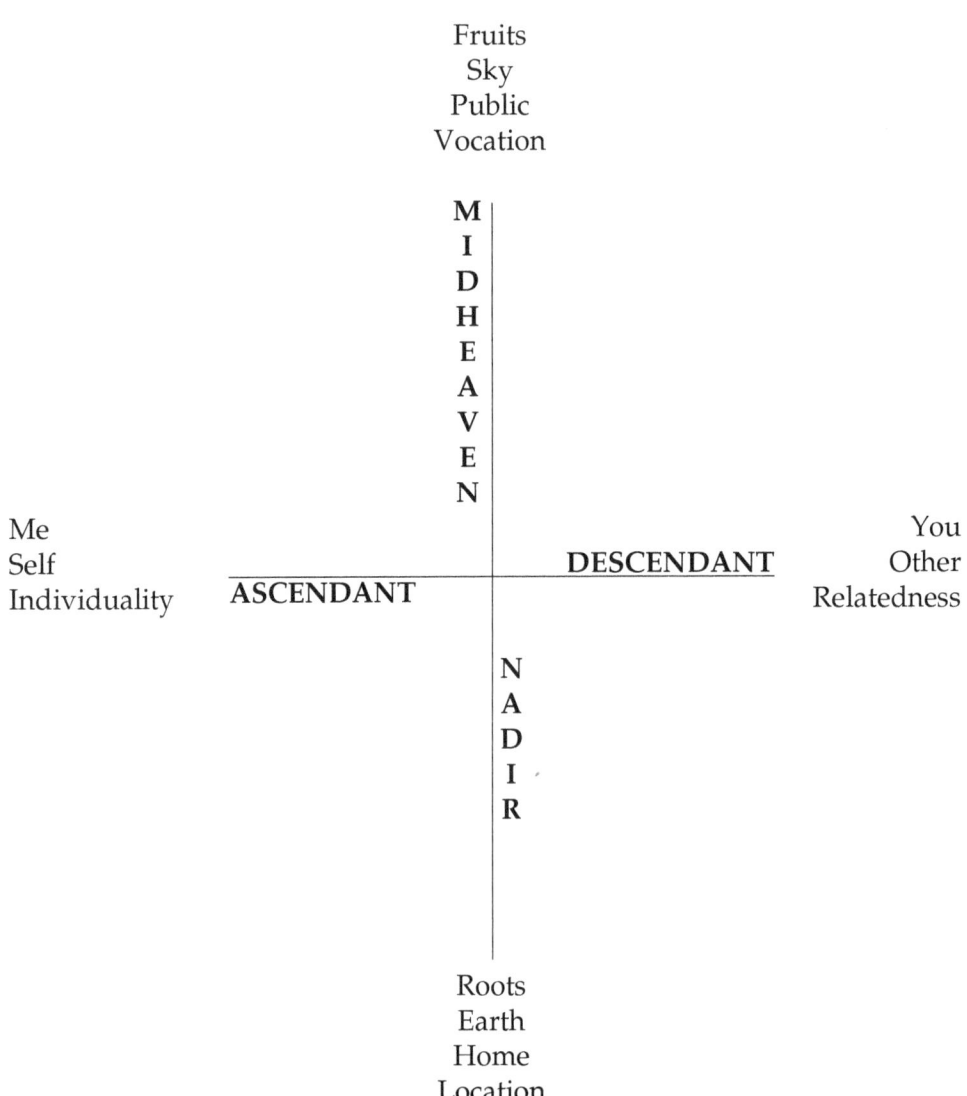

Figure 1. Four Axes of Consciousness

House 1: self-image and formation of identity.

House 2: money, ownership, and acquisitions, finances and assets.

House 3: thinking, reading, learning, speech and communication, transportation, driving, mobility; interaction with siblings, neighbors, and others we encounter in daily life.

House 4: family life, housing and domestic matters, connection to a sense of place, locale, memory, and ancestral heritage.

House 5: self-expression, creativity, play, enjoyment, and children.
House 6: health, employment, skill development, apprenticeship, jobs and training situations, self-purification, and self-improvement.
House 7: significant relationships, friendship, and marriage.
House 8: deepening of relationship through exchange of financial, emotional and sexual energies, and developing the capacity for intimacy, commitment, and responsibility to another.
House 9: education, study, travel, definition of theories, concepts, and beliefs that bestow meaning upon experience.
House 10: profession, vocation, career, and contribution to society.
House 11: awareness of social and historical circumstances and our response to them; participation in groups, teams, collectives, conferences, community activism, social movements, political causes, professional organizations, or any gathering of consciousness concerned with the future and human welfare.
House 12: solitude, retreat, introspection, altruistic activity, awareness of karmic forces and the collective unconscious, and inner exploration through meditation, dreams, fantasy, and astrology.

Each house has a *dispositor*, a planetary ruler determined by the sign on the cusp of the house. If Leo is the sign on your tenth house cusp, then the Sun (ruler of Leo) is dispositor of your tenth house. If you have Pisces on the second house cusp, then Neptune is dispositor of that house and has symbolic rulership over the realm of personal finances.

Cycles

Astrology is based on understanding the cyclical nature of existence. All of life follows a cyclical pattern of birth, growth, decay, and new beginnings. Dane Rudhyar popularized the metaphor of the vegetation cycle to illustrate this point. In spring, seeds sprout, put down roots, and grow stalks and branches. During summer flowering, fruits are produced. In autumn, leaves wither and fall to the ground to become raw material for future cycles. Finally, seeds are released that lie dormant through the winter, waiting to sprout in the spring, when a new cycle begins.

The monthly phases of the Sun and Moon exemplify this cycle of growth, decay, and rebirth. At New Moon, an impulse is released as the Moon receives new light from the Sun. This impulse develops during the first half of the lunation cycle, which emphasizes *growth of form*. A turning point is reached at the First Quarter phase, which Rudhyar called a *crisis in action*, a moment when decisive action is required to overcome the inertia of the past and to carry forth the new impulse into actuality. At the Full Moon phase the process culminates in an *illumination of purpose*, a lucid, objective awareness of the meaning of this cycle of existence. The plant, or the cycle of development, has reached its symbolic and existential fruition.

The second half of the cycle features reevaluation of the structures developed in the first half. We experience *change, dissolution of form, altering of structures,* and *reorientation of purpose,* and hopefully a *growth in awareness*. At the Third Quarter phase, a *crisis in consciousness* occurs. Aspects of the past need to be repudiated and our beliefs and priorities are adjusted or relinquished. Finally, the cycle nears completion during the Balsamic Moon phase—the waning crescent Moon—marking release of the past, letting go, and a period of waiting in preparation for a new cycle that will commence at the next New Moon.

A human life follows a similar pattern of development. The entire lifespan constitutes the individual's cycle of existence, in which there are beginning, middle, and ending phases. The first half of life is often a process of striving to establish a stable personal identity and material existence and can be broadly characterized as a phase of growth of form. Later in life, while growth of form may continue, it's also common to reevaluate the pursuits and achievements of youth and to give greater attention to questions of meaning and growth of awareness.

The birth moment is the inception of a new life-cycle, containing an implicit pattern of development that can potentially unfold during the remainder of the life-cycle. Thus, Rudhyar taught, the birth chart operates as a "seed pattern" for the person's life, portraying major themes and areas of activity that are likely to be emphasized over the course of a lifetime. The birthmap also enables us to understand the numerous, interconnected subcycles operating within the life-cycle as a whole, defined by the transits of the planets—each of which has a particular purpose and intention.

All events and experiences gain heightened significance when situated within the context of cycles. Just as each month there's a New Moon, a First Quarter Moon, a Full Moon, and a Third Quarter Moon, so, too, there are identifiable phases in human experience. There are moments of new beginnings, moments requiring decisive action, and moments of completion and preparation for the future.

Through reflection on astrological symbolism we come to understand that everything is cyclical and occurs in phases. From this perspective, enlightenment means understanding these cycles of development and cooperating with them. We know when to plant and when to harvest, when to nest at home and when to embark on journeys and adventures.

Interplanetary Aspects

Just as Sun and Moon go through the monthly phases of the lunation cycle, all planets enact cyclical relationships with one another. The significant phases of interplanetary relationships are called *aspects*. Aspects show how the various planetary functions link up and work together within the personality. Two planets placed together (like the New Moon) are in *conjunction*, whereas if they're directly opposite one another (180°), they're in *opposition* (like the Full Moon). Planets 90° apart form a *square*. The *trine* is a 120° aspect. The sextile is a 60° aspect between two planets. Other important aspects include the *quincunx* (150°), the *semi-square* (45°), and the *sesquiquadrate* (135°). Each aspect has a slightly different flavor. The trine and sextile show innate skills, talents, and harmonious interplay of planetary energies. The opposition, square, semi-square, and sesquare represent dynamic linkage of planetary energies and some tension between different facets of the self that have to learn how to cooperate and work with one another. With the quincunx, conscious changes and adjustments are needed to coordinate two (or more) discordant planetary forces. Even when two planets aren't in a classical aspect, they're related through their midpoints, the point midway between their zodiacal placements. Bill Tierney's *Dynamics of Aspect Analysis* provides a brilliant explanation of aspects.(5) For discussion of midpoints, refer to Harding & Harvey, *Working With Astrology*.(6)

The study of aspects is a vast topic. In this chapter I'll briefly discuss aspects of the Sun and Moon, which have special importance.

Aspects of the Natal Sun

The natal Sun's sign, house placement, and aspects are general determinants of personality type, showing the defining marks of identity. Planets aspecting the Sun are archetypal energies seeking embodiment through us. To simplify for a moment, we can say that natal aspects of the Sun define the basic signatures and potentials of the self:

Sun-Moon: an emotional, highly sensitive, feeling, caring person.
Sun-Mercury: a cerebral, verbal, thinking, communicative person.
Sun-Venus: an affable, friendly, affectionate, or artistic person.
Sun-Mars: a competitive, assertive, fiery, motivated, energetic, or aggressive person.
Sun-Jupiter: an expansive, optimistic, intellectual, or well-traveled person.
Sun-Saturn: a serious, responsible, hard-working, conscientious person; a person who must strive to overcome self-doubt, to achieve goals, and to gain self-respect.
Sun-Uranus: an unconventional, inventive, unique, free-spirited person; or a rebellious, high strung, eccentric, or very funny person.

Sun-Neptune: a sensitive, spiritual, imaginative, mystical, idealistic person.
Sun-Pluto: an intense, magnetic, or socially dominant person.

There is a wide spectrum for expression of any of these solar aspects, and sometimes we manifest our less evolved selves. With Sun-Neptune in aspect we can become the realized mystic, the visionary, or we can be an aimless, disorganized, helpless lost soul, someone who lacks motivation, exhibits disordered behavior, struggles with drugs, alcohol abuse, and self-numbing, vegetative TV and video game viewing. Sun-Pluto in hard aspect may represent self-hatred or self-deprecation, cynicism, someone exhibiting some degree of resentment, hostility, or negativity; yet, Sun-Pluto aspects can also signify profound self-transformation. It's up to us to develop our solar potentials, to be as exceptional as we're capable of becoming.

Let's consider an example that features vivid solar symbolism. Ken Wilber has Sun opposite Pluto, which can be a signature of a person of intensity and immense world impact. Wilber's Sun conjunct Mercury, ruler of the ninth house, is the signature of a widely published writer, teacher, and theorist—one of the foremost modern mystic philosophers. With Sun conjunct Mercury and Mars, Wilber is a person who constantly exercises his mind—reading, writing, and public speaking. A prolific writer, he often uses the spear of his discerning mind to refute the views of others. The Mercury-Pluto opposition represents the power of persuasion. With Sun-Mercury-Mars conjunct, Wilber can be verbally aggressive and contentious; there's plenty of humor, argument, and occasional pointed sarcasm in his writing. Wilber's Sun in Aquarius is sesquare (135°) its ruler, Uranus, symbolizing genius and inventiveness, someone very political, progressive, and forward-thinking, interested in many sciences and innovations. He's a promethean figure, someone very individuated, a quirky individual. Sun ruler Uranus in Gemini is placed in the ninth house, symbol of an intellectual genius and innovator synthesizing new forms of knowledge, creating a new intellectual paradigm of Integral Theory. Aquarius Sun aspecting Uranus denotes his interest in launching a social movement through his Integral Institute. Wilber's Sun is aligned with all three outer planets, as well as Mercury and Mars, showing a highly complex and multi-faceted individual. With Sun trine the ascending Neptune (as well as Jupiter square Neptune), Wilber is a mystic who has been a lifelong practitioner of meditation, dedicated to enlightening spiritual and holistic knowledge.

Look at how the Sun is powerfully configured in the natal charts of four remarkable women: Buddhist guru Pema Chodron; Roshi Joan Halifax, director of Upaya Foundation; gentle, luminous advaitin sage Gangiji; and visionary educator, Jean Houston. Although I have no birth times for any of them, I've constructed Noon charts that in each case reveals a highly cohesive solar personality ray.

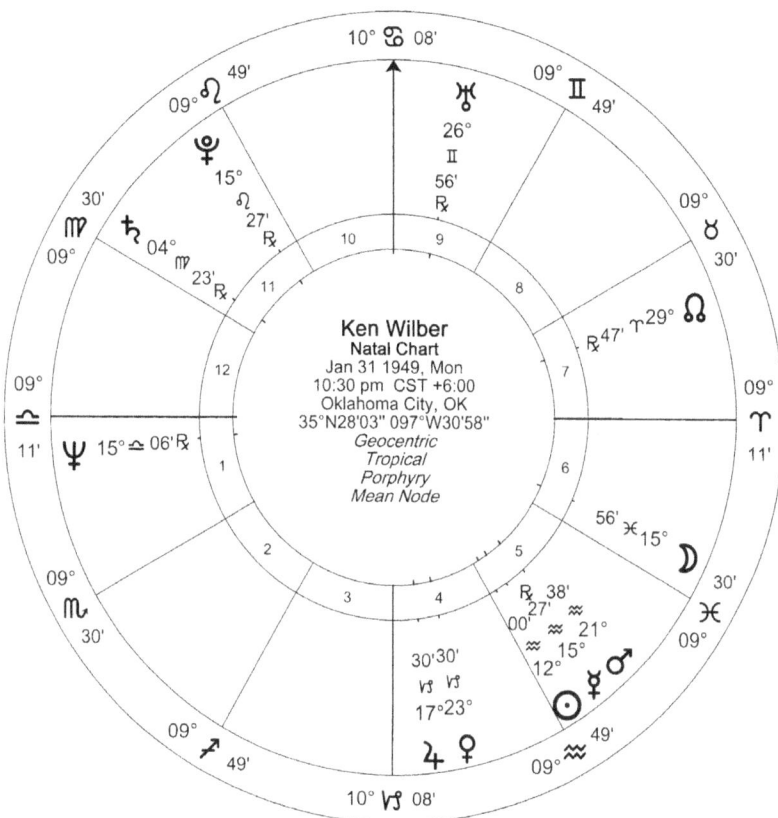

Pema Chodron's (see chart on page 14) Cancer Sun conjoins Mercury, Mars, Venus, and Pluto in a steady water trine to Saturn, showing her soothing, comforting emotional presence. With four planets in Cancer, she grew up on a farm and lived a family life with two children. Sun trine her Saturn in Pisces, and sextile her Neptune, signifies flowing self-discipline and immersion in spiritual practice, and cultivating the feeling of compassion. She's a fully ordained Buddhist nun who spends much of her time in meditation retreat under the guidance of her gurus (Saturn in Pisces opposite Neptune). Sun conjunct Venus in Cancer signifies warmth and nurturing care offered to benefit all beings. Sun-Pluto conjunction signifies strength, influence, renunciation, purification, and urge for transformation and spiritual empowerment in a state beyond the ego. Gemini Moon opposite Jupiter in Sagittarius shows her learned discourses and engaging stories. Jupiter square Saturn represents her ability to organize and constructively present Buddhist teachings through ongoing study, lecturing and publications (Jupiter in Sagittarius).

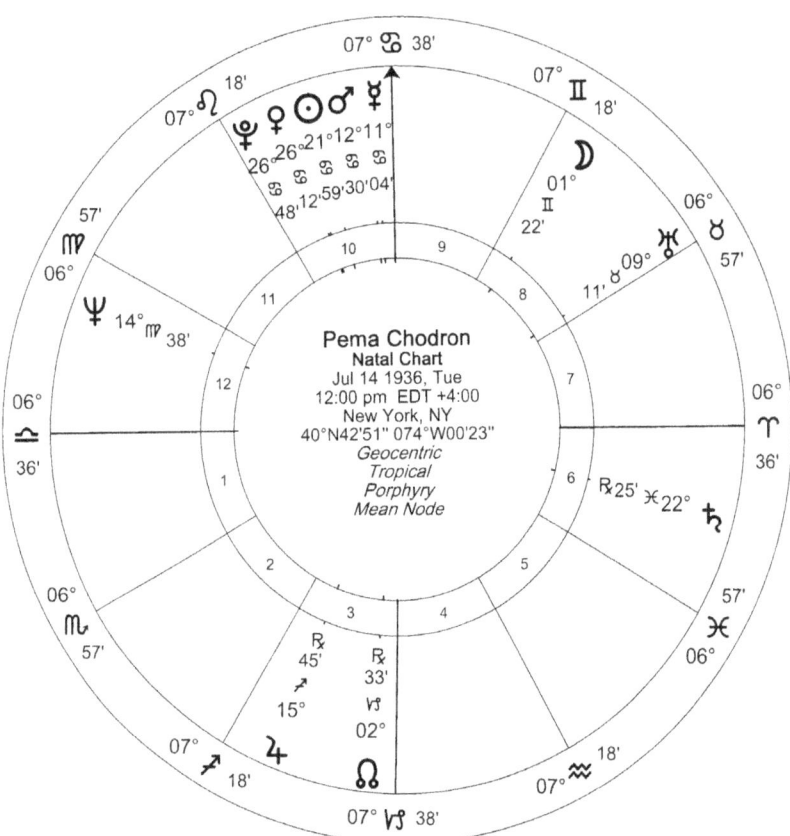

Roshi Joan Halifax has Sun conjunct Mercury and Pluto. With Sun-Mercury-Pluto, she's a captivating speaker and teacher of socially engaged spirituality who emanates tremendous intensity and force of personality. She has done pioneering work on compassion and empathy in care for the dying. She's an inspiring example of a Sun-Pluto personality with fiery soul strength. Her books reflect her Sun-Pluto aspect, with titles such as *Shamanic Voices*; *The Fruitful Darkness*; and *The Human Encounter with Death*.

Gangaji's Sun is conjunct Uranus, Saturn, Mercury, and Jupiter and squares Neptune (see chart on page 16). With four planets in Gemini, she engages in deep conversations and relaxed teaching dialogues with her students and audiences. Sun-Mercury-Jupiter signifies intelligence and skill in lecturing and storytelling. Sun–Mercury square Neptune denotes compassion and freedom from the cogitating mind in Self-realization.

Sun is conjunct Moon, Mercury, and Uranus in the chart of Jean Houston (see chart on page 17), human potential movement philosopher and educator, prolific author

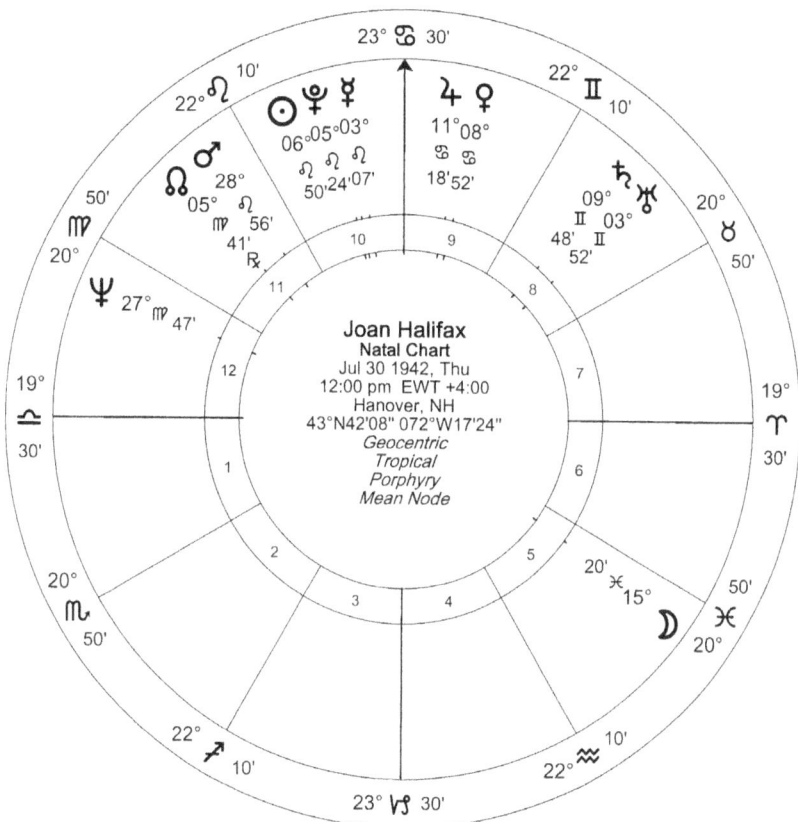

of 26 books, including: *Listening to the Body*; *The Possible Human*; *Mind Games*; and *The Varieties of Psychedelic Experience*. With her strong stellium in Taurus (including the exalted Taurus Moon) trine Neptune, Houston's teachings emphasize the potentials of the body and sensory awareness, earth and goddess mysteries, sacred psychology and mythology, and the spiritual value of connection to animals and nature.

Examining the placement of the natal Sun is typically the starting point for birth chart interpretation. Sun is also what I call the *primary vocational indicator* as its sign, aspects, and house position are central indicators of the personality essence that's trying to be actualized.

Transits

The sign, house placement, and aspects of the Sun and other natal planets form a symbolic portrait of the individual. And by studying ongoing cycles of various planets we sense the optimal internal schedule for our development. The potentials indicated

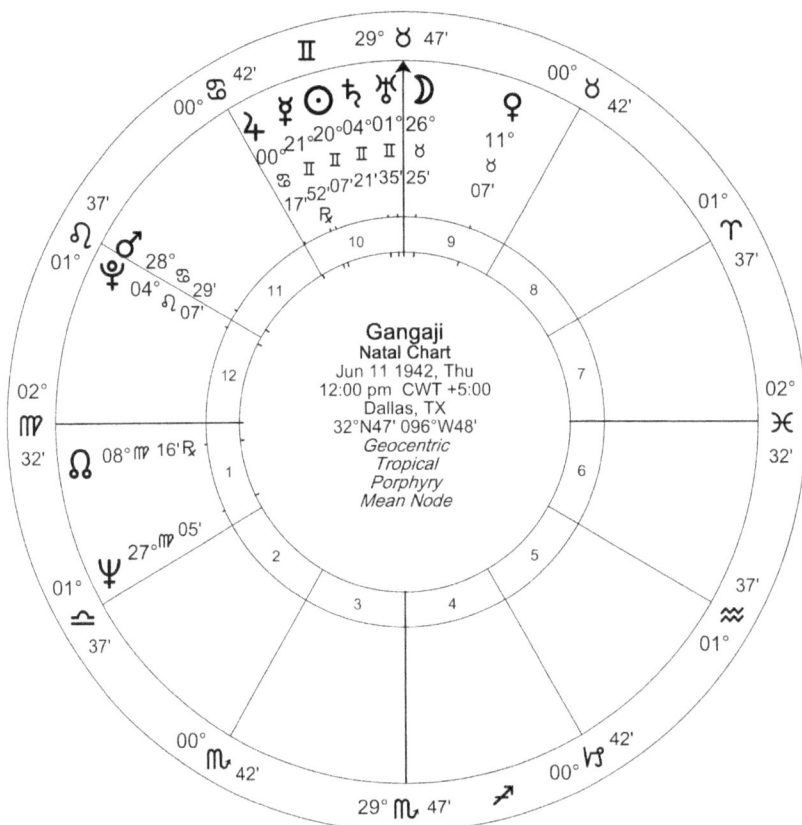

in the birth chart are brought to life by transits, the continuing movements of planets through the sky, which activate the planets and angles of the birthmap. The Moon's transit through the twelve signs each month symbolizes our constantly changing emotional lives. The Sun, Venus, and Mercury pass through the entire chart every year; the transits of these inner planets show, respectively, the changing focus of our vital energy, our affections, and our mental attention. Mars takes two years to transit through the entire birth chart; its movement through the signs and houses shows where we need to take the initiative and assert ourselves vigorously, even when this leads to frictions, tensions, and irritations. Jupiter takes twelve years to transit through the twelve signs and houses and marks the growth of our plans and aspirations, setting attainable goals, and strivings for growth and improvement. Saturn, Uranus, Neptune, and Pluto are slower-moving planets, and their transits are momentous, producing deep changes in a person's life. The study of transits illuminates where change is happening at any given time in acordance with specific archetypes. For example, Saturn's transits through the houses, Saturn's aspects to other planets, and Saturn's aspects to its natal

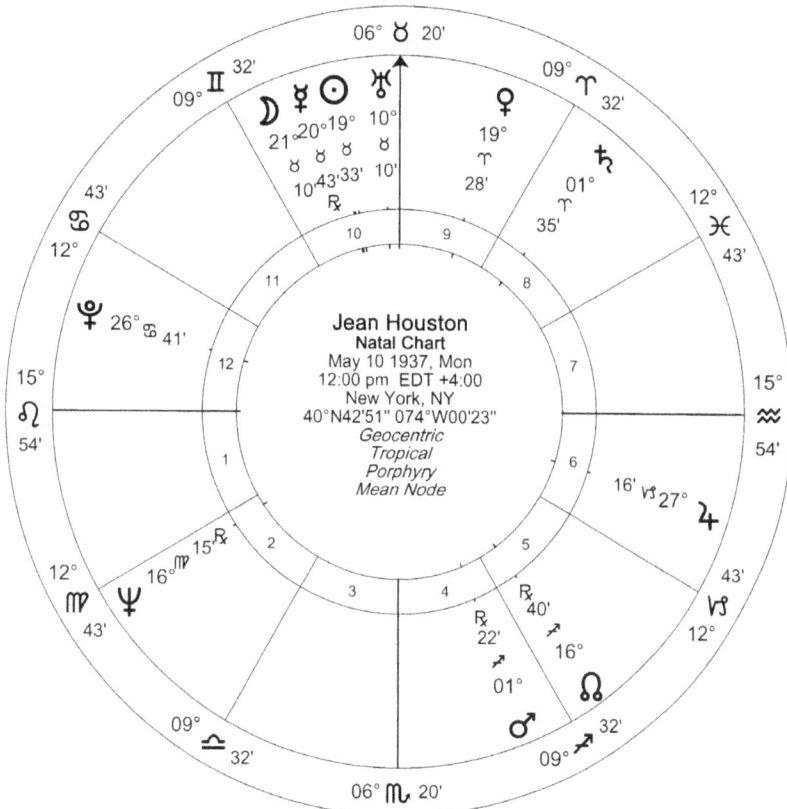

position are maturational processes that press us to become focused and responsible. In contrast, Uranus transits electrify and stimulate and creatively reorganize, pressing us to make major structural, behavioral, or attitudinal changes.

Another dimension of transits focuses on *interplanetary* cycles, examining the phasic aspects formed by pairs of transiting planets—following two transiting planets in relation to one another—from their conjunction, to their first quarter square, to opposition, to third quarter square, to their subsequent conjunction. The monthly solunar cycles measure phases of the relationship of Sun and Moon, from the New Moon (conjunction), representing the beginning of a cycle, to the Full Moon (opposition), representing the climax or culminating moment of the cycle, and back to the New Moon, marking the inception of a new cycle. We similarly follow cycles of other planetary pairs. For example, the cycle of Venus and Mars represents the rhythmic pulse of affection and physical desire; their periodic alignments are times of heightened affectional and sexual attractions.(8) We also watch the twenty-year cycle of Jupiter and

Saturn, which represents the journey of pursuing goals within the social sphere, within the domain of culture and society.(9) The phases of the Jupiter-Saturn cycle measure stages in the growth of a career or a calling in life, over decades. This principle is illustrated in the astrobiography of Tagore (Chapter 11). Also see "Understanding the Jupiter-Saturn Cycle" in *Astrology and Meditation*.(10)

We experience momentous changes through the powerful outer planet transits. But transits of the inner, personal planets are also equally important. For example, whenever Mars is retrograde we tend to experience various stresses, discordances, and pressures of life. I recall how once transiting Mars was retrograde in Virgo, which can indicate a time of anxiety, stress in the workplace (Virgo), health complaints (especially digestive upset), and feeling cranky, angry, and dissatisfied. A man named Trent (see chart on page 120) had transiting Mars in Virgo near his Midheaven, square natal Sun, Saturn, and Ascendant in Sagittarius, for four weeks. Trent was under tremendous stress. He had pain in all his joints; Mars often signifies physical pain or discomfort. Trent's boss was on his case and he felt constantly criticized in the workplace. His job involved working with people experiencing workplace injuries and workman's compensation cases (Virgo: health concerns and issues of employment and the workplace). He felt angry and dissatisfied at work. Then his girlfriend Kiko got scratched by a feral cat and had to undergo antibiotic treatment to prevent rabies. Mars retrograde brought some highly unruly energies. But knowing astrology helped Trent keep his peace of mind even in the midst of all that trouble. Knowing about the Mars retrograde transit helped him ride it out and not get overly stressed and upset, so he remained at ease.

One night while Mars in Virgo was turning direct in motion, Kiko was in a fiery, testy mood. Transiting Mars was passing through Kiko's first house, so she was feeling quite irritable. I'd explained Mars retrograde to Trent, and he made an effort to remain calm and didn't try to dissuade Kiko from being angry, aggressive, and belligerent. He accepted this energy coming from her without resisting. Knowledge of the Mars transit—knowing that there might at this time be some angry energy in his atmosphere—helped Trent reduce his reactivity, staying calm. This change in his demeanor affected Kiko, who suddenly had a moment of self-reflection in which she saw herself with more clarity and discernment (first-house Mars in Virgo). This is an example of how astrology helps us achieve a more refined consciousness. Trent realized during the big Mars transit that he doesn't have to get angry just because somebody is angry at him. He can take the heat and survive the attack without further inflaming the situation. In my opinion, that is a moment of enlightenment. Transits portray the constantly changing quality of the time moment and allow us to align with it intelligently.

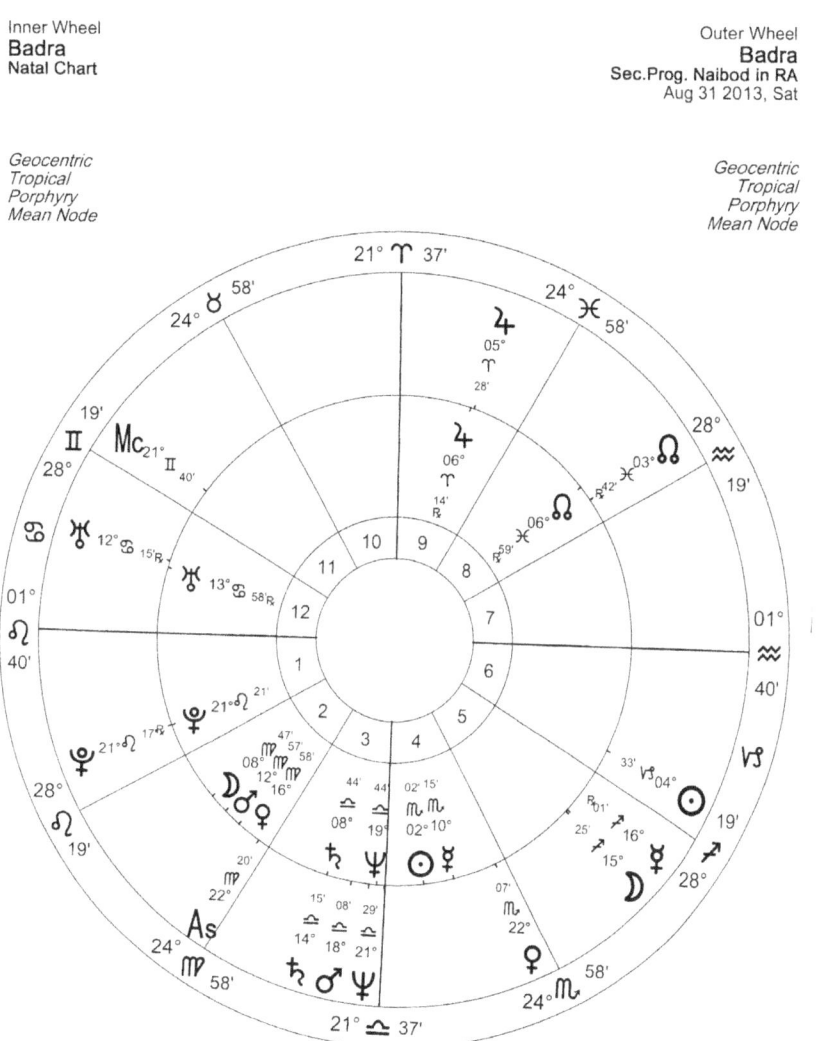

Progressions

Transits indicate how environmental pressures activate the inherent personal characteristics and potentials indicated by the natal chart. However, most astrologers don't view human beings as fixed and static entities, but rather as persons who continually grow and change. The birth pattern is like a snapshot of the sky frozen in time, which contains an implicit continuation and resolution of the birth moment. Astrologers posit a correspondence between the planetary positions in the days after birth and developments in the corresponding years of the individual's life. Thus, if we examine the positions of the planets in the days immediately after birth, we observe changes in the birth pattern, showing the continuation or follow-through of the birth moment. This method is called *secondary progressions*, using the formula *one day after birth equals one year of life* to measure changes occurring within the birth pattern and the personal life-world that it symbolizes. The combination of transits and progressions give astrologers two means of measuring the kinds of experiences and evolutionary development a person may face during a particular period. We pay special attention to the sign, house, and aspects of the progressed Sun and Moon.

Look at the chart of Badra, who at the time of consultation was 62 years old. I began explaining her progressed chart to her by tracing the motion of the progressed Sun, which moves at the reliable rate of one degree per year. At birth, her fourth-house Sun is 8° away from Mercury, so at age 8 her progressed Sun was conjunct Mercury. Her parents divorced, she and her mother moved to a new place, and she spent a lot of time traveling between the two homes. She remembered that was the year she won a school spelling bee and was quite verbally precocious. I noted that once the progressed Sun completed the remaining 28° of Scorpio and traveled an additional 9° to reach 9° of Sagittarius, it squared her natal Moon at 9° Virgo—at age 37. The Sun travels 1° per day and 1° per year by progression, thus the progressed Sun travels 37° in 37 years. At age 37 Badra gave birth to her only child, transforming into a mother (progressed Sun square Moon). Four years later the progressed Sun reached 13° Sagittarius, square natal Mars. At that time she was embroiled in marital conflict with constant domestic disputes and fiery arguments, leading to dissolution of the marriage. Four years later, when her progressed Sun squared Venus, Badra began painting, found a boyfriend, and started a loving relationship that lasted for many years. At age 56, her progressed Sun reached conjunction with Chiron—planet of the guru, the wounded healer, and the mentor. At this time she apprenticed with a teacher who trained her in a healing art and holistic philosophy (Chiron in Sagittarius). The aspects of the progressed Sun demarcate pivotal turning points and should be closely studied. Also note the position of progressed Mars at the time of consultation. I observed that Mars was 10° past conjunction with natal Saturn in the third house of siblings, and 4° past conjunction with progressed Saturn. Approximating that progressed Mars moves about a half degree per year, I estimated on the spot that progressed Mars had been conjunct natal Saturn 18–20 years earlier and also conjunct progressed Saturn. Badra had been having problems with one of her siblings for close to 20 years. They had argued and disagreed repeatedly, had been business partners, then bitter rivals and enemies. He had led her to commit funds to a business enterprise that failed and Badra ended up losing a lot of money. The long progressed Mars-Saturn conjunction in her third house represented this extended conflict with a sibling. It was immensely helpful for Badra to examine the symbolism in her progressed chart and how it had manifested in her life. Progressions of the birth chart are a key to understanding the unfoldment of personality over time.

Lunar Cycles, Aspects, and Transits

Astrologers walking the spiritual path gain innumerable insights through attunement to the Moon, which constantly influences our mood and emotional wellbeing. Tracking the monthly lunar phases, as well as the progressed lunation cycle, we follow the rhythms of nature. We feel a cycle's inception at New Moon. At the beginning of a new cycle we can relax if our efforts haven't born fruit; things are just getting started, something is set in motion. But we need to energize and sustain our efforts during the cycle's formative waxing phases, overcoming inertia. Cycles culminate at the Full Moon's moment of peak intensity and luminosity, as the meaning of this cycle of life is clarified. The Moon's reorganizing waning phases reorient consciousness as we reconsider our goals and attitudes, and dismantle structures. Lots of success coaches teach people to energize the waxing phase of initiative, heroic effort, and motivation. In waxing phases of a cycle we need to strive and get out there. But wise astrologers also honor the waning phases of cycles, the need to bring things to a close, to consciously deconstruct something, to let go and allow forms to change. Astrologers embrace the balsamic phase of endings, the silences, lulls, periods of waiting and gestation. Maybe it's a waning Moon or transiting Moon is conjunct Neptune and you're vegetating in front of the TV in your preferred pose of the lounge lizard. You could start to get down on yourself for feeling so unmotivated and like such an inert slug and get all depressed about that. Or you can say, it's a waning Moon, or a void of course Moon, or the Moon is conjunct Neptune and it's okay to relax and do nothing. It's not a great time to launch a major initiative. There isn't any energy. By the same token, when the waxing phase comes you're ready to get activated. That's no problem because you allowed yourself a moment of stillness, you got your time to rest. You relaxed and recharged. This is the essence of astrology: alignment to the rhythmic movement of consciousness, to the natural movement of energy. We know when to wait and gestate an idea, and when to act decisively, without hesitation; we know when to let go of the past and look forward to the future. We know that cycles of nature are ever-flowing, ever replenishing. There's always another cycle, another chance to begin again, to try again.

The Moon is a constant focus of our attention as astrologers. Our state of wellbeing is affected by *natal Moon's house position*, an emotionally laden zone of the horoscope and life-world, something we care about deeply; *natal Moon's aspects*, showing innate emotional structures and recurrent feeling states; and *transits to natal* Moon, indicating crucial phases in emotional life.

Moon represents mother and the archetypal experience of being held and cared for. Moon shows our capacity for emotional attachment to others. It represents caring for our living space and work space, caring for ourselves by cooking and eating nourishing meals, healing the mother wound, and achieving emotional reconciliation with ourselves.

A basic astrological technique is to follow transiting Moon's aspects. Moon represents our embodied felt experience in the present moment. Natal lunar aspects condition us to respond emotionally in consistent patterns, both conscious and unconscious. But we also learn to fluidly move through a series or spectrum of emotional states, shown by transiting Moon's conjunction, opposition, and square with other transiting planets. In this way, we expand beyond the range of our habituated emotional responses, becoming more flexible and evolved beings. Similarly, we track aspects of the progressed Moon to other planets. The Moon's natal, transiting, and progressed aspects give astrologers a precise symbolism for developing emotional intelligence, showing our evolution through a range of feeling states.

During contacts of Moon and Mercury we're busy, nervous, high strung, talkative, focused on thinking, writing, communication, documents, and traveling from place to place.

When Moon aspects Venus we feel serene, loving, affectionate; emotional needs are well satisfied through friendship, relationships, beauty, art, music; love can be expressed through tender physical touch, caressing our existence.

When Moon aspects Mars we feel more energy, anger, annoyance, impatience, and sexual fire. We can be emotionally excitable, reactive, irritable, or volatile, expressing fiery emotions if needs aren't being met.

The same principles can be applied to the *progressed* Moon's aspects, except progressed Moon's aspects typically influence us for a year, not just a day. A concerned mother consulted me about her teenager daughter, Hannah, who had progressed Moon conjunct natal and progressed Mars in Scorpio in her second house, for a full year. During this phase, Hannah was angry, willful, selfish, emotionally volatile and difficult. She was very sexual, seductive, and magnetic; also quite acquisitive and materialistic (Mars in second house). She was waking up her Mars energy. Her mother said, "Now I guess I can relax, it's just going to be that way this year."

Moon-Jupiter aspects bring a mood of optimism, expansion, kind and nurturing demeanor; and interests in learning, education, planning. Our mood and attitude brighten as we see ways to satisfy our needs.

Under the influence of Moon-Saturn aspects we're focused, task-oriented. We have to stay on schedule, create order, do our chores, get organized, and follow through to finish and accomplish things. Sometimes Moon-Saturn aspects are linked to sadness, depressed moods, the feeling of unsatisfied needs. We exhibit serious demeanor and emotional strength; we have to take responsibility. When transiting Saturn aspects Moon, we may experience some moodiness and insecurity; we need to satisfy our needs for comfort, holding, and emotional attachment.

In contrast, with transiting or progressed Moon-Neptune aspects we feel like spacing out, taking a bath, meditating, reading fiction or mysticism. This is the moment to let our boundaries melt, become an amorphous jellyfish, feel how we're part of everything. Sometimes boundaries between self and other are fluid and enmeshed. We're capable of empathy, selflessness, and devotion. We may feel weak, indecisive, vague, or unclear, or engage in rescuing or caretaking of others. Moon-Neptune aspects signify the importance of extending compassion toward self and others who are suffering. Neptune transits to the Moon can evoke confusion and uncertainty or a wide, expansive feeling, an ecstatic, blissful mood. Later on I'll recount the story of a man who got arrested for driving while intoxicated during a progressed Moon-Neptune conjunction. I've also seen examples of people who did significant spiritual and psychological growth work during similar aspects.

Moon-Pluto aspects mark emotional upsets, surfacing of buried feelings or memories; bitterness, resentment, and negativity may build up and erupt and need to be released. Impurities of body, speech, mind, and action can be flushed out now. Pluto transits to Moon bring emotional catharsis and release, intensification of feeling and nurturing capacities, and desire for emotional closure and completion. Emotional attachments with others may feature themes of power, control, or domination. We feel our emotional agonies and work them through to completion.

While her progressed Moon was conjunct Pluto in Leo in the eleventh house, a woman filed a wrongful termination lawsuit against her former employer, which was a small corporation in which she'd been an officer. This action ripped the skin off an old wound and reopened many long-buried emotions, grievances, and revelations of conniving plots within this organization. For her this was an epic battle against the forces of evil. She told me, "I never stood up to injustice before." With progressed Moon in Leo, she filed this lawsuit as an act of self-respect and preservation of her dignity (Leo). The case was resolved out of court and she got a sizable settlement.

Natal, transiting, or progressed aspects of Moon and Uranus signify emotional excitability or an urge for freedom and independence. While Moon-Venus contacts shows a need for closeness, Moon-Uranus shows a need for distance or emotional separation.

Transiting Uranus aspects to Moon awaken a restless urge for change, freedom, breaking out of ruts, a move or changing the home. One seeks more emotional freedom, separation or differentiation from others.

Studying the Moon's aspects is a foundation of psychologically-oriented astrology, generating self-insight and awareness of our inner feeling life. At the conclusion of Chapter 3, I'll describe an example illustrating analysis of lunar aspects and the profound effect of transits to the natal Moon.

Saturn and the Practical Business of Life

Another key to chart interpretation is study of the influence of Saturn. Conscious astrologers attend to the practical business of life in accordance with natal Saturn's position, its current transiting sign and house position and aspects; and during major phases of Saturn's transit cycle: the waxing square at age 7–8, when hopefully a child gains self-control, focus, and capacity for industrious activity and learning; the Saturn opposition in adolescence; the waning square at 21–22; the Saturn Return at age 29; Saturn's waxing square in our mid-thirties; Saturn opposition at age 43–44; waning square at age 51; the Saturn Return at 58–59; waxing square at 65–66, and opposition phase at 72–73. At these times, life challenges us to be responsible, pragmatic, strategic—to form and sustain our commitments. We work our way through a series of practical life lessons.

During major Saturn transits when you're working your tail off and there's pressure on you and so much work to do, then knowledge of Saturn can bring inner peace and clarity of purpose. It doesn't bother you that you're not having much fun; you expect that from Saturn. But if you have defined goals, you don't feel so stressed out or conflicted about doing all that work. You're doing what you need to do. Saturn is often viewed as a depressive influence. But I don't think Saturn intrinsically makes people depressed. People become depressed when they're not meeting the challenges of Saturn—not working, not achieving. Saturn energy is about taking care of business and building our personal edifice. People who love their work and their commitments are less susceptible to depression. People who successfully accomplish a series of developmental tasks become steady and strong. They become *intentional* beings. This is how highly developed people live, with clearly defined intentions, and the maturity to slowly bring them to fruition.

Astrologers prepare to meet the challenges of Saturn's natal placement. For example, if Saturn is in our second house we prioritize saving and managing money. With Saturn in the fourth house, we have ongoing responsibility for a home or family, an office or property. With Saturn in the ninth house, it's important to study or travel, to be a teacher, scholar, or intellectual. With Saturn in the tenth house, our life path may involve becoming an accomplished professional, or a conscientious, authoritative parent.

Attunement to Saturn's transits through each house is essential. Here we're working hard, experiencing pressure to commit, organize, and accomplish things. I remember how, when I was 25, Saturn transited into my second house (finances), and I was down to my last dollar, twice. I put my last dollar on an altar and meditated quietly, feeling my innate value, even though I was totally broke. I was aware of the Saturn transit and knew I had to do whatever was necessary to get some money, so I worked various temp jobs. Once I went to work in the kitchen of an Indian restaurant. Ostensibly I was hired as a dishwasher, but they had me put on an apron and climb onto a tall ladder with a bucket of soapy water, to clean filthy grease off the walls above the stove. It seems that the next morning the health inspector was coming, and these walls had never been cleaned in thirteen years they'd been in business. After several hours I was covered in slop from head to toe. I was thinking about whether this was a good use of my college education. Right at that moment, the owner said to me, "You have done your job well. My son never visits me here at the restaurant anymore because he's in medical school and thinks he's so much more important than I am. But in the eyes of God it makes no difference if you are some big, important doctor or if you are cleaning the grease off these walls." Then he gave me a classic Indian head waggle and told me to go home and get cleaned up. I liked that man very much, and I learned the lesson that all jobs done well and with consciousness and gladness can bring satisfaction. I soon moved on and found better ways to make a buck. Each Saturn transit is a challenge to become more mature, more grounded and self-disciplined. Some astrologers would tell clients Saturn entering the second house is a difficult transit for money. But we can frame it differently and say Saturn poses a task of maturation and intelligence about money. In other words, it's a constructive process, not an affliction or malefic influence. It's a *purposeful challenge*. We have to refine the language we use if astrology is to be transformative.

Prediction, Destiny, and the Symbolic Attitude

A perennial question in our field is whether or not we're fated to experience certain events. Most people who engage in a serious study of astrology realize that a great deal of predictive acumen is possible using the methods of transits and progressions. (11) But this doesn't mean that all events are predestined or can be foreseen astrologically.

Liz Greene's book *The Astrology of Fate* is an extended meditation on the nature of fate, prediction, and destiny in astrology. Greene recounts the story of King Henri II of

France, who went to two different astrologers, both of whom predicted that on a certain date the King would die in a duel from a blow to the head. Sure enough, his death occurred exactly as predicted. Greene examined the king's chart to see if she could figure out what the astrologers had looked at to predict his death. She concluded that they'd focused on the king's Aries Sun square Saturn (Aries rules battles, duels, and the head). However, Greene reasoned, she herself had done many charts of people with the same planetary configuration but none of them suffered a fate similar to that of King Henri.

How could this be? Is it possible that the predestined, fated quality of planetary combinations no longer holds for modern persons? Perhaps, Greene wonders, the modern psyche has changed in such a way that we longer need to exteriorize events in order to experience planetary energies and archetypes. Greene contends that through the mediation of symbols we can overcome the compulsion to externalize events as an expression of planetary forces and can instead internalize and transform these energies through the magical power of symbols. She writes:

> Psychic energy tends to transform from instinctual compulsion to meaningful inner experience through the mediation of the symbol. In other words, psychic energy "introverts" if the image which corresponds to the outer compulsion emerges within the individual and if he is able to contain that compulsion through the mediating power of the image. . . . We are ultimately the inheritors of Ficino and the alchemists, who believed that the transformation of one's own substance was the only possible answer to fate. Paradoxically, this entails an embrace of one's fate.(12)

In the study of astrology, we learn to work cooperatively with the planetary archetypes, viewing each of their tests as means of embracing our fate and transforming our inner substance.

The Influence of C. G. Jung on Modern Astrology

This alchemical attitude toward the transforming power of symbols was originally inspired by the work of C. G. Jung, who made a number of important contributions to modern astrology. Many people are aware that Jung was an avid astrologer who cast birth charts for many of his patients. His library included books by authors such as Alan Leo, Charles Carter, and Sepharial. One of Jung's 1911 letters to Freud reads, "At the moment I am looking into astrology, which seems indispensable for a proper understanding of mythology. There are strange and wondrous things in these lands of darkness." (13) Maggie Hyde, author of *Jung and Astrology*, notes, "Jung therefore took up astrology alongside his work on *Symbols of Transformation*, and a month later he had well and truly got the astrology bug. On 12 June he told Freud he was coming across 'incredible things' in astrology. His evenings were taken up with chart calculation. . . ." (14) Jung later wrote, "Astrology, like the collective unconscious with which psychology is concerned, consists of symbolic configurations. The planets are the gods, symbols of the power of the unconscious."(15)

Astrology influenced Jung through its demonstration that we can anticipate precisely the timing of appearances of the archetypes. At the same time the astrological worldview, often reviled for being deterministic, unscientific, and confused in its attempts to predict events, has become more palatable to the public when viewed through the lens of Jung's ideas, especially the view that astrology is a form of religion, less a predictive science than a mythological language, a language of the psyche. (16) From this perspective, planets and zodiacal signs represent mythical, recurrent patterns of experience, universal human situations and motivations; and astrology is a practice of feeling, and merging with, the patterns of change and evolution symbolized by the planets and signs. We observe how at various times different archetypes imprint themselves on us and seek embodiment through us. Jung directly influenced Dane Rudhyar to formulate modern humanistic astrology, emphasizing personal growth, psychological awareness, integration of opposites, and the idea that the birth chart is a map of individuation and the tasks it entails.

A further example of how Jung transformed our understanding of the birth chart pertains to the psychological meaning of the Ascendant. The house immediately preceding the Ascendant, the twelfth house, was traditionally seen as a house of imprisonment and loss. Jung's work offers us a different understanding—that this house represents the realm of the unconscious mind, inclusive of the personal unconscious, biographical memories, hidden secrets, private, guarded areas of the psyche; and the collective, transpersonal unconscious of archetypal forms, mythological themes, and angelic, etheric, and spiritual realms. Through dreams, fantasies, imagination, and meditative states, and through contemplation of mythology and metaphysical principles, we widen our aperture of consciousness to encompass material from these imaginal and transpersonal domains. In his pivotal book, *Symbols of Transformation*, Jung described how the hero's mythic encounter with a monster, a dragon, or a great serpent represents the individual's transformative encounter with the deep unconscious (twelfth house), and emerging from this encounter as an individual, with clear boundaries, with awareness of my identity and my defining features (first house). The psychological meaning of the Ascendant is that it represents birth, self-awareness, the dawning of consciousness, the emergence of a sense of I, a subjective consciousness. It's the point of differentiation of my personal consciousness from the collective unconscious. On the opposite side of the horizon, the Descendant marks awareness of the

Other, and an objective viewpoint. It conveys feedback that comes to us directly from people and encounters in the outside world. The horizon of the birth chart depicts the character and behavior of the self and of others, and the interaction of self and others. The birth chart portrays who I am, archetypes I embody, and how I perceive others. What Jung's writings didn't address is how astrology describes self-unfolding over the course of time. In astrology, Time is the central archetype, the rhythmic template of nature and evolution.

The Archetype of Time, and the Birth Chart as Archetype

Jung's colleague Marie-Louise Von Franz noted the centrality of reflections on the meaning of time in the ancient cultures and religions of Egypt, Greece, India, and China. She wrote:

> Time . . . was originally looked upon as a Deity. . . . In man's original point of view time was life itself and its divine mystery. . . . Aion, the [Greek] god of time, is . . . an image of the dynamic aspect of existence. . . . All opposites—change and duration, even good and evil, life and death—are included in this cosmic principle. . . . . This same archetypal symbolism of time, as the godhead and also as an unending stream of life and death, can be found in India. . . . In the *Bhagavadgita* . . . Vishnu says: 'Know I am Time that makes the worlds perish, when ripe and come to bring them destruction.' Not only Vishnu but also Shiva represents time. He symbolizes the energy of the universe increasingly creating and sustaining the forms in which he manifests himself. Shiva is called *Maha kala*, 'Great Time', or *Kala Rudra*, 'all-devouring Time'. . . . [In China,] Yang and Yin are not static cosmic principles but alternating cosmic rhythms. . . . The word for time, *che*, means . . . a circumstance favourable or unfavourable for action. . . . Time in China was . . . a . . . continuum containing qualities or fundamental conditions. . . . [In] the *I Ching* . . . [t]ime consists . . . in certain time-ordered phases of transformation of the cosmic whole. (17)

Studying the divine mystery of time, astrology instructs us in the conditions that are favorable or unfavorable for action. We seek the auspicious moment. We follow the *alternating cosmic rhythms* and *time-ordered phases of transformation*. Called by many names—Aion, Vishnu, Rudra, Maha Kala, Che—time is our deity, our domain of contemplation, our teacher of spiritual liberation.

Building on the work of Jung, Dane Rudhyar elucidated the archetype of time, the cycle and its orderly phases, the principle of cyclical development, and the meaning of specific planetary cycles and transits. Rudhyar showed that there's a structure and organization to the flow of time, and the unfolding of personality also has a structure and organization defined by the horoscope. He observed that the birth chart itself forms an archetype, and made this astute comment:

> The symbolic meaning of the birth chart of an individual ... is actually, and as far as its psychological value is concerned, an archetype in his unconscious. It is perhaps the most powerful of all archetypes, when it is brought up to the light of consciousness, inasmuch as it can determine the entire conduct of the individual, his entire attitude toward himself and his life, and the quality of his expectancy with reference to future events and his destiny as a whole. (18)

The symbolism of astrology can positively shape and inform our conduct, our objectives, and our spiritual practices. Our task is to sharpen our alignment with the formative structure of the birth chart by understanding its component planets, signs, and houses, so we can fulfill the individual pattern of growth that it portrays.

To conclude this discussion of basic astrology, let's consider these words of the Sufi master, Hazrat Inayat Khan:

> It matters little whether you are on the top of the mountain or at the foot of it, if you are happy where you are. . . . The one who is able to keep his [her] equilibrium without being annoyed, without being troubled, gains that mastery which is needed in the evolution of life. . . . Stand through life firm as a rock in the sea, undisturbed and unmoved by its ever-rising waters.(19)

Astrologers strive to meet each event and experience consciously, with the noble attitude toward the changes of time invoked by Inayat Khan. Through reflection on astrological symbols and the nature of cycles, we develop equanimity and composure as we go through life's changes. Study of the birth chart shows us how we can express the different components of the personality (the planets) and navigate wisely all phases of the wheel of life symbolized by the twelve signs and houses. Astrology aids us in the practical affairs of life and also guides us on the path of spiritual awakening. That's the topic of this book.

Chapter 2

Finding a Spiritual Path: The Twelve Yogas of the Zodiac

ALL MYSTICAL TRADITIONS SPEAK OF A CONDITION OF ENLIGHTENMENT, expanded consciousness, and fully actualized spiritual potential. This has been called by names such as *Atman*, *nirvana*, *moksa* (liberation), *satori*, cosmic consciousness, and God realization. All traditions agree that this enlightened condition represents the highest stage and goal of human evolution. To reach this condition, it's helpful to do a *sadhana*, a discipline or practice of some kind, such as meditation. But how do we know which spiritual path is right for us? In our era we have access to a wide range of practices and teachings, such as yoga, vipassana meditation, bodywork and movement therapies, lucid dreaming, brain-wave synchronization soundtracks, channeling, Tantra, rebirthing, ayurvedic medicine, mystical Judaism and Christianity, Buddhism, Sufism, shamanism, out-of-body travel, macrobiotics, fasting, and transpersonal psychotherapies. While seekers now have more access to information about various traditions and practices than ever before, the array of options for spiritual growth can be confusing, making it difficult at times to know which path to follow.

Astrology provides invaluable guidance in finding and following a road to spiritual growth that's in alignment with who we are as individuals. The birth chart helps us to discern which approach to spiritual awakening is most suitable, both on a long-term basis and for the duration of particular transits or progressions. Studying our natal and transiting planets can inspire us to practice sadhana and take conscious steps to advance spiritually.

Every aspect of our incarnations as human beings is sacred and an aspect of the spiritual path—not just meditating, following a guru, or studying ancient mystical texts. From an astrological perspective, every event, every circumstance, and every relationship in our lives offers an opportunity for expansion of consciousness. Astrology confirms the fact that extraordinary spiritual pursuits (Kabir, the Indian poet-saint, calls them "spiritual gymnastics") aren't always necessary; and that "ordinary" aspects of human existence—such as childbirth, performing occupational roles, and working the earth to grow food—can be noble spiritual paths. Any road followed with consciousness and reverence can take us to the Light.

In many spiritual traditions, a teacher prescribes contemplative practices that match a student's personality and stage of development. Similarly, our birth charts help us determine for ourselves which methods or paths will be most fruitful to pursue. Moreover, the birth chart's complex symbolism accurately reflects the way we must integrate many facets of our lives and identities to develop an individualized sadhana and way of living. Typically this means we need to blend several different pursuits, for example a combination of gardening, meditation, parenting, music, and martial arts.

Study of the birth chart illuminates the stages of the path leading to transformation of awareness. The great sages of ancient India understood this, and there was a strong connection between astrology and the practices of yoga.(20) In Indian Vedic astrology certain planetary combinations are known as *yogas*, suggesting that particular natal configurations represent karmically determined patterns that serve as an individual's evolutionary path toward enlightenment.(21) The ancient Indian sages recognized that no single approach to spiritual growth is suitable for everyone, that there are numerous yogic paths leading to enlightenment or higher consciousness, and that astrology can assist each person in finding the most suitable practices and path. The planetary yogas in the natal chart were utilized to discern the proper approach to yoga or spiritual life for that individual.

The Twelve Yogas of the Zodiac: A Model for Spiritual Development

This chapter explains my own conception of how zodiacal signs demarcate twelve essential yogas or paths of spiritual development. I associate the signs with Sanskrit terms from the Indian yogic tradition that describe different facets of the spiritual path. I relate these zodiacal motifs with themes of corresponding houses of the birth chart, for example noting affinities between the sign of Cancer and the horoscope's fourth house.

The symbols of the zodiac can be understood in an almost infinite variety of ways. Figures 2, 3, and 4 feature some keywords describing the zodiacal signs. I try to avoid

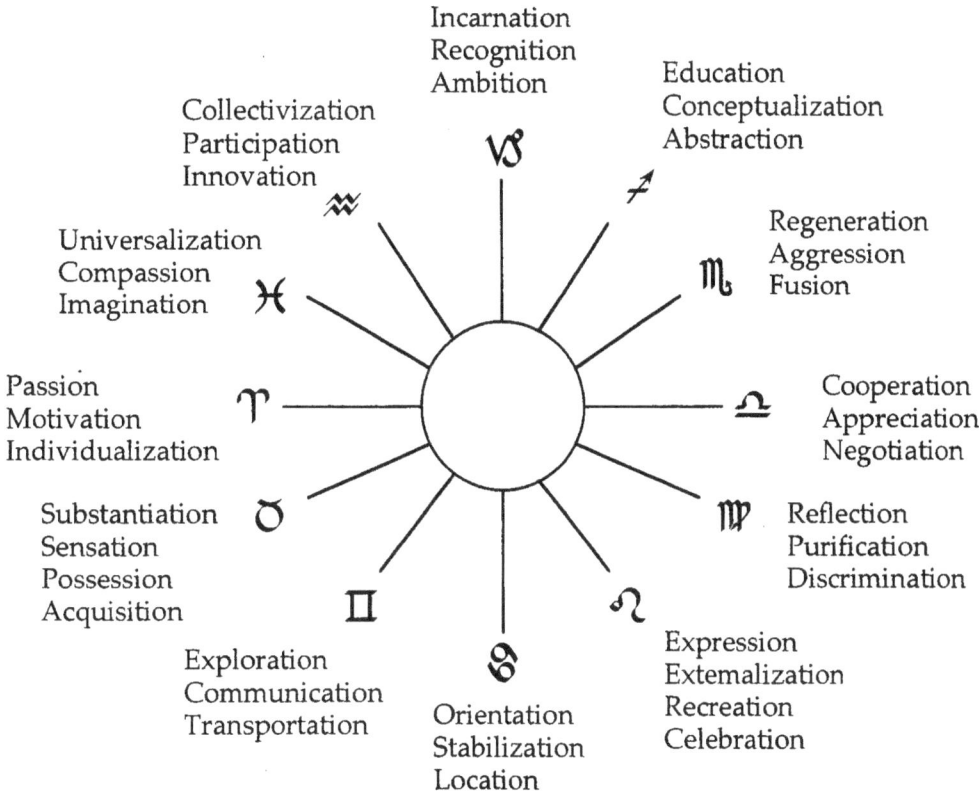

Figure 2. Zodiac as Twelve Phases of Evolution

using traditional descriptions of the qualities of each sign, such as equating Taurus with stubbornness or Leo with vanity and egotism, to suggest alternative ways of understanding these endlessly fascinating symbols. I link the meanings of the signs with their ruling planets and the twelve houses of the birth chart in a manner similar to the astrological alphabet popularized by Zipporah Dobyns.(22) In this system the first sign, Aries, house 1, and the planetary ruler of Aries, Mars, all refer to similar themes, which she describes as "self will in spontaneous action; initiative, impulse, ... pioneering spirit, vitality, ... enthusiasm for the new...." Taurus, its ruler Venus, and the second house comprise the second letter of the alphabetical alphabet: "Pleasure in manipulating the physical sense world; comfort, ... contentment, love of beauty in tangible possessions...." While some people feel this approach oversimplifies, Dobyns's model is a useful way of thinking that makes astrology easier to understand.

In the model of The Twelve Yogas of the Zodiac, the signs, their planetary rulers,

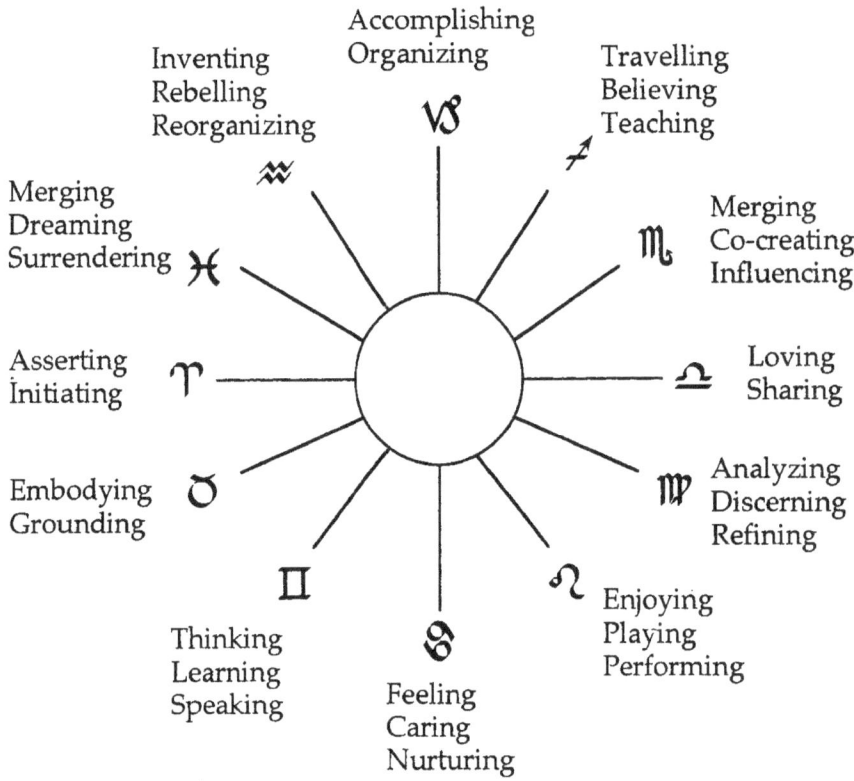

Figure 3. Mandala of Twelve Modes of Activity

and the house corresponding to each sign are viewed as specific dimensions or phases of the journey of awakening (Figure 4). This model suggests approaches to spiritual growth that you might pursue if you have emphasis in your birthmap on particular signs, houses, or planets. For example: having Sun in Taurus and Saturn in the second house; or Moon in Pisces and Neptune (ruler of Pisces) conjunct the Ascendant; or having several planets placed in the same sign or house. Planets are accentuated if they closely aspect the Sun, Moon, or Ascendant ruler, or one of the birth chart's angles. Contacts to the Moon's nodes also link us to planetary energies that need integration.

This chapter utilizes brief examples to convey the themes of these twelve yogas. As you read through these stories, reflect on your own birthchart and what it says about the path, or combination of paths, that's most appropriate for you. According to the makeup of your particular horoscope, one or more of the yogas described below will be emphasized. A natal chart featuring Sun in aspect to Saturn, Moon in Capricorn,

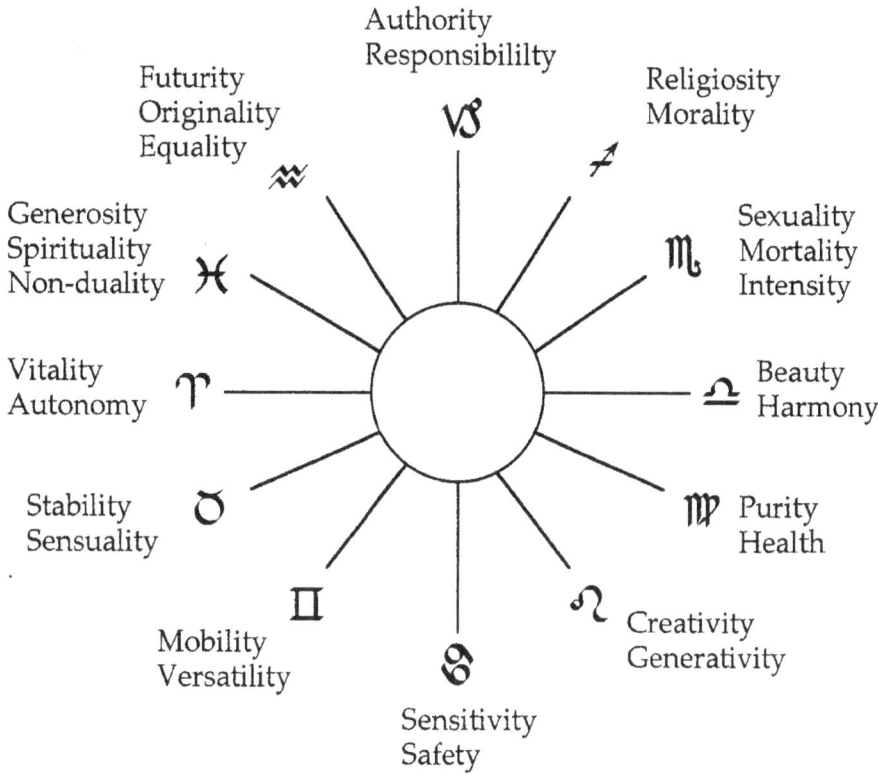

Figure 4. Mandala of Central Human Concerns

and several planets in the tenth house clearly emphasizes the Capricorn/tenth house yoga. More typically, the natal chart indicates a need to focus on several of these paths. And due to the influence of transits and progressions, we need to grapple with, and hopefully master, all twelve yogas over the course of life. Note that each planet's placement suggests themes deriving from both the planet's sign and house. So if your Sun is in Scorpio in the fifth house, refer to the issues pertaining to both Leo/fifth house and Scorpio/eighth house.

Aries/Mars/First House: Prana:
The Yoga of Identity, Vitality, Will, and Self-Assertion

If your birth chart emphasizes the sign Aries, its ruler, Mars, or planets in the first house, your spiritual path centers around instinctual energy, desire, exercising your will-power, self-assertiveness and self-definition. If your chart features Sun or other

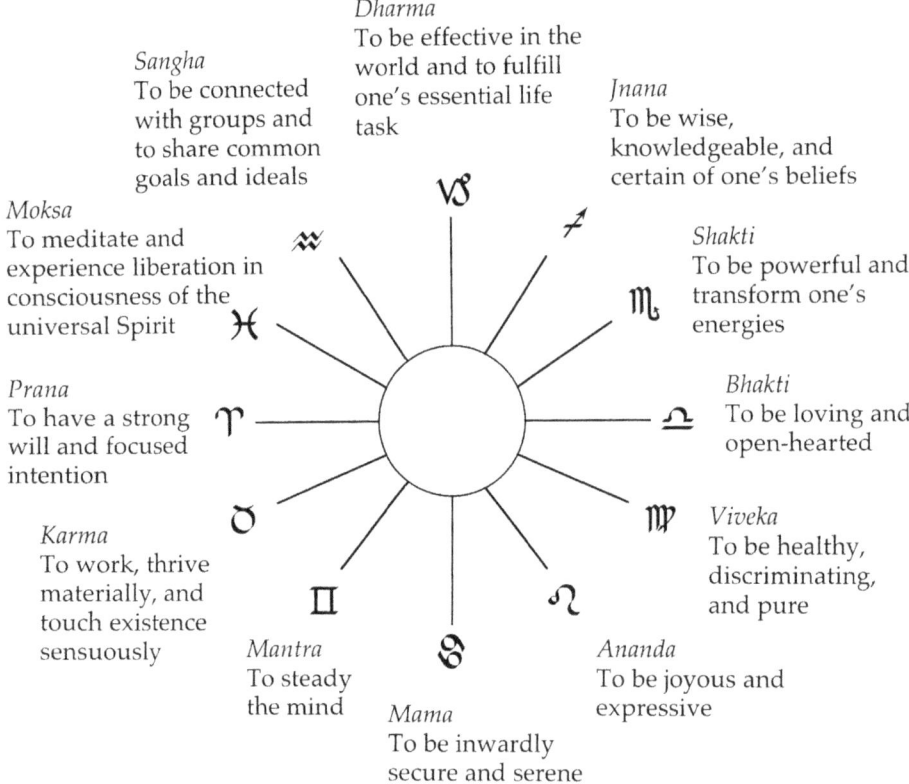

Figure 5. Mandala of the Twelve Yogas of the Zodiac

planets in Aries, or prominent placement of natal Mars, your way of being accentuates individuality, initiative, fiery determination, and a search for a feeling of vitality.

A man with Aries Sun in the fifth house gave up his meditation practice because it made him feel "dead." Instead he took up acting classes and weight lifting, both of which, he said, made him feel energetic and alive.

Aries signifies instinct and desire, thus, sexuality is a central issue. Wilhelm Reich had Sun in Aries square Mars in Cancer. His psychological theories and therapeutic practices focused on sexual healing, development of the capacity for orgasmic potency, and release of "character armor" embedded in our physical musculature.

Aries is not at all intellectual, but represents our physicality and force of will. Ogden, a man with Moon-Saturn conjunction in Aries in his fifth house had a very willful

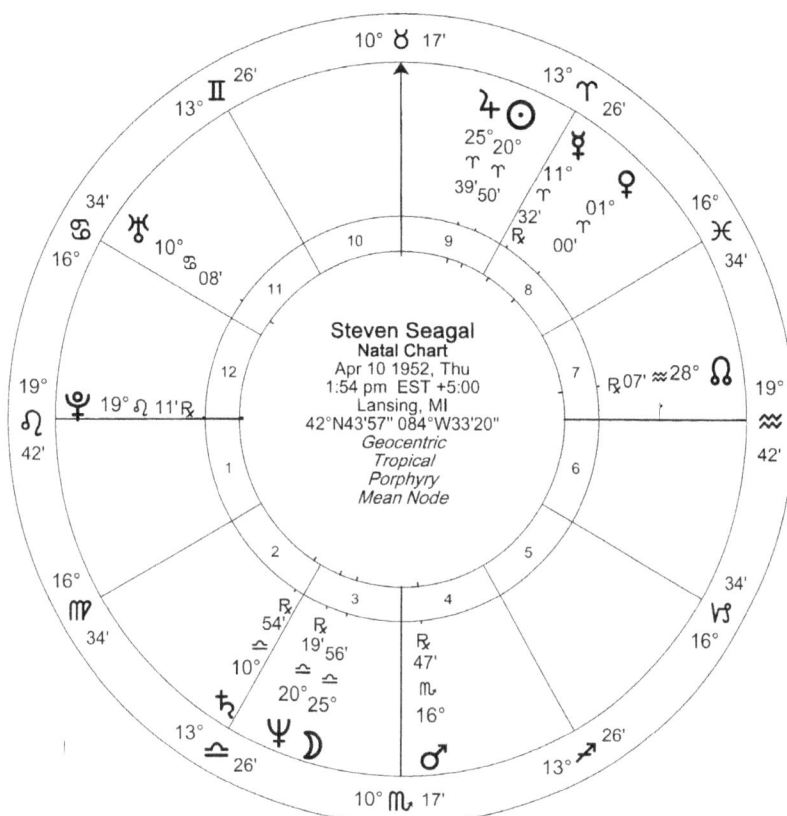

mother (Aries Moon) who pushed him into playing sports as a child, and he went on to compete in the Olympics and later became a professional athlete. More on Ogden later.

Action hero and martial artist Steven Seagal was born at a Full Moon opposite Sun, Jupiter, Mercury, and Venus in Aries; and he has Mars in its domicile, Scorpio, square Pluto at the Ascendant—a symbol of strength and power as well as violent combat. A true warrior, Seagal is an Aikido expert, a sixth degree Black belt Sensei in Aikido, and is also skilled in Judo, Karate, and Kendo knife fighting. He studied in Japan, spent 15 years in Asia studying Eastern philosophy (Sun-Jupiter in the ninth house), became a bodyguard (Aries) and eventually a Hollywood superstar known for his fight scenes. He considers himself an environmentalist and protector of the Earth.

People with aspects of Mars and Uranus need a strong physical outlet through some kind of exuberant or vigorous practice such as a martial art or competitive sport. People with prominent Mars-Jupiter aspects can be drawn to adventurous, outdoor activities, or situations requiring bravery, heroism, and valor. A man who'd spent years meditating said his most powerful enlightenment occurred while fighting a huge forest fire in Oregon, while transiting Uranus was conjunct his natal Mars and Jupiter. He experienced an emergence of bravery and valor in the heat of crisis, a significant initiation into being a warrior.

Film icon Clint Eastwood has Scorpio Ascendant and its ruler, Mars, in Aries conjunct the north node. Eastwood projects a rugged, macho tough-guy, Aries persona. With Mars conjunct the node, Eastwood is an archetypal hero figure, always portraying a gunslinger, adventurer, detective, enforcer, or warrior.

Prominent placement of Mars or planets in Aries indicate that it's important to strengthen or restructure your physical body through vigorous exercise or practices such as *hatha yoga*, Postural Integration (Rolfing), bioenergetics, weight training, or any other strenuous physical discipline. The focus here is on developing a stronger, more vital and balanced, and less obstructed physical vehicle. The practice of yoga postures (*asanas*) generate an intense *prana* (vital energy), which can propel one into deeper states of consciousness. People with natal aspects between Mars and Saturn may be especially attracted to hatha yoga because of the increased strength and vital energies this practice generates. For example, yogi Bikram Choudhury was born with a close Mars-Saturn conjunction in Cancer, quincunx his natal Sun.

B. K. S. Iyengar, the most creative, intense practitioner of hatha yoga of our modern era, has Mars exalted in Capricorn, opposite Jupiter, signifying strength and vigor. Mars is conjunct the Nadir and squares the Moon, showing access to deep reserves of physical strength as well as tireless effort and emotional involvement as a husband and father who supported a large family. Mars is quincunx Saturn, signifying an intensity present from birth, a tension to achieve the focused expression of will power, an interior buildup of energy that could only be satisfied by assuming innumerable yoga postures allowing a full circulation and release of energy. His natal Sun is in a fire grand trine with Moon in Aries and Saturn in Leo. Iyengar has a fiery, lionlike personality and a thick mane of hair typical of someone with strong Leo energy. Saturn trine Sun signifies intense self-discipline, and Neptune culminating at the Midheaven is appropriate for a yogi, a mystic personality. Chiron in Pisces is placed in the sixth house of health issues and health disciplines. He experienced profound healing and self-transformation through the practices of yoga and became the ultimate mentor and trainer of yoga students. With Sun, Mercury, and Venus in Sagittarius, Mr. Iyengar is a dynamic teacher who has given thousands of public demonstrations and lectures and achieved excellence in writing books lucidly expounding the philosophy of yoga. The Sagittarius emphasis is reflected in the fact that he refined and popularized standing yoga poses that thoroughly stretch and strengthen the legs (Sagittarius). Saturn and

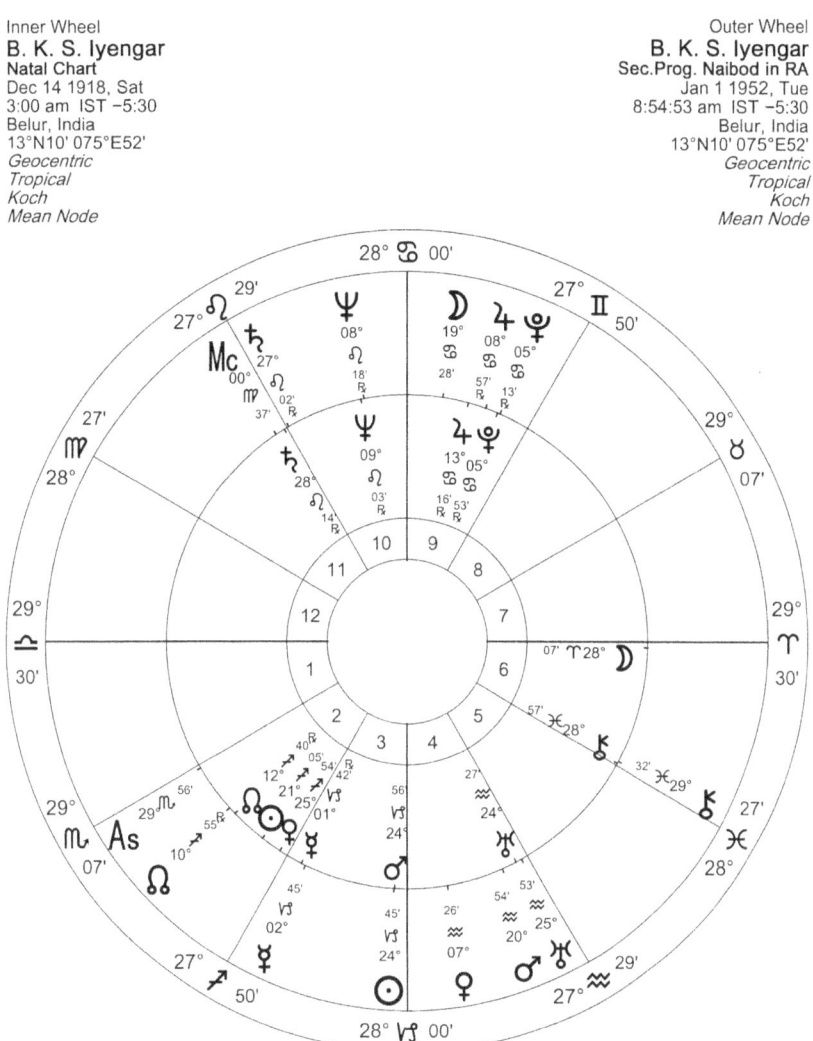

Neptune trine the natal Sun reflects his background as a man of humble origins who overcame poverty and physical weakness, worked extremely hard, and grew up to be a great teacher who traveled internationally. With Sun sextile Uranus in Aquarius in the fifth house, two of his children, Geeta and Prashant, became great teachers and yoga innovators.

In his teenage years immediately before he was initiated into yoga, Iyengar suffered from multiple ailments, including malaria, tuberculosis, and typhoid fever, corresponding to the time when transiting Saturn was conjunct natal Mars, activating the quincunx to Saturn. Through disciplined practice of hatha yoga he regained his strength and became the triumphant master of the body and a radiant embodiment of vitality and fearlessness. Iyengar was on fire with yoga from the age of 15 when transiting Saturn reached conjunction with his natal Uranus and he began working creatively within and beyond the traditional structure of hatha yoga discipline (Uranus opposite Saturn). He practiced in an evolutionary way that revolutionized yoga. In 1952, Iyengar was discovered by the great violinist Yehudi Menuhin, who took classes from him. From this time on, Iyengar became a world force in yoga. In 2004, Time Magazine named him one of the 100 Most Influential People. Looking at Iyengar's secondary progressed chart for 1952 is quite illuminating. His progressed Sun was exactly conjunct Mars, planet of the graceful yogi and his poses of the warrior (Virabhadrasanas I, II, and III). In addition, this was the time of Iyengar's progressed Full Moon in Cancer, a culminating moment. The progressed Full Moon was approaching his Midheaven, suitable symbolism for a period that raised him to public prominence. Also, his progressed Mars in Aquarius was soon to pass over Uranus and oppose Saturn; this represented how the internal evolution of his Mars energy through intensive yoga led to a restructuring of his entire being over a number of years. Every aspect of his consciousness was activated by this powerful influence of progressed Mars, culminating in his publishing *Light on Yoga*, sometimes called the bible of yoga.

When Mars is prominent in a natal chart, we need to strengthen or redirect the expression of physical and sexual energies. Yogi Amrit Desai, originator of Kripalu Yoga, has Mars (ruler of Aries) placed in the tenth house near his Midheaven (using a birth time given to me by one of his longtime devotees). Amrit's teachings emphasize awakening and directing vital energy (prana) through yoga postures (asanas) and breathing practices, combined with aerobic exercise such as running. Amrit Desai's natal Sun is in a Grand Cross with Pluto, Saturn, and Uranus. Sun square Pluto signifies his power to bestow *shaktipat*, awakening *kundalini* energy in others. Sun square Saturn symbolizes his intense discipline and lifelong commitment to yogic practices. Sun opposite Uranus symbolizes his innovative approach to yoga, especially his introduction of "meditation in motion" and the "posture flow" in hatha yoga, where instead of performing isolated and static asanas, the practitioner's body flows spontaneously through various poses under the liberating impetus of the inner shakti. More on Amrit Desai later.

The first house of the natal chart is the realm of personal identity. In the first house my goal is to make myself happy, to be who I am without apology. At the Pisces or twelfth house stage of evolution you transcend identification with a particular self-construct or self-image. The focus here is on consciousness of your identity, your motives, and your desires. In the first house we work on creating a well defined personality so that particular archetypal energies can express and be embodied through us. As spiritual

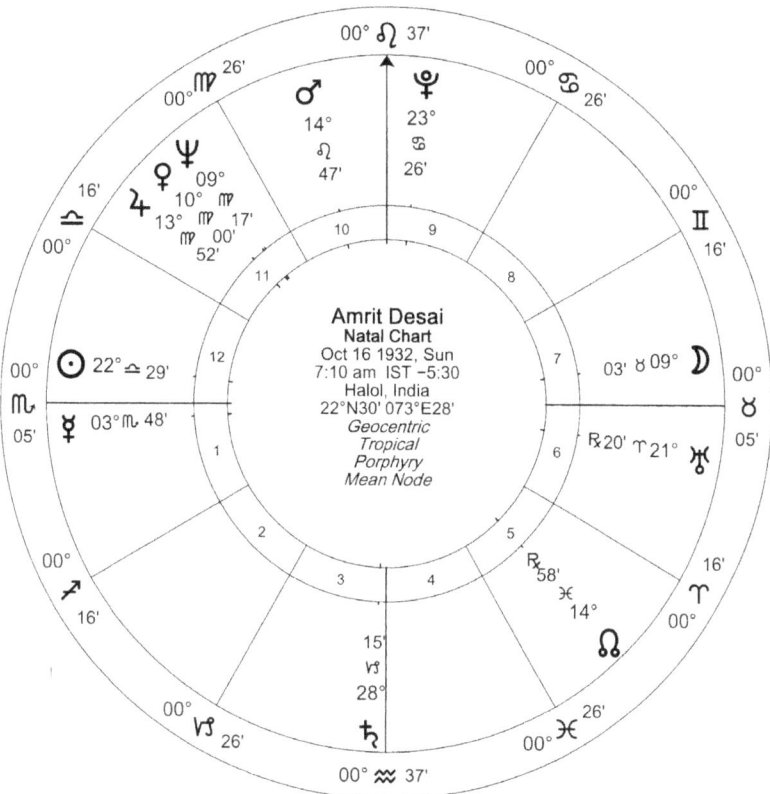

teacher Ram Dass once said, "You have to be somebody before you can be nobody."

Planets in the first house describe central facets of our self-image, personality characteristics, and visible behaviors. Mercury in the first house often indicates a strong communicator, a highly verbal and mentally alert or inquisitive individual. Jupiter is found in the first house of many teachers and educators. Ram Dass (Chapter 12) has Jupiter and Pluto in his first house, apt symbolism for a powerful, influential (Pluto) teacher (Jupiter). A man with Uranus conjunct his Ascendant gradually outgrew the oddball self-image of his youth and emerged as an inventive computer science wizard. A young woman with Mars in her first house pursued a career in gymnastics and thrived on the excitement of competition. A woman with Neptune in her first house had many prophetic, psychic dreams, was unmotivated to pursue worldly goals, and was guided by faith and intuition.

A man whose unconventional parents raised him in a psychedelic commune had Saturn in Taurus placed in his first house. He vehemently rejected his parents' values and lifestyle, was a serious student of history and economics, became a dentist, and got involved with a conservative (Saturn) political movement. His central priorities in life were to achieve social status and financial stability. This was his appropriate life path.

When natal or transiting planets are in your first house, it's important to stand consciously in your aloneness and your wholeness, in a state of conscious personality integration. You have to know who you are and stand in the truth of that identity. Here it's important to feel in charge of myself, to feel "I am who I will myself to be."

With Sun in the first house, we strongly project our distinctive personality. A man with Scorpio Sun in the first house was a radio talk show host renowned for his sarcastic comedic personality. Kristine, with Sun-Mercury-Venus-Neptune in Scorpio in the first house, was formerly a model (Venus) and is now a spiritual artist and educator who projects a refined aesthetic image through her colorful and expressive wardrobe. A man with a Sun-Saturn conjunction on the Ascendant in Sagittarius is a magazine publishing executive.

A teenager with natal Saturn in her first house in Leo and a Sun-Venus conjunction in Aries in her tenth house was physically beautiful (Venus conjunct Sun), gifted as an artist and musician (Venus), performing music and painting with an inspired exuberance and vitality that were awesome to witness. She also had a painfully shy streak and a negative self-image (Saturn in first house) that at times inhibited her creativity (Saturn in Leo). Her spiritual path focused on resolving these identity issues so she was ultimately able to express herself, in many media, as a spirited, lively, passionate individual (Sun in Aries).

John Lennon had an Aries Ascendant and its ruler, Mars, conjunct the Moon's north node and widely conjunct the Sun. John had periodic problems with his fiery temper, and in his youth his angry outbursts at times were quite violent. John married Yoko Ono in 1969 while transiting Uranus and Jupiter were conjunct his natal Mars in Libra, the sign of the couple. Soon after their marriage John and Yoko held a bed-in for peace. They lay in bed naked and gave interviews talking about peace and war, like a pair of stoned mischievous angels. Their unprecedented, brash, and open celebration of love was a revolutionary act, a proclamation of sexual and human liberation (Uranus conjunct Mars in Libra), and a longing for peace (Libra) and the end of war (Aries). There was in all of this a strong element of self-assertion by Lennon, who was separating and differentiating from his identity as a member of the Beatles. Using Porphyry house system, Moon is in the tenth house, but near the eleventh cusp and in the eleventh sign from the Ascendant. I believe it can be helpful to look at charts through the lens of different house systems, and casting Lennon's chart using the Koch house sys-

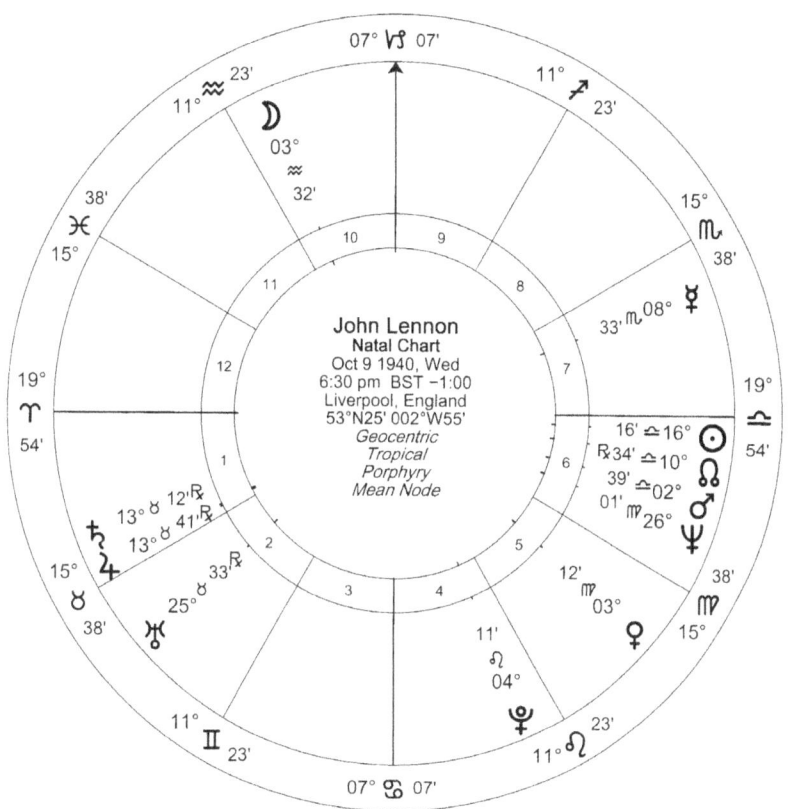

tem places his Moon in the eleventh house. Lennon's Aquarius Moon in the eleventh house, opposite Pluto in Leo signifies his membership in the most influential musical group in history. Also note Saturn's co-rulership of his tenth and eleventh houses, and the strength of Saturn conjunct Jupiter in Taurus and also conjunct Uranus, ruling the Aquarius Moon. The Beatles, as a group, expressed the feeling of freedom and liberation that marked the 1960s. We'll return to John Lennon later.

Taurus/Venus/Second House: Karma:
The Yoga of Action and Reward, Money, and Enjoyment of the Body

With a natal emphasis on Taurus, its ruler Venus, or the second house, money and physical comfort are central priorities. Here we develop a pragmatic attitude to life, striving to achieve a prosperous material existence, and to cultivate self-esteem and a sense of competency. Here the path is to enjoy the serenity that comes from financial and material stability and sensuous enjoyment. Although these aspects of human life are reviled by some religions and spiritual teachings, they're an important facet of our incarnate existence. It's important not to become totally preoccupied with glutting oneself with sensual experience and material possessions and to remember that, as the Buddha taught, everything is impermanent, including pleasure. But moderate enjoyment and satisfaction have a place in a balanced spiritual life.

Taurus and the second house are both concerned with satisfying basic material needs, embodying our core values, and following the path of *right livelihood*. Emphasis here indicates a need to understand the laws and principles of money and to manage resources effectively. In Taurus and the second house our spiritual growth is centered around the principle of *karma* and *karma yoga*, the path of work and action. The law of action and its results gives us immediate feedback about the quality of our effort and attitudes. The Taurus and second house yoga is a path of generating abundance and practicing what David Spangler calls *the laws of manifestation*.(24) Spirit infuses and interpenetrates this visible, physical world, filling it with radiance, light, and magic. And money is the energy of spirit made manifest. Ideally, our attunement to the spiritual forces of life enables us to have the right relationship with money so that our material needs are satisfied adequately. If you offer something positive in the universe, someone will pay you for it, whether it's for goods or services. Of course, sometimes our material path is difficult, and we have to live frugally and within a budget, appreciating the simple things. In Taurus, we learn the principles of money—the value of working hard, saving, spending wisely, creating an environment of prosperity. In Part III we'll study the astrobiographies of Tagore, Kriyananda, and Muktananda, all of whom had Sun in Taurus.

John Lennon, with Jupiter-Saturn-Uranus in Taurus in his first house, was fantastically wealthy.

A man with Taurus Sun in his second house drifted away from his involvement with psychic readings and channeled teachings, and became focused on the pursuit of a lucrative job. He proclaimed, "Making money is my spiritual path."

A man with Sun, Moon, and Venus in Taurus and Saturn-Pluto conjunct in Leo in the second house is a multi-millionaire with a large stock portfolio who has spent a lifetime managing his investments. With his Sun and Moon in Taurus placed in the twelfth house (altruism), he's a philanthropist who anonymously gives away large sums of money to aid others.

A socially conscious woman with a Sun-Mars conjunction in Taurus in the eighth house (joint resources), square to Saturn and Pluto in the eleventh house (social awareness, organizational involvements) is married to a very wealthy man. While she enjoys the comfort that this marriage affords her, she's troubled by the contrast between their opulent, luxurious lifestyle and her awareness of the pervasive poverty and suffering in the world (Saturn-Pluto in the eleventh). She has had many arguments with her husband because of her desire to contribute money to social causes, and she only agreed to stay in the marriage after he reassured her he'd make regular financial contributions to charitable organizations.

A man with Sun in Taurus opposite Neptune was quite spaced out and reported that he felt like he was not in his body. He began to feel more grounded when he reduced his daily pot smoking (Neptune) and began practicing sensory awareness exercises that made him more aware of his body and helped him function more effectively in the world.

With Sun in the second house, a person's self-worth seeks to be validated by solid earnings. A man with a Leo Sun in the second house focused on earning money to support having children. He made creative use of resources, for instance, by financing the construction of an elaborate display at the Burning Man festival. A man with the Sun, Mercury, and Venus in Leo in the second house was a successful salesman who, according to his wife, is obsessed with money and investments.

Jiva (see chart on page 46), who had Moon in Taurus, Venus-Jupiter on the Ascendant, and Sun, Moon, and Mars in her second house in Capricorn, worked for a large international bank and was deeply immersed in the world of finance. Because the Capricorn planets squared Neptune in her eleventh house (groups), Jiva often dreamed of quitting her job and living in a rural spiritual community. However, as a single mother with two children (Mars, ruler of fifth house, conjunct Sun), she recognized that for the time being her path was to sustain her family materially, and to pay occasional visits to the yoga ashram. She resolved the tension between her need to be a strong provider (Taurus Moon and second house emphasis) and her Neptunian spiritual ideal. With Sun conjunct Mars in Capricorn, she studied in her spare time and became licensed to practice acupuncture, the science of using needles to alter the flow of *chi* energy.

Alicia had Neptune in the second house. She had terrible financial problems because she made bad financial decisions, spent indiscriminately, didn't keep financial records, didn't file her tax returns, couldn't balance her checkbook, and was constantly overdrawn in her bank account. I'll return to Alicia later.

Major aspects of Venus—dispositor of Taurus—often represent a person's relationship to wealth and possessions. Financial tycoon Donald Trump has natal Venus conjunct Saturn and square Jupiter. Venus-Saturn aspects show the importance of saving and gradual accumulation of funds. Venus-Jupiter aspects are a planetary indicator of wealth, comfort, expensive tastes, and opulent lifestyle. Microsoft founder and philanthropist Bill Gates has a Venus-Saturn conjunction, square Jupiter and Pluto in the

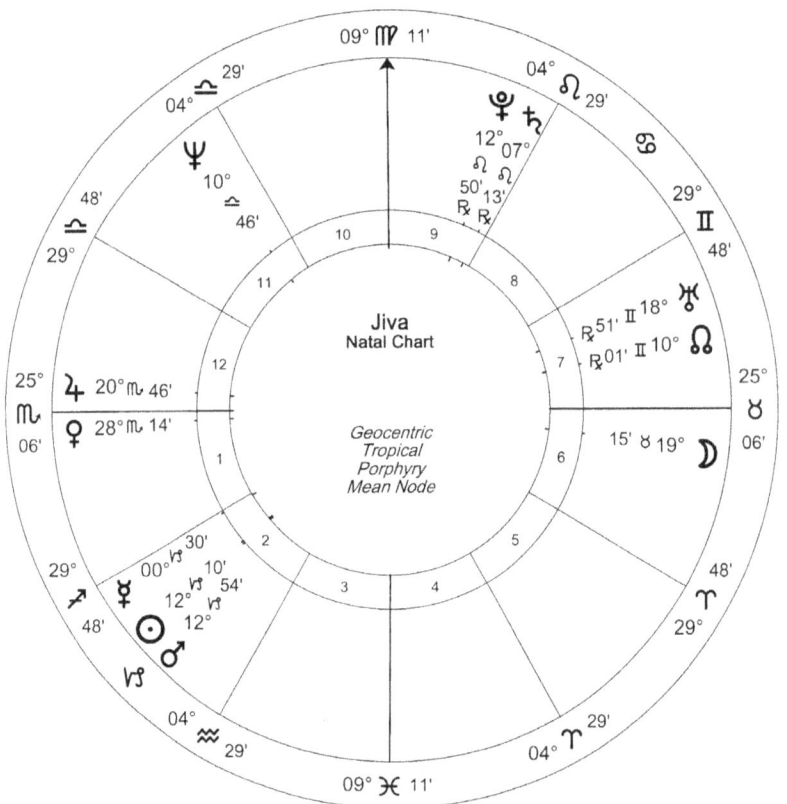

second house, symbolizing his immense fortune. Billionaire Steve Jobs had an exact Venus-Jupiter opposition. His Venus was in a Grand Cross involving Mars, Neptune, Jupiter, and Uranus, which suggests to me the aesthetic genius that led Jobs to design sleek, attractive products that the whole world wants to own and enjoys operating. Apple products have a magnetism, elegance, and ease of use that generates fervor, excitement, and devotion among customers, reflecting the aspects of Venus, Mars, and Neptune. The charts of Jobs and Gates appear in Chapter 4.

A contrasting example: Sufi master Hazrat Inayat Khan had Saturn conjunct Neptune in his second house. Although he longed for solitude and retreat from the world, his path was to ground his enlightened awareness in the material world by establishing the Sufi Order. He underwent considerable material challenge and austerity in order to serve this spiritual life mission. Note how impeccably this expresses the energy of Saturn-Neptune. Inayat Khan's teachings apply the principles of Sufi mysticism to everyday life, and celebrate the splendor and sacredness of Nature (Neptune in Taurus).

Gemini/Mercury/Third House: Mantra:
The Yoga of Mind, Thought, and Speech

If Taurus represents the body, then Gemini and the third house represent the mind and our language and communication skills. If you have prominent placements of planets here (or an accentuated Mercury), your spiritual path may focus on learning, thinking, writing, verbal fluency. It's helpful to pursue the practices of mental concentration through meditation, forming positive thoughts and mental images; also the practice of right speech. Most spiritual traditions emphasize techniques for focusing and cleansing the mind, for example observation of the flow of thought in *zazen* or *vipassana* (mindfulness) meditation; or the practice of *mantra yoga* using sound vibrations to change and uplift our state of consciousness. In Buddhism we learn to consciously form thoughts of peace and extend compassion toward others. (See the Metta Sutra in Pisces section below.) Other Gemini/third house practices include affirmations, reading of sacred texts, chanting and repetition of mantras, sacred sounds, and prayers. Gemini and the third house also refer to the narrative faculty, so planets here show a need to communicate your ideas and tell your story. Gemini and the third house correspond to what Kashmir Shaivism calls *maitrika shakti*, the power of language—which both emanates and describes the manifest world of form, and ultimately leads to liberation from its grasp through the vibratory power of mantra. We'll discuss this in Chapter 5.(25)

A woman with Venus, Mercury, and Jupiter in Gemini discovered that her preferred spiritual practices were story-telling and the Progoff Intensive Journal method. A man with Sun and Moon in the third house, opposite Neptune, wrote poetry and fiction in his spare time and found this quite satisfying. A man with Mercury conjunct Saturn in the tenth house is a landscape architect who devises solutions to practical problems in the home and garden. Another man, with Mercury conjunct Neptune, enjoys reading mystery novels to relax his mind. A woman with Mercury square Neptune is deeply immersed in reading and writing poetry, and considers this her main spiritual discipline. A man with a Sun-Saturn-Neptune conjunction in his third house experienced deep states of meditation through intense, concentrated practice of *mantra yoga*. Gurumayi Chidvilasananda has Mercury conjunct Venus in Gemini at the Midheaven, square her Ascendant, trine Neptune and sextile Pluto. She is a captivating speaker who gives lucidly articulated discourses on yogic texts describing the nature of the mind. Her melodious voice is a refined instrument.

Dane Rudhyar (see chart on page 48), who published 52 books and innumerable articles, had Sun in the third house and a conjunction of Mars, Jupiter, Neptune, and Pluto in Gemini. Rudhyar's dynamic personal identity was expressed in writings encompassing astrology, philosophy, and poetry.(23)

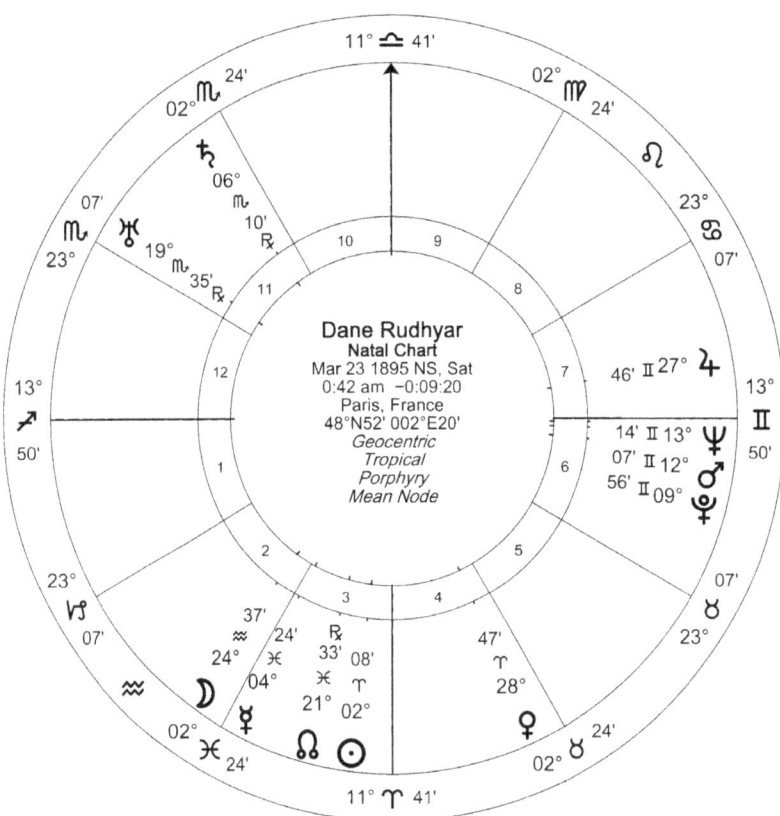

Poet Gary Snyder has Mercury, Venus, and Jupiter in Gemini, and Saturn in Capricorn in the third house, trine his Taurus Sun. A master of naturalistic description, his words are filled with a fierce, incantatory power (Saturn in third house opposite Pluto, square Mars-Uranus). Poet and translator Robert Bly has Mercury near his Ascendant. Novelist Joyce Carol Oates has Sun and Mercury in Gemini. Mystical poet and essayist Andrew Harvey has Sun, Moon, and Mars in Gemini. William Butler Yeats, with a Sun-Uranus conjunction in Gemini in the fifth house (creativity), crafted words into completely original poetic utterances. Salman Rushdie was born with Sun-Moon in Gemini conjunct Uranus, apt symbols for a highly original writer and storyteller whose work has been controversial and a focal point for social change and heightened political awareness. Allen Ginsberg had a Sun-Mercury conjunction in Gemini. His writings featured detailed, "close to the nose" descriptions of events, feelings, people, and places. When I met Ginsberg in 1980 he helped me with my writing, telling me to be less abstract and theoretical and to stay close to what Wallace Stevens called the "concrete particulars."

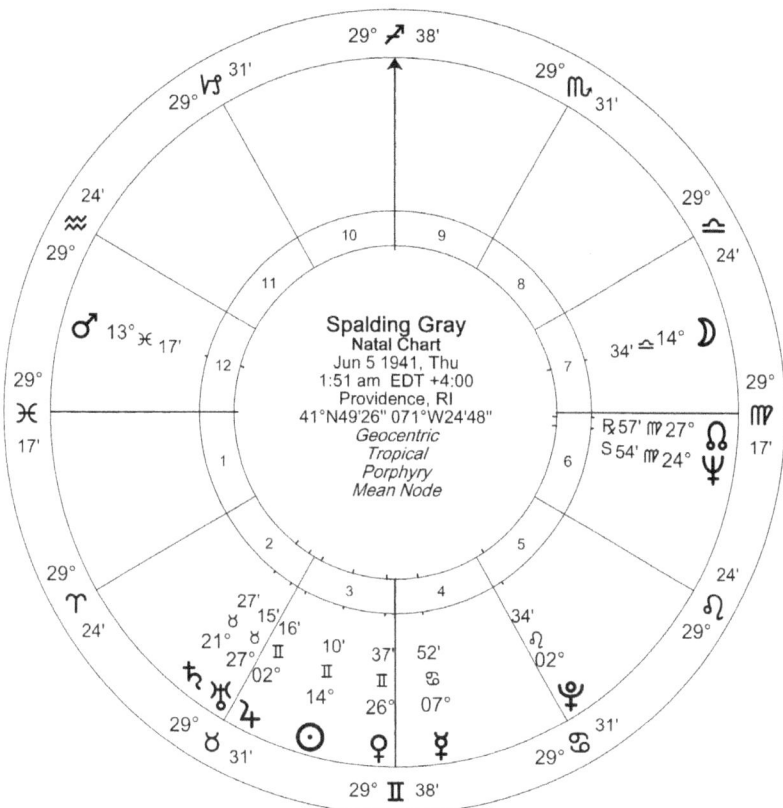

Performance monologist Spalding Gray had Gemini Sun in the third house, along with Venus and Jupiter in Gemini. He was the ultimate raconteur, one of our finest storytellers. With Sun square Mars, Gray was witty, a firecracker, always edgy, and he needed to tell his story. It's noteworthy that Gray had Neptune conjunct the north node at his Descendant, and his work describes a suffering that could never be expunged, perhaps stemming from the suicide of his mother. Neptune-node conjunction and Sun square Mars in the waters of Pisces and in the twelfth house are symbols of the loneliness and despair that drove Gray to his own act of suicide, which occurred through drowning—the tragic end of a brilliant and wickedly funny person.

The third house governs our sibling relationships and, more broadly, our experience of speech and communication. Louise, a woman with Neptune in Scorpio in the third house, had an argument with her husband over his failing to follow through with a household task he'd promised to complete. It reminded her of other occasions when agreements weren't honored, when people didn't do what they said they were going

Astrology and Spiritual Awakening, Part I 49

to do. That reminded Louise that she had twelve siblings, so she felt keenly what it's like to not be listened to, saying, "I felt totally lost and invisible in that family. Because I was my dad's favorite I drew the wrath of my siblings. They resented me and said mean things behind my back." Her third-house Neptune is in Scorpio, signifying the nastiness, undermining aggression, and insidious sniping of her siblings. Louise said, "None of my siblings would listen to me and they'd always forget things we'd talked about." Neptune represents a vulnerability, a sensitive point. Louise was sensitive about her voice not being heard and feeling invisible and forgotten. Attention to the importance of right speech and listening to each other in conversation is a significant yoga when this house is emphasized.

With Sun in the third house we're greatly interested in reading, writing, and communication skills. For example, Fred's natal Sun is in Libra in the third house, conjunct Saturn and Neptune. Fred's calling is to become a novelist, musical composer (Libra), and songwriter (third-house Sun). With Sun in Libra (sign of relationships) conjunct Saturn–Neptune in the third house, he writes romantic love songs and is working on a novel about relationships. He has interesting observations (third house) about people and their relationships (Libra). Fred asked me whether he should quit his job to pursue writing. Fred has natal Jupiter in Taurus in the tenth house. In alignment with Jupiter's rulership of Sagittarius (law), Fred works as a legal secretary, a position he obtained in 2000, when transiting Jupiter and Saturn were conjunct in Taurus at his Midheaven, conjoining his natal Jupiter. He does this job to make good money (Jupiter in Taurus). His career in the legal field had developed and advanced while transiting Jupiter and Saturn were conjunct in his tenth house. This fortunate opportunity enabled him to establish the professional and life structures needed for long-term prosperity. Fred gained from this job the financial comfort that allowed him to continue pursuing his imaginative writing (third-house Sun-Neptune).

Cancer/Moon/Fourth House: Mama:
The Yoga of Emotional Attachment, Caring, and Family

Cancer, its ruler Moon, and the fourth house concern emotional life, our sense of place, feelings of rootedness, and our ability to draw sustenance and inspiration from ancestral roots and our family, ethnic, or national heritage. Some spiritual traditions denigrate the entanglements of family life and encourage detachment from emotions. But with natal emphasis here, spiritual life may center around following the path of the householder, and experiencing the emotional intensity of family life. One may need to explore some form of "emotional yoga" or psychotherapy, to heal the past, to develop the capacity for bonding and attachment, to understand family dynamics and intergenerational issues. Cancer and the fourth house are areas of the chart that focus on emotional dynamics, memory, and resolution of early developmental issues. Natal

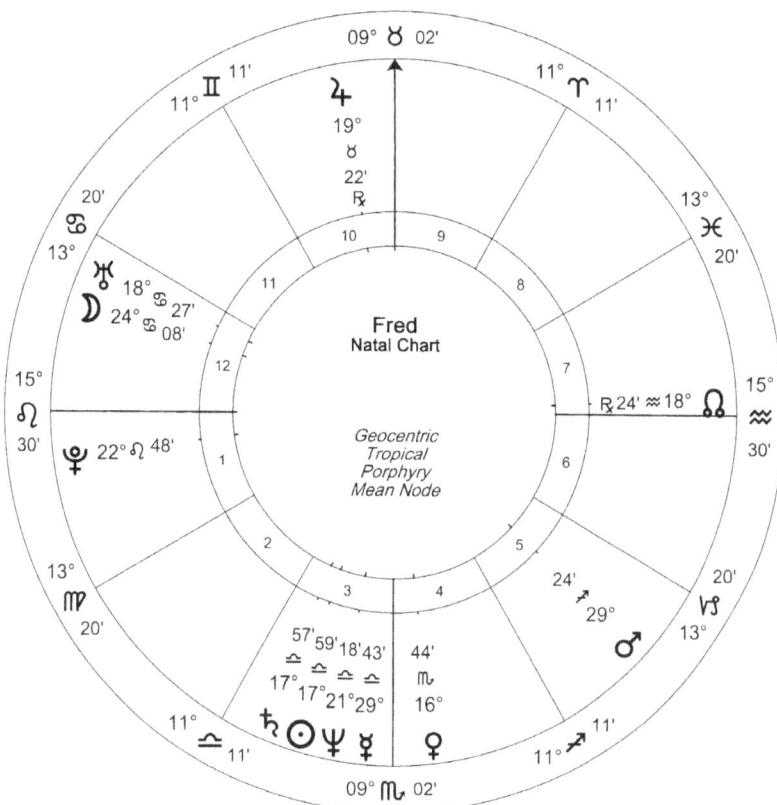

placements here can indicate emphasis on the path of *mama yoga*, clarifying emotions and connecting with one's emotional and family roots. You may also flourish through cultivation of the domestic arts, such as cooking and gardening. This is true for men as well as for women.

Novelist and essayist Wendell Berry (see chart on page 52) has written extensively about agricultural issues and is a proponent of the values of family, farm, local community, and land conservation. He has natal Sun in the fourth house and Mercury, Venus, and Pluto in Cancer in the third house. His Gemini Moon and third-house Mercury show the emphasis on writing.

Victor, a thirty year-old Buddhist meditation practitioner, came into therapy during his Saturn Return in the fourth house. He'd been estranged from his family for several years while he traveled and practiced meditation on retreat in India. He was feeling a need for greater stability, and he wanted to buy a home. He went to visit his family and had a meaningful exchange with his father, who agreed to loan him money for a

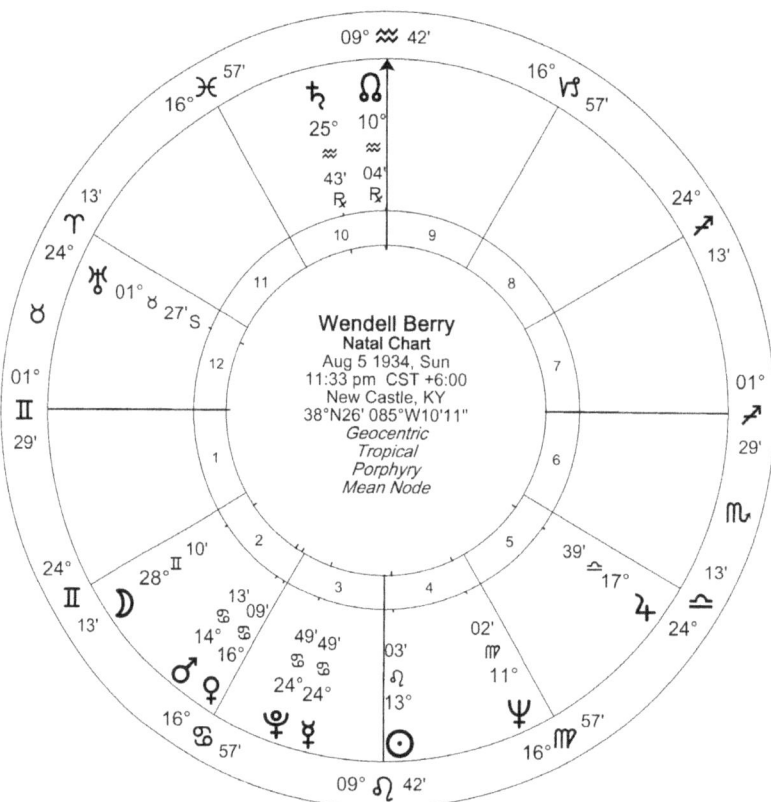

down payment on a house. By the end of his Saturn Return, Victor brought his parents and five siblings together for several sessions with a family therapist. Many old scores were settled, and for the first time he felt like he had a close family. He felt more emotionally stable due to the new respect, acknowledgement, and support he received from his family. Over time, working to renovate, furnish, and gratefully inhabit the home became one of his preferred forms of meditation practice.

A woman with Sun, Venus, and Mercury in Cancer confided that her boyfriend wanted her to participate in fire walks, psychedelic drug journeys, and intense breathing exercises. Only gradually was the boyfriend able to appreciate that the spiritual path she felt drawn to involved gardening, studying herbs and flower remedies, and cooking sumptuous meals.

A woman with Cancer Sun in the second house found fulfillment in drying, canning, storing, and cooking food she grew in her garden.

A woman named Barbara with Sun, Venus, and Uranus conjunct in Cancer in the eighth house (house of joint finances, interpersonal disagreements) assiduously avoided marriage despite many proposals that had been offered. She was resistant to being trapped in traditional female roles as wife, mother, and homemaker (Uranus, planet of freedom, rebellion, and independence, conjunct Venus-Sun in Cancer). She was particularly uncomfortable with the idea of caring for children and being expected to cook for a family. Now, at age 40, she was considering marriage and moved to a new city to live with her boyfriend, Ed. Although Ed had planned to sell the house that he'd lived in with his ex-wife and his children, he'd been unable to do so, and Barbara was unhappy living in the place that had been the scene of Ed's previous marriage. Feelings of insecurity (Cancer) about her centrality in Ed's life were aroused by the constant, nagging presence of Ed's ex-wife, Laura, who constantly called and dropped by the house to discuss finances and childcare arrangements. Barbara felt that this wasn't really her home and was emotionally distraught as she had been financially dependent on Ed for several months while she found employment in the new location (Cancer: dependency; eighth house: money received from another person).

A person with many planets in Cancer thrives in a cozy, comfortable home, with strong familial bonds. However, for Barbara this house felt laden with memories of Ed's prior marriage, and she had mixed emotions about living with Ed's son, William. Gradually Barbara accepted her stepson, and Laura, as part of her family. With Uranus in Cancer she needed to adjust to the inevitable tensions of a blended family. As she became clearer about her feelings, she could offer Ed her emotional support during this difficult transition. She realized that if she wanted to be the "woman of the household" she'd have to make room for herself in this family. To her amazement, she found a deep inner reservoir of mama energy that grew as she nurtured Ed and William, and discovered that she truly enjoyed cooking and baking bread. She rebelled against the use of cookbooks, however, and began developing her own strange but unique recipes (Sun-Uranus in Cancer).

With Sun in the fourth house, one's life path is influenced by family heritage, or there are interests in real estate, land and property development or management. A woman with Sun, Venus, and Mars in Cancer in the fourth house found a fulfilling career in hotel management. A man with a Taurus Sun in the fourth house is a contractor who buys, renovates, and sells houses and specializes in designing and constructing bathrooms and kitchens. He's an expert on home improvement. Natal Sun in the fourth house can indicate working from the home, the importance of living and working from our deepest emotional center, and strong ties to the family that influence our sense of purpose.

Uma and Arjun, recent immigrants from India, called to consult with me. Uma had Saturn in Cancer in the first house, closely conjunct her south node, thus family and home (Cancer) were her core values. She also had a natal Sun-Pluto conjunction in Virgo in the fourth house. Her father was a very controlling patriarch (Pluto in fourth). Uma worked in the family business—geographic mapping (fourth house: the sense of place). This is an occupation requiring great Virgo precision and attention to detail. Uma very much wanted to buy a house (fourth-house Sun, and Saturn rising in Cancer), but she and her husband had no money. At the time of consultation, transiting Saturn was conjunct her Ascendant. She needed to face the limits of their situation, be patient, slowly save money, and make the best of their current small dwelling (Saturn in Cancer), which at least was safe and quiet, she said. During her Saturn Return in Cancer, she and Arjun were able to fulfill their dream of buying a house, with financial help from her family.

Leo/Sun/Fifth House: Ananda:
The Yoga of Self-Expression, Creativity, and Joy

Leo represents the phase of evolution in which the radiance of the individual shines forth. With an emphasis on Leo or the fifth house, one's goal is not transcending the self (as in Pisces/twelfth house) but expressing oneself and demonstrating one's talents and creativity. If your chart accentuates these domains then highly serious and ascetic approaches to spiritual growth may not be appropriate for you, as you'd prefer paths of festivity, celebration, parties, and play; relationships with children; or self-expression through artistic works, athletics, theater, drama, or other performance arts. Here we develop extraverion, warmth, enthusiasm, and outward expression of *ananda* (joy). In the philosophy of Kashmir Shaivism (see Chapter 5), ananda shakti refers to the inherent bliss of Supreme Consciousness, which is self-arising and self-fulfilling, finding intrinsic satisfaction in its own being and joyous emanation. Emphasis here in the birth chart refers to the capacity to feel pride, joy, and satisfaction in one's own being and pursuits. We want to feel sunny and wonderful and creative, and enjoy being the center of attention. Great personalities are able to project themselves with creative flair and an inner feeling of dignity and self-respect. At our core, each of us is the golden child. The inner Sun shines with its own intrinsic light and extends its warming ray of love.

A woman with a Moon-Mars conjunction in Leo in her tenth house felt that her true calling in life was to have many children; she eventually gave birth to four of them.

A woman with Jupiter and Mars in Leo in her tenth house leads workshops for children and adults on creativity, involving mask-making, dance, music, drawing, and the recovery of playfulness.

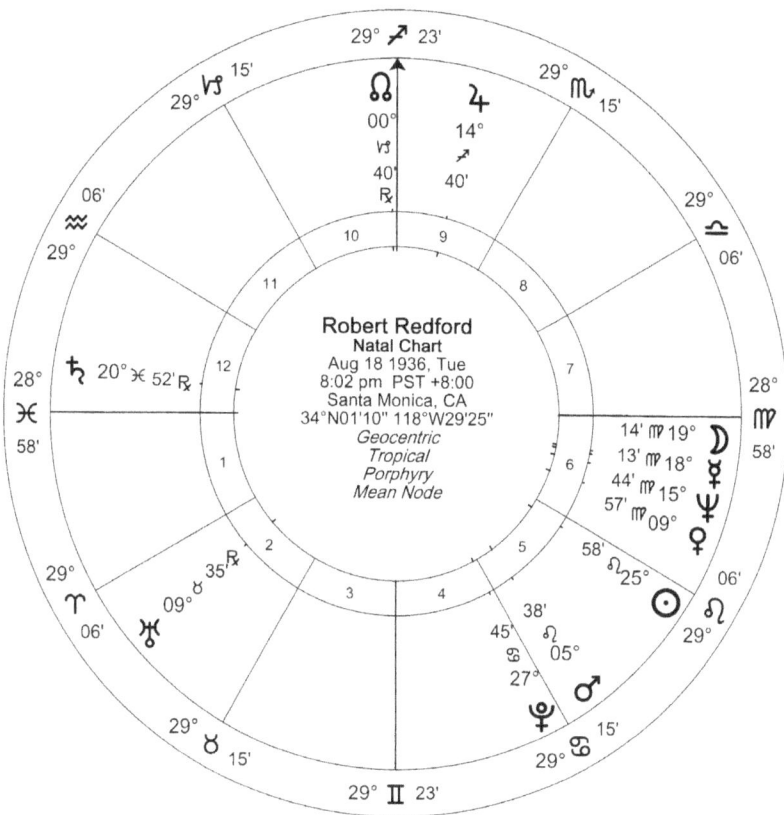

A woman with natal Pluto in Leo in her fifth house, opposite Sun, had an intense orgasmic surge of energy while giving birth and felt that she herself was reborn in the process.

Leo emphasis indicates interests in creativity, play, acting, dance, performance. For example, Robert DeNiro has Sun, Jupiter, Pluto, and north node in Leo—a vivid astrological signature for a great actor. Tom Cruise has Moon and Venus in Leo in the tenth house. David Crosby has Sun-Mercury in Leo in the fifth house. Crosby's appearance and aura have a golden radiance and warmth. With his Leo Sun trine Mars in Aries on his Ascendant, Crosby is brash, creative, and free-spirited. With Venus and Neptune in Virgo conjunct the north node, Crosby made some of the pivotal music of the 1960s and 70s, including songs of delicate beauty such as "Guinevere." Another radiant solar personality, Robert Redford, has Sun-Mars in Leo with Mars in the fifth house of acting and performance. Note Redford's Mercury-Moon conjunction opposite the rising Saturn in Pisces. This combination of Moon-Mercury-Saturn near his natal horizon

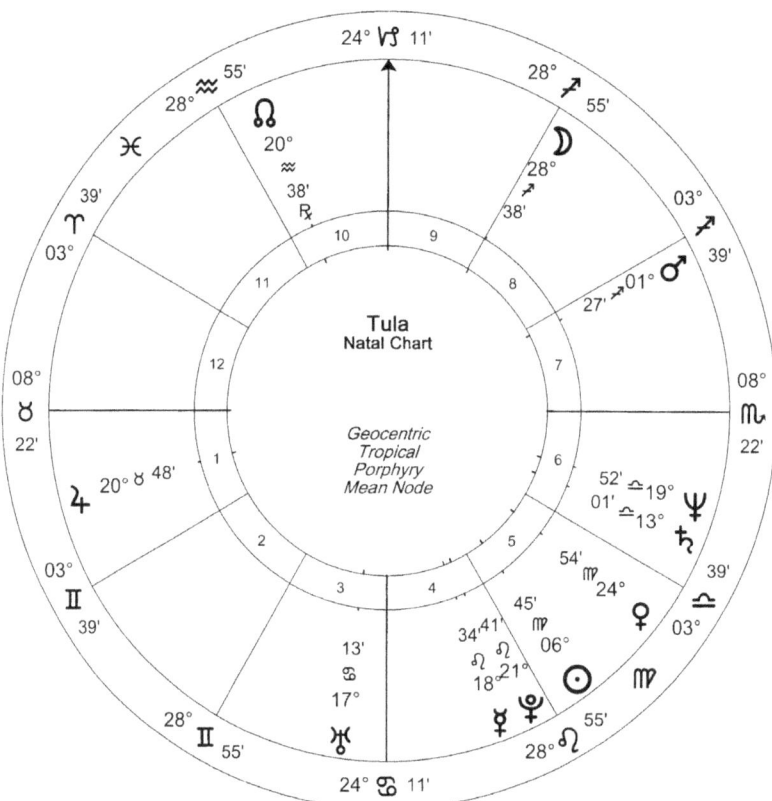

represents Redford's intelligence, emotional sensitivity, his serious gaze and circumspection. In his performances and his public demeanor Redford exhibits emotional composure and containment; you rarely see him lose self-control. The Moon's north node conjunct the Midheaven signifies his fame, and Midheaven ruler Jupiter is strengthened by placement in its home sign Sagittarius and in the ninth house. With Mars and Pluto in his fifth house, Redford has faced several crises involving his children.

The fifth house of the birth chart is a realm of creativity and performance. A woman with Venus and Mars in the fifth house decided at age 41 to take piano lessons and by age 48 was performing in jazz clubs.

With Sun in the fifth house, we're drawn to fun, play, performance, creativity, the arts, places of entertainment, or living or working with children. A musician with Sun–Venus in Leo in the fifth house and Mars in Capricorn in the tenth is driven to succeed and has the ambition and initiative needed to get ahead in the competitive field of entertainment.

Tula has Sun and Venus in Virgo in the fifth house. I began her consultation by asking whether children were central in her life. Tula replied that she has three children and six stepchildren. Indeed, kids are the center of her life. She works as a child advocate, promoting children's health and nutrition (Virgo Sun in the fifth house). Tula's Moon squares Venus. She's a loving mother, and has great relationships with all of her kids. Motherhood is a focal point of her life path (Moon-Venus). With Jupiter rising in Taurus, square Mercury-Pluto, Tula had been a foreign correspondent for a news magazine for over a decade (Jupiter: journalism; Sagittarius Moon). Also, fundraising is a big part of her work (Jupiter in Taurus). She writes grants and gets large sums of money for children's organizations and schools.

Jim, an accomplished composer and concert musician, had Sun–Mercury in Aries in the fifth house (performance) and a Venus–Jupiter conjunction in Aquarius in the third house, symbolizing someone with abundant musical ideas. Jim's Saturn in Virgo in the tenth house brought a strong dose of the reality principle, and the reality was that Jim's work in music didn't generate much income. Jim had to bear the tension of the fact that he needed to hold various jobs (waiter, taxi driver, night security guard), none of them glamorous but necessary for his survival. With Saturn in Virgo in the tenth house, quincunx Sun–Mercury, his path was not only to be a musician, but also to be a worker, to sustain himself while he continued to pursue music. During a period of almost eight years of obscurity and hard work during which he rarely performed, Jim's spirits were buoyed by the awareness that Uranus would soon transit from Pisces into Aries and would eventually pass over his Sun–Mercury in the fifth house, which he hoped would bring more opportunities to express his talents as a concert artist. To his great joy, when transiting Uranus reached conjunction with his Sun, Jim began receiving new offers to perform publicly and record his music.

Norwegian stage and film actress Liv Ullman (see chart on page 58) has Sun and Mercury conjunct in the fifth house, and Pluto in Leo conjunct the Ascendant. Many of her film performances, such as *Cries and Whispers* and *Scenes from a Marriage*, depict the intense emotions, passions, and discordances of love and family life, of marriage and parent-child relationships (Venus and Mars in Scorpio in the fourth house; Libra Moon in fourth house). Ullman brings philosophical depth (Sun in Sagittarius) to her work as a creative artist (fifth house). With Sun conjunct Mercury, her verbal elocution is exquisite. With her natal Sun closely square Neptune, Ullman has worked extensively with Unicef and the Women's Refugee Commission, involved with charitable and humanitarian works.

Bruce Springsteen has Sun, Moon, Mercury, Venus, and Neptune in his fifth house (in Libra) and Mars-Pluto in Leo in his third house. He's renowned for his energetic

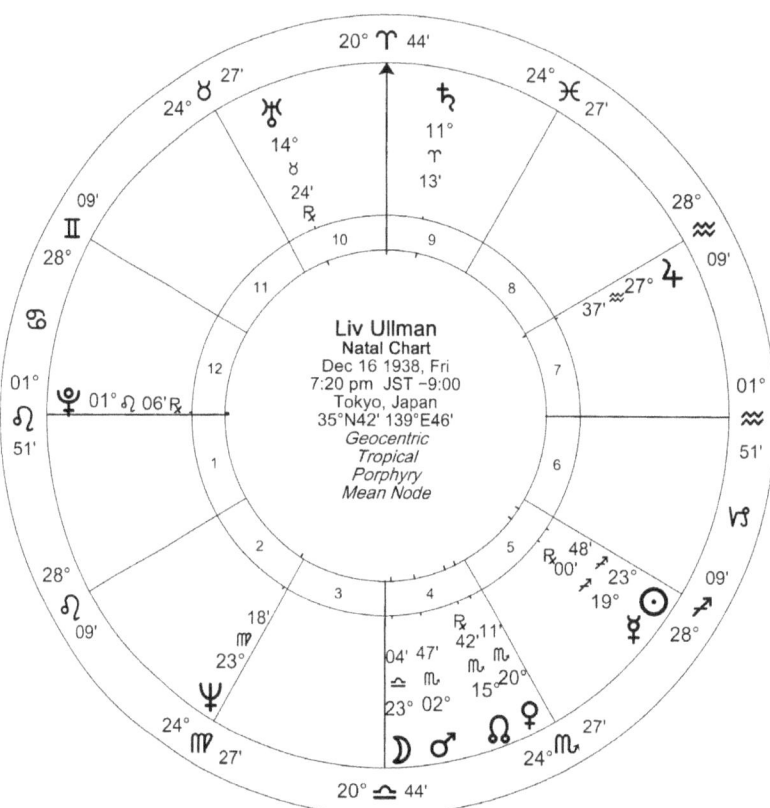

and heartfelt concert performances (fifth house), his passionate voice and song lyrics (Mars-Pluto in third house). His signature song, "Born to Run," expresses the vibrant third house call to the road, to adventure, searching, and widening of horizons. Jerry Garcia of the Grateful Dead had Sun, Mercury, and Pluto in Leo. Mozart, a unique creative genius, had Aquarius Sun, Mercury, and Saturn in the fifth house. William Blake, the visionary poet and artist, had Sun, Mercury, and Jupiter in Sagittarius in the fifth house. Pablo Picasso had Moon in the fifth house.

Angelica, a woman with Sagittarius Sun in the fifth house, had a long career in early childhood education and also did acting jobs on the side. When transiting Neptune in Pisces squared her Sun, she was chosen by her guru to give a lecture about their spiritual practice tradition at an international science and religion conference; note the many Sagittarian themes. Angelica hadn't seen her guru in person in seven years, yet she was selected over thousands of the teacher's other followers and disciples for the honor of representing their entire movement at a large meeting receiving extensive press and media coverage. She said she had no idea what she was going to say but she got up in front of the audience, smiled, and shared her joy. She said she felt that the talk came through her fluidly and spontaneously from a place above and beyond the rational mind (Sagittarius: teaching, lecturing; fifth house: performance, innate dignity, poised demeanor; Neptune: grace, inspiration).

Virgo/Mercury/Sixth House: Viveka:
The Yoga of Health, Discipline, and Apprenticeship

An emphasis in the birth chart on planets in Virgo or the sixth house indicates the importance of work and health issues, making wise choices regarding nutrition and exercise, striving for excellence and self-betterment, and following a technique or regimen—for example by practicing a *sadhana* or spiritual discipline. Virgo can signify worry and anxiety but also the ability to manage anxiety and stress, as it's a discerning energy that can cut through confusion and make accurate, refined assessments of our situation. At times physical illnesses provide opportunities for transformation through changes and adjustments in our personal habits and routines, and by learning principles of healing. For example, Deirdra, with Sun-Mars-Neptune in Virgo in the sixth house, suffered from Chronic Fatigue Syndrome. After becoming disillusioned with traditional medical treatments, Deirdra adjusted her diet and underwent treatment with nutritional supplements and naturopathic medicine, acupuncture, and herbology. These efforts to regenerate her body were a primary focus of her spiritual quest.

Virgo emphasis in a birth chart can indicate an interest in activities requiring meticulous attention to detail, analysis, classification, systematizing, diagnosing problems, and any highly technical, skilled occupation or pastime. It signifies the enjoyment of precision and thoroughness in each and every activity. Personally, I try to use transits of planets here to organize my work and my home, undergo treatments, cleanse, take supplements, and increase the intensity of my efforts in any path requiring self-discipline, such as a program of yoga poses or practicing scales on the guitar, increasing my refinement of movement, breathing, and musicianship.

Planets in Virgo indicate a need to develop and practice *viveka*—discrimination, learning to discern for oneself what foods, habits, or activities are healthy and which are unhealthy. In Virgo we question how much drinking, pot smoking, sex, TV watching and other pleasures of life are okay for us, and when these become obsessions and distractions. Viveka is the capacity to discriminate the real from the unreal, the eternal from the transitory. In yoga psychology, a discerning, discriminative intelligence, called *buddhi*, differentiates from the mind (*manas*) and its stream of thinking, perceiving, memory and fantasy, turning us toward Brahman, the eternal Being. Consciousness becomes reflective, experiencing a turn toward *self-recognition* and intuitive perception of the etheric, subtle realms signified by Pisces. Virgo is the refinement of awareness that invites release into an expanded space of the mind in Aquarius and into the pure waters of Pisces. Virgo is the effortful aspect of sadhana where we undergo the heat of testing and struggling to rein in impulses and our chaotic, slovenly tendencies, striving to become more impeccable in our way of being. To develop discrimination and inner purity we can voluntarily adopt a path or code of moral discipline and precepts such as those taught in Patanjali's *Yoga Sutras*, the Bible's Ten Commandments, and Buddhist *abhidharma* texts. Hazrat Inayat Khan said, "A pure life and a clear conscience are like bread and wine for the soul."(26)

If your chart highlights Virgo or the sixth house, strive to be discriminating and pure; but try to avoid the pitfall of becoming overly anxious or wracked by guilt about your imperfections or impurities. Virgo represents honest self-assessment, but also a tendency to engage in harsh self-judgements. Nobody is perfect, and we need to let go of the *addiction to perfection*. According to Angeles Arrien, it's also important to achieve freedom from the *addiction to intensity; addiction to the need to know; and addiction to fixating on what's not working rather than what is working*.(27) Releasing these addictions helps liberate us from debilitating anxiety and stress. Virgo represents efforts to heal our life and heal ourselves. We can practice what Arrien calls the *eight universal healing principles*: balanced diet; regular exercise; time for fun, play, and laughter; music, sonics, and chanting; love, touch, and support systems; engagement in hobbies and creative purpose; nature, beauty, and healing environments, trees, plants, and animals; faith and belief in the supernatural.(28) In all of these ways, we become better able to handle the stress of life, and to have a sense of humor about our imperfections, even as we hold ourselves to high standards and try to meet them as best we can.

Resonating with these Virgo themes, the horoscope's sixth house is the realm of health consciousness. A man did an extended fast at a rural holistic health center during a transit of Jupiter through his sixth house.

A man with Mars conjunct Saturn in Virgo in the sixth house became seriously ill while traveling in India during his Saturn Return in the 1970s. This experience caused him to change his diet and to learn about homeopathic medicine, in which he became quite skilled. During this time he learned hatha yoga, which he has practiced vigorously for decades. In time he became a renowned and much beloved yoga teacher with many trainees and apprentices.

Virgo and the sixth house represent training, apprenticeship, or discipleship. In yogic traditions *guru seva* (service to the Guru) and mindful labor are important spiritual disciplines. Virgo and the sixth house signify developing and demonstrating our abilities in job-related tasks and may point to the need for skill development or vocational training in order to procure better employment. A woman with Saturn conjunct the

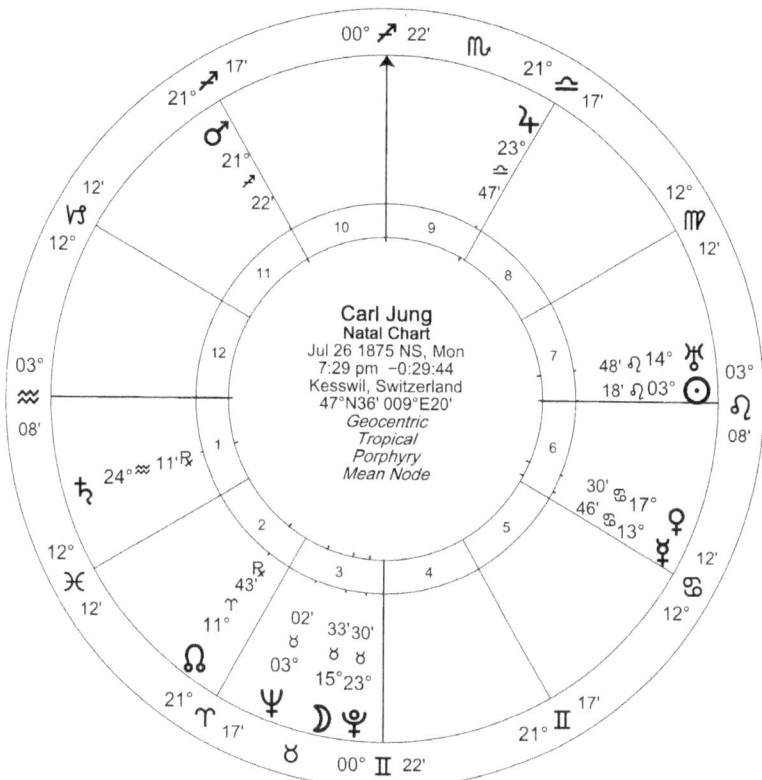

Ascendant in Virgo often complained about the drudgery of having to work for a living. However, with a Sun-Jupiter-Venus conjunction in Aquarius in her sixth house, she was always able to find employment in new and unusual fields that gave her a range of skills in a variety of trades.

Sun in the sixth house represents interests and concern with health issues; it also suggests being identified with one's workplace role or trade. A man with the Sun in Scorpio in the sixth house was known to everyone as Ted the Plumber. A woman with a Sun–Pluto conjunction in Virgo in the sixth house is a disciplined practitioner of yoga and is very health- and diet-conscious. She's very involved with her job as an auditor and investigator (Pluto) for a large health insurance company (Virgo).

The sixth house governs the workplace and our need to develop our work-related skills through training and apprenticeship. Transits through the sixth house denote changes in workplace conditions, changes in relationships with co-workers or employees, or a need to enhance one's skills. A graduate student in psychology found a paid internship working with children when transiting Sun, Venus, and Jupiter were conjunct in Leo in her sixth house. A man experienced stress in the workplace while transiting Mars was retrograde in his sixth house. A woman fell in love with a co-worker when transiting Venus and Mars were conjunct in her sixth house.

Carl Jung had a conjunction of Mercury and Venus in Cancer in the sixth house. For an important period of his life Jung was a protégé and associate of Sigmund Freud. In 1907, while transiting Neptune passed over Mercury and Venus, Jung first corresponded with Freud. At the time of their first meeting, during which they conversed for 13 hours without a break, transiting Jupiter was in Cancer conjunct natal Venus. Their relationship intensified between 1908 and 1911 while transiting Neptune passed over Mercury-Venus. Simultaneously transiting Uranus in Capricorn opposed Mercury-Venus. The opposition of two transpersonal planets, Neptune and Uranus, symbolized a revelation of new insights about the nature of religion, myth, symbols, and the unconscious mind that had a transformative effect on Jung's thinking and consequently influenced the consciousness of all humanity. The power of the Uranus-Neptune opposition was focused through Jung's Mercury and Venus in the sixth house. Jung's training and association with Freud, and also his work under the supervision of Dr. Eugen Bleuler at Switzerland's famed Burgholzi asylum, generated new ideas (Uranus and Neptune aspecting Mercury) that were a major contribution to modern culture. This illustrates how transits of the outer, trans-Saturnian planets operate through individual personalities and lives to bring about changes that impact the collective.

Libra/Venus/Seventh House: Bhakti:
The Yoga of Love, Cooperation, and Relationship

Libra represents the experience of love, harmony, and beauty. It's the sign of friends, lovers, and couples. With planets placed in Libra or the seventh house, your evolution emphasizes friendship and relationships. You may have a strong urge for a partner in love. These areas of the chart accentuate a need for human affection and companionship; and whether we're talking about friends, siblings, roommates, or romantic partners, learning to live and grow in harmony with another person can be a most challenging and satisfying path. (29) With emphasis here, you may experience the couple's journey, learning to love, cooperate, and accommodate another person. Your path could also focus on *bhakti*, opening your heart through devotional practices and through worshipping the spiritual light in all of your beloveds. You may also draw inspiration from art, music, aesthetics, and beauty. These themes are also relevant when Venus is an accentuated planet in the birth chart or transits. For example, Vera, an artist who runs a vibrant art studio and gallery in the basement of her home, has Venus in Aquarius in the fourth house, closely trine her Libra Ascendant.

A woman with four planets in Libra in the fourth house began a new career in hotel management, giving her the opportunity for many friendly, pleasant interactions with others. She also finds great pleasure in painting.

Tom Petty has Sun-Saturn-Neptune conjunct in Libra, and Moon closely opposing Venus. In addition to writing innumerable songs about relationships, Petty is remarkable as a rock star who realized the dream (Saturn conjunct Neptune) in collaboration with friends, keeping the same band together for decades, apparently with no major drama or problematic egos disturbing these friendships.

A man with Venus in the tenth house conjunct the south node is a successful recording artist who had the conviction since his early childhood that he'd one day be a famous musician.

A man with Venus in the tenth house and Sun, Moon, Mercury, and Neptune in Libra in the eighth is a talented painter and computer graphics artist. His challenge has been to professionalize his art (Venus in tenth) and to win grants and procure financial investments from others (eighth house) to fund his artistic business projects.

The seventh house is the birthmap's relational zone. A woman who spent eleven years as a Hindu monk got married when transiting Saturn passed through her seventh house, conjunct her natal Moon, Venus, and Jupiter.

A woman with Uranus in the seventh house in Cancer found that marriage inhibited her freedom too much, parted with her husband, and made a conscious decision to remain alone. Some years later, she and another woman decided they wanted to raise a child together, and, with her ex-husband's assistance, they conceived a child and expanded their family. Uranus in the seventh carries the potential for an infine variety of liberating, socially unusual relationships.

With Sun in the seventh house, there's an impetus to live or work with others, to sustain ongoing relationships. Our spiritual path is shaped by partnerships, friendships, and marriages. Ed, a music producer with Sun–Moon in Leo in the seventh house, helps other people realize their creative aspirations. A woman with Sun–Venus in Capricorn in the seventh house managed her husband's medical practice.

Dave, who had Sun–Venus in Taurus in the seventh house, square Saturn in Leo in the tenth house, made a good living in computer technology sales. Dave felt that his path was to supply the material comfort and luxuries his wife desired, and to provide financial security for his children (Saturn in Leo). Dave built his success by working tirelessly to cultivate lasting relationships with his business clients (Saturn square Taurus Sun in the seventh house).

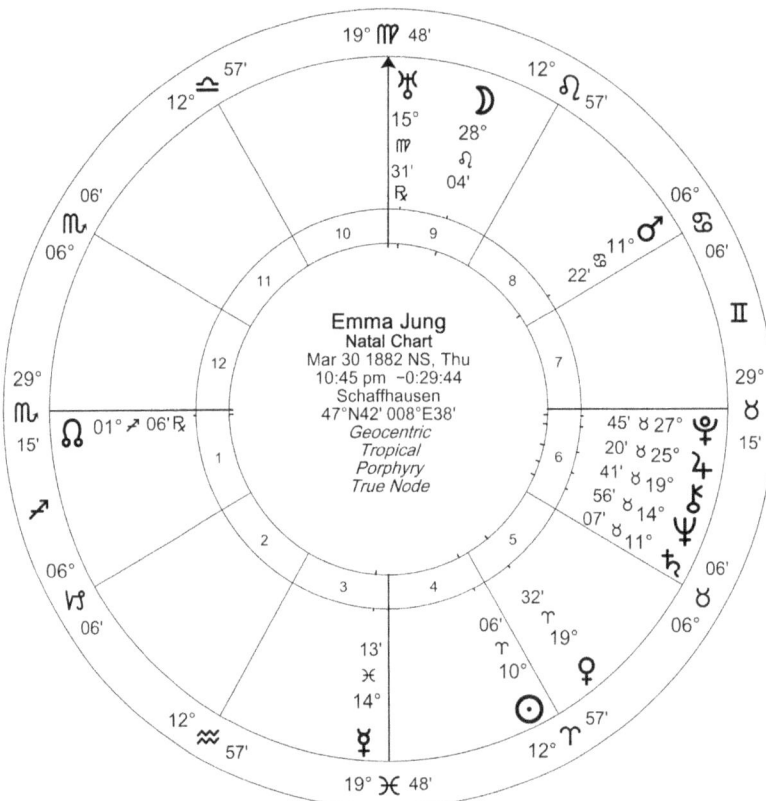

Jean Paul Sartre, who had a long-term relationship with Simone de Beauvoir, had a Venus-Jupiter conjunction in his seventh house. Sufi Master Hazrat Inayat Khan (see chart on page 148) had a close natal square of Venus and Neptune. He began his career as a performing musician and experienced awakening of God-consciousness through music. He married and was loving and devoted (Venus-Neptune) to his wife, children, and his many mureeds (disciples).

Carl Jung had a Sun-Uranus conjunction in his seventh house. Returning briefly to the relationship of Freud and Jung, tension between the two men began to grow when transiting Uranus crossed Jung's Ascendant and opposed natal Sun-Uranus in 1911, until they broke off all communication and had no further contact. Jung started to express a more independent viewpoint that was viewed as radical and rebellious by Freud. Jung's development as an original thinker required freedom from this relationship, connection to a new circle of associates, and freedom to explore an unconventional marriage with his remarkable wife, Emma.

With her Sun–Venus conjunction in the fifth house, Emma Jung's chart portrays her as a warm, affectionate woman who was very involved with her five children. Moon in Leo square her Ascendant and also squaring Jupiter–Pluto indicates that she was a strong matriarch. With her Mercury–Uranus opposition near the MC/IC axis, Emma was an innovator and free thinker in the field of depth psychology and mythology. The conjunction of Pluto, Jupiter, and the South Node at her Descendant depicts her husband, C. G. Jung, a powerful, influential, and world-transforming personality who lived an underground life as an alchemist, astrologer, and student of esoteric knowledge. Emma's five-planet conjunction of Saturn, Neptune, Chiron, Jupiter, and Pluto shows the immense, concentrated power of her chart and her personality, her spiritual clarity and wisdom. With five planets in Taurus, Emma had quite a bit of money, which was of great benefit to the couple during the period when Carl largely withdrew from public life and devoted himself, for several years, to his inner imaginal journey. By derived house analysis, Emma's stellium in her sixth house is in the twelfth house from the husband-seventh house. Thus it represents her husband Carl's twelfth house, signifying his journey into the unconscious, into dreams, symbols, religion, gnosis, and mysticism. Her chart portrays her husband as a Plutonic figure who fully delved into a mythic, archetypal inner journey where he experienced a form of spiritual initiation (Jupiter-Chiron-Neptune). Both of their charts feature Neptune and Pluto in Taurus. C. G. Jung's Taurus Moon was conjunct Pluto and Neptune in Taurus. Pluto in Taurus can be seen as a symbol of alchemical transformation of matter—a central theme in Jung's work.

Emma Jung remained devoted to her husband despite his esoteric leanings in the direction of mythology and alchemical studies, his longterm love affair with Toni Wolff, and the extensive time he spent apart from his wife while on retreat at his castle at Lake Bollingen. Emma exhibited Uranian openness, adaptability, and an admirable loyalty and dignity, embodying the most evolved qualities of her Leo Moon and her husband's seventh house Leo Sun. Emma was so magnanimous that she was able to accept Toni as her friend and ally. She allowed another woman to love her husband and apparently wasn't threatened by this. Emma became a highly accomplished analyst and scholar, authoring her masterpiece, *The Grail Legend*. C. G. Jung's seventh-house Sun-Uranus represents his wife Emma as a genius and the central light of his life.

John Lennon's Libra Sun was placed near the cusp of the seventh house, symbolizing his life-purpose and identity as a lover, husband, musician, artist, and songwriting collaborator with Paul McCartney. Lennon's unparalleled worldwide fame and popularity may be traced to the Uranus-Pluto conjunction during the mid 1960s, which occurred in Virgo, near John's natal Venus, dispositor of his Sun sign. In 1967, during Saturn's transit opposite his Libra Sun, John became involved with Yoko Ono, an artist who encouraged the full range of John's artistic activity. Some years later, while transiting Uranus was conjunct his Sun, John separated from Yoko and his role and identity as a marital partner went through changes and major upsets as John experienced his "lost weekend," featuring public drunkenness and rowdiness, unruly and belligerent behavior in bars, and estrangement from Yoko.

John returned to Yoko in 1975 when Jupiter in Aries transited opposite the Libra Sun. And transiting Saturn was also squaring his natal Sun, indicating a desire to recommit to his marital relationship. Although Saturn is traditionally said to create suffering, sorrows, and difficulties, it only tends to do this if we're totally unwilling to accept responsibility and commitments. If we're willing to embrace the virtues of sobriety and realism, and to straighten our lives out, Saturn can help us build structures that will endure. During this stabilizing Saturn transit to his natal Sun, John settled down, reduced his drug use, began eating a macrobiotic diet, and became more mature as a husband and father.

To conclude our discussion of the Venus-ruled sign of Libra, allow me a brief digression on the charts of musicians. Musical talent can be indicated by strong placement of Venus near the angles or in prominent aspects to other planets. Jazz guitarist John Scofield has Venus conjunct Pluto, an apt symbol for his intense, biting, bluesy sound. Jeff Beck has Sun-Venus conjunct in Cancer. Singer-songwriter Richard Thompson has Aries Sun conjunct Venus, Mars, and Mercury. His songs are passionate, furious, witty, and sarcastic. Jazz pioneer Ornette Coleman had Venus-Uranus conjunct in Aries; he invented a new conception of music that was wholly original. Donald Fagen of Steely Dan has Venus in Aquarius exactly square the Moon's nodes, and opposite Saturn-Pluto in Leo. David Crosby has Venus closely conjunct the north node in Virgo. Miles Davis had Venus in Aries square the nodal axis, trine Neptune in Leo. Jimi Hendrix had Sun-Venus conjunct in Sagittarius, opposite Uranus and Saturn; no musician has ever been more electrifying (Venus-Uranus). Thelonius Monk had Sun-Venus-Mercury conjunct in Libra. Willie Nelson has Sun-Venus in Taurus in the fifth house. Gypsy jazz virtuoso Django Reinhardt had Venus in Pisces semisquare Saturn, sextile Mars, trine the Moon, square the Moon's nodes, and sesquare Jupiter and Neptune. Elvis Presley was born with Venus conjunct Sun, Mercury and the north node, opposite Pluto, and squaring Uranus in Aries on his fifth house cusp.

Eric Clapton (see chart on page 68) has Libra rising and Ascendant ruler Venus in Taurus opposite Moon in Scorpio, square Pluto in Leo in the tenth house (public impact and artistic influence), and sextile Mars on the fifth house cusp (performance and creativity). Venus in a T-square with Moon square Pluto signifies the power and soul of the music, the heart of the blues, the energy and vitality and spirit of his music. Clap-

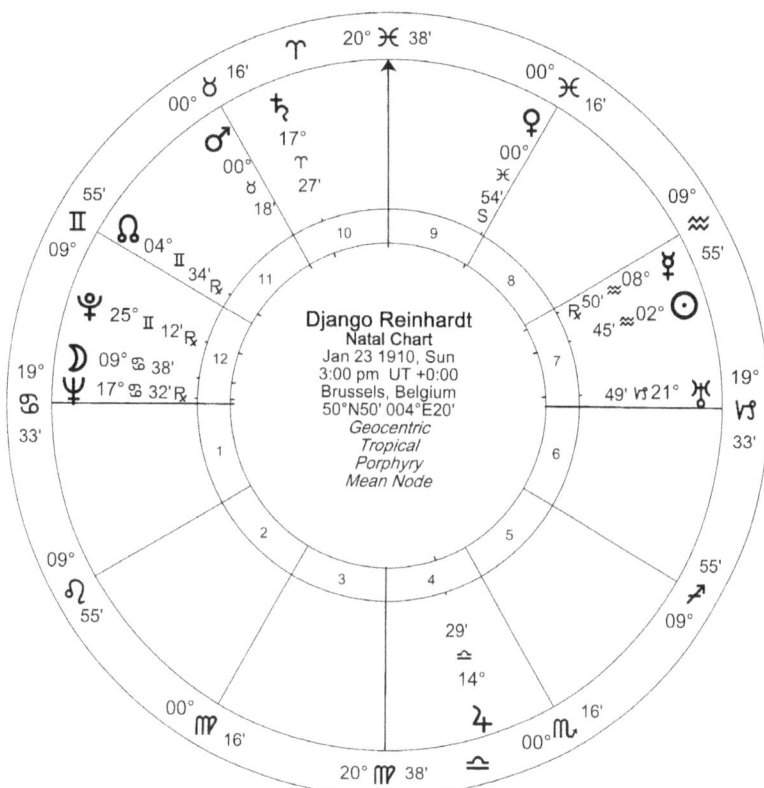

ton expresses Plutonian emotions of grief, loss, and tragedy in songs such as "Leyla" and "Tears in Heaven" (his song about the death of his son), featuring an almost unparalleled depth of feeling and poignancy clothed in music of tender beauty (Moon-Venus). With Sun opposite Neptune he has grappled with addictions and learned to rise up from his sorrows and sufferings, becoming a heroic figure of spiritual redemption. He has been laid low and always come back with a beautiful song that heals him to sing and heals us to listen to. In the 1960s people used to say "Clapton is God" and there has always been some sense that he is musically and emotionally a conduit for higher forces. A highly gracious person, with Venus sextile Mars he exudes a positive, attractive energy that's magnetic. With Mars in Pisces aspecting both Venus and Moon there's a calm strength that drives his serpentine electrifying riffs.

Ravi Shankar (birth time unknown; see chart on page 69) had a fire trine involving Sun in Aries, Moon in Sagittarius, and Jupiter-Neptune in Leo, symbolizing how much joy there was in his performances, how sunny and radiant his face as he plucked magical

Astrology and Spiritual Awakening, Part I

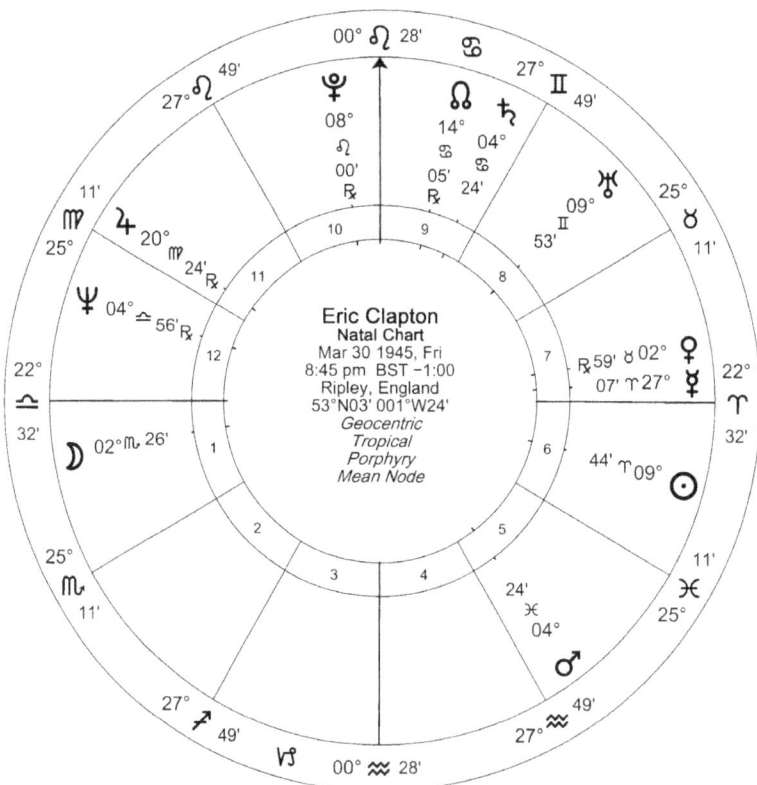

tones from his sitar, producing wave after ecstatic wave of raga rivers of sound. Scorpio Mars square Jupiter gave drive, vitality and impetus to the music. Mars square Neptune represents the pranic, energic, blissful aspects of yoga and meditation, which inspired and called forth his music. His Venus in Pisces in exact tri-octile aspect (135°) to Jupiter and Neptune signifies heightened aesthetic subtlety as well as devotional love (Venus-Neptune).

Ravi Shankar was a master of bhakti, spiritual devotion. His music was an offering from the heart. He was beyond the glamour of being a star, a celebrity performer. His face emanated peace, one-pointed absorption, and spiritual communion. As you watched him play he would get out of the way and become the instrument of transmission. Once I saw and heard him at New York's Cathedral of Saint John the Divine and he filled the space with magical, celestial sounds. Everyone in the room was transported into a state of meditation as light poured through the Cathedral's stained glass windows and through Ravi's beautiful upward reaching gaze.

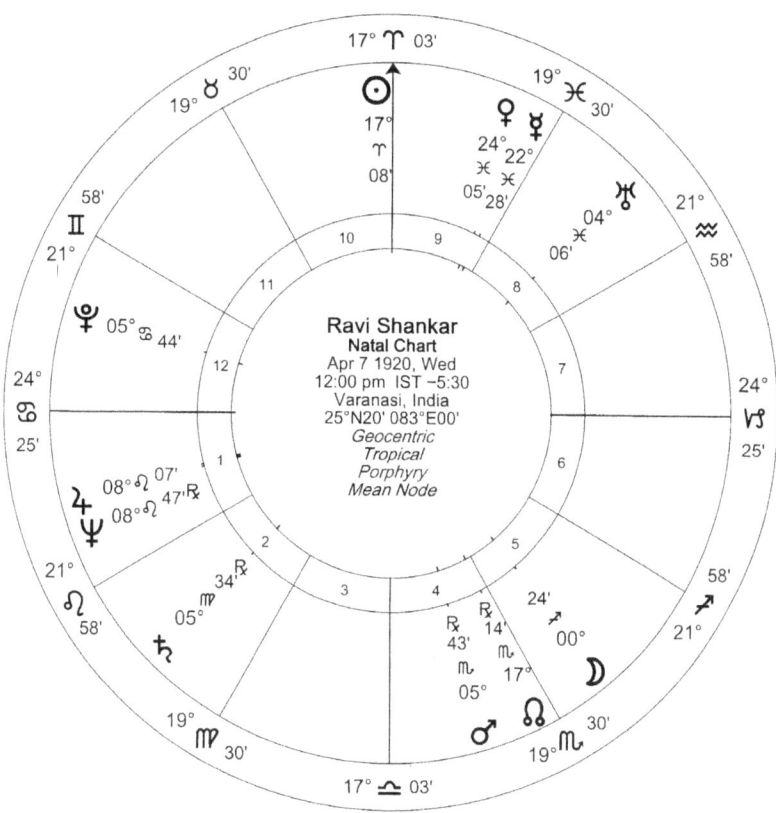

Scorpio/Mars/Pluto/Eighth House: Shakti:
The Yoga of Power, Sexuality, and Regeneration

Natal emphasis on the sign Scorpio, its rulers Pluto and Mars, or the eighth house indicates a focus on transformation and generation of power through the intensities of human interaction and experiences of interpersonal crisis. Traditional astrology books often state that Scorpio and the eighth house are concerned with death and rebirth or occult power, not making it sufficiently clear that experiences of death-rebirth or of the dynamics of power often occur in the context of interpersonal relationships. With major placements in Scorpio or eighth house, you may be deeply moved by encounters with others, have powerful confrontations with the existential reality of death, or need to learn lessons about cooperation and the ability to work together with others. Through situations involving joint finances, business ventures, and financial and emotional investments, you may come to better understand the dynamics of human aggression, disagreements, conflicts of will, resentment, hostility, possessiveness, and jealousy. These circumstances can give rise to a deeper maturity about sexuality, interpersonal commitments, and the capacity for intimacy. With Scorpio or eighth house emphasis you may be drawn to a spiritual path focused on generation of *shakti*—spiritual power—through sexuality, tantra, magic and ritual, *kundalini yoga*, or *shaktipat* initiation. We'll delve into these fascinating topics later.

Planets placed here indicate the importance of transforming sexual issues and transmuting aggression and anger. One may decide to commit to the principle of non-violence and to developing conflict resolution skills. Julia, who had transiting Saturn conjunct her natal Sun in Scorpio in the seventh house, had been arguing with her new husband Luke for several months. Their conflicts and hostilities had been escalating. In couples therapy they were both able to let their negative feelings surface. They both harbored resentments about their sexual life that needed venting, and at times their words stung one another. This is the nature of Scorpio. They also acknowledged the many ways their lives and energies and finances were intertwined and testified to each other their gratitude and longing for each other. Once they began openly communicating they became a very sexy couple. Julia said finally she had someone in her life she trusted enough to truly experience deep desire. During Saturn conjunct the Scorpio Sun, sexuality became central to Julia's spiritual life. She and Luke achieved the alchemical union and fusion that Scorpio represents.

Three men—one with Sun in the eighth house, the second with Scorpio Sun in the first house, the third with Moon-Mars conjunct in Scorpio—had very active sex lives and were highly focused on their sexuality. A man named Devin had Sun conjunct Mars and Neptune in Scorpio. When transiting Saturn was conjunct Sun-Mars-Neptune he had a transcendent mystical experience while making love with a woman who was not his wife. It was like a force seized them in pleasurable waves, and this connection had continued for a few months. Not surprisingly this led to a great deal of conflict, anger, and jealousy in Devin's marriage. Heated circumstances sometimes do come up during a transit such as Saturn conjunct Mars in Scorpio. Devin experienced many facets of encounter with the instinctual forces and furies of Mars in Scorpio.

Singer Rickie Lee Jones was born with Scorpio rising and Saturn and Sun conjunct Venus in Scorpio, which was closely square Pluto. Jones burst onto the music scene in the 1970s and 80s with a sultry, sexy vibe and a completely original sound (Venus trine Uranus) and sang in sly, moody, liquid tones about love, desire, betrayal, endings and renewals in relationships. Her voice, her music, and her songwriting have an emotional and vibrational power that moves people.

With natal Sun in the eighth house, we may work in areas related to sex, death, or trauma or any field connected with business, credit, loans, investment, or the sharing of assets. Management of trusts, estates, or other shared funds or resources can be a personal focal point. A woman with Sun in Capricorn in the eighth house felt that owning her own business was the most fulfilling thing she'd ever done. She procured funding from a bank to expand her enterprise. A prominent oncologist had natal Sun and Pluto conjunct in the eighth house. A sex therapist had Sun-Mars in Scorpio in the eighth house. A woman with Sun-Moon in Scorpio, square Pluto in Leo in the eighth house, is a pastoral counselor whose work involves providing emotional support for bereaved individuals and families. A woman with Sun–Mercury in Gemini in the eighth house is a data clerk (Gemini: data processing) for a statewide Workers Compensation fund. She manages the funds of others on a large scale.

The eighth house can be a realm of interpersonal crisis, endings, and renewals. Jeff, a man with Sagittarius Sun in the eighth house, used family inheritance money to start a chain of retail stores, and enjoyed applying his Taoist philosophical beliefs in the field of business. When transiting Saturn passed over his eighth-house Sun, he experienced a sudden falling-out with his longtime business partner. Simultaneously his marriage spiraled into a crisis that led to a divorce and a separation from his wife and her entire side of the family. During this time of Saturn conjunct Sun, Jeff sold his stock in the business, and lost his home and much savings in the divorce settlement. Nevertheless, he met this crisis as a necessary process of cleaning house, as many latent conflicts in his marital, family, and business relationships were eventually aired. Several years later he made a fresh start in a new business and began rebuilding his assets.

The eighth house represents funds received through loans, credit, and inheritance, and funds we generate in business and spousal partnerships. Travis, a man with Mercury, Jupiter, Uranus and Pluto in the eighth house, inherited some money and invested all of it in a business venture, remaining fully committed to this venture for over 20 years, at which point it finally became profitable. At the same time, after many years of tumultuous and changeable relationships in which he'd been the sole or primary breadwinner, he met a woman who was financially successful, who contributed resources to household improvements and his business. Eventually they married and enjoyed joining forces as a "power couple," a force in the world.

Spiritual teacher Da Avabhasa (aka Da Free John) had Sun in Scorpio in the tenth house, and Moon-Pluto conjunction in the seventh house. He was known for his capacity to transform others through dynamic energetic transmissions, his powerful *satsang* that conveyed a living ray of consciousness. During his career he often dealt with issues regarding power and sexuality, and his teachings describe in detail the transformative alchemy and intensity of the guru-disciple relationship. With Sun and Moon aligned with Pluto, he was said to emanate a unique magnetism.

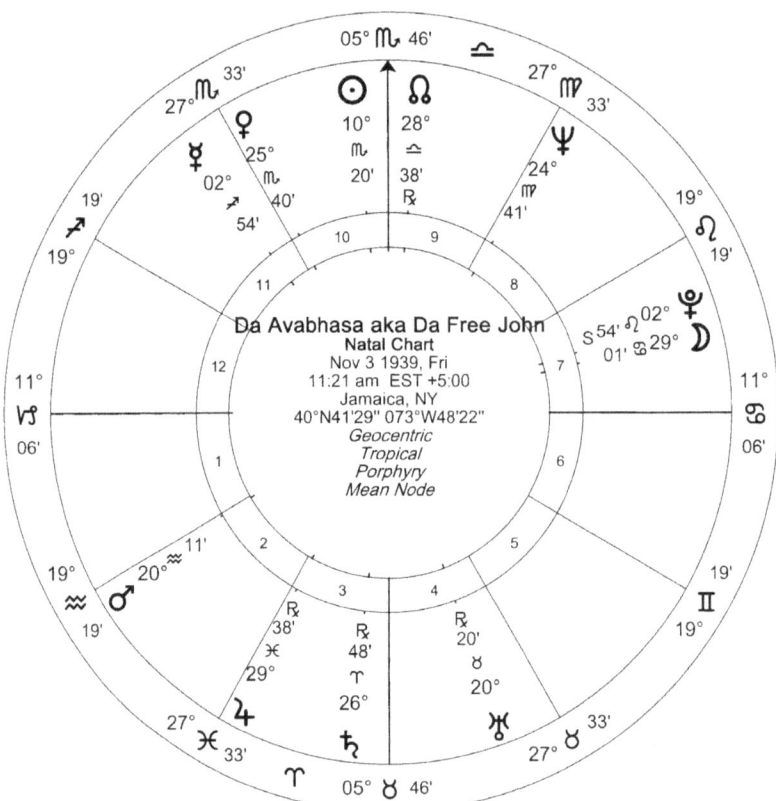

Dr. Elizabeth Kubler-Ross, who worked to promote more humane care for the dying, had Sun conjunct Pluto in Cancer, trine Saturn in Scorpio in the eighth house. With Saturn square both Jupiter and Neptune, her writings described how one must overcome the fear of death (Saturn in Scorpio) and pass through stages of denial, anger, bargaining, depression, and acceptance, to experience serenity and wisdom (Jupiter and Neptune) through the dying process.(30) With Uranus in Pisces in the first house, Dr. Kubler-Ross revolutionized how our society, our medical professionals, and institutions care for the terminally ill. As a child, she rebelled against her father, who told her she should be a secretary or a maid. Defying her family, she left home at age 16, volunteered during World War II in hospitals, caring for refugees. She candidly interviewed dying people about their feelings and needs. Later she became interested in issues of life after death, spirit guides, and spirit channeling, which met some resistance from her peers in the field of medicine. She campaigned vigorously for better treatment and care for the terminally ill, and brought consciousness and spirituality

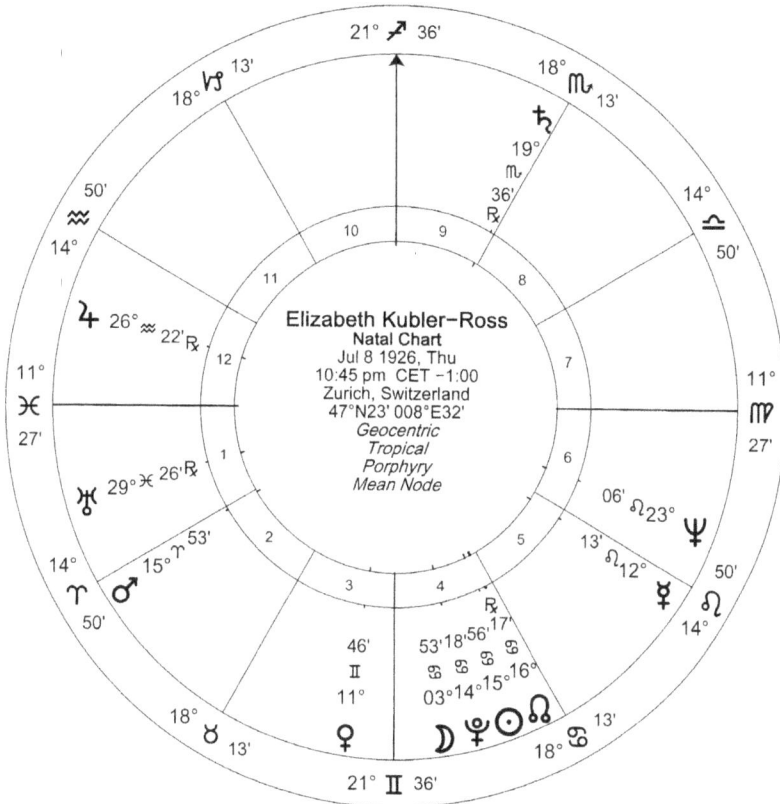

into the practice of medicine and thanatology. In all of this one sees vivid expressions of Sun conjunct Pluto and her eighth-house Saturn in Scorpio. Her Sun-Pluto conjunct the Moon's nodes signifies the impactful social influence of her work.

Dr. Stanislav Grof (see chart on page 74), the visionary psychiatrist whose ideas shaped the field of transpersonal psychology, has Sun, Mercury, and Jupiter conjunct Pluto in Cancer, opposite Moon and Saturn. Jupiter and Pluto are in the eighth sign from the Ascendant and near the eighth house cusp, thus I view these as eighth house planets. The strength of Pluto in his chart signifies that the essence of Grof's life's work has been to illuminate the human experience of birth and death. The Full Moon opposite Jupiter-Pluto signifies Grof's emphasis on emotional discharge and release, utilizing intense, cathartic methods such as LSD psychotherapy and holotropic breathwork to activate and resolve prenatal and perinatal memories and experiences, to breathe and struggle through inner agonies and ordeals, to experience death of the ego and to be reborn in the light. The zodiacal sign of Cancer represents

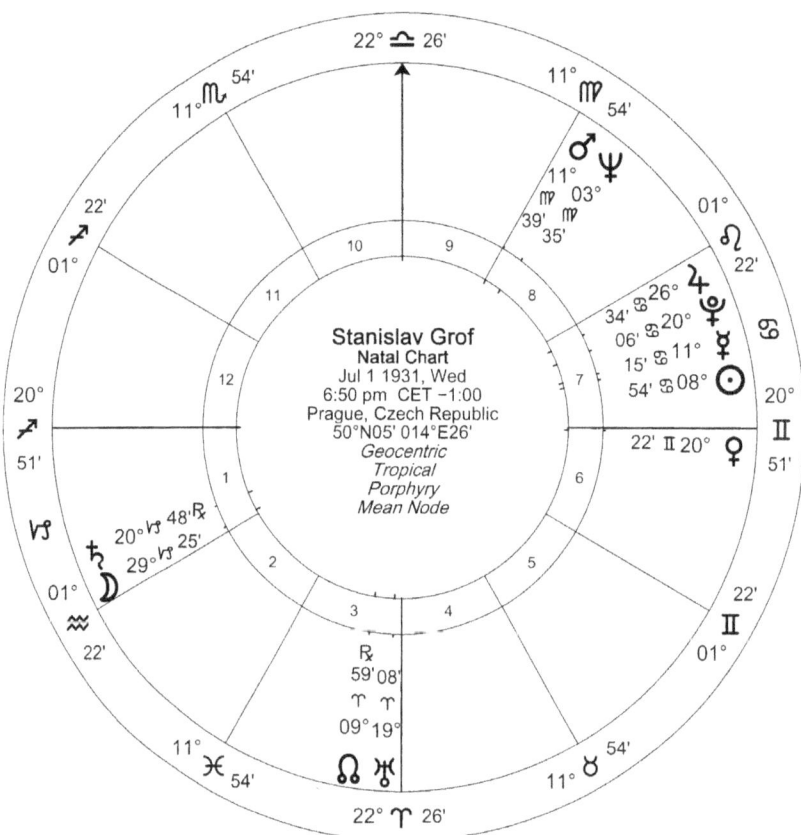

memory and emotional connection with the mother, which is the central focus of Grof's cartography of the perinatal matrices. In holotropic breathwork, rhythmic breathing, evocative music, focused bodywork, and the presence of an emotionally supportive guide facilitate reliving crucial phases of the birth process, liberating bound or dormant energies within the psyche and the body, activating expansive transpersonal states of consciousness.

The great sage Ramana Maharshi experienced a dramatic transformation that led to spiritual awakening. One day when he was 16 years old, Ramana Maharshi suddenly was gripped by a fear of death and began diving inward to inquire into his true nature, asking Who am I? He soon passed suddenly into a state of enlightenment and permanent Self-abidance. Soon thereafter, he left home and traveled to Mount Arunachala in Southern India, where he lived for the rest of his life. At the time of his enlightenment, transiting Uranus in Scorpio and Neptune in Gemini were in a quincunx

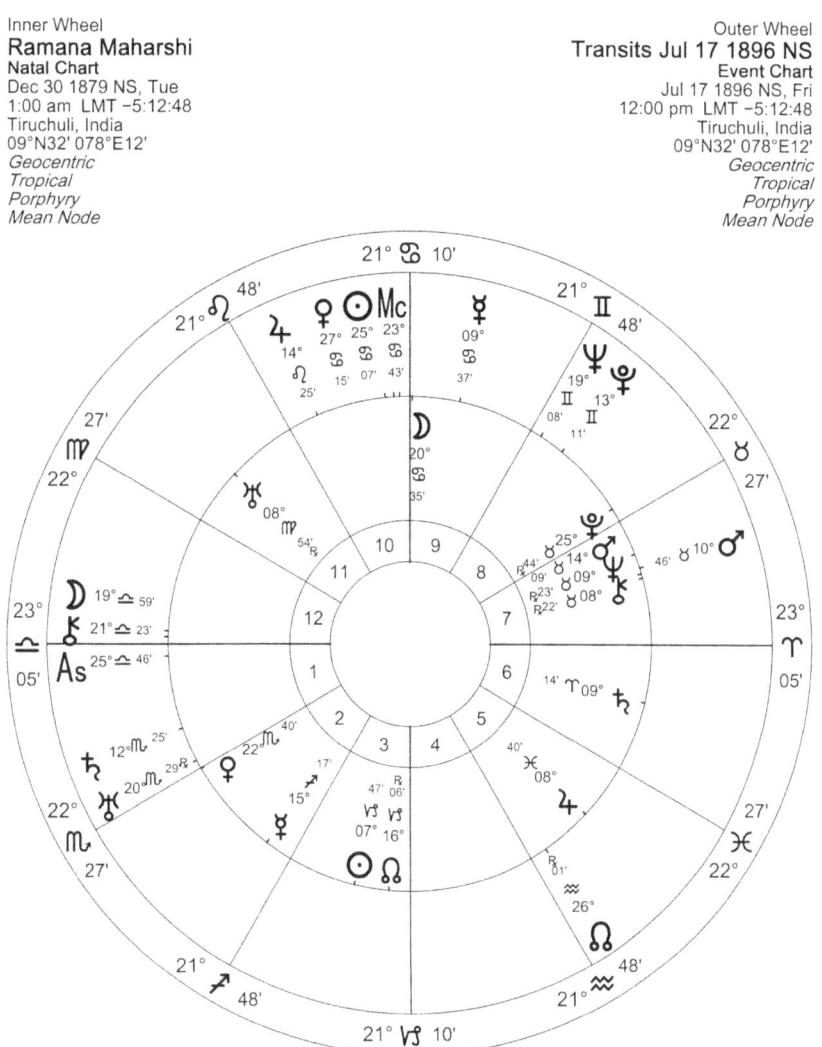

aspect between his natal first and eighth houses. Transiting Saturn and Pluto were also forming a quincunx. Uranus was beginning a long transit opposite natal Pluto in the eighth house, signifying a crisis experience of death and rebirth. At this time, Ramana's progressed Sun was trine Pluto and anticulminating near the IC, showing the way he spontaneously dropped down into the Self, into his deep center. There was a conjunction of progressed Moon and Jupiter in Pisces, zodiacal sign of *moksha*. Chiron, planet of initiation and the Guru, was transiting in Libra conjunct his Ascendant at this time of awakening. Natally, Ramana had Sun trine Neptune and sextile

Astrology and Spiritual Awakening, Part I

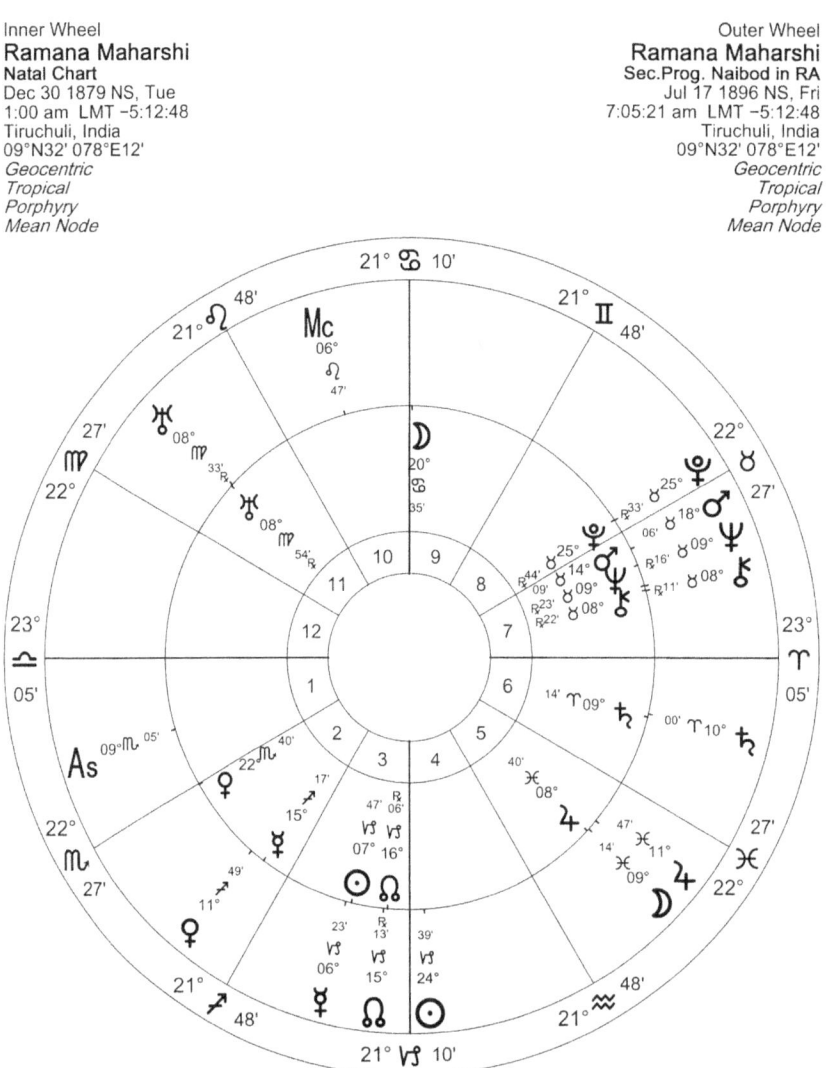

Jupiter in Pisces, signifying spiritual wisdom, sagely presence, and ease of being. The significant contacts of the natal Sun and Full Moon conjunct the Moon's nodes show his destiny of drawing attention and connection with the public, becoming a beloved world figure. Ramana's energy was lunar, soft, round, soothing, gentle, reflecting his amazingly full Cancer Moon conjunct the Midheaven. He conveyed his influence in silence, emanating calm, loving concern, and wakeful presence.

Sagittarius/Jupiter/Ninth House: Jnana:
The Yoga of Knowledge, Truth, and Philosophy

Sagittarius represents the formation of concepts, theories, beliefs, cosmologies, and religious, philosophical, and ethical principles that enable us to find meaning in life. With natal emphasis in Sagittarius, prominent placement of Jupiter, or planets in the ninth house, you pursue a quest for meaning and purpose through philosophical reflection, travel, education, teaching, or publishing. Your spiritual path might focus on keeping the company of enlightened teachers; going on a pilgrimage or vision quest; developing *jnana*, knowledge of the Real, *gnosis*, enlightening spiritual knowledge that brings freedom and deliverance. All of us need a philosophy of life or guiding doctrine to give meaning to our experience. Of course it's possible to become overly wrapped up in lofty, abstract concepts or dogmatic beliefs, but developing the higher intellect can be an important facet of spiritual growth.

Sagittarius and ninth house emphasis often indicates an orientation to travel, adventure, international contacts and interests, teaching and education, scholarship, publishing, law, journalism, philosophy, religion, promotion, and advertising. A woman with Sun-Venus-Mars in Sagittarius traveled around the world in her twenties on a quest for enlightenment, and then embarked on a career in educational publishing.

Professor Noam Chomsky has the Sun, Mercury, and Saturn conjunct in Sagittarius, an apt symbol for this intellectual genius.

Gershom Scholem (see chart on page 78), the eminent scholar of Jewish mysticism, was born with Sun, Mercury, Mars, Saturn, and Uranus in Sagittarius, in exact opposition to Pluto and Neptune at the Midheaven. Jupiter, dispositor of his Sagittarius stellium, was in the first house, symbolizing a man of knowledge. Scholem devoted his life to the study of Jewish Gnosticism, Hasidism, and Kabbalistic teachings.

Anthropologist Margaret Mead had Sun, Mercury, and Uranus conjunct in Sagittarius and an exact conjunction of Mars and Jupiter. Mead spent much of her life traveling around the world, writing about other cultures and anthropological theory. Many great writers with philosophical orientation have prominent placements of Sagittarius ruler Jupiter. Thomas Mann had Gemini Sun trine Jupiter. Herman Hesse had Jupiter in Sagittarius in the first house opposite Mercury. D. H. Lawrence had a conjunction of Sun and Jupiter in Virgo. Alfred North Whitehead had natal Sun opposite Jupiter. Deepak Chopra has Sun conjunct Jupiter and Venus in Sagittarius in the ninth house, signifying his beautiful teachings and publications.

Arundhati Roy (birth time unknown, noon chart shown on page 79), Indian writer, activist, fighter for social justice, was born at the Gemini Full Moon opposite Sun-

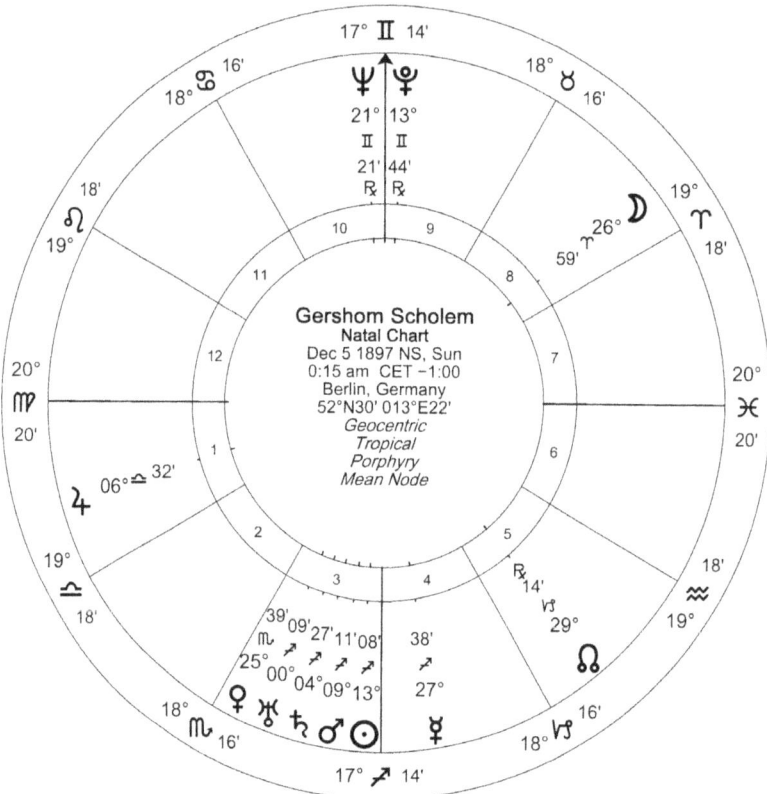

Mars in Sagittarius. Her books include *The God of Small Things*, *Power Politics*, *War Talk*, and *An Ordinary Person's Guide to Empire*. An exquisitely lucid thinker and inspiring educator, her Sun is sextile Jupiter. Jupiter in Aquarius conjunct Saturn in Capricorn signifies her commitment to leadership for political and social change. With the fiery intellectual sword of Mars in Sagittarius square Pluto, she engages in probing analyses, confronting corporate and government power with intense intellectual force.

Stanley Krippner (see chart on page 80) has Moon in Sagittarius and Jupiter conjunct Neptune and sesquiquadrate (135° aspect) Saturn in the tenth house. His cutting edge research in parapsychology, dream telepathy, cross-cultural healing methods, and shamanism have advanced knowledge of mystical, transpersonal, and healing phenomena (Saturn aspecting Jupiter-Neptune; Saturn ruling the ninth house of scholarship, and dignified by placement in its own sign and in the tenth house). Krippner has published 17 books and innumerable articles and travels the world constantly, teaching and learning from indigenous healers and shamans. With his Sun-Mercury

The Twelve Yogas of the Zodiac

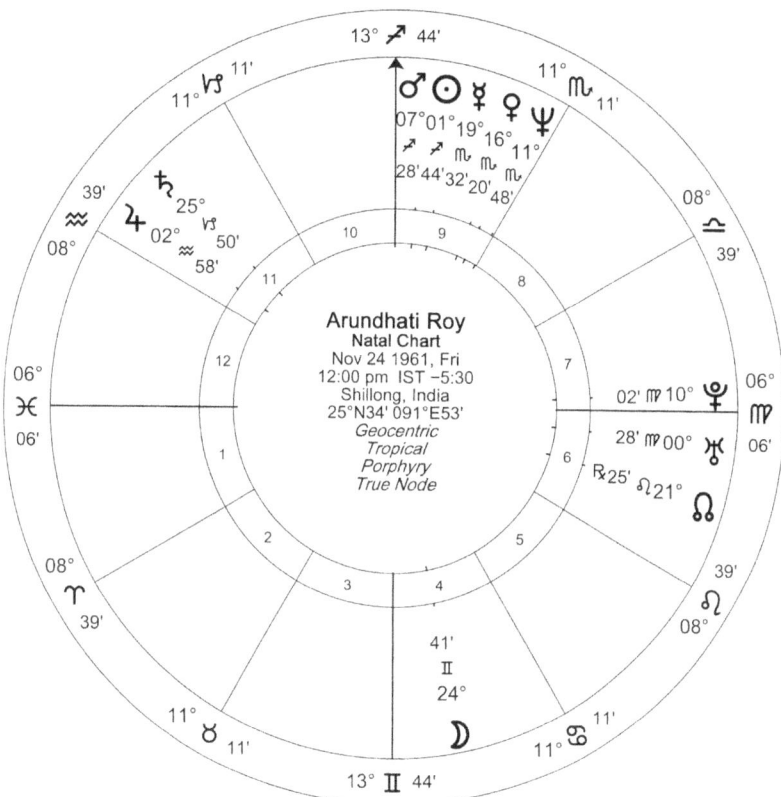

conjunction opposite Uranus, Krippner has an inventive mind and is a lively, funny, learned, and lucid speaker. Also note his Jupiter-south node conjunction, symbol of scholarship, intelligence, and intellectual productivity.

Sri Aurobindo (see chart on page 81), modern India's great philosopher and mystic seer, had Sun conjunct Jupiter in the first house in a Grand Trine with Moon in Sagittarius and Neptune in the ninth house. Well educated during his travels abroad in England, Aurobindo returned to India and became a journalist (ninth house and Sagittarian emphasis). He later wrote inspired volumes expounding the philosophy of Integral Yoga.

Spiritual philosopher Paul Brunton had a conjunction of Sun, Mercury, Venus, Saturn, and Uranus in Sagittarius. He was famous for his books on the great guru Ramana Maharshi, and describing his quest for sacred knowledge in India and Egypt.

Sun in the ninth house can indicate an intellectual focus or interests in education, trav-

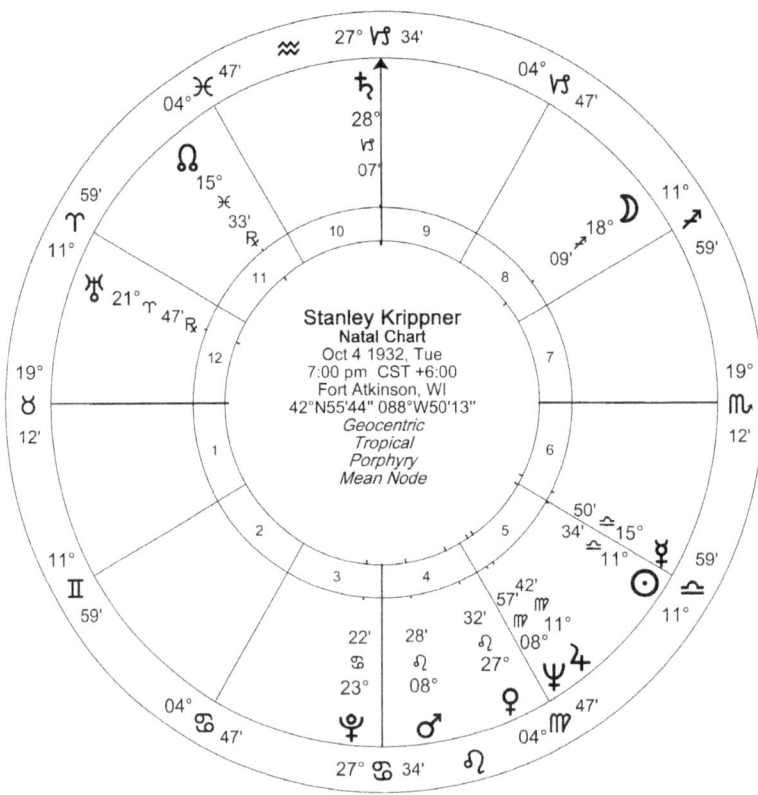

el, or law. A man with a Sun-Neptune conjunction in the ninth house was a theoretical physicist who wrote and researched cosmology theories. A woman with Sun-Mars in the ninth house is a university administrator known for energetic and decisive educational leadership. A man with Sun in the ninth house, trine Jupiter in the first house, is a university librarian who also enjoys teaching. A woman with Sun-Mercury in Virgo in her ninth house was director of a city Department of Education.

Ted, a visionary photographer interested in the philosophy of art and film, has natal Sun–Venus in Leo in the ninth house, in a T-square with Moon in Taurus and Jupiter–Neptune in Scorpio in the twelfth. Ted's ninth-house Sun symbolizes his identity as an intellectual, but with Moon in Taurus in the sixth house of trades and workers, Ted supports himself using his practical skills as a carpenter and handyman. Sun square Jupiter signifies his interest in philosophy and theory. Sun-Venus square Neptune shows the interests in film and its mythic symbolism.

The ninth house is also the house of legal proceedings and courtrooms. A woman with

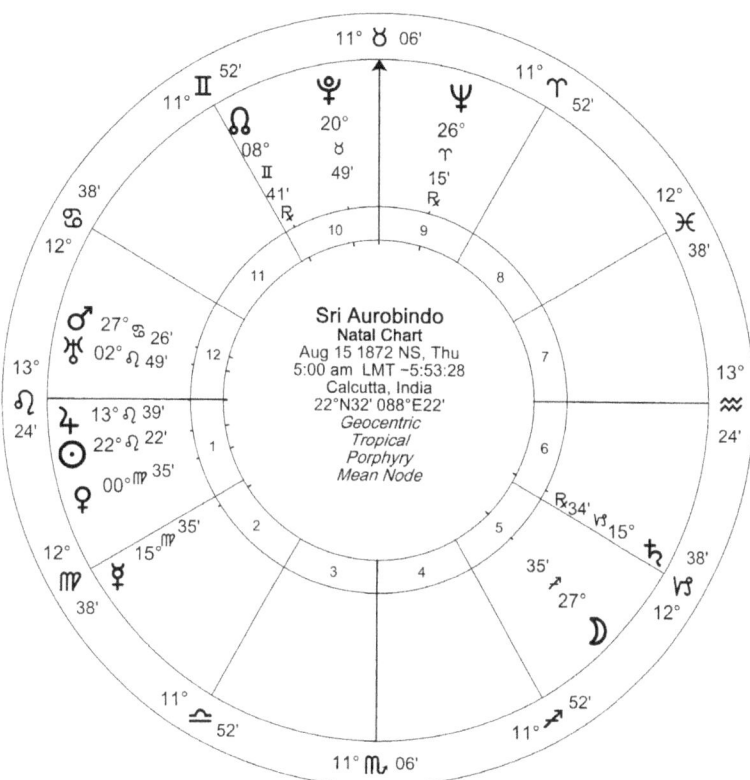

Virgo Sun in the ninth house is a highly principled person who served on a grand jury, even though her boss was upset about her missing several weeks of work. She said she felt greater integrity for having the experience of jury service.

The ninth house signifies education and the influence of teachers. A man met his guru when transiting Saturn passed into his ninth house, and he traveled with this teacher on a national tour for two years, listening to his lectures and studying philosophical texts.

Stanislav Grof's Mars-Neptune conjunction in Virgo at his ninth house cusp represents his work as a prolific author, teacher, and a theoretician of great persuasive power and imagination (ninth-house Mars-Neptune). Grof describes the use of breathwork and other spiritual practices to explore the farthest regions of mysticism, transpersonal realms, and visionary experience. Grof has also written extensively about spiritual emergencies, crises of awakening.

Astrology and Spiritual Awakening, Part I

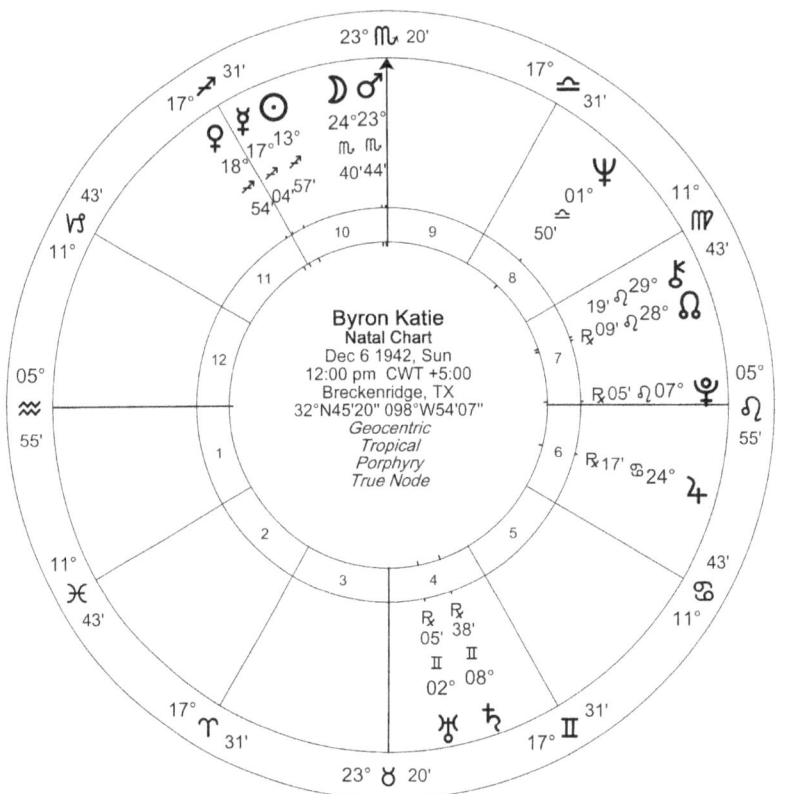

Spiritual teacher Byron Katie (time unknown; noon chart shown) became severely depressed in her early thirties. For almost a decade she spiraled down into rage, self-loathing, and thoughts of suicide. She seemed fully possessed by the emotionally turbulent energies of Moon conjunct Mars in Scorpio. For the last two years of this period she was often unable to leave her bedroom. This corresponded to the period when Saturn was transiting in Scorpio, tapping the intense Moon-Mars energy and effectively exhausting it. Then one morning in February 1986, while in a halfway house for women with eating disorders, Katie experienced a life-changing realization, which she calls "waking up to reality." She says, "I discovered that when I believed my thoughts, I suffered, but that when I didn't believe them, I didn't suffer, and that this is true for every human being. Freedom is as simple as that. I found that suffering is optional. I found a joy within me that has never disappeared, not for a single moment. That joy is in everyone, always." Katie realized that what had been causing her depression wasn't the world around her, but her beliefs about the world. Instead of trying to change the world to match her thoughts about how it should be, she could

The Twelve Yogas of the Zodiac

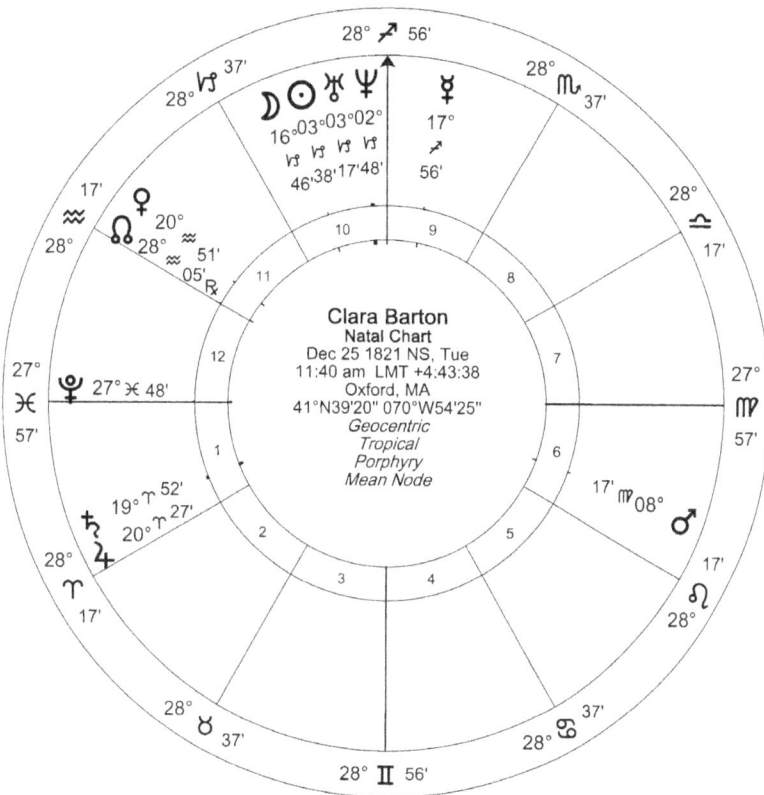

question these thoughts and, by meeting reality as it is, experience freedom and joy. "As a result, a bedridden, suicidal woman was instantly filled with love for everything life brings."(31)

In February 1986, Saturn had recently entered Sagittarius, zodiacal sign of knowledge, and it would pass over her Sun-Mercury-Venus within a year, signifying the awakening of wisdom and articulation of her teaching and philosophy. Transiting Pluto squared natal Pluto, representing untying the knots of ignorance, a death-rebirth experience, shedding old skin, a death of the ego. Pluto was also quincunx natal Saturn, showing significant tensions. Subsequently, during the Saturn-Uranus conjunction in Sagittarius in 1987–88, Katie underwent a revolution in her understanding and became a teacher. Transiting Saturn had been opposite natal Saturn and Uranus, showing a high stress period of trying to break out and experience freedom from old patterns and structures. Chiron is conjunct Katie's natal Saturn, showing a powerful initiation, resolving her own woundedness, and coming to hold the scepter of pristine knowledge and spiritual authority. The transit of Saturn opposite Saturn signified maturing, coming into her own, developing a steady consciousness. If Byron Katie can achieve this degree of life transformation during transits all of us pass through at midlife (Pluto square Pluto, Uranus opposition, Saturn opposition), then all of us are capable of fully awakening our innate potentials. For Katie that meant living the Sagittarian archetype, becoming the wise teacher.

Capricorn/Saturn/Tenth House: Dharma:
The Yoga of Mastery Through Accomplishment

Emphasis on Capricorn, its ruler Saturn, or the tenth house suggests a need to define and pursue your professional ambitions and to follow what Hazrat Inayat Khan calls the path of "mastery through accomplishment." Some spiritual seekers become sensitive and want to withdraw from the world and from personal ambitions. However, with planets here your task is realize your goals and ambitions, to become an incarnation of your ideals, and to assume your appropriate position within the social and spiritual hierarchy of humanity, through tangible achievements. These areas of the chart emphasize embodying personally meaningful archetypes, defining and actualizing your dharma or personal vocation and assuming authority or a position of leadership. The tenth house and tenth sign Capricorn represent striving and achievement, so planets placed here call forth efforts to succeed in our career or occupation.

Daman, with Sun, Jupiter, and Saturn in Capricorn in the tenth house, spent his twenties drifting around touring with the Grateful Dead but began to feel anxious during his Saturn Return because he hadn't accomplished anything or established a profession. Daman became quite serious about finding a career and eventually found a position in a corporate environment. His entire life changed from that point on.

Clara Barton, founder of the American Red Cross, had Sun, Moon, Uranus, and Neptune in Capricorn and in the tenth house, as well as Saturn conjunct Jupiter in the first house. This highly capable, committed, and ambitious woman worked tirelessly to alleviate the sufferings of others (Sun-Neptune in tenth), risking death on the battlefields of the Civil War to care for the wounded. She served as the President of this important relief organization for twenty-two years. The Sun-Uranus-Neptune conjunction represents selfless service of humanity and commitment to organizing for social change (Uranus). The rising Saturn is dispositor of the eleventh house of organizations.

When Saturn transited over his Midheaven and into his tenth house, a man who had spent many years dithering and procrastinating while trying to complete a historical novel stopped wasting time, finished his book, and found a publisher. He began to speak publicly and gradually established his reputation as an authority in his field.

In the tenth house it's not necessary to achieve fame or notoriety. What we strive for is to accomplish our own goals and feel satisfied with those accomplishments. That is success.

A woman was appointed director of a school of metaphysical studies and developed a following as a psychic counselor and healer when transiting Saturn and Pluto in Scorpio passed over her natal Jupiter-Neptune conjunction in the tenth house.

California Governor Jerry Brown has Sun in Aries conjunct Saturn, showing managerial and executive ability, and a Mercury-Venus-Mars-Uranus conjunction in Taurus in the tenth house. He has been exceptionally inventive with governmental fiscal policies and budget management (Taurus). In his terms as governor he has allocated funds to the development of new technologies (Uranus) such as renewable energy sources. As a practicing Catholic and Zen Buddhist, Brown has a strong spiritual orientation, shown by his natal Sun quincunx Neptune. Yet his path in the world is to be a progressive, futuristic, and pragmatic politician (Mercury-Mars conjunct Uranus in Taurus).

Sri Aurobindo, with natal Pluto in the tenth house square Sun-Jupiter, experienced a "death-rebirth" crisis that changed the direction of his career and his life path. A period of imprisonment for alleged seditious acts against the British rulers in India led him to end his former life and activities as a political journalist and social activist.

> I was taken from Lal Bazar to Alipore and was placed for one month in a solitary cell apart from men. There I waited day and night for the voice of God within me, to know what He had to say to me, to learn what I had to do. . . . I remembered that a month or more before my arrest, a call had come to me to put aside all activity, to go into seclusion and to look into myself, so that I might enter into deeper communion with Him. I was weak and could not accept the call. My work [for the liberation of India] was very dear to me and in the pride of my heart I thought that unless I was there it would suffer or even fail and cease; therefore I would not leave it. It seemed to me that He spoke to me again and said, "The bonds you had not the strength to break, I have broken for you, because it is not my will nor was it ever my intention that that should continue. I have had another thing for you to do and it is for that I have brought you here, to teach you what you could not learn for yourself and to train you for my work. . . . [D]ay after day, He showed me His wonders. . . . That knowledge He gave to me day after day during my twelve months of imprisonment.(32)

While in prison in solitary confinement Aurobindo heard this inner voice suggest to him that there was a secret, occult purpose behind his crisis of imprisonment, which

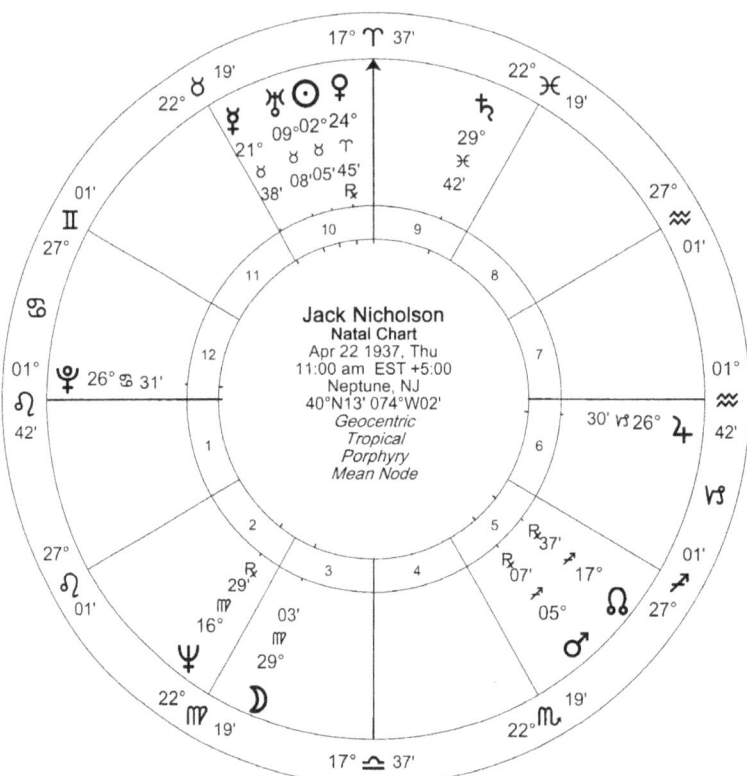

was mysteriously orchestrated to free him from worldly and political entanglements to prepare him for the "adventure of consciousness." He underwent an inner transformation from activist to integral yogi. Aurobindo used the prison time for deep meditation and study of yoga. Subsequently his capacity for leadership (Sun square Pluto in tenth house) was redirected into a career as a spiritual teacher who wrote and taught about the descent of supramental, world-transforming energies. Pluto represents transmission of power from the supramental plane of consciousness to purify and transform the body, the personality, and this physical plane of existence.

Sun in the tenth house denotes the potential to gain notoriety and recognition. People with Sun in the tenth may attract prominence, exceptional reputation, and visibility in their career. Jack Nicholson has a Sun-Uranus conjunction in the tenth house. He is a true original, a person unlike any other; he is his own archetype. Sun rules his Ascendant, exactly squaring the Ascendant from the tenth house, representing gaining attention and notoriety. Venus, ruler of his Taurus Sun, is conjunct the Midheaven, signifying how he's widely loved—as well as wealth. With Venus square Pluto on his Ascendant, Nicholson also has a reptilian energy that's part of his captivating persona. Mars quincunx Sun-Uranus signifies his self-confident, slightly arrogant, unruly air of freedom, independence, and rebelliousness.

Natasha, a film and stage actress with a Sun–Venus conjunction in Capricorn at the Midheaven, quincunx Pluto in Leo in the fifth house, enjoyed a period of fame and success, but later withdrew from the public eye because she disliked the egotism and ruthless competitiveness of the entertainment industry (Pluto in the fifth house) and the childish petulance, vanity, and image-consciousness that this world evoked in her. She struggled with a narcissistic streak, a desire to be treated as special (Pluto in Leo in the fifth house). This made it hard for her to endure the competition and frequent disappointments of auditions. She felt that she should be chosen for roles without having to audition, because of her past work and reputation. After several years of retirement, she made a successful comeback when transiting Jupiter passed through Cancer, opposite her tenth-house Sun–Venus. Her talent naturally drew attention from the public. She was cast in several excellent theatrical roles and appeared in a television series.

Sue, with Sun-Mercury in Aquarius in the tenth house, opposite Pluto, is an administrative secretary for a large corporation, serving upper management. She has a visible position and is a well-known figure at her company. Within her organization she's a star. With Sun opposite Pluto in Leo, Sue takes pride in working under important people, and within her sphere of influence she's a powerful person. One day Sue called to tell me that she was quitting her job after thirteen years. Transiting Uranus was exactly conjunct her Sun. She'd had a revelation after a weekend workshop where she walked on hot coals. She said, "This experience woke me up. I realized I had to break free in order to realize my teenage dream of becoming a great writer." Uranus acted here in its classic role as the awakener. Sue decided to go back to college to complete her bachelor's degree, studying creative writing (Sun-Mercury in the tenth house), with an emphasis on futuristic science fiction (Uranus conjunct her Aquarius Sun). She was individuating rapidly. With Sun-Mercury in the tenth house, opposite Pluto, Sue wanted to have her own career and life's work, and to be recognized for her own ideas.

Let's consider a few other planetary placements in the tenth house. The Moon in the tenth house may signify careers involving caring, cooking, nurturing, feeling, and empathy, as well as nurturing parenting and professional roles. A man with Moon in Cancer in the tenth house is a psychotherapist who exudes emotional empathy and sensitivity. Mercury in the tenth house often symbolizes a career in writing, communications, and public speaking. My mother had Mercury in Gemini in the tenth house;

she was a professional journalist and editor. Venus in the tenth house is sometimes seen in the charts of bookkeepers, financiers, or anyone with a career in which people skills and maintaining business relationships are essential to success. Venus in the tenth house may also signify a career in music or the arts, as I noted earlier. A pianist with Venus conjunct the South Node in Aries in the tenth house was a child prodigy who went on to tour internationally and recorded many albums.

Jupiter placed in the tenth house is commonly seen in the charts of people involved with law or education. Mars in the tenth house indicates strong energy for the pursuit of career and ambitions. Prominent placement of Mars, aspecting the Sun, or placed in the tenth house, is sometimes seen in the birth charts of athletes, mechanics, plumbers, engineers, fighters, firemen, and people employed in law enforcement or the military. It may signify any occupation involving bravery, heroism, or strong motivation and initiative. A salesman with Mars–Mercury in Taurus in his tenth house is a tireless worker who won Salesman of the Month awards 18 times.

Aquarius/Uranus/Eleventh House: Sangha:
The Yoga of Groups, Community, and Organizations

Aquarius and the eleventh house represent awareness of historical forces and social conditions and participation in groups, organizations, teams, communities, coops, meetings, conferences, political causes or gatherings concerned with social change and creating a better future for humanity. With an emphasis here, some form of political activism or organizational involvement can be an important facet of your spiritual path. You may also seek to understand social movements, historical cycles, and current social trends. Pursuing solitary spiritual practices feels incomplete and you recognize the importance of *sangha*, involvement in a community or group, or socially engaged forms of spirituality such as those informed by Engaged Buddhism or Liberation Theology. Scientific experimentation and interests in technology and innovation may also be of great interest with prominent placement of Uranus, or planets in Aquarius or in the eleventh house. President Barack Obama has Saturn in its domicile, Capricorn, conjunct Jupiter in Aquarius, ruler of his eleventh house of politics and social activism. Obama's Sun is conjunct Ascendant-ruler Uranus, which is closely conjunct the Moon's north node, symbol of a person whose personal identity is merged to a social consciousness and collective enterprise, inspired by a vision of the future and human potentials. Note Obama's Sun-Mercury in a T-square with Neptune and Jupiter, signifying his compassion, refined spirit, intellectual brilliance, clear thinking, and poised, articulate speech.

A woman with Aquarius Sun in the fourth house purchased property in order to found an intentional community.

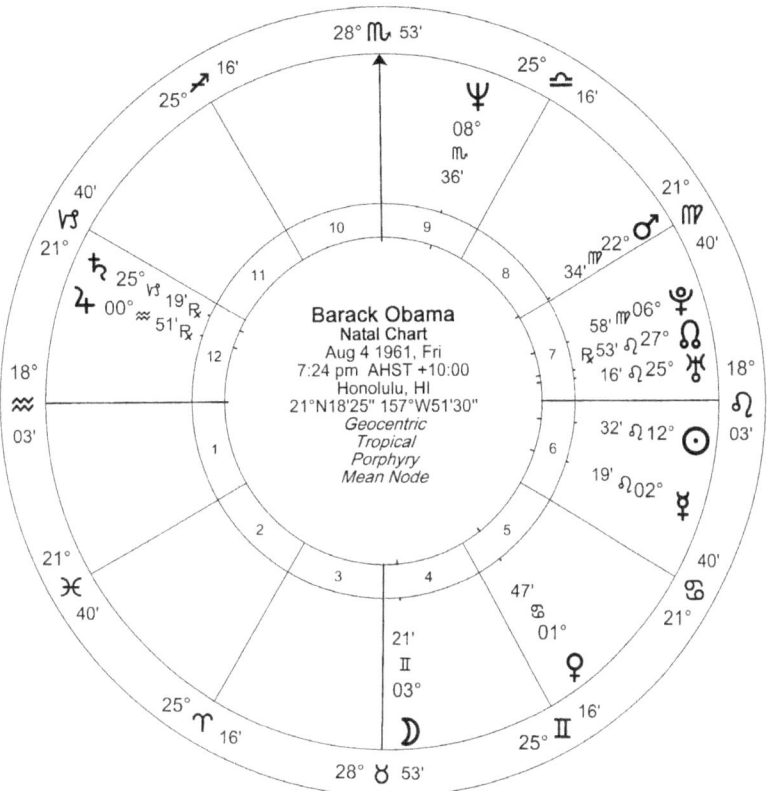

A woman with Sun-Saturn conjunction in her eleventh house found a new sense of purpose during her Saturn Return when she joined a yoga ashram community and assumed a position of leadership and responsibility in this group (Saturn in eleventh).

Doris, an African-American woman, had an eighth-house Sun in Taurus square Saturn-Pluto in Leo in her eleventh house. Doris repeatedly confronted racism and sexism (Pluto square Sun) during her years of education and professional life, which generated a commitment to social activism in her community, investing her own money (Taurus Sun) in the struggle against discrimination and oppression of minorities, and violence against women.

A man with Uranus in the tenth house and Sun conjunct Pluto in the eleventh house is a scientist and futurist who is involved with several scientific organizations and conferences and lived for over three decades in a large communal household.

Jiddu Krishnamurti was the spiritual leader of an organization within the Theosophical movement called Order of the Star. He unexpectedly dissolved this order in August, 1929, while Saturn transited over his eleventh-house Moon in Sagittariuis.

President Franklin Roosevelt had Sun in Aquarius and Uranus conjunct his Ascendant, and made part of his mark on history through the innovative policies of the New Deal. President Bill Clinton's Leo Sun is placed in the eleventh house. He has been dedicated to progressive social causes since his youth. Physicist Albert Einstein, with Uranus in the third house opposite Jupiter in the ninth house, revolutionized science and modern thought with his revolutionary theories. Inventor and futurist Buckminster Fuller had a natal grand trine of Sun, Moon, and Uranus.

Tibetan Buddhist teacher Chogyam Trungpa Rinpoche was born on a Full Moon with Sun in Aquarius closely squaring Uranus (ruler of Aquarius). He was an unpredictable, revolutionary, crazy-wisdom teacher who broke with Tibetan traditions in many respects, whose controversial actions were sometimes shocking and unsettling, and who renewed Buddhist teachings by translating them into contemporary terms.

Dane Rudhyar had Moon in Aquarius, square Uranus, and natal Saturn in the eleventh house. In 1916, at the age of 21, while transiting Uranus was conjunct his natal Moon and square natal Uranus, Rudhyar cut himself loose from the past. He left his native France, sailed to America, and changed his name to Rudhyar, derived from Rudra, the fiery, creative aspect of Shiva. He left behind the culture and consciousness of the European past and became a vehicle for expression of creative energies with a sense of futurity. He dedicated his life to cultural transformation through a multi-faceted career as an avant garde musical composer, painter, philosopher, poet, and astrologer. He was involved in progressive artistic movements, multimedia performance art, and catalyzed a significant social trend by inspiring the growth of modern astrology, founding the International Committee for a Humanistic Astrology.

Sun in the eleventh house may signify an interest in politics or social activism. One's lifepath may be defined by commitment to a cause, social movement, or collective enterprise or by involvement in the activities and agendas of a particular group or organization. A woman with Sun in Taurus in the eleventh house is a fundraiser for a large spiritual organization.

Rami, a yoga teacher with a natal Sun–Moon-Jupiter-Mercury conjunction in Cancer in the eleventh house, was asked by her guru to move to a distant city and start a yoga center. For her, Sun–Jupiter in the eleventh house symbolized teaching and leadership in a community. However, things were not going so well. There was a transiting Saturn–Pluto opposition across her Gemini Midheaven and Sagittarius IC. She was facing obstacles, classes were not filling up, and she was losing money. Jen was wonder-

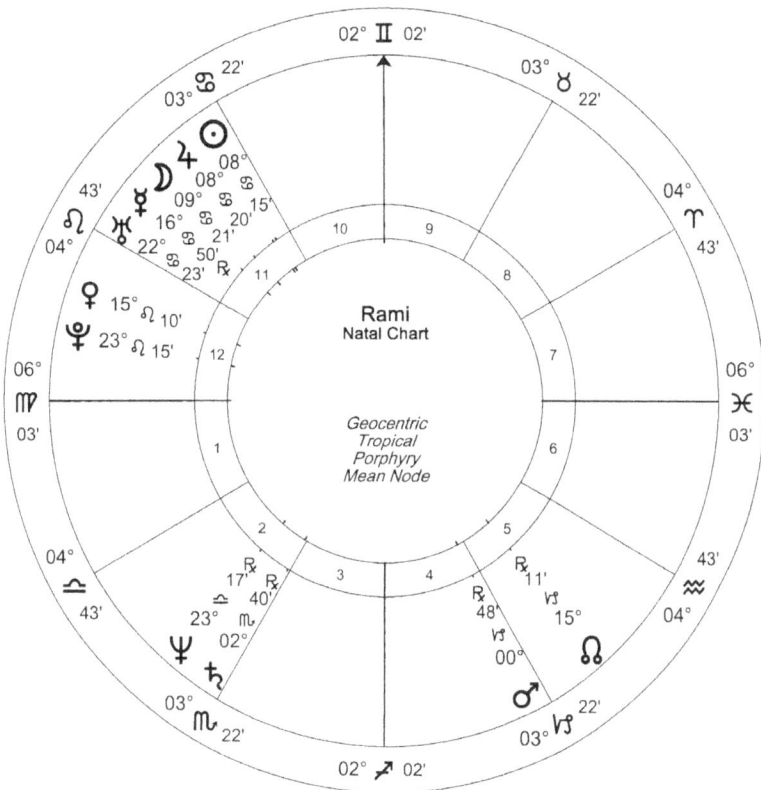

ing whether she should accept defeat and close the center. I noted that, nine months in the future, transiting Saturn in Cancer was going to be conjunct her natal Sun–Jupiter. The unfolding of her goal to become a teacher and create a vibrant yoga community could be expected to come to fruition at the time of this transit. Astrology teaches us the importance of patience, faith, and right timing. It was also pertinent that Jen had a progressed Sun–Pluto conjunction in Leo in her twelfth house. She was burning with resentment and hurt pride (Leo) because other, more glamorous yoga teachers got all the public attention, while she felt unappreciated and overlooked (twelfth house). These feelings seemed to reflect a certain wounded pride and unfulfilled desire for attention (Sun-Pluto in Leo).

I suggested that Rami could develop her own feminine, Great Mother, Cancerian style as a teacher, for example, by offering food at her yoga center, seasonal celebrations, child care, a family environment, and warm hospitality. Her calling was to create more sense of family and community: Sun, Jupiter, and Moon in Cancer in the eleventh house. Nine months later, Rami's center was written up in the newspaper and suddenly became a popular yoga hot spot in her city. The contribution of astrology here was to affirm her path and to give her faith in a positive outcome. Saturn's transits are times to approach our tasks with focus and sustained effort. This example illustrates the importance of visualizing the most desirable outcome of our current and upcoming transits.(33)

**Pisces/Neptune/Twelfth House: Moksa:
The Yoga of Tranquility and Self-Realization**

In Pisces we open up and feel the stillness and ease of Being, the peace of existing as pure consciousness without form. The Pisces/Neptune/twelfth house yoga is to move beyond ego-centered awareness, and to experience *moksa*, liberation, interior spiritual freedom. It's important here to yield, trust, surrender, and let go of grasping to form, to ego, to attachments—to inwardly merge one's being into a larger whole. This is the intelligent culmination of our evolutionary journey. Here we overcome our feeling of separateness and limitation, experiencing a state of union and limitlessness, enlightenment, illumination, and Self-realization. One may experience what Buddhists call the "radiant light of consciousness," or what the Sufis call *fana* (annihilation of the ego) and *baqa* (Self-realization). The great Tibetan Buddhist guru Padmasambhava taught that the goal of spiritual practice is the remembrance of "intrinsic awareness." He said, "When you look into yourself. . . nakedly (without any discursive thoughts) since there is only this pure observing, there will be found a lucid clarity without anyone being there who is the observer. . . . This is the real introduction to the actual condition of things." (35). Pisces, Neptune, and the twelfth house are the astrological symbols associated with awakening to this enlightened condition.

If your chart emphasizes planets placed in Pisces or the twelfth house (or accentuates Neptune) you may be drawn to mysticism and spirituality, interiorization of consciousness though meditation, visions and trance states; altruism and selfless service; contemplative prayer; retreat and solitude. You may experience the emergence of symbolic material from the deep unconscious through dreams. You may have experiences of the void, nothingness, or states of ecstasy.

Occasionally there are less pleasant manifestations of Pisces, its ruler Neptune, or twelfth house planets, such as hospitalization, convalescence; in some cases people manifest problems with their mental health, including hallucinations, inflation, or psychosis. This can be the realm of a *dark night of the soul*. Thomas, who had Moon, Saturn, and Mars in the twelfth house, left his family to spend several months on retreat in the desert fasting and practicing strenuous austerities. During this time he experienced visions that he was destined to become the Messiah, the World Saviour.

Months of therapy with a psychiatrist who prescribed medication, and a period of meditation practice under a teacher's guidance helped bring his delusional ideation under control. Thomas did have great psychic sensitivity, which he began to express through offering psychic readings.

Sometimes there's a disorganizing tendency with Pisces energy that can create inertia, delusions, or confusion. More typically, one may grapple with loneliness, addiction, or feelings of weakness, victimization, ineffectiveness, powerlessness, abandonment, or grief. With planets here, you may find refuge and liberation through meditation, dreamwork, hypnosis, visualization, active imagination, symbolic amplification, Jungian analysis, transpersonal psychotherapies, shamanic journeys, past life regression, or use of psychedelics. Planets here can also indicate strong interests in metaphysical truths and mystical arts such as astrology. The capacity to work with symbols and the higher mind through these spiritual methodologies can help alleviate our psychological suffering, our neuroses and pathologies.(34)

Individuals with a strong Pisces/twelfth house emphasis, or with Sun, Moon, or Ascendant ruler in strong aspect to Neptune, may be drawn to meditation, silent contemplation, and periods of solitude and retreat. During Sri Aurobindo's 1908–1909 imprisonment and his subsequent inward turn toward meditation, transiting Jupiter passed through his twelfth house, then contacted his Ascendant and natal Sun-Jupiter, awakening knowledge. Transiting Saturn was conjunct Neptune in his ninth house of teachers and spiritual realization; he came under the influence of two great teachers, Swami Vivekananda, who visited him in prison, and Vishnu Bhaskar Lele, who instructed him in meditation. It's also noteworthy that his friendships with these two *mahatmas* who initiated him occurred during Chiron's transit in his seventh house, directly opposite his natal Sun. Chiron is the planet of the guru, the mentor, the initiator. Transiting Uranus in Capricorn was conjunct natal Saturn in the sixth house of yogic sadhana. Transiting Neptune in Cancer entered his twelfth house of seclusion and the interior journey into divine life. Uranus and Neptune had reached their opposition phase, showing the potential to raise and expand consciousness. Uranus and Neptune both activated natal Saturn in the sixth, and hereafter Aurobindo's life was centered in austere spiritual practice.

Pisces and the twelfth house are concerned with transcendence of a limited, egoic perspective and awakening of compassion. An emphasis here can generate a desire to express the spirit of service and lovingkindness in daily life. A woman with Mars in Pisces in the first house worked with disadvantaged children and as a nurse on an intensive care ward, and spent much of her spare time caring for an elderly neighbor. Her identity (first house) was formed around her desire to serve others (Mars in Pisces).

In Buddhism, the altruistic, selfless, compassionate attitude of Pisces is called *metta*, described in the *Metta Sutra—The Buddha's Discourse on Loving-kindness*:

> This is what should be done/ By those who are skilled in goodness,
> And who know the path of peace; / Let them be able and upright,
> Straightforward and gentle in speech. / Humble and not conceited,
> Contented and easily satisfied. / Unburdened with duties and frugal in their ways.
> Peaceful and calm, and wise and skillful, / Not proud and demanding in nature.
> Let them not do the slightest thing / That the wise would later reprove.
> Wishing: in gladness and in safety, / May all beings be at ease.
> Whatever living beings there may be; /Whether they are weak or strong, omitting none,
> The great or the mighty, medium, short or small, / The seen and the unseen,
> Those living near and far away, / Those born and to-be-born—
> May all beings be at ease! / Let none deceive another,
> Or despise any being in any state. / Let none through anger or ill-will
> Wish harm upon another. / Even as a mother protects with her life
> Her child, her only child, / So with a boundless heart
> Should one cherish all living beings; / Radiating kindness over the entire world:
> Spreading upward to the skies, / And downward to the depths;
> Outward and unbounded, / Free from hatred and ill-will.
> Whether standing or walking, seated or lying down, / Free from drowsiness,
> One should sustain this recollection. / This is said to be the sublime abiding.
> By not holding to fixed views, / The pure-hearted one, having clarity of vision,
> Being freed from all sense desires, / Is not born again into this world.(36)

Acharya Buddharakkhita commented:

> The thought-radiation must be 'willed' well. . . . If . . . the wishing is performed in a perfunctory or mechanical way, the practice will be of little avail, for then it will be merely an intellectual pastime of *thinking about metta*. One must clearly understand that to *think about metta* is one thing and *to do metta*, to actively project the will-force of loving-kindness, is quite another.(37)

In Pisces and the twelfth house we experience spiritual ordeals and awakenings. Freya had a conjunction of Sun-Moon-Mercury-Venus-Saturn in Pisces and in the twelfth house, opposite Mars-Uranus-Pluto in Virgo in the sixth house. She experienced a religious conversion in her early twenties as transiting Uranus and Saturn squared

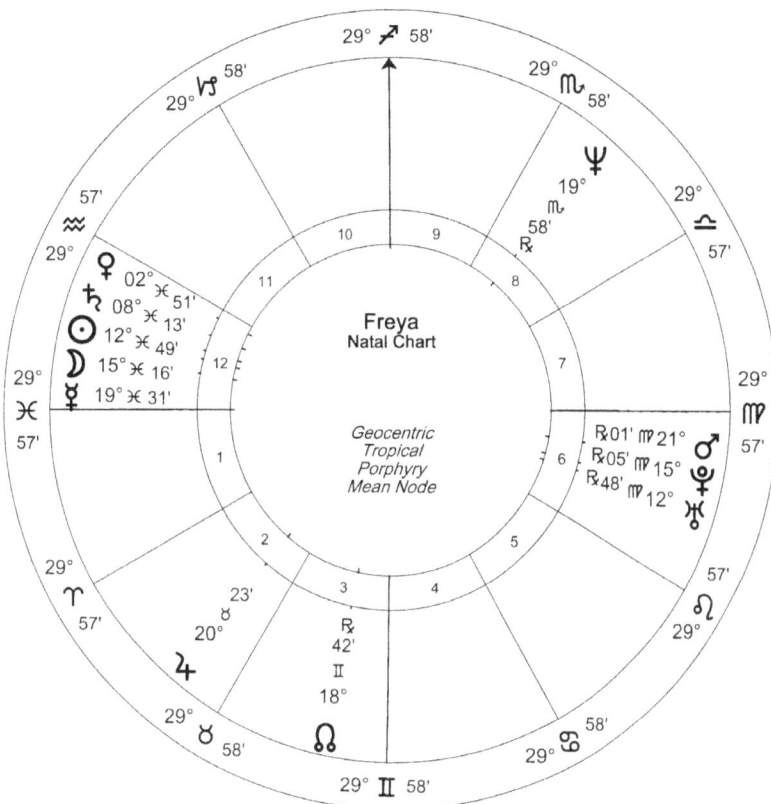

these planets from Sagittarius. Freya had visions of Christ and the Virgin Mary and oscillated between states of ecstasy and feelings of loneliness and abandonment. She also experienced an acute conflict between her spirituality (Pisces planets) and her sexuality (Mars-Uranus-Pluto conjunction). She forced herself to undergo strict religious penances (Virgo-sixth house emphasis), which she felt were necessary to purify herself of her desires. She tried meditation but was unable to make progress as she suffered from severe anxiety, mostly stemming from stress and worries about work (Virgo, sixth house emphasis). She struggled for many years to find stable and satisfying employment. Slowly she gained skills that enabled her to advance in a career in retail store management, which stabilized her life. She learned accounting and moved into a role where she was earning more money (Jupiter in Taurus in second house). Freya began to thrive in her forties when she got married. Finally she had someone with whom she could share her affectionate nature (Sun-Venus) and experience passionate sexual fire (Mars conjunct Uranus and Pluto). She realized that, for her, sex and spirituality were one and the same.

Jeff, a 24-year-old man, with natal Sun and Moon in Virgo in the twelfth house square his third-house Saturn, sought counseling during a period of confusion and disorientation. He was preoccupied with his dreams, and spent most of his time meditating, and reading books about spirituality, astrology, and mysticism. He had no inclination to work or be involved in relationships. Transiting Saturn was in his twelfth house, conjunct natal Sun-Moon. Many people thought there was something wrong with Jeff and expressed concern about his withdrawal and preoccupation with his inner world. Through studying his birth chart Jeff realized this was a crucial period of inner work, reorientation, and preparation for rebirth. The twelfth house can be a zone of uncertainty, transition, gestation, the condition of a caterpillar in a crysalis. Jeff recognized the necessity of this phase of interior exploration, and allowed himself to immerse in it, trusting that eventually the period of confusion would come to an end. By the time Saturn transited over his Ascendant, he became more grounded and began exploring avenue for becoming a writer (natal Saturn in third house). This led him to return to journalism school during his Saturn Return, after which he got a job as a newspaper reporter and found his place in the world.

Ogden, who had a fifth house Aries Sun, struggled with how to channel his physical and competitive drives after retirement from his Olympic and professional athletic career; and he began to experience depression during a progressed Moon-Neptune conjunction in his twelfth house. He was having a hard time with isolation, invisibility, being out of the public eye. At this time, he got a ticket for driving while intoxicated. His driver's license was suspended, and, not being able to drive, he had to slow down his life considerably. At first he wallowed and felt sorry for himself and started drinking more. I played him a Robbie Robertsong song, The Code of Handsome Lake, which tells the story of the Seneca Indian chief who was afflicted with alcoholism. "He drank your poison, swallowed your fire, and lay with fever four long years." Handsome Lake had a vision that three messengers with painted faces appeared and taught him the principles of healing, purification, and self-forgiveness that helped free him from the fever of drinking and inner soul agony. They told him, "When the dark moon has come to live in your soul, get in touch with your Creator, you are not alone." Listening to this song helped Ogden touch some deep emotions, and he became willing to talk about how drinking was a way he'd been trying to numb his feelings. He started attending Alcoholics Anonymous meetings and learned to meditate. He underwent an inner ordeal and inner healing, forgave himself inwardly, and cultivated a feeling of tranquility through prayer and meditation. Ogden found his way through this confusing period with faith and a feeling of grace.

Sun in the twelfth house signifies an orientation toward service and charitable activity, occupations in which one can remain behind the scenes, or an interest in metaphysics and spiritual practices. One is less motivated here by egoic strivings, and spiritual aspirations become central to one's sense of purpose in life. Arjun, the husband of Uma (discussed earlier), was a software engineer. With a Sun-Neptune conjunction in early Sagittarius in the twelfth house, Arjun wasn't highly ambitious and enjoyed quietly doing his job, then dedicating the rest of his time to meditation. His interest in spirituality grew stronger when transiting Uranus squared natal Sun-Neptune. With natal Sun in the twelfth house, spirituality and self-realization were his central life goals.

Astrologer and occultist Manly Palmer Hall had natal Sun in Pisces square Neptune, and Moon trine Neptune. The great astrologer Evangeline Adams had Sun in the twelfth house, Mercury, Jupiter, and Venus in Pisces, Pisces Ascendant, and Neptune in the first house; one can hardly imagine a more mystical chart symbolism. Prophet and trance channel Edgar Cayce had a Moon-Neptune conjunction on his Midheaven and Pisces Sun in the ninth house. Visionary philosopher-mystic Rudolph Steiner had Sun, Mercury, and Neptune in Pisces. Mystic-seer Sri Aurobindo had Sun trine Neptune, Mars-Uranus in the twelfth house, and Mars square Neptune, all symbolizing an evolutionary pull toward enlightenment and a life of expanded consciousness.

Mata Amritanandamayi, known as Ammachi (see chart on page 98), showed a mystical inclination from childhood, capturing attention for her devotional singing, compassionate acts, ecstatic demeanor, and immersion in meditation. As a teenager, while transiting Saturn opposed natal Sun-Mercury-Saturn-Neptune in Libra, she met the wrath of her family when she refused to marry, devoting herself to a life of meditation, contemplation, and social service (twelfth house emphasis). Transiting Saturn was in Aries: She had her own will; she was her own autonomous person. She was banished by her family, and taunted and threatened by stone-throwing neighbors. She slept outdoors without possessions. Her stripped-down state of simplicity and renunciation reflects the conjunction of Saturn-Neptune. Apparently a dog brought her food to eat and a cow stayed near her so she could drink milk from its udder. With Taurus Moon in the seventh house, she met the infinite abundance, nurturance, and protection of nature, the divine mother. As transiting Uranus was conjunct her natal Sun, squared natal Uranus, and was conjunct natal Neptune and Saturn, she pursued a very different and unconventional lifestyle free of conventional family roles, dedicated to spiritual life and altruistic works. In 1975 she prayed fervently for divine union and began to manifest saintly qualities and became known as Mata Amritanandamayi. From 1981, when Jupiter and Saturn in Libra were conjunct her natal Sun, she began to be recognized and pursued by devotees attracted to her wisdom, her advanced yogic state, her radiance and unconditional love. She is known for her sanctity, selflessness, simplicity, and her organizing of hospitals, orphanages, schools. With Mars semisquare Neptune she emanates bliss energy. With her Libra emphasis, Venus

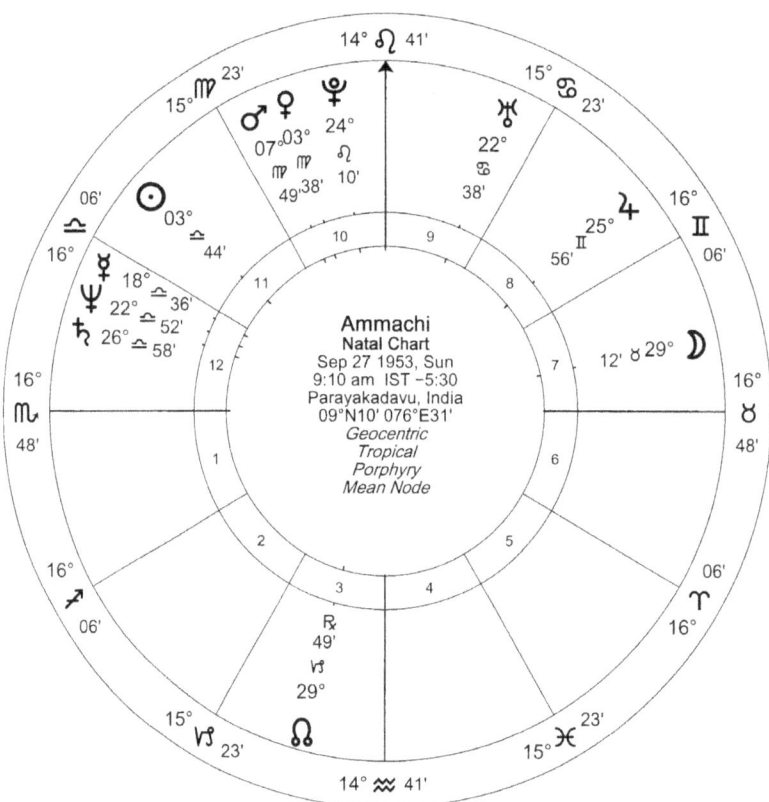

conjunct Mars, and exalted Taurus Moon in the seventh house, she is very sociable, related, loves people, hugs everybody, is the Mother of All. With Sun in the eleventh house, she inspired the forming of spiritual communities internationally and founded a worldwide organization, Mata Amritanandamayi Mission Trust.

Bengali saint Sri Ramakrishna had a Mars-Neptune conjunction in the twelfth house, and Sun in late Aquarius conjunct Uranus in early Pisces, along with Moon and Mercury in Pisces in the first house. At age 6–7 Ramakrishna experienced his first ecstatic state, became detached from worldly matters, and began exhibiting behaviors that others viewed as abnormal, peculiar, or crazy. This occurred when transiting Jupiter and Neptune were conjunct at 20° Aquarius, near his Ascendant, and when Jupiter conjoined natal Sun and Uranus (strange behavior). At age 9 he began to lose himself in meditation and worship of the Goddess Kali; transiting Saturn was in his twelfth house, conjunct natal Mars and Neptune. Between 1856–1859 he passed through a period of "divine madness," experiencing a feverish longing for union with God, intense

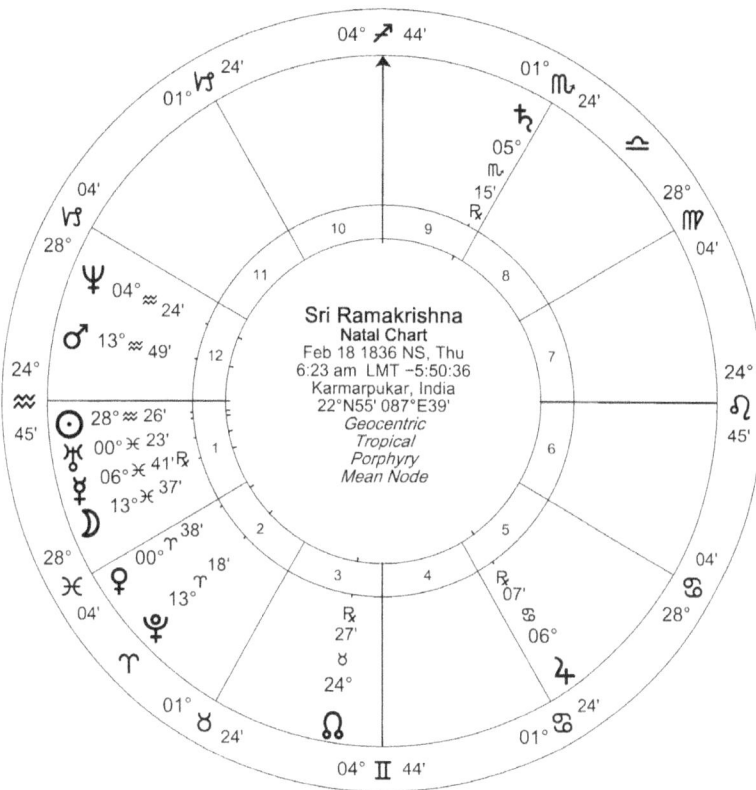

physical heat and pain, and a spiritually intoxicated condition (Mars-Neptune). Transiting Pluto was square to natal Neptune; he frequently entered states of samadhi, complete inner absorption in meditation. Simultaneously, transiting Saturn opposed Mars-Neptune from the sixth house and he began practicing *sadhanas* (spiritual disciplines) from many different traditions.

Ramakrishna's spiritual awakening occurred over the course of many years of meditation, prayer, and devotion—while transiting Pluto squared natal Mars-Neptune; transiting Neptune in Aries sextiled Mars-Neptune; and progressed Venus squared natal and progressed Neptune (awakening of bhakti, divine love). While Saturn transited through his seventh house, Ramakrishna formed relationships with two teachers, Brahmani and Totapuri, who were the only people who understood his unusual condition and could guide him. Under Totapuri's tutelage he was able to reach the highest pinnacles of mystical experience, remaining in samadhi continuously for six months—while transiting Jupiter in Sagittarius was conjunct his Midheaven, square natal Sun-Uranus. His final enlightenment occurred during his first Saturn Return and while transiting Uranus was conjunct natal Jupiter; both Uranus and Saturn were activating his natal Grand Trine of Jupiter-Saturn-Uranus. Ramakrishna's path was to surrender or dissolve his personal ego in the ocean of divine consciousness. He was one of those rare beings who fully embodied the ideal of egolessness and self-surrender into the ocean of divine consciousness.

With Sun and Moon in Pisces, Master Charles Cannon is a pure embodiment of Piscean energy. A teacher of meditation and nondual philosophy, he's the originator of Synchronicity High-Tech Meditation, and an illumined mystic. I first met him in 1975 when he was known as Arjuna, Swami Muktananda's secretary. He gave me guidance and brought me to meet Baba at the end of the Arcata, California retreat, where Muktananda initiated me into *siddha yoga*. He told me two details about his life. Apparently he was a child prodigy musician (a drummer) who performed in nightclubs in his pre-teen years. Jupiter-Chiron-Neptune in the fifth house opposite his Sun and Moon represent this early manifestation of heightened creativity. With this amazing conjunction directly opposite his natal Sun, he has a blissful, expansive demeanor and emanates a vast and peaceful inner light. Also, during the 1960s he was a successful astrologer in New York. It was Master Charles who first recommended in 1976 that I study astrology in college. It was the first time anyone had suggested this to me. I was skeptical about astrology but he told me, "It is a divine science." That seed thought marked the birth of my interest in this subject. I used to spend time with Master Charles in 1976 at the New York Siddha Yoga ashram and he told me that he would soon be taking sannyas initiation into an ancient order of Hindu monks. This occurred in 1977 when transiting Saturn was conjunct natal Pluto in Leo, symbolizing his connection to an unbroken yogic lineage (fourth house), vows of renunciation of attachments and ego, cutting his ties to worldly ambitions and possessions, and undergoing a profound initiation. With Sun and Moon in the eleventh house, Master Charles has lived most of his life at the center of various spiritual communities. He has devoted himself to realization of divine consciousness. When I was 20 and staying in the Ganeshpuri ashram, apart from darshans with Muktananda, Master Charles was my favorite person to spend time with. He was a friendly, funny, liberated swami. He once described kundalini as sounding like "a form of Hindu linguini," which is hilarious. With Uranus in Gemini on the Ascendant, he is tricksterish and unpredictable, a true original. Master Charles is originator of sound technologies that unfold the brain, balancing its two hemispheres, making deep meditation natural and accessible.

This chapter has examined twelve facets of the conscious spiritual life. Reflecting on the twelve yogas, identify the major themes of your own birth chart to discern what paths or practices are most suitable for you. Let the symbols of your birthmap help

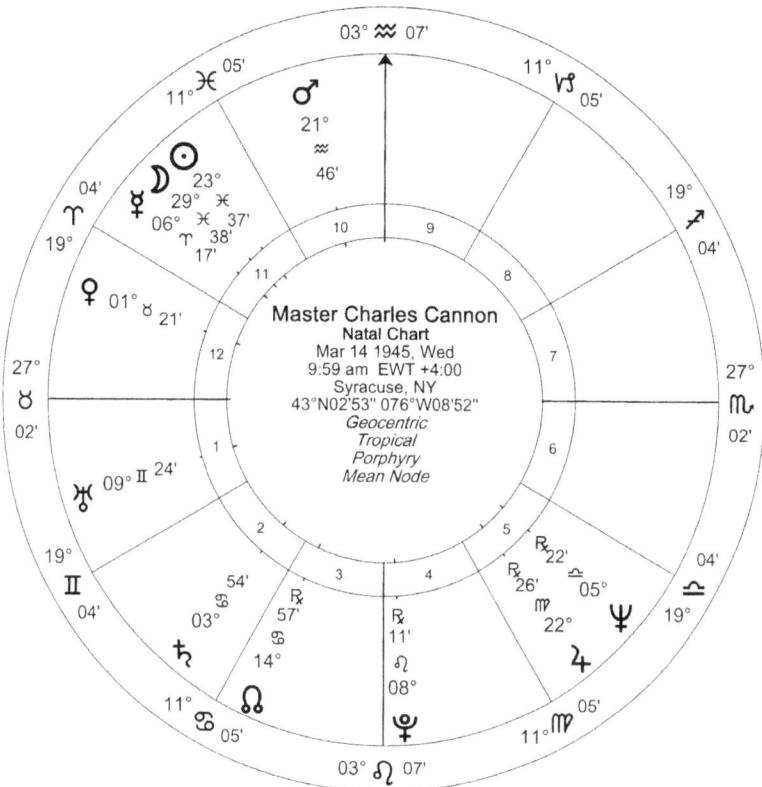

you envision and commit to your unique evolutionary road. As planets constantly travel through the signs and houses your attention will return to these lessons again and again. Astrologers follow these archetypal templates, which define central evolutionary pathways.

Astrology and Spiritual Awakening, Part I

Part II

Transpersonal Astrology and the Path of Transformation

WHEN I SPEAK OF A TRANSPERSONAL INDIVIDUAL. . . [I am speaking] of an individual person who has. . . taken steps on the path of radical and total transformation. The transpersonal way refers to this path which symbolizes a long and arduous process that can take a variety of forms, yet which has a definite, nearly universal structure—just as the embryonic development of a future human being, within the mother's womb, takes place according to a series of clearly marked phases. This process of rebirth is difficult and often requires intense phases of catharsis because of the inertia of the biological past and the socio-cultural and individual karma that must be overcome. All individuals whose minds have opened themselves to the messages or visions that the soul reveals in symbolic forms, and who have accepted the challenge of total transformation, have to undergo such a process of rebirth.(38)

Chapter 3

From Predictive to Humanistic Astrology

ASTROLOGY CHANGES AS HUMANKIND AND OUR CONTEXTS OF INTERPRETATION CHANGE. In agrarian societies, astrology was used to determine the times of planting and harvesting of crops. In the eras of great Kings, it was used to foretell the political fortunes of monarchs. In our psychologically-oriented era, astrology is used for self-reflection and self-awareness, and to navigate complex crises and metamorphoses. Utilizing astrology as a means of spiritual guidance is known as transpersonal astrology. Although it has precedents in Indian culture, where a spiritual approach to astrology was developed to a high degree of refinement, this is a relatively new approach that was envisioned in the writings of Dane Rudhyar.

In the next several chapters I examine the humanistic and transpersonal astrology described by Rudhyar, and its relevance to the contemporary practitioner. I'll comment on the importance of creating our own conceptual foundation for this work rooted in our own spiritual practice traditions, and I'll describe my own synthesis of astrology with the yogic philosophy of Kashmir Shaivism.

The Four Levels of Astrological Interpretation

To understand the emergence of humanistic astrology, we should note that the symbolism of astrology can be interpreted on four levels: biological, socio-cultural, individual (humanistic), and transpersonal.(39) These four levels aren't hierarchical; they are four different interpretive lenses one can look through, and an evolving astrologer can utilize all of them to some degree.

At the biological level, medical astrology can help resolve difficulties in maintaining a healthy physical organism. Applied at the biological level, astrology has also been used for weather prediction and coordination of agricultural planting and harvesting.

I personally have little knowledge of medical astrology and avoid offering clients anything remotely ressembling medical advice. But I do pay attention to a few planetary influences that consistently impact my own physical health. For example, under the influence of Mercury (transits to natal Mercury, or periods of Mercury retrograde), life becomes exceptionally busy and it's difficult to slow down and relax; sometimes I have difficulty sleeping. I accept that I'm going to feel wired at this time, and I allow myself to focus on mental, cognitive tasks: thinking, reading, learning, and writing. I note that during periods emphasizing Mars (by transit or progression), health conditions can flare up and become inflamed. Injuries and cuts sometimes occur, with sprains, bruising, or contusions; sometimes there's a head cold or fever or a rash; there are symptoms of acute or chronic pain; or heated life circumstances create physical stress and discomfort. For example, once I had progressed Sun square natal Mars in the third house of writing, and my overuse of computers while writing books, articles, and lecture notes led to tendonitis in my arms, which felt as if they were on fire. It was so bad that I couldn't click a computer mouse. This problem was only resolved by greatly reducing the repetitive stress over a period of two years, and through undergoing lots of physical therapy. Periods strongly influenced by Mars can also bring an invigorating energy, vitality, and aliveness, a desire and a capacity for more strenuous exercise. We may have an interest in developing muscular strength and greater range and agility in movement. A woman who had transiting Uranus conjunct her Mars in Aries at the Midheaven said she'd been on an absolute tear in recent tennis tournaments, triumphing with intensity; she couldn't believe how fierce her competitive drive had been. In contrast, during periods with a prominent Neptune influence, our bodies may sometimes feel fatigued, lightheaded, faint, short of breath, lacking energy and motivation, or susceptible to allergies or environmental sensitivities.

A woman named Jen was bitten by a tick and developed Lyme Disease right as Saturn entered Scorpio and was conjunct her natal Neptune and opposite natal Mars in Taurus. Jen embarked upon a massive fight against the pathogen for control of her body. This was resonant with the Scorpio symbolism: bites, neutralizing a poison, a struggle for dominance. Jen's symptoms were especially difficult during a three-month period when transiting Saturn in Scorpio went stationary retrograde on the exact degree of her Mars-Neptune midpoint, signifying weakness, susceptibility, being knocked out by medications, needing to rest and convalesce; being the innocent victim of the illness; having to suffer a period of debilitatation when she was relatively helpless and couldn't go to work. For several weeks she had to rest and let herself go through this

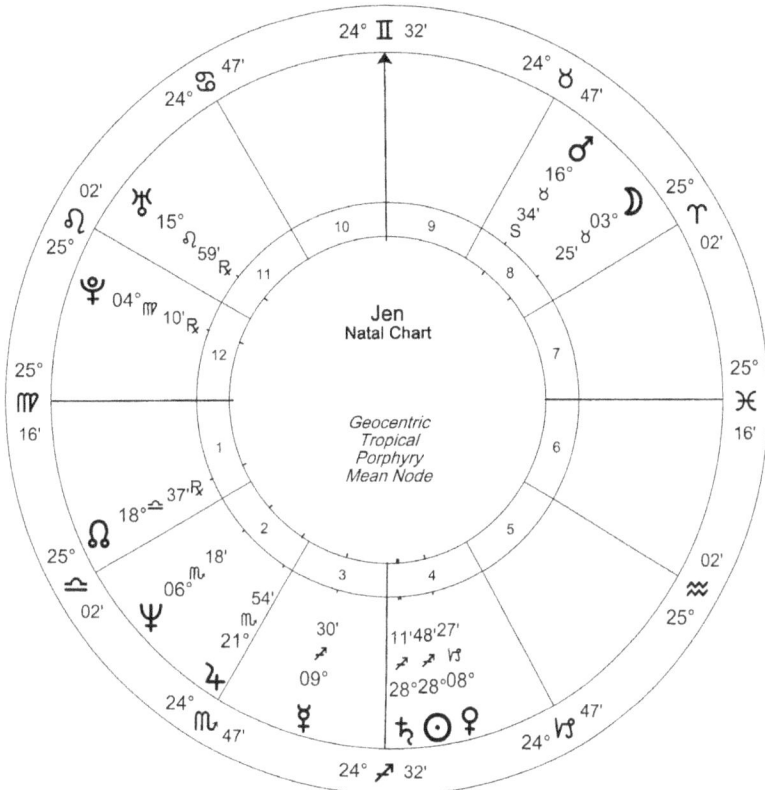

difficult period, temporarily collecting disability (second-house Neptune). Mars-Neptune also manifested as tingling associated with neuropathy, but through acupuncture treatments Jen was able to feel inside her body and work at the level of subtle energetics. As the midpoint transit ended, and as transiting Saturn moved on to oppose natal Mars, she began to feel somewhat stronger.

For those seeking to study medical astrology, I recommend Lee Lehman's *Traditional Medical Astrology*.(40) Every human being has their own story of the body—its growth, mishaps, and changes, its gradual or sudden demise. Each of us could devote a lifetime to the study of the biological level of astrology.

At the socio-cultural level, astrology helps us find the most suitable vocation, and to resolve problems of work adjustment, social adaptation, and interpersonal relationships. One of the most important skills for an astrologer to master is the art of guiding ourselves, our loved ones, and our clients to fulfillment and success in our vocation, in our careers, in our creative projects and endeavors, in the path of our heart's desire.

All astrologers, no matter what methods we use, advise people about how to find their way in the world of work and vocation, where most of us spend much of our adult lives as we earn money, serve others, perform roles in society, and invest our energy in creative activity. Through our success in handling our practical affairs, we demonstrate the ability to apply astrology in a grounded way, in the real world. Vocational astrology guides us in what Hazrat Inayat Khan called the path of *mastery through accomplishment*.(41).

In vocational astrology, we're concerned with two distinct tasks: finding a way to earn our livelihood, and finding our calling, our true vocation. Sometimes these tasks are synonymous, so we learn to translate what we love doing most into our source of income. But frequently the path of our calling isn't the only way we earn our living. Think of Jim, the brilliant musician who had to work as a taxi driver and security guard for periods of time. And Fred, the paralegal who loved to write stories and music. I like to use vocational astrology for help in both tasks—finding a job and pursuing a calling. To find our vocation is to identify the central project or projects of our life, an activity that's intrinsically fascinating and satisfying to us, regardless of whether we earn money or recognition for it. To actualize our vocation is to find an expression of the true self, the natal Sun, in alignment with our solar zodiacal soul path, and the evolving pattern of progressions and transits.

There are five core vocational astrology books I think are worth studying, beginning with Charles Luntz's classic, *Vocational Guidance by Astrology*, first published in 1942 and now reprinted in Noel Tyl's anthology, *How to Use Vocational Astrology for Success in the Workplace*. Also, Tyl's *Vocations: The New Midheaven Extension Process* is essential reading. I also recommend Joanne Wickenburg's *In Search of a Fulfilling Career*, and Faye Cossar's *Using Astrology to Create a Vocational Profile*.(42)

Luntz says to pay special attention to planets in the tenth house and planets near the Midheaven (MC) or aspecting the MC, and also planets in the ninth house but within 5° of the MC.

> If Saturn has not already appeared in one of the above categories, viz., in or within 5° of the tenth, ruling the tenth cuspal sign or aspecting the MC, he should next be considered, as he is the normal planetary ruler of the tenth. Examine the sign he is in. . . . If Capricorn has not similarly appeared, his sign is now up for consideration together with planets occupying it. Capricorn is the normal tenth house sign. . . . We must then look to the sixth house and its affiliates. The sixth house governs employment, whereas the tenth is concerned with the nature of the occupation. In the horoscope of

an employee, the sixth represents the employers. If and when he becomes an employer, it then has reference to his employees. (43)

In vocational assessment, as with any other type of chart interpretation, we look at what planets were dominant in the sky at the birth moment—what planets were aspecting the Ascendant, the MC, the Sun and its dispositor, and the Moon. We also look at any planet that is the *final dispositor* of a group of other planets. For example, if you have a stellium of planets in Sagittarius, Jupiter is the final dispositor of those planets, because it governs Sagittarius. With a stellium in Taurus, Venus is final dispositor.

Regardless of what path we choose, for vocational success we need to awaken the powers associated with each planet. *Mercury*: good language and communication skills. *Jupiter*: expansion through education, planning, goal-setting, and taking advantage of moments of opportunity. Mars: energy, drive, initiative, motivation. *Moon*: Caring and showing our concern for others, sustaining emotional attachments, and being in our emotional center in whatever we're doing. *Venus*: having good people skills, dressing well, and exhibiting tact, diplomacy, and social appropriateness. Highly skilled or talented individuals with underdeveloped Venus functions may be hampered in their progress, because they don't know how to mingle easily with others and make a positive impression. And it's important to develop the *Saturn* functions of focus, commitment, hard work, conscientiousness, and organization.

Ultimately, the natal Sun is the primary vocational indicator. In addition to studying the dispositors of the Ascendant and MC and the overall sign and house emphasis of a chart, I closely examine natal Sun's house and sign, solar aspects, and the placement of the Sun's dispositor. This provides abundant symbolism for guiding self and others at the socio-cultural level.

The socio-cultural level of astrology also encompasses the study of Mundane Astrology, which examines social issues, political trends, and historical cycles, including the astrology of nations and political leaders. These topics are outside the scope of this book.

The individual, humanistic level of interpretation we'll be exploring in this chapter refers to a psychologically-oriented astrology that describes personality dynamics and helps us to actualize our individual potentials. Humanistic astrology illuminates the challenges of individuation, the process of becoming an individual and enacting one's identity. It sheds light on struggles and crises we experience when we question and evolve beyond the collective mentality of our times and pursue interests or activities that are at odds with Saturnian social norms, traditions, and demands for conformity.

Transpersonal astrology goes even further, illuminating the process of self-transcendence and spiritual awakening. In Rudhyar's view, the process of becoming free, autonomous individuals sometimes causes us to fixate on money, status, and materialism.(44) We grow very attached to the ego, to getting what we want, fulfilling our desires. But sometimes we must accept, and yield to, the existence of forces greater than the ego, greater than our powers and free will as individuals. Seen through the lens of planetary symbols, we find meaning in our moments of loss, suffering, and defeat, experiencing hope and the birth within us of a luminous wisdom. We can face and understand various tests and ordeals of the spiritual path.

This perspective makes it possible for us to evolve through adversities in ways we wouldn't have expected. For example, a woman had transiting Saturn turn stationary direct conjunct natal Neptune and Ascendant in Libra for several months. At this time she underwent some shared sorrows and suffering in her marriage (Neptune in Libra) as she learned that her husband had Parkinson's disease and came to terms with what it meant to care for him. She had practiced Buddhist meditation for several decades and now she was faced with a situation that invited her to practice the teachings of egolessness and lovingkindness, to manifest true enlightenment (Neptune). Seeing her very challenging test in this archetypal light gave the process nobility and sanctity.

The Ancient Attitude of Dread Toward the Planets

Traditionally, astrology was practiced at the biological and socio-cultural levels and was predominantly predictive or *event-centered*. For centuries people have approached astrology to unlock the mysteries of the future, eager to know, Where's my life headed? What will happen when Saturn crosses my Midheaven? When will I get married? What's going to happen with my health? Will my career be successful? And who will win the election? Astrologers try to shed light on these questions using transits and progressions to understand the timing of life trends. (45) But predictive astrology can be associated with a fatalistic attitude that weakens us. I know astrology practitioners who remain very stuck in their lives. They always say it's because they have one or another afflicted planet, or they're having "terrible transits," so they feel there's nothing they can do about their situation.

The fatalistic viewpoint permeated ancient astrology and was evident in the doctrines of the Gnostics, mystical sects of the ancient Middle East.(46) The Gnostics' worldview was radically dualistic. They believed God was transcendent, completely separate from the cosmos, and that the material world was a realm of darkness created by a second, evil God called the Demiurge.(47) Like the dualistic Samkya philosophy of ancient India, Gnostics believed that repudiation of the physical world was required to achieve spiritual freedom and return to the Light, the realms of splendor, the *Ple-*

roma. The Gnostics were mystics who sought salvation through knowledge of what lies beyond this physical world. Yet their spirituality was extreme. Instead of viewing incarnation and embodiment as sacred (the viewpoint of the Book of Genesis, where God affirms that Creation is good), Gnostic mystics adopted ascetic lifestyles, seeking to free themselves from the bondage of matter and time, including the realm of the planets. To the Gnostics:

> The universe, the domain of the archons [cosmic rulers] is like a vast prison whose innermost dungeon is the earth, the scene of man's life. Around and above it the cosmic spheres are ranged like concentric. . . shells. Most frequently these are the seven spheres of the planets surrounded by the eighth, that of the fixed stars. . . . The religious significance of this cosmic architecture lies in the idea that everything which intervenes between here and the beyond serves to separate man from God, not merely through spatial distance but through active demonic force. (48)

Thus, the planets were considered malevolent beings that imprisoned humans and actively sought to separate them from their creator. The Gnostics' view of astrology was colored by their sense of exile from the transcendent God and their desire for liberation from the world. From the Gnostic, anti-cosmic perspective, celestial bodies were objects of hate, contempt, and fear. The planets were viewed as causing bondage to an oppressive cosmic fate (*hiemarmene*), the prison of the Demiurge God. Because celestial bodies were thought to dispense hiemarmene, the inexorable law of the universe, the stars and planets became associated with tyranny rather than divine providence.(49)

The view that the planets were gods controlling the destinies of human beings was prevalent in many ancient cultures, and, insofar as the planets were considered malevolent, astrology was approached with an attitude of dread. This fearful attitude toward celestial bodies led to the development of magical practices, such as using talismans, gemstones, and mantras to ward off and counteract the influences of certain planets, such as for protection from Saturn, known as the great malefic.

Humanistic Astrology

Occasionally I meet people who approach astrology with dread, viewing their birth charts as a curse they must endure. Certainly each of us becomes aware of areas of tension and challenge in charts and in ourselves. However, astrology has evolved beyond the ancient belief that the world is a "vast prison" ruled over by planetary forces determining our fate. The humanistic turn in astrology begins with an emphasis on choice, free will, and a non-deterministic attitude in our response to celestial influences. The planets describe certain formative, structuring influences, but it's always within our powers as human beings to make something of our situation. Humanistic astrology, which Rudhyar describes as *person-centered*, illuminates our process of emergence as self-determining individuals. Planetary symbolism helps us envision what we can become and guides us through the steps needed to actualize ourselves. Humanistic astrology views the birth chart as a *mandala*, a blueprint of the individuation process for that person. As Rudhyar put it, astrology can "help any individual to gain a clearer and more objective consciousness of the law of his being." (50)

The birth chart represents our internal organization and our orientation to experience. Viewing the chart holistically, we discover that even our most challenging natal placements, aspects, and transits have purpose, intention, and evolutionary potential. Even the unsettling effects of the outer planets are understood as intelligent forces seeking to bring about needed changes and growth in consciousness.

> [A]ll planetary factors in a birth-chart have to be developed, and . . . the chart must be understood as an organic whole, as a symbol of the totality of the human personality. The total development of that personality may occur through relatively smooth interactions or sharp tensions between the various functions; but there is no sense in calling the former types of relationships (i.e. planetary aspects) "good" and the latter "bad," or even "fortunate" and "unfortunate."(51)

According to Michael Meyer, one of Rudhyar's closest students:

> In humanistic astrology, a birth-chart is . . . approached aesthetically. First it is seen and "felt" as a whole, then its individual functional parts are examined and analyzed, . . . and finally the chart is perceived again as a whole consisting of interactive and interrelated functional processes.(52)

This aesthetic appreciation of the chart as a whole includes analysis of hemisphere emphasis, planetary groupings, focal points and singletons in the chart, planetary patterns and midpoints, and the lunation cycle. The chart can be viewed as an instrument of self-actualization, "a discipline of mind, a technique for the development of holistic thinking."(53)

Approached in this way, astrology is an ally in the process of human liberation. Instead of imprisonment, we experience freedom through alignment with planetary energies. Humanistic astrology promotes the development of an organized consciousness, one that becomes self-determining even while operating within the structuring pattern of the horoscope. A birth chart isn't just a description of random events or personality traits; it's a portrait of a life world, a psyche with particular organizing themes and areas of emphasis. The chart defines a particular archetypal form that gives shape and definition to identity, to the person's life path and relationships. Rudhyar wrote:

> From the Jungian point of view, the birth-chart can be considered an "archetype of the unconscious." It is a visible recording of the inner voice—of what God has wrought for us as a blueprint of what we could (thus, should) become. To earnestly consider this blueprint—this symbolic Name of our fulfilled personality—to give it a determining importance in our everyday living; to know ourselves as a concrete incorporation of its structural harmony—this constitutes a most serious, most vital, and irreversible step.(54)

To study the horoscope's blueprint and to follow the birth pattern with consciousness is to walk what Rudhyar calls the Conscious Way, a path of wholeness, of actively fulfilling one's potentials. Consider this example:

Jed, a 64-year-old man, has Sun-Moon in Aries in the seventh house, with Mars, ruler of Aries, conjunct Saturn and Pluto in Leo in the tenth house. Jed was constantly irritated, if not outright enraged, with his wife of 25 years, Bella, and expressed resentment about his responsibilities and the arduous labor and expense of raising three children. Jed wondered if he should get a divorce and find a new, easier relationship. He'd spoken to an astrologer who told him his Mars was "afflicted" and that because Mars, the seventh-house dispositor, was conjunct Saturn and Pluto in Leo, marriage and parenting would always be difficult and unfulfilling for him. It always pains me to see people approach astrology in a way that instills fear and negativity about the defining features of their lives; so as a humanistic astrologer, it was important to me to offer Jed a more helpful, constructive interpretation.

It's true that this combination of Mars-Saturn-Pluto (none of them lightweights) involves symbolism traditionally considered to be malefic. Certainly parenting involves tremendous exertion and sustained effort, and Jed did indeed have a fiery relationship with his wife. He found her difficult and egocentric, and sometimes they locked horns and butted heads like a couple of rams (Sun-Moon in Aries). But Jed had successfully walked the path of marriage, involved fathering, and conscious parenting, and he was proud of these accomplishments. With Sun-Moon in the seventh house, and their dispositor Mars conjunct Saturn in the tenth house, work, marriage, and fatherhood were the building blocks of Jed's existence. He was a tremendous provider and an authoritative parent whose children knew what his expectations were, but also felt his warmth, affection, and support. Jed embodied the best of Saturn, the archetypal father, provider of order, security, and protection. The same astrological symbolism that from one perspective seems to indicate doom and gloom can also be viewed as representing Jed's crowning evolutionary achievements. The birth chart doesn't just describe a fate we're trapped in. It indicates challenges that can be freely chosen. I wanted Jed to see the combined energies of Mars-Saturn-Pluto as defining his greatest capacities and strengths, his nobility of character, forged through tests of responsibility. Also, regarding his allegedly afflicted Mars, Jed was an athlete who still competed in several sports well into his sixties. His Mars energy was strong, focused, and productive. Humanistic astrologers believe that challenging planetary placements and alignments have an evolutionary purpose. Jed had become the man the universe intended him to be.

The fact that Jed's path involved total involvement in his family and occupational roles illustrates that socio-cultural activity is a key domain in which we realize our purpose as individuals. Individual and socio-cultural influences in development constantly intermingle.

Dane Rudhyar is a very different type of example. A strongly Uranian person, no conventional social role or identity could adequately define him. He was a composer of avant-garde music, poet, painter, and philosopher, as well as a revolutionary astrologer. Rudhyar was self-defining, an embodiment of his own archetype as an individual.

In his book, *From Humanistic to Transpersonal Astrology*, Rudhyar emphasized that the chart helps us understand the individual's configuration and relationship to other individuals and to the universe.(55) In studying the horoscope, our aim is to achieve an individualized consciousness, actualizing the particular potentialities that make us a person, even when this involves challenging or leaving behind aspects of collective attitudes and norms. The birth chart indicates the best paths and possibilities for action, describing not only what is but also what *should* be if we're to fulfill the purpose of our births. Rudhyar wrote:

> The first principle is that the individual person should be able to stand, erect and open, at the center of the universe around him. Erect in the "tallness" of his or her own truth of being; open to the downflow of the "star" at the precise zenith of his own destiny—what he was born on this earth-surface to perform for the sake of mankind and the whole earth. When I speak of a person-centered astrology I refer to a kind of astrology, and to the type of astrological tools, which can be used to assist the individual to stand, consciously and deliberately, at the center of a great mandala: *his own particular universe....* A person-centered astrology has only this one essential purpose: to clarify the meaning and purpose of what daily existence and daily relationships bring to the individual who is committed

to significant and purposeful living. Such a commitment implies a "structured" living. . . . I mean a kind of structuring which is the concrete manifestation of an individual's essential relationship to *his* universe. To work out this relationship consciously and in utter intellectual and emotional honesty—beyond all tricks of the ego—this is what fulfilling one's destiny actually means.(56)

Humanistic astrology is a practice of standing tall in the truth of who we are, carefully considering the structuring forces of our involvement in our culture and its social institutions while also being true to our own internal, archetypal structure. Rudhyar adds:

The humanistic label . . . was selected in 1969 to indicate a stand which somewhat paralleled that of the humanistic psychologist. It essentially indicated an alternative to the superficial game of fortune-telling, and to the serious business of statistical research and quantitative devices for chart-interpretation. . . . My ["person-centered"] approach is oriented to the possibility of developing in every person a steady eagerness for self-transformation and independence from the socio-cultural patterns of the past. On the belief that there is latent in every man and woman the power to be greater than they are, more creative, freer, yet more deeply committed to a process of world-transformation, I stand. I hope to awaken the sleeping god in every person. By sounding the true "name" of an individual one may arouse to life the divine in him.(57)

In noting that humanistic astrology has parallels to humanistic psychology, and invoking the individual's capacity to achieve greatness, freedom, and creativity, Rudhyar is implicitly posing *self-actualization* as a fundamental goal of the work. This term was popularized by Abraham Maslow, a pivotal figure in humanistic and transpersonal psychology, who studied self-actualizers, people who stand out for their creative intellectual, moral, artistic, and spiritual achievements, leadership, and wisdom. In the 1950s and 1960s, the prevailing behaviorist model of American psychology, based on the principle of operant conditioning, promoted a form of psychological determinism, the idea that all behavior is conditioned by the environment. Countering this view, Maslow emphasized the importance of each person's values, purposes, goals, intentions, and plans as driving forces of growth. He showed that greater psychological health and productivity are possible when we strive to actualize our inner nature. Humanistic psychology's focus on discovering the real inner self of the person gave birth to the human potential movement, with its emphasis on full embodiment, celebration of sexuality, removal of inhibitions to natural organismic expression; and the importance of *self-disclosure*, the process of revealing ourselves, allowing ourselves to be known by others.(58) This psychology is rooted in the study of self-actualized people who have developed their human nature to its higher limits. There's so much we can all learn from the examples of individuals such as Abraham Lincoln, William James, Franklin and Eleanor Roosevelt, Albert Einstein, Mohandas Gandhi, Pablo Picasso, Albert Schweitzer, Nelson Mandela, the Dalai Lama, Barack Obama. Maslow found that self-actualized individuals exhibit boldness in living, courage, freedom, spontaneity, integration, self-acceptance, humor, effortlessness, playfulness, and the ability to identify with others. They can transcend their own personal perspective and needs, their own culture and life situation. They're realistic but not held back by present realities; they're autonomous and also capable of loving deeply. They have peak experiences—powerful moments beyond time that bestow glimpses into reality's mysteries, moments of ecstasy, mystical union, spontaneous artistic creation, or spiritual fulfillment. These impactful experiences are catalysts for raised consciousness and refined personal comportment. Paradoxically, self-actualization makes possible the transcendence of self and selfishness. Such people experience themselves as part of a larger whole than themselves. Astrology promotes self-actualization, aiding us in overcoming obstacles to the unfoldment of our full human potentials.

Humanistic astrology can be considered a form of *karma yoga*, revealing the kinds of experiences and actions (karma) necessary to actualize our *dharma*, our "truth-of-being." Rudhyar wrote:

> [T]he basic purpose of studying a birth-chart and discussing it with the person to whom it refers is to help this person become more positively, more meaningfully, more creatively, more totally what he potentially is. . . . [Astrology] is a method of "self-actualization" . . . and. . . a kind of yoga—a yoga with one's destiny. . . . The birth chart is an archetypal form, and through the study of progressions and transits we can foresee its evolution, that is, the process according to which what is potential at birth becomes actualized through life-events. . . . The fundamental concept of which astrology is based is that everything that is "born". . . at a particular time and point of space is organized according to a particular seed-pattern or archetype symbolized by its birth chart. This seed-pattern defines what that organism. . . SHOULD be if it fulfills its function in the universal scheme of things, or one might say according to God's Plan. . . . [A]strology does not tell us what will happen, but what would happen should the person act consciously and earnestly according to the celestial instructions represented in code by the birth chart.(59)

Meditation on the natal seed pattern clarifies our life paths and the tasks leading to realization of our innate potentials. None should imitate the life path of another—"to one's own self be true." Like Jed, we can engage in challenging labors and relationships and commit to following our own pattern of existence.

The Astrology of Meaning: Cyclical Awareness and Life Interpretation

In contrast to the traditional "astrology of events," Rudhyar calls his humanistic, person-centered approach "the astrology of meaning," because the aim isn't to predict exactly what will happen but to reveal the meaning of events. (60) Astrological self-study is a process of interpreting our past, present, and anticipated future life experiences, viewing them as coherent and purposeful. We can describe the major themes of a given time period, not the exact experiential content. We can feel each moment of life as a phase of larger cycles and an enactment of mythical motifs, which allows us to *harvest meanings* from our varied experiences. Rudhyar wrote:

> Life, when lived in terms of meaning and purpose, is. . . to be considered a ritual, or, in more modern terms, a structured process whose every phase is filled with significance.(61)

Astrology is an interpretive discipline that reveals archetypal dimensions in every moment and phase of life. Interpreting our life histories astrologically, we employ what Rudhyar calls *eonic consciousness*, awareness of "the cycle in its essential unity."

> He who does not really "transcend" time, but rather includes in his greatly extended perceptions the whole of the cycle of his living as a person. . . has developed eonic consciousness. He understands the meanings of and the unfolding interconnections between all the phases of his evolution as a center of consciousness and of power. (62)

In eonic awareness, we're not seeking transcendence of time and history, or release into eternal Spirit or a realm of Emptiness devoid of material form or temporal limitations. Rudhyar clarifies:

> An eternity is a complete cycle of time. The consciousness which can perceive things in their eternal nature is one which sees every happening as definitely related to a particular phase of some more or less vast cycle of existence.(63)

An eonic consciousness derived from study of planetary cycles gives specific meanings to each phase of time. This is in contrast to transcendentalist philosophies, such as Vedanta and Gnosticism, that view the world of time and manifest form as a prison or an illusion. Such doctrines provide no basis for responding to the pressures of life—the personal challenges and social upheavals we encounter—except to promote detachment and renunciation. From that perspective, temporal events have no inherent significance, except insofar as they generate a longing for an atemporal state of salvation or liberation. This approach actually serves to dissociate and distance us from our present experience embedded in this material world.

Humanistic astrology is a practice of sanctifying earthly life by interpreting events within the context of planetary cycles. We expand our consciousness to simultaneously encompass the beginning, middle, and end of each cycle. Rather than seeking to escape from the prison of time, we search for meaning and significance in our incarnate existence within time and history. Astrology teaches us to reflect upon events from a cyclical perspective that, in a sense, allows us to transcend time, but also helps us to live consciously and effectively *within* the realm of time. That's why I like to say, "Astrology is the Yoga of Time." These ideas are in accord with a basic tenet of Western religions, namely that a divine or spiritual intelligence enacts its relationship to humanity through, not despite, the events of time and creation. These principles satisfy our longing for a "salvation" realized within history, rather than outside of it.

In humanistic astrology, the individual human being is the focus of attention, in much the same way that gods and goddesses have elicited devotion and veneration throughout history. As astrologers we contemplate the emergent face of our own unfolding identity reflected in the birthmap mandala, and we shape ourselves into the envisioned image through our choices, effort, and focused will.

Meditating upon our astrological birth charts, we become our own deities. Studying the symbolic patterns that informed our births, we discern our unique creation myths. By enacting these myths, our lives become theogonies, performances through which deities create themselves. In this way, the human and divine planes begin to interpenetrate, the aim of all sacred traditions.

A Humanistic Approach to a Saturn Transit

A crucial feature of modern humanistic astrology is the constructive attitude we adopt toward Saturn, the planetary architect of enduring accomplishments in life. In astrological lore, Saturn was customarily considered a malefic, unfavorable influence, but humanistic, psychologically-oriented practitioners take a different view, approaching Saturn as the planet of maturation, adaptation, and stability. Saturn's natal and transiting influences call forth situations requiring groundedness, realism, sustained effort, and steadiness under stress. Saturn signifies the principle of self-control, self-discipline, and self-cohesion needed to adapt socially and to achieve authorship of one's own life. It signifies mastery of form and the spirituality of work and everyday life. Natal Saturn defines a task, a series of lessons that are a major focus in this lifetime, requiring effort, commitment, and investment of the self in works, structures, and chores—our conscious labors. Natal, transiting, and progressed influences of Saturn are opportunities to master our fears and work toward steady accomplishment.

Humanistic astrologers don't see chart symbols such as Saturn as simply malefic or "bad," nor do we make overly definitive pronouncements about someone's chart. If a client has a Venus-Saturn conjunction, we don't tell them they'll have big problems with love, relationships, and money. This kind of interpretation is superficial, and most often it's plain wrong. My mother had Venus conjunct Saturn in Cancer and she was married for 57 years. She did well in love and with finances. Donald Trump has Venus-Saturn conjunct in Cancer, and obviously he made a fortune in real estate (Venus-Saturn in Cancer). Astrological symbols don't have fixed meanings or fixed outcomes. The conscious astrologer contemplates the meaning of chart symbols through dialogue and meditation, actively striving to unfold the planets and look for multiple expressions. We're less concerned with predicting events than with understanding how planetary symbols present us with a series of tasks; we can think of them as *assignments*.

Here's another Venus-Saturn example. Trent (see chart on page 120), a man with transiting Saturn conjunct Venus at 26° Libra 22', was depressed about his relationship with Kiko, his girlfriend of twelve years. At Saturn's first pass over Venus, Trent bought Kiko an engagement ring, but he wasn't sure he could go through with it; he wasn't sure she was the one. Then, while Saturn turned retrograde, he was uneasy because Kiko hadn't said yes. His attitude toward her was tepid and ambivalent; he said they stayed together out of loyalty and friendship. But something in him was seeking a clearer definition of the relationship and greater commitment to it. Many people feel this urge while Saturn transits in Libra, the sign of coupling, and also when Saturn transits natal Venus. However, Trent wasn't conveying his warm affection in a way that would seal the deal. With his Sun-Saturn conjunction, he was very serious, and was frequently preoccupied with various failures and personal shortcomings. Jupiter in Virgo at his MC showed his self-criticism. He was also critical of Kiko's faults and limitations; he was often dissatisfied. At the same time he realized that Kiko steadfastly loved him, believed in him, encouraged and sustained him. For example, she gave him the money to rent time in a recording studio, and to hire several supporting musicians to produce a CD, allowing Trent to fulfill his natal Venus in the eleventh house. Trent clearly saw the value of her love and support. Then he asked me, "What do the planets say is going to happen?" I said, "The planets indicate it's time for you to decide. This is the moment of truth. Are you just going through the motions, or do

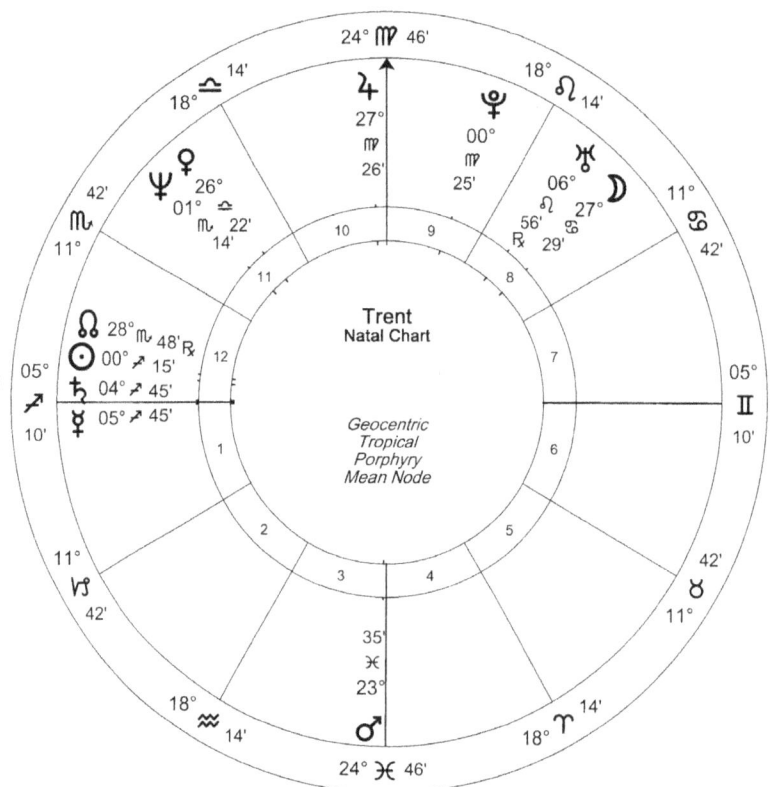

you really mean it? The Hawaiian Huna teachings state, 'To love is to be happy with.' During this transit, you choose whether you can be happy with Kiko, and love her just as she is, see her as your beloved, and feel genuinely happy to see her. You bought her a ring, but your feelings and actions have to back up the gesture. Saturn conjunct Venus says your feeling emanation toward Kiko really matters. This moment is when you establish the patterns of your future existence. You can remain half-hearted, or you can forge a lasting love."

This is an example where we can't predict a precise outcome. He either will or will not get married during this transit. To a large extent that's up to him. This is the attitude of person-centered astrology. With Saturn conjunct natal Venus, we face our fears and resistance in love; we can also learn to enhance our relationships in practical ways—by expressing fondness, seeing the good in each other, learning tolerance, listening, being responsive to each other. Over several months of Saturn retrograde, Trent worked on his relationship skills, warming up his way of interacting with Kiko. At the end of Saturn's retrograde phase, as Saturn turned stationary direct, Kiko said yes! They celebrated their wedding at the time of Saturn's third pass over Venus. It's always nice when two people say "we like what we have; we'd like to preserve this and make it last." Progress in life and love is a maturational process. For Trent, learning to love deeply and achieve the refined emotional state of marriage has been a significant stage in his self-actualization. Humanistic astrology's focus on the psychology of the individual also helps us increase our intelligence in relating effectively with other selves, respecting their integrity and the relationships we share.

Example of a Transit to Natal Moon

Let's look at an example that illustrates a number of core principles in chart interpretation—analysis of Moon's natal aspects, Moon's house placement, and transits to the Moon; natal Sun as vocational indicator; the importance of seeing the chart as a whole, chart synthesis, and attention to how complex information is conveyed in the counseling session. This story illustrates how astrology helps us find a spiritual viewpoint to address urgent life issues, orienting us in the process of change, strengthening our will and sharpening our choices. This example again involves a relationship crisis, including a confluence of elements and variables that need to be considered simultaneously—emotional, familial, relational, vocational, financial, and transpersonal.

My client Amy (see chart on page 122) has Sun conjunct Mercury in the sixth house of employment. She was very involved in her workplace role as a director of communications (Gemini) for an international charitable and social service agency (Neptune in tenth house). Jupiter and Pluto near the cusp of her ninth house represent the international scope of the work and Sun-Mercury in the sixth house represents the healthcare emphasis. Natal Venus in Cancer is placed in the seventh house, showing a desire for a harmonious relationship, to live with someone she loves.

I noted that transiting Pluto in Capricorn had recently been in opposition with natal Venus, which was my first clue that Amy had been going through a time of relational crisis or reevaluation. With Saturn transiting in Libra, the sign of couples and relationships, it wasn't surprising that she was in a period of relational challenges. Transiting Saturn was stationary retrograde conjunct natal Neptune at 28° Libra 56', in the tenth house, square her Moon in Capricorn in the second house of finances, and square Uranus in the eighth house (joint finances). Amy had just broken up with her boyfriend Rob a month earlier, and was sad and upset (Saturn square Moon). She'd broken up with Rob because he was shifty about money and didn't contribute financially, wasn't committed to her, wouldn't pay for anything; and because he did weird things for money, like selling old electronics gear and sundry garden and kitchen items at flea markets (Uranus in Cancer). None of this was helpful to Amy at a time when she was facing her own monetary difficulties.

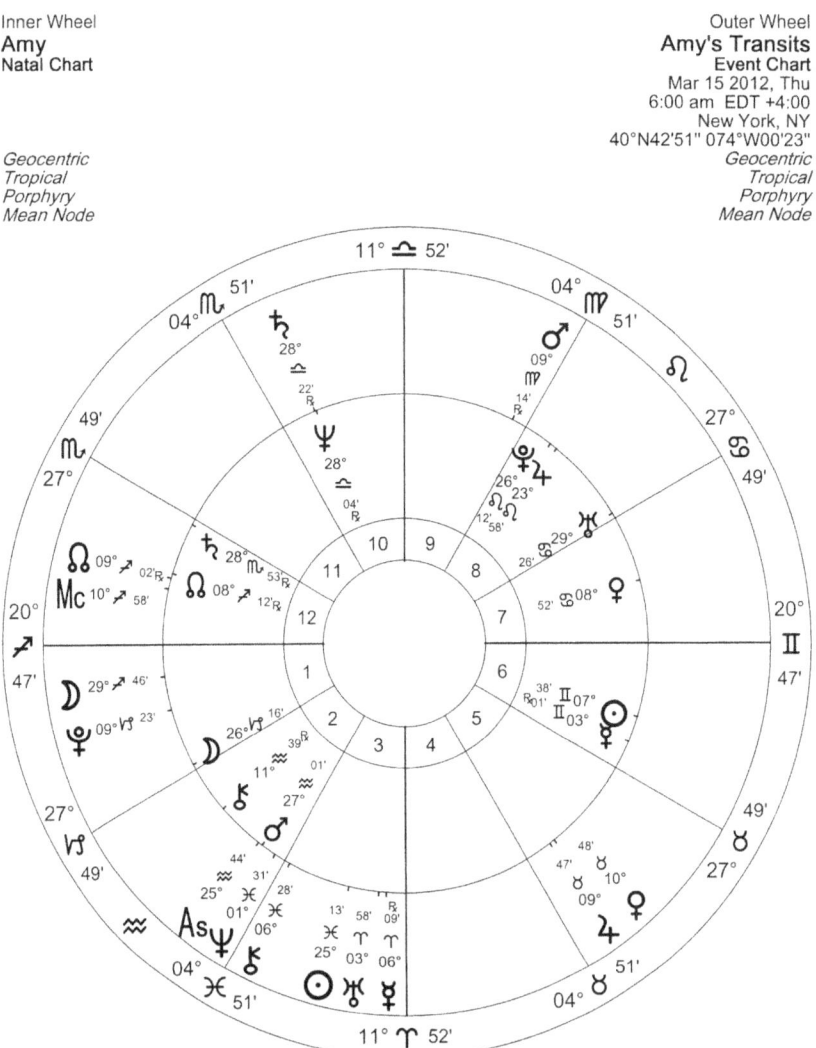

Amy had just declared bankruptcy because a previous boyfriend, Don, who was still her business partner, ran up huge credit card debts. This was devastating and depressing, especially because her second-house Capricorn Moon signified the importance she placed on financial management and a need for monetary security. She said, "When Don and I were together, we always had disagreements about money. Don didn't contribute to our house payments. At one point he stopped working. He was always financially irresponsible." All of this reflected Saturn's transit to natal Uranus in the eighth house of business and shared resources. Now Amy was starting over and assuming responsibility for herself financially (Saturn square Moon in second house).

From Predictive to Humanistic Astrology

I said, "Moon opposite Uranus in the eighth house describes how you've faced stormy changes in relationships due to financial issues. It seems that men act wily and tricksterish when it comes to money. They seem emotionally icy and detached, like they don't care about you." Her response: "It reminds me of how my father and mother always flaked on me financially. I can never trust that somebody is going to be there." This statement reflects her natal Moon opposite Uranus, showing the feeling of parental inconsistency. The interpersonal crises around money reactivated this sensitive issue and clarified the emotional need for someone she could count on.

With Moon square Neptune, Amy often felt that others ignored or denied her needs. She also has Saturn in Scorpio in the twelfth house (secrets and inner life), square Mars in Aquarius, signifying feelings of abandonment and a great deal of buried rage that she couldn't openly express in her family and relationships (Mars square Saturn). With this suppressed anger came fears and insomnia. It was difficult for Amy to relax enough to fall asleep with anyone, which increased her feelings of emotional separation and estrangement in relationships. I said, "This twelfth-house Saturn in Scorpio suggests hidden fears, hidden demons. You've always had to hide your resentment. Then you feel hurt and angry and withdraw." "Yes, I withdraw." That played directly into Amy's Moon opposite Uranus and her tendency to create distance and break off contact. Moon-Uranus is a symbol of what John Bowlby calls insecure-avoidant attachment, where a person exudes false self-sufficiency, the attitude that "I don't need you. I don't need anybody." Amy said, "I always project that I'm ultra self-reliant." She minimized her needs, through what Bowlby calls "defensive exclusion" of feelings. Her Moon-Uranus-Neptune T-square manifested as emotional reactivity and sensitivity, and a tendency to end relationships abruptly, then to feel empty and bereft. These behaviors had been working against her longing for a loving emotional union (Venus in Cancer in the seventh house).

I told Amy I saw Saturn in her twelfth house as a key to her unfolding: She needed to find an inner cove of safety and privacy where she could feel safer around her fear of aggressive energies in relationships (Saturn in Scorpio). Perhaps by connecting Saturn in the twelfth house to the Mars pole of the square she could gain the energy to be more verbally assertive (third-house Mars) to let people know she sometimes felt abandoned by them, especially when they played games and wreaked havoc on her finances. Saturn in the twelfth validated her need for alone time to balance the demands of relationships. Maybe it was okay if she needed to sleep in her own bed; that needn't preclude her loving somebody. With Venus trine Saturn in the twelfth, she could find inner support from her spiritual life and deep faith in existence that could help her sustain a relationship over the long term.

Amy's bankruptcy occurred with Saturn stationary direct conjunct natal Neptune. Sometimes with Neptune, everything dissolves into nothingness and we experience the reality of impermanence. We face situations that require surrender, serenity, and acceptance. We undergo a spiritual baptism. We need to go to the water for renewal, hold a space of prayer and deep meditation, and spend time in silence, forests, and pools, in a state of detachment and freedom. Sometimes the fish has to flow with the ocean, so that we accept a defeat and humbling of the ego and meet it with tranquility and equanimity. It is an initiation into a free, detached, and transcendent consciousness. At the same time, with Saturn conjunct Neptune in the tenth house, squaring the second-house Moon, Amy felt financially supported by her current job with a social service agency, where she was actively working to benefit others, a fine and compassionate expression of her Moon-Neptune energy.

Amy was conflicted about breaking up with Rob. With Uranus in the eighth house, she missed the sexually stimulating energies he brought into her life. With a natal Venus-Mars conjunction in Gemini conjunct Amy's descendant, she experienced Rob as affectionate, passionate, and loving toward her. She really didn't want him to go away, and realized she could either choose to be single again, or find a way to transform within this relationship. Based on Amy's placement of Uranus in Cancer, I intuitively suggested that Rob look for a job related to new sciences, perhaps some sustainable, green technologies related to homes and housing. Amy took that suggestion home and reported back to me that Rob had applied and interviewed for a job with a company specializing in biomass and biofuels, and had begun learning about the politics of fracking and the search for alternative fuels for automobiles and home heating. He even seemed interested in signing up for several college science classes that would help him get started in this industry. She started seeing him again and is hanging in there with the relationship, viewing Rob differently, through the lens of a person with Venus in Cancer in the seventh house, someone capable of having a loving relationship. Amy's story illustrates that astrology is alchemical. We can transform coals into diamonds, lead into gold. Also of note: it's amazing to witness what effects and consequences can emanate from our spontaneous interpretation of a chart symbol such as Uranus in the eighth house. Humanistic astrologers cultivate a feeling of freedom and creativity in how we interpret the planets, and in how we live and craft our lives.

Chapter 4

The Transpersonal Level of Chart Interpretation

AT THE HUMANISTIC LEVEL OF INTERPRETATION, astrology aids us in becoming choiceful, self-defining individuals meeting the challenges of social adaptation. In the 1970s, Rudhyar began to state that astrology could also be practiced at a transpersonal level, to guide individuals through various stages and tests of spiritual life. Here astrology becomes a way to attain the truths and levels of consciousness described by mystical and mystery traditions, which describe a path and a state of enlightenment and harmony with Spirit and a transcendental order. The objectives and techniques taught in these traditions can greatly enhance our astrological work.

At a transpersonal level, the context of interpreting planetary symbols changes. One's concern is not only with establishing a distinctive identity and well-functioning ego, but also with higher evolution beyond the perspective of the ego and the realization of one's connection to a larger whole. Rudhyar explained:

> [E]very truly individualized human being is a responsible aspect of Humanity-as-a-whole. The whole acts not only in the individual, but *through* the individual. The whole realizes itself in and through the acts, feelings, and thoughts of its individualized participants who have become open to its descents of power. As this occurs, the transindividual state of existence is reached. The way to such a state is what I call the transpersonal path. In no basic sense is it different from what esoteric traditions have spoken of as the Path of Initiation. . . . [T]he word transpersonal . . . implies a 'descent' of power that meets . . . the aspirations or 'ascent' of the human person. . . . A transpersonal approach to both astrology and psychology. . . can only be

> successfully practiced if based on a . . . thorough understanding of what is really at stake once the individual opens up to the descent of spiritual, supramental forces. Such an understanding requires an at least partial or tentative realization of the nature of the spiritual Source from which the subliminal light and the transcendent power flow. This light and power may be directly experienced by the fully open individual consciousness, but the Source itself can only be envisioned or evoked through the intermediary of some kind of symbol, image, or mythos. . . . The basic concept of transpersonal astrology . . . is that when a human being has reached a truly individualized and autonomous state of being and consciousness, he or she becomes a 'place' at which two currents of opposite directions will eventually meet: the 'descent' of spirit and the 'ascent' of matter. . . . Mind simply represents the possibility for spirit and matter to unite within a definite area of experience. . . . After the final union—at first there may be only brief and temporary meetings—spirit as the positive factor determines the character and function of the being that results from the union of the two currents. This being . . . is now a transindividual being. [The] mind as yet does not realize that in the cosmic scheme it is meant to be the consecrated place—a sacred enclosure, a temple—in which a . . . crucial type of integration, that of spirit and matter, has to occur. . . . A factor existing within the human psyche beside the mind has somehow to act directly upon the mind, or to serve as a hidden gate through which 'inspirations' of a spiritual nature may enter and gradually transform the mind.(64)

Astrology practiced at a transpersonal level guides and facilitates the metamorphosis that Rudhyar calls "the transpersonal way," which leads the individual to become increasingly transparent to energies that seek expression *through* the personality. The individual personality is transformed as it becomes responsive to the higher mind and creative intelligence signified by Uranus; as it spreads peace, healing love, compassion, and altruism (Neptune); and as it becomes the instrument of a transpersonal will, energy, and impetus (Pluto). The seeker strives for clarity and expansion through inner journeys and deep meditation while also practicing an active mysticism that's accomplished in works, in service of a more encompassing whole. On the transpersonal way, the goal is transformation of the personality so that we can serve a cause, a *dharma*, a mission or a calling greater than the desires and whims of the ego.

Traditionally, the path of initation that led to spiritual transformation and enlightenment was brought about through training in mystery schools and monasteries. In our present world this process often takes place outside the protective enclosure of the temple, ashram, or zendo, and requires our understanding of its structure and phases.

Astrology is a means of *guiding oneself* through rites of passage that lead to spiritual awakening. It was with reference to this guiding function that Rudhyar called astrology a form of "threshold knowledge," knowledge that enables individuals to step over a threshold.(65) Reflection on the birth pattern is a process of "self-education," a contemporary path of "chela-ship" (discipleship) that facilitates our initiation into the transpersonal life. (66) Astrology is also a catalyst that accelerates our evolution and activates previously unconscious energies and potentials.

> The birth chart is very different indeed from a mere scientific tabulation of factors. Once it is studied and given vital attention, the chart begins to act as *a dynamic power within the unconscious*. It "does things to the astrologer." It forces tendencies into the consciousness (and thus produces events) which otherwise might have remained latent and hidden.(67)

Transpersonal astrology is meaningful for those looking beyond narrow individual and material preoccupations and following a spiritual path. Thus it shares common interests and goals with the field of *transpersonal psychology*, which investigates nonordinary, mystical states of consciousness, methods to induce them, and how they may be beneficial. (68) Professors Glenn Hartelius and Mariana Caplan described transpersonal psychology as a psychology beyond ego; a holistic psychology of the person in an interconnected world; and a psychology of transformation.(69) *As a psychology beyond ego*, it describes states beyond the ego and its pathologies and neuroses—states of self-transcendence, wholeness, and non-duality. Transpersonal astrologers share this focus as we observe how outer-planet influences, especially Neptune, call forth experiences of expanded consciousness and an impetus toward transegoic life.

Transpersonal astrologers are in accord with the need to evolve a *holistic psychology of the person in an interconnected world*, viewing the individual within the context of family, nature, our environment, community, and cosmos. The inclusive, multidimensional life-world depicted in zodiacal signs and the horoscope's circle of houses clarifies how the individual evolves in tandem with larger wholes and systems—through investment of the self in relationships, financial agreements, occupational roles, institutions and groups. From this perspective, we can face life decisions with awareness that we're part of everything, part of nature, part of the Whole, asking, How shall I act in resonance with this wholeness I'm a part of? What does the universe want or intend right now? We try to act based on what the wholeness of life wants. It's not always the path we expect, so we have to be willing to give up some of our attachments and let change happen.

Transpersonal psychology emphasizes human potentials; it's *a psychology of transformation* rooted in practices that enable us to become more expansive, greater than the ego. It studies how our evolution is accelerated through the doctrines and disciplines taught in yoga and dharma lineages, schools of esotericism, metaphysics, and spiritual psychology. The transpersonal approach to astrology shares this interest. As we saw in Chapter 2, planetary symbols can direct us toward specific practices and paths that are best suited to the individual. In an astrology of transformation, the process of chart interpretation can be informed by spiritual teachings. For example, in my work I often refer to Haridas Chaudhuri's description of three inseparable goals sought in Integral Yoga: *individuality* (personal identity and uniqueness); relatedness (belonging to the social organism); and *transcendence* (union with the ground of existence). (70)

In this chapter I develop some operating principles for transpersonal astrology and consider what it means to add a transpersonal lens to our multilayered interpretation of astro-symbolism. I link Rudhyar's conceptions to the ideas of three transpersonal psychologists: Roberto Assagioli, Stanislav Grof, and Michael Washburn. I explain how we transform through crisis and ordeals, consciously lived. I'll detail the meanings of Uranus, Neptune, and Pluto, and how they operate as archetypes that shape our transformation. We'll consider how astrological symbols can aid us when our goal is a state of enlightenment, described here from the perspective of Buddhism. We'll reflect on the astrology of death, our existential horizon; and we'll follow the story of a woman undergoing a crisis and rebirth. I begin with several ideas from Roberto Assagioli, one of Rudhyar's close friends; they were linked through their mutual involvement in Theosophy.

Psychosynthesis, Meditation, Visualization, and the Act of Will

On the path of astrology we're constantly working to awaken various basic faculties: Sun: forming and expressing an identity; Moon: feeling, caring; Mercury: cognition and communication; Mars: energy, vitality, and self-assertion; Saturn: coping, working, structuring; Jupiter: planning, assimilating culture, morals, and philosophy; Uranus: the faculty of invention and creative intelligence. But under the influence of Neptune, our task is to develop our faculty of relatedness to a larger field of existence—the Self, a state of nonduality or non-egoic consciousness. Roberto Assagioli calls this *spiritual psychosynthesis*, the reorganization of personality around the Transpersonal Self—a state of pure awareness, a center of inner guidance, a Higher Power that communicates from within us, from which we may receive an inner call. He also called this the *higher unconscious*, the source of mystical experience, intuition, compassion, genius, and illumination.

To develop an alignment with the Self, meditation is recommended. Through periods of inner silence we repose in a tranquil, clear state of consciousness and can begin to conduct our whole lives in the awareness that this is who we really are. While occupy-

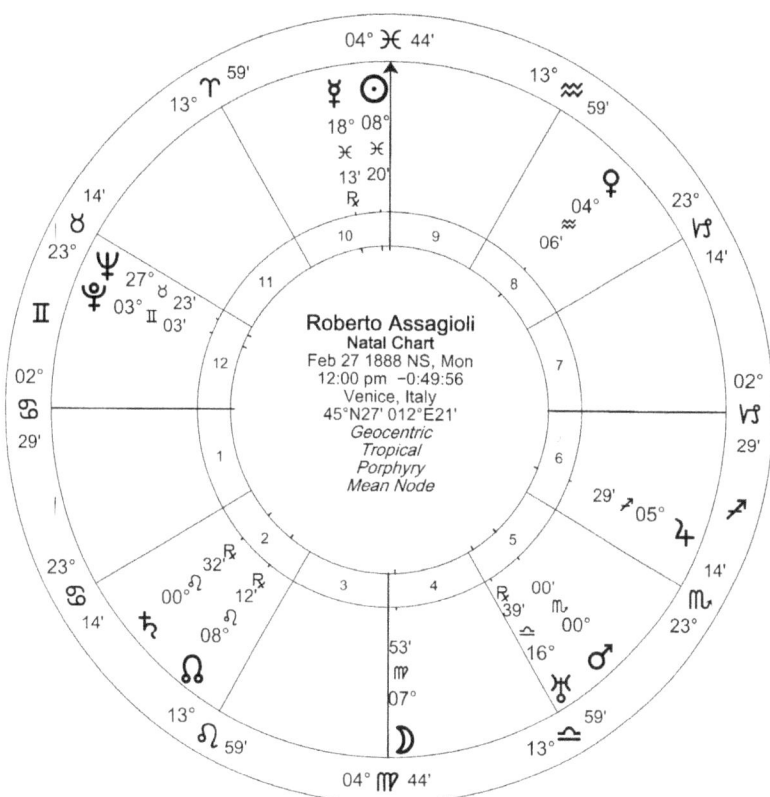

ing and developing our social roles and identities, we also enjoy inner peace, the feeling of being a silent witness. Meditation is the practice of quieting down, centering, immersion in the Self, the *Atman* of the yogis. I consider meditation the inner foundation for practicing astrology at a transpersonal level.

Astrologers centered in meditation learn to witness, and interpret, the effects of transits, even difficult ones, in a dispassionate manner, with equanimity, evenmindedness. With a quiet mind one can intuit the spiritual meaning and purpose of planetary energies. Then it's possible to discern, Why is this happening to me? What can I learn from this situation?(71)

This witness perspective promotes a state of calm in all circumstances. Assagioli practiced this himself during several years when he was persecuted by the Italian Fascist government because of his involvement with liberal thinkers and spiritualists. In 1940 he was arrested and kept in solitary confinement for a month, during which he undertook focused psycho-spiritual exercises. Over the next several years he tried to live a quiet, secluded life in the country, staying out of sight, hiding in remote hamlets. He had two narrow escapes from Fascists who pursued him and sacked and destroyed his family's country house near Florence. His natal Pluto square Sun manifested as encounters with dictatorial power, a reign of terror, and suffering active persecution. At the time of his imprisonment, his progressed Sun had just entered Taurus and was exactly opposite natal Mars in Scorpio (people trying to harm him). His progressed Sun also closely squared Saturn in Leo; in addition, the progressed Moon was conjunct Saturn, and transiting Pluto was conjunct natal Saturn. Talk about pressure! These were difficult, tense circumstances that tested his courage, poise, and self-mastery. Through all of this crisis, he meditated and was devoted to the practices of theosophy and *raja yoga*. Transiting Uranus and Saturn passed through Taurus and were conjunct his natal Neptune, and eventually conjoined natal Pluto in the twelfth house, opening up higher centers of awareness and forming a vision of psychospiritual transformation that would impact the future consciousness of humanity (Uranus conjunct Neptune-Pluto). With his Full Moon in Virgo, Assagioli developed a series of techniques and practices to facilitate Piscean spiritual joy, bliss, union, and ascension. His Sun is T-squared with Jupiter and Pluto, representing the powerful knowledge that came to a focus through his prodigious intellect (Sun square Jupiter in Sagittarius). Pluto in the twelfth house square the Pisces Sun shows introversion, inward movement of awareness, developing a quiet and vast mind space and the power of creative will. With his Sun opposite the Full Moon and squaring Pluto (which was conjunct the Sun's ruler, Neptune), Assagioli taught that a seeker can attain Self-realization by consciously emanating transpersonal qualities such as tranquility, lovingkindness, eternity, detachment, generosity, gratitude, bliss, luminosity, mercy, silence, and wholeness. In the practice of psychosynthesis, one actively visualizes these qualities and strives to embody them in the face of life's challenges.

Psychosynthesis was an expression of Assagioli's own birth chart and the spiritual aspirations and potentials implicit in its symbolism. Rudhyar made this evocative comment:

> [A] person's ideal creation is the exteriorization of the goal to which his total personality reaches out. His ideal is exteriorized as a doctrine; his strivings are generalized into a method; the blueprints of the perfected type, which is himself as a perfected person, are projected as a "vision," or even "revelation"—even though the man himself is yet far from becoming in actual concreteness of living all these things which he . . . visualizes, and strives toward. . . . . Dr. Assagioli's psychosynthesis is an answer to the chaos . . . which our generation has created. The multiplicity of energies and stresses, and the complexity of a global openness, are facts which must

be met. Assagioli has had to meet them in his own person. . . . According to Dr. Assagioli, his "conception of the structure of our being . . . permits of a wider and more comprehensive understanding of the human drama, of the conflicts and problems that confront each one of us; it indicates the means of their solution, the way of our liberation." The way to such a liberation, . . . to "peace, harmony, and power" is four-fold. The four stages on the path are defined by Assagioli as: 1. A complete knowledge of one's personality. 2. Control of its various elements. 3. Realization of one's true self, . . . the creation of a unifying center. 4. Psychosynthesis: the formation or reconstruction of the personality around a new center.(72)

These four stages form a basis for astrological self-study, which is a means to understand "the human drama, . . . the conflicts that confront each one of us." The birth map is the blueprint of the individual's perfected type, and the astrologer projects this as a vision and strives to concretize it. Contemplating the horoscope orients the personality to the unifying center of the Transpersonal Self, which Assagioli taught is a *silent witness* and also *a center of will and intention*, coordinating our various faculties, as a conductor conducts the orchestra's many instruments, weaving many voices into one unified composition. The Self, in its expression as the will, actively brings about changes in the personality and in our circumstances. Assagioli showed that the will possesses multi-spectral qualities: energy, dynamic power, intensity; mastery, control, discipline; concentration, attention, one-pointedness, focus; determination, decisiveness, resoluteness, promptness, organization; persistence, endurance, patience; initiative, courage, and daring.(73) A psychosynthesis practitioner exercises the will in daily life, from *intention to realization*, passing through stages of *deliberation*, *choice*, and *decision*, a*ffirmations*, *planning*, and *execution* of *the act of will*.

These stages and facets of the will are relevant to the practice of astrology, insofar as I choose to not just passively suffer the effects of the planets. I exercise my will to transform in accordance with planetary patterns and archetypes. I utilize these symbols to imagine, visualize, and craft a more evolved personality and lifepath, sculpting myself into new shapes, engaging in conscious, intentional character development. Seeing a potential taking shape in the sky, I deliberate on its meaning and choose how to respond. Then I plan and execute my response. I synchronize my actions and development with the celestial order, and from this alignment my actions flow. Assagioli wrote:

> [T]here are volitional acts which do not necessarily require effort. It can be said that particularly the stages of intention, evaluation, and choice can be effortless. Moreover, there is another and higher condition in which the

personal will is effortless; it occurs when the willer is so identified with the Transpersonal Will, or, at a still higher and more inclusive level, with the Universal Will, that his activities are accomplished with free spontaneity, a state in which he feels himself to be a willing channel into and through which powerful energies flow and operate. This is wu-wei, or the "taoistic state," mentioned by Maslow in *The Farther Reaches of Human Nature*.(74)

Astrology aids us in attaining this free-flowing, Taoistic state where our actions are spontaneous expressions and gestures of a universal will. Constant exercise of our personal will remains important in pursuing our goals and desires, driven by the energy of Mars. But actions have a different meaning when they're called forth through alignment with the universal will, which is *transpersonal*; its motives and goals are not only those of the ego. Something larger than us is trying to enact its Self-organizing plan; and we learn that making room for the operation of transpersonal forces often means yielding to experiences and changes that seem antithetical to the goals, intentions, and attachments of the ego.

According to Rudhyar, a transpersonal astrologer interprets each life event and each astrological aspect "as an opportunity for transformation on the way to the 'star.'" (75) The process of metamorphosis takes us outside of our secure comfort zones as we receive transpersonal influences (mediated by Uranus, Neptune, and Pluto) that precipitate crises and transformative passages. The great value of astrology is that when we encounter stress points in development, when our lives get turned upside down, we sense the inner purpose of events, so we can meet these experiences as initiations that result in growth in consciousness. Astrology can also heal wounds and sufferings we carry from the past. In *The Astrology of Transformation*, Rudhyar wrote:

> a transpersonal astrological and psychological interpretation. . . can help the client gradually to re-interpret all the events of his or her past. By giving a new and transformative purpose to past events—especially past traumas, frustration, and psychic injuries—the past is actually changed. It is transpersonalized. Every tragic occurrence may be consciously understood as a necessary step in the process that may eventually lead to the transindividual state.(76)

A Call to Transformation in Early Adulthood

When I was 21–22, I reached a crucial developmental convergence: Transiting Saturn squared natal Saturn; Uranus reached the waxing square to its natal position in my tenth house, and also squared my Sun and Moon; and transiting Neptune was conjunct natal Saturn in Sagittarius. Saturn square Saturn at age 22 is a transit of maturation into adulthood. At this age most people are becoming more responsible and self-reliant, entering occupations and forming the elements of an adult life. For me, the intense Uranian influences radically eclipsed my striving for stability, structure, or conventional ambitions. With Neptune conjunct natal Saturn, I had no idea who or what I wanted to be in the world. In the summer of 1980 I wandered around in Oregon, experiencing an awakening in nature, in the forests of Crater Lake, Three Sisters, Cougar Reservoir, the crystal ocean and blackberry vines of Coos Bay. This was when I discovered astrology. I distinctly remember several weeks during a transiting Sun-Venus conjunction in Gemini in my ninth house when I read many books and met several teachers in Eugene. At this time I made it my job to live in a tent and hitchhike around, filling notebooks with poems, dreams, songs, drawing horoscopes and horary charts and psychedelic mandalas. Migrating to Boulder, I got intensively involved in my spiritual practices of hatha yoga, mantra, meditation, dreamwork, astrology, and music. I absorbed the writings of C. G. Jung, M. L. von Franz, and James Hillman, which were totally fascinating. I met Andres Takra, who became my astrology teacher and mentor. I was singing and playing guitar in nightclubs and on street corners, under the name Laughing Coyote. I had long hair and was somewhat freaky looking.

I was opening my inner eye through pranayama, doing Rebirthing sessions, practicing mind training and affirmations. I sat by streams, under trees, on top of rocks and mountains, prayed in sweat lodges, melted in hot springs, chanted at the rose tinted dawn. Inwardly activated by the combined ray of Neptune and Uranus, I felt an irresistible urge toward transformation. I walked in forests at all hours, found the sacred river and bathed in it, listened to hooting owls nestled in midnight trees. I was changing in ways I didn't understand, but I let it happen, even though my parents and many of my friends thought I was totally weird. At this point I realized what Rudhyar meant when he said that a person on the transpersonal way has to emerge from the womb of culture and conformity. I was responsive to the Uranian call to freedom and the Neptunian call of the Spirit. I was a seeker of truth, but I wasn't what you'd call socially well adjusted. I was experiencing the urge to live an unconventional life and follow my calling to a spiritual mode of existence.

I suppose one could say it was "bad" to have Neptune conjunct natal Saturn for a couple of years. I had little inclination to work and make money. From a sociocultural perspective my life was a mess and I appeared completely aimless. But this was exactly when I discovered astrology. It was a crucial time of immersion in spiritual scholarship (Neptune conjunct Saturn in Sagittarius). I had to go into the woods, into the unknown, in order to find myself. This is why we need astrology, to help us find that deep center during periods of confusing and tumultuous changes.

An Astrology of Crisis and Transformation

Transpersonal astrologers study how outer-planet energies precipitate realignments of our life structures, objectives, and priorities, so transformations can occur. For example, when transiting Pluto in Sagittarius squared his tenth-house Virgo Sun, a man named Paul experienced an unpleasant, unsettling period of professional power struggles and decided to drop out of the corporate world. Having achieved many of his ambitions, and realizing the emptiness of craving further wealth and influence, he felt that entire phase coming to an end. Pluto sometimes marks endings and completion. Paul embarked upon a spiritual quest, seeking a more meaningful way of living. He learned that money isn't everything. However, he'd prudently put aside enough to sustain him in retirement. Paul simplified his material lifestyle, divested himself of many possessions (Pluto: getting rid of things), and took an extended break from relationships for the first time in many years. Paul's goal was no longer to accumulate more things, more power. He wasn't ambitious anymore, nor was he restless and inflamed by desires. He happily passed his time walking, cooking, meditating, gardening, hanging out on the beach, sitting on his porch, listening to birds and crickets, enjoying the simple pleasures of this present life. With Pluto square his Virgo Sun, Paul enjoyed having time to exercise every day. He let go of the past and walked on a different path.

Study of the outer planets illuminates how transformation occurs through crises and ordeals. For example, in 1957, John Coltrane had a religious experience that led him to overcome the heroin addiction and alcoholism he'd struggled with since 1948. In 1948, transiting Saturn in Leo came into conjunction with Neptune near his seventh house cusp; undoubtedly a friend or acquaintance introduced him to heroin. With Neptune in Leo, he moved amidst the royalty of jazz, but addiction caused his career to suffer several times, when he was fired by Miles Davis and Duke Ellington. He was fortunate to have people in his life who held him accountable to higher standards of conduct. He continued to abuse his body with drugs and alcohol during the years when transiting Pluto was opposite natal Jupiter in his twelfth house, signifying retreat into his drug habit. Things reached a crisis point in 1957 as Pluto reached conjunction to natal Neptune, when he was able to find the true spiritual source that could lift him out of the bondage of chemical dependency. In the liner notes of *A Love Supreme*, Coltrane states that, in 1957, "I experienced, by the grace of God, a spiritual awakening which was to lead me to a richer, fuller, more productive life. At that time, in gratitude, I humbly asked to be given the means and privilege to make others happy through music." Pluto conjunct Neptune was the final crisis that allowed him to throw off the toxic addiction. He had to purge that negative influence, expiate his soul, and receive spirit's grace and healing—which also coincided with Neptune in Libra transiting opposite

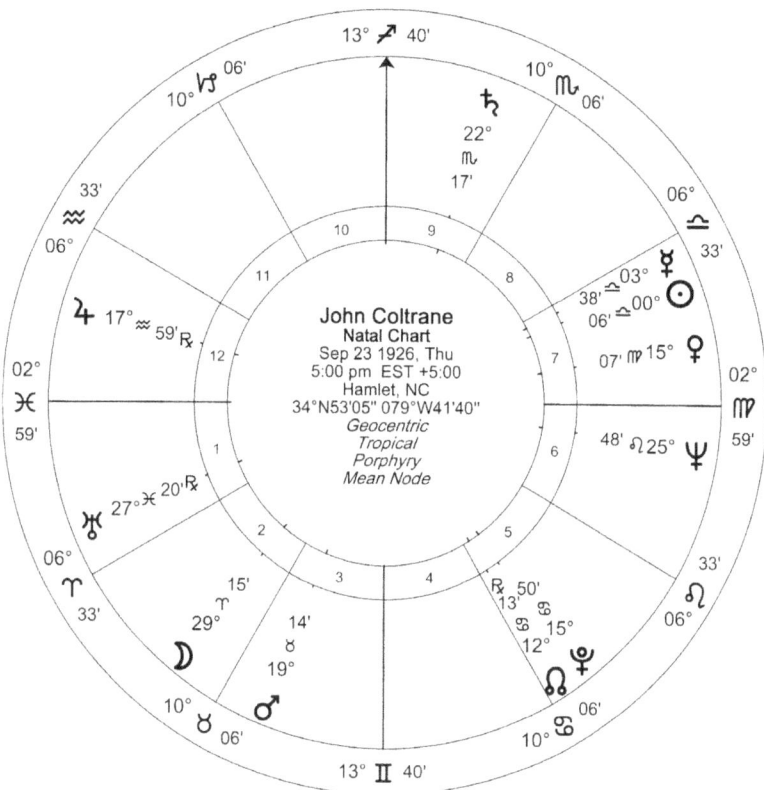

natal Moon. His spiritual redemption and awakening occurred over the next several years as transiting Uranus conjoined natal Neptune in 1961–62, coinciding with the release of *A Love Supreme*, an artistic and spiritual pinnacle. Coltrane's advancement through music was meteoric as transiting Uranus came over his Descendant and was conjunct Venus and Sun, and there was no impediment to the expression of his brilliant solar essence in electrifying fluid sheets of sound. The story of Coltrane's purification and offering of self to the music that was his divine purpose is inspirational.

Planetary symbolism clarifies how one can best transform through adversities, crisis, and ordeals, gaining wisdom and compassion that can serve as the basis for future roles of helping and service. Addicts or alcoholics on the path of recovery may go through a healing process that leads them to become inspiring role models and to offer support to others, sometimes in the role of sponsors in 12-Step programs. Recall the story of Ogden in Chapter 2. A man who survived prostate cancer during a long transit of Pluto in his sixth house now volunteers as a counselor to others who are battling this illness. Another example of this was a woman born with a close Moon-Neptune conjunction who was put up for adoption at birth. In her twenties, when transiting Saturn squared her Moon-Neptune, she had an emotional crisis when she realized, during a guided meditation, the vast scope of the abandonment she felt. At first she was deeply upset as she revisited and acknowledged her own suffering, re-experiencing the distress of an insecure infant. She went on to become a compassionate psychotherapist and agency administrator who works with families and children around adoption issues. She has helped many people. Her personal wound became the basis for her life's work. Similarly, Rudhyar notes, "a repetitive pattern of frustrating or tragic interpersonal relationships" can teach us lessons that awaken a compassionate, non-clinging, steady and inclusive love.(77)

> In transpersonal living, an individual should not be concerned with "success" and especially with what from the socio-cultural point of view would be called a constructive achievement. . . . An individual on the transpersonal path should realize in what way a present occurrence is an *effect* of the past, and at the same time, understand the *purpose* of the event in generating power to move ahead in the process of transformation. . . . [T]he real issue is whether [one remains] as unaware as before of the inherent *transformative purpose* of the events, or whether the individual will be able to meet these happenings as tools for the cutting and grinding of the coarse and dull stone of personality into a clear and translucent jewel.(78)

At the transpersonal level of interpretation, we evolve beyond a predictive emphasis on "good" versus "bad," malefic or benefic planetary influences, and a black and white assessment of success or failure. When facing planetary challenges over the course of our lives, we're able to find the strength and clarity to meet these experiences as purposeful phases of transformation.

A Turbulent Spiritual Metamorphosis

The next example is one we'll trace through a number of stages into the next chapter. Sonia, in her early forties, had natal Sun conjunct Jupiter in Sagittarius in the tenth house, trine to Pluto, Mars, and Saturn in Leo in her seventh house. In the 1980s, during the transits of Saturn and Uranus through early Sagittarius and Sonia's tenth house, she enjoyed a period of success and achievement as a university professor (Sun-Jupiter and Sagittarius emphasis). However, from 1988–1990 she passed through some challenging transits: Saturn and Uranus in late Sagittarius were conjunct natal Venus and opposite the Moon. Then Saturn and Neptune in Capricorn transited into her twelfth house and squared natal Neptune. Pluto in Scorpio approached conjunction with natal Chiron in Scorpio and began a prolonged square to Pluto-Saturn-Mars

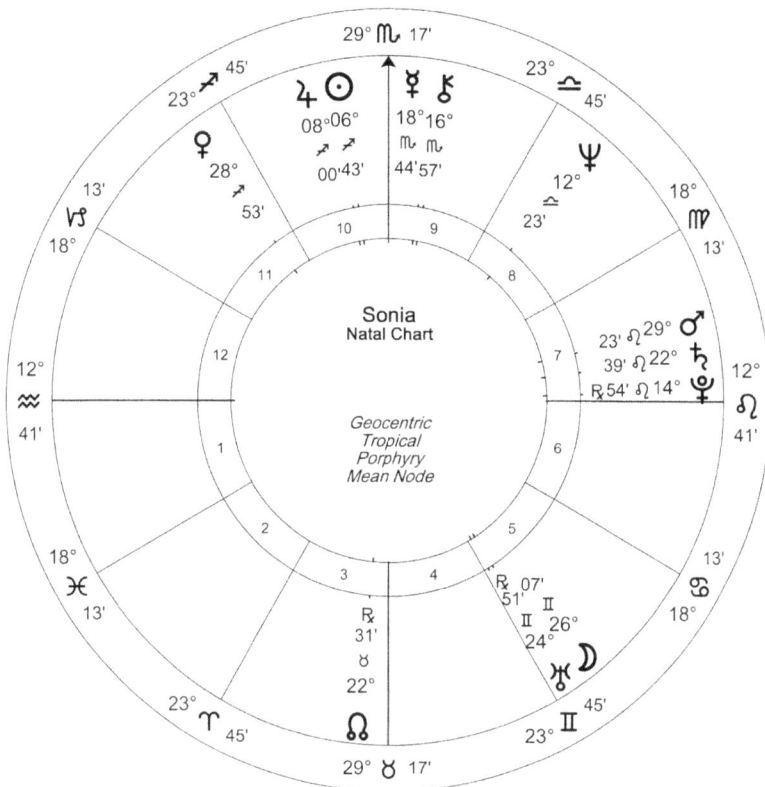

in the seventh house. Transiting Chiron entered her sixth house, the horoscope's realm of work, employment, health, personal crises and adjustments.

During these transits, Sonia experienced a period of inward and outward upheaval so severe that she had to take an extended, unpaid leave of absence from her university teaching position. With transiting Pluto conjunct natal Chiron (symbol of the wounded healer), while Chiron transited in her sixth house, she was in the midst of a health crisis, including chronic fatigue, severe allergies, headaches, and a stomach ulcer. With Neptune square Neptune, Sonia was lethargic and sleeping a lot. She couldn't concentrate and had lost interest in her research. An uncompleted book was long overdue, despite an unproductive sabbatical year, during which she fretted, worried, distracted herself, and argued with her husband instead of doing any writing. She tried various medical treatments, but her symptoms continued unabated. She felt helpless, confused, and worthless because she felt so debilitated that she was unable to work.

With transiting Saturn and Uranus conjunct Venus, and Pluto square natal Pluto in the seventh house, Sonia was also going through a marital crisis. Pluto square natal Pluto was hugely important for her because natal Pluto was conjunct Mars and Saturn; relational stress and discord were practically unavoidable. Both she and her husband had affairs and it felt like their marriage was cracking. There were constant power struggles, with unpleasant storms of resentment and negativity. Pluto was surfacing many deep feelings and a great deal of long-suppressed anger. Sonia was also becoming aware that she was a survivor of incest, a subject no one in her family had ever acknowledged, covering over the whole matter in a haze of denial (Neptune in her eighth house of sexuality; Pluto, planet of trauma and coercion, in her seventh house in 135° aspect to Venus, ruler of the fourth house of family).

Added to this, with Saturn and Uranus opposing her fifth-house Moon-Uranus, Sonia was having an emotional crisis about not having children and coming to terms with the fact that she'd chosen independence and freedom from motherhood in order to be a free-spirited scholar, an intellectual force. She was doing some intense self-examination accompanied by emotional upheaval and frequent tearfulness. Major transits to the natal Moon indicate important times for emotional healing, deep inner reflection, and increased responsiveness to our own needs. With these transits to her Moon, the sixth-house dispositor, Sonia had been constantly changing her diet and was feeling highly unsettled about what she was supposed to eat. I encouraged her to find out from within herself what foods were nourishing to her body.

With her body, her self-esteem, her career, and her marriage in disarray, Sonia was confused about her downwardly spiraling situation. She was distressed to discover that the spiritual disciplines of yoga, pranayama, chanting and meditation she'd practiced for many years didn't shed any light on what she was going through. They didn't touch the pain she was feeling or calm the energies agitating inside her, yearning for an as yet undefinable state of freedom. Sonia came to consult with me in a state of considerable fear and anxiety.

Astrology is first and foremost a centering practice that orients and illuminates us at moments of chaos and confusion. (79) In that spirit, I attempted to help her make sense of her situation. An astrological counselor could approach such a crisis situation in various ways. A medical astrologer, focusing on the biological level, might try to determine the nature of Sonia's illness from the birth chart. Again, lacking much knowledge of medical astrology, I limited myself to the briefest comments. Because the sign of Cancer, on her sixth-house cusp, rules the stomach, I wondered if there was some emotional basis for her ulcer symptoms and suggested that it was important for emotional conflicts to be processed and resolved. With transiting Pluto square natal

Mars, she was under a lot of stress at work, especially with a colleague in her department who'd become a hostile professional rival. She was angry and tense about this, possibly contributing to her headaches. Protracted stress can certainly affect our immunity to illness and could have been a source of Sonia's chronic fatigue symptoms.

Alternately, one could view Sonia's situation as primarily a problem of socio-cultural adjustment and a need to adapt better to the demands of her occupation. Thus, one could address her predicament through the lens of a traditional career counseling model. For example, Work Adjustment Theory, developed by Rene and Lloyd Lofquist at the University of Minnesota, describes how workers achieve or maintain a good relationship with a work environment.(80) It examines *work satisfaction*: being satisfied with the work one does, the extent to which work fulfills our needs and requirements; and *work satisfactoriness*—our job performance, the appraisal of supervisors and colleagues, and the extent to which we complete the work assigned to us. Indicators of the degree of work satisfaction and satisfactoriness include job turnover, absenteeism, tardiness, job morale, devotion to a job, and productivity. All of these are indicators of our degree of work adjustment, or show work adjustment problems. The work environment must satisfy the individual's needs and the employee must satisfy the job's needs. For Sonia, not returning student papers, turning in grades late, showing up to classes unprepared, and blowing off academic committee meetings were signs that her capacity to perform her job was significantly impaired. Sonia had gotten some tough, critical teaching evaluations and performance reviews that shook her self-confidence. She also reported a low level of job satisfaction, which made it appropriate to consider major changes in her occupational role. At the socio-cultural level, we seek a sense of *role salience*, a feeling that our jobs and families and other social roles are meaningful ones, that what we do genuinely matters to us. Being a professor at this university had become a less salient role than it once had been for Sonia.

At a humanistic level of interpretation, we could emphasize that Sonia's tenth-house Sun-Jupiter indicate that an expansive professional life in the Sagittarian realm of academia was central to her lifepath. Now, however, she'd reached a crossroads moment when her self-actualization required authenticity and being honest with herself; it required that she undergo a period of uncertainty, a rite of passage that would hopefully, in the end, be redemptive. Neptune square Neptune is a symbol of transition and liminality. During the chaos, destructuring, and rising tides of Neptune transits, it's possible to yield inwardly and welcome the opportunity to reevaluate commitments and life structures. Letting go can be a conscious choice. I wanted Sonia to recognize she wasn't the victim of her situation; she was still a self-determining person. She could make this decision to take a leave of absence, with her future job status unresolved, not only out of necessity but also with deliberate intention, as an act of individuation, to make room for new energies being activated inside her—more artistic and body-oriented. One initial expression of this was that Sonia joined a contact improvisation theater group, satisfying Uranus's conjunction to her eleventh-house Venus. This allowed Sonia some new experiences of connection with others and a greater freedom from self-inhibition.

A transpersonal approach builds upon the other levels of interpretation and also seeks to understand how crises can be catalysts for spiritual awakening. Planetary symbolism helps us understand the conflict we experience between socio-cultural functioning—our efforts to achieve or maintain occupational, financial, and material stability—and a growing receptivity to transpersonal influences that can be disruptive or destabilizing. This reflects the energetic tension between Saturn and the outer planets. We need to keep some resilient life structures in place and meet our earthly responsibilities. We need a strong vessel, forged by the tests of Saturn, which promote pragmatism, self-discipline, and grounding. But sometimes the small vessel has to break so that one can be enfolded by a greater vessel, contained by a greater whole. In this feeling of containment, one can experience healing and a new vision of the purpose of this life.

In Sonia's case, the situation was complex. She clearly had some work to do on emotional issues related to her marriage, sexuality, and memories of incest, which could be addressed in psychotherapy. She also needed to come to terms with her crisis of professional identity. These weren't, in themselves, transpersonal concerns. But planetary symbolism could influence Sonia's level of consciousness during this process. Amidst all the changes and confusing symptoms, I asked Sonia to *imagine and know* that she was transforming according to a secret design inscribed in her chart; and that alignment with this design could help her evolve within her present circumstances. There are moments when maintaining stability isn't the all-important goal that we often assume. Sonia had performed her role in society; it wasn't that she still needed to prove herself. She had already been there. But current planetary influences showed that previously unconscious evolutionary forces were at work, trying to initiate her into a new consciousness, informed by new priorities. These unconscious and transpersonal energies precipitate changes, assigning new and challenging tasks, as they increasingly guide and influence the seeker, the individual in transformation.

Outer Planet Rites of Passage

Transpersonal astrology sheds light on the competing needs and developmental strivings of individuals transitioning from "personhood" (socio-cultural success and self-actualization) to "seedhood" (self-transcendence, transpersonal creativity, and service). The influence of Uranus incites actions and choices that are surprising, spontaneous, and unconventional. Uranus is the forward movement of each generation's collective consciousness. During transits involving Neptune, mystical, transpersonal, interests grow stronger and we may at times become spacy, incompetent, or unfocused, if our Saturnian functioning doesn't remain crisp. In his book, *Culture, Crisis and Creativity*, Rudhyar posed the question, "Which do you want, security or transformation?" Spiritual awakening under outer-planet influence can generate some turbulence and disruption of one's social adjustment and feeling of security, such as Sonia leaving her comfortable job for a period of self-exploration. The story of Richard Alpert transforming into Baba Ram Dass is a perfect example of this (see Chapter 12).

Astrology aids us in reorganizing our lives during the passages shaped by Uranus, Neptune, and Pluto, which are intelligent agents of evolution. Note how all three outer planets were active by transit during Sonia's spiritual crisis. To guide oneself or other persons through chaotic periods requires that we understand the specific purpose of these planets. Rudhyar wrote:

> As an individual begins to experience his attunement to the spirit, he always has to face a crucial choice: to be a Sun, while dreaming of identification with the Supreme Spirit or, as a star among companion stars, to dedicate to the whole community whatever spiritual inflow has sought in him a focal point and channel for expression. . . . There are three fundamental kinds of test, . . . three levels at which the decision has to be made during the process of transformation of the individual. . . which can be referred to the specific character of the three trans-Saturnian planets, Uranus, Neptune, and Pluto. . . . [These symbolize] the hunger for spiritual experiences, the desire for display of miraculous powers surrounding one with transcendent glamor, and the deep yearning for self-glorification and power over other human beings.(81)

Now let's examine the specific character of these planets.

Uranus

Transits or progressions involving Uranus precipitate an urge for change, self-liberation, creative autonomy, and freedom from rigid cultural conditioning and beliefs. Old certainties are questioned; fresh perceptions and novel conceptions are formed. We imprint new pathways, experiment, and implement intelligent changes. Uranus stirs a person to pursue new directions, embrace alternative identities, and break free from unquestioning conformity to family and social norms and traditional modes of thought.

Sometimes to follow the path of our individuation we have to break away, alter some aspect of our life structure, or undergo a crisis of severance, such as my client Sonia's decision to take an extended leave from her university teaching job, which provided status, prestige, and financial stability. She held a position in the world that many people would envy and hold onto at all costs. With transiting Uranus opposite her Moon, Sonia was restless for a change of direction and dissatisfied with her occupational role and its attendant lifestyle. She longed for freedom from the limitations of her professional activities (teaching large lecture classes, grading papers and exams, and pressure to publish research and procure funding), and she became emotionally and intellectually unable to fulfill her academic responsibilities during this time. She admitted that she'd secretly wanted to make a career change for a long time, but had been afraid of the uncertainty and of what others would think. The transit of Uranus liberated her from attachment to stability and propriety. It gave her the boldness to face the harsh judgements of parents, friends, and colleagues that her decision to leave her job would inevitably elicit.

Also, Sonia questioned and reappraised her prior values regarding marriage. When Saturn and Uranus transited over natal Venus, she and her husband attended meetings of a group promoting polyamory (Venus in the eleventh house), and she began exploring new relationships outside her marriage. This was a major reversal of her prior sensibilities and values internalized from her family and religious upbringing. Eventually Sonia realized she much preferred a monogamous lifestyle, but she felt this period of experimentation had been valuable and that several new friendships resulted from it. Although the whirlwind of change that was set in motion was frightening, Sonia experienced the exhilaration of living at the edge of freedom and new, uncharted possibilities. Uranus signifies an embrace of the open space of discovery and innovation, freedom from former commitments and self-definitions, and a willingness to reorganize one's life.

Uranus typically generates excitement, controversy, social disapproval, or stigma for our unconventional beliefs, pursuits, ideologies, and lifestyles. Born with a conjunction of Sun-Uranus in Leo in the seventh house, C. G. Jung's life featured controversies and drama centered around his uranian marriage to his amazing wife, Emma; his relationship with his lover, Toni Wolff, and his devoted circle of women, known as the Valkyries.(82) People responsive to Uranus take bold steps beyond culturally sanctioned values and beliefs. Uranus can also manifest as defiance and obstinacy. It frees us to shapeshift, innovate, and transform, to become change agents, instruments of invention and social transformation. Gandhi had Uranus conjunct the Midheaven. Our noble U. S. President, Barack Obama, has a natal Sun-Uranus conjunction; he was born to become an instrument of social change. Physicist Niels Bohr had a Sun-Mercury-Uranus conjunction. Bebop saxophone avatar Charlie Parker was born on a full Moon conjunct Uranus in Pisces. John Coltrane had Uranus opposite Sun and Venus,

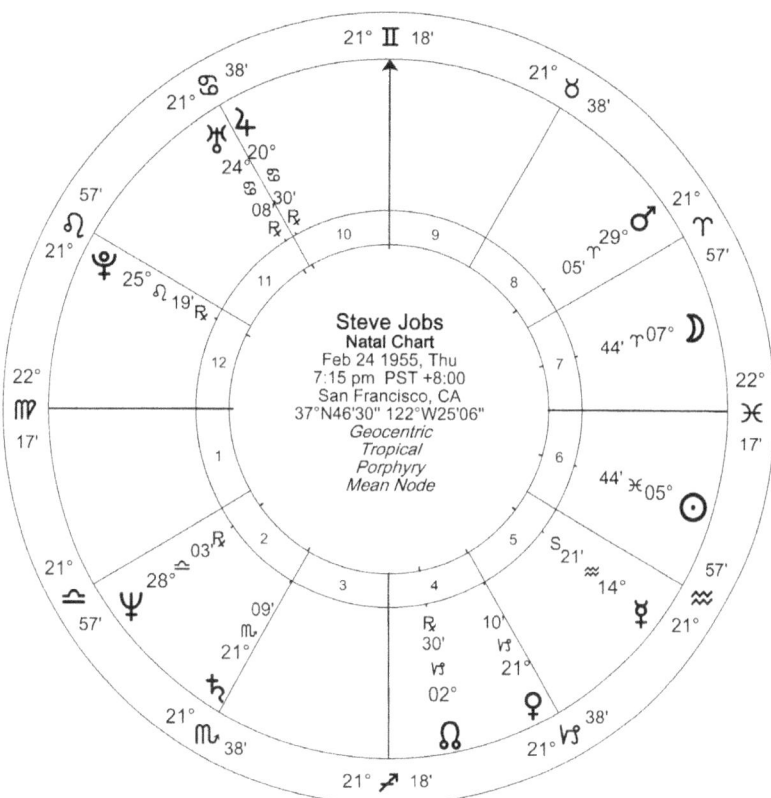

apt symbolism for a musical genius and innovator. Bob Marley had Sun in Aquarius and Uranus conjunct the Descendant. A revolutionary figure, his songs gave voice to an urge for freedom that can't be subdued or subjugated.(83)

Three key figures in the computer revolution have charts strongly emphasizing Uranus. While these aren't people we ordinarily think of as spiritually oriented, they're clearly agents of social innovation. Apple Computer founder Steve Jobs had Uranus conjunct Jupiter, with Jupiter in the tenth house. Uranus was also square Mars, trine Saturn, opposite Venus, and formed a sesquiquadrate to his natal Sun. Jobs developed intelligent technological inventions that changed the world. Jobs also had Sun and Jupiter in an exact 135° aspect.

Microsoft founder Bill Gates (see chart on page 144) has natal Uranus conjunct the Ascendant. With his natal Sun-Neptune square Uranus, Gates embodies that visionary blend of technology and imagination that the personal computer revolution made possible for the masses (Uranus square Neptune). With his powerful Jupiter-Pluto

Astrology and Spiritual Awakening, Part II

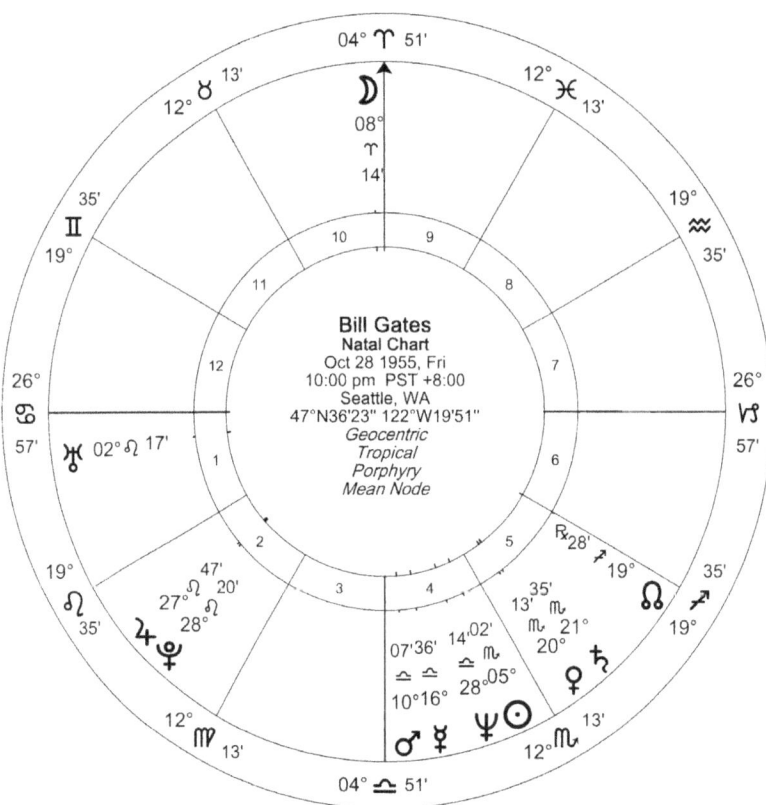

conjunction in the second house of money, Gates holds vast wealth, and has made unprecedented monetary contributions through his charitable foundation.

Facebook founder Mark Zuckerburg has Uranus conjunct Moon's south node. Uranus on the nodal axis represents capturing the zeitgeist of the times, formulating new conceptions such as inventing a new form of social media. Those who are consciously responsive to Uranus challenge old ways of thinking and conceive new ideas and innovations. In whatever realms of life they touch, they work for change, especially in the social-collective sphere.

With natal Uranus in my tenth house, after the period of wandering described earlier I created an unconventional professional identity as a psychotherapist openly using astrology in my counseling practice. I work for change by telling my clients that astrology, yoga, meditation, dreamwork, visualization, music, and aerobic exercise can be effective antidepressant agents, in many instances more helpful than the long-term use of pharmaceutical medications. As a licensed mental health professional, I'm will-

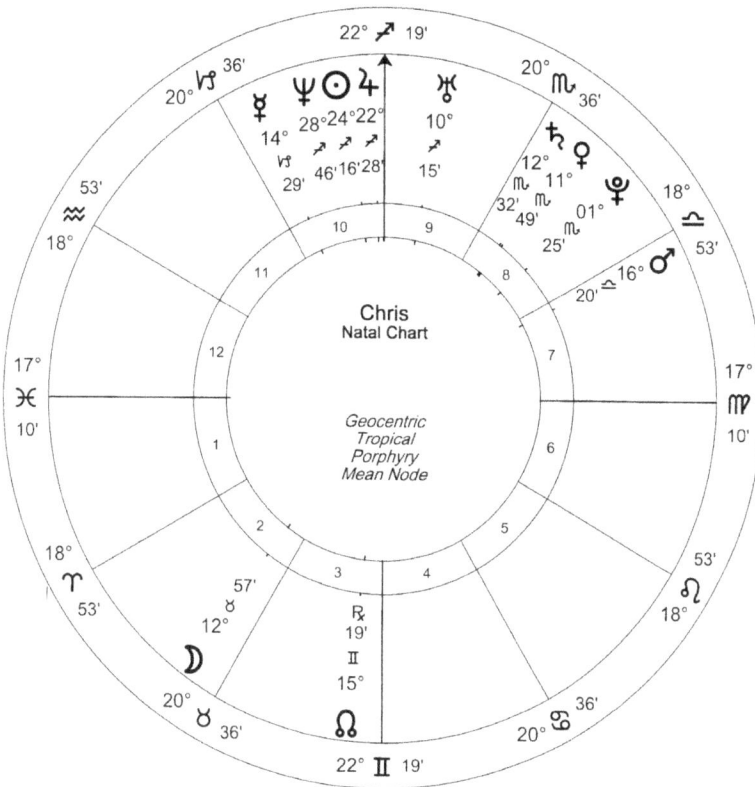

ing to stand up and say this and publish case studies to support my convictions.(84) This is my humble revolution.

For example, Chris, age 27, had a natal conjunction of Sun-Jupiter-Uranus-Neptune in Sagittarius. He'd been diagnosed as schizophrenic by doctors and was on two antidepressants, an antipsychotic medication, meds for attention deficit disorder, and sleep meds. He'd been fired from his last two jobs and was on the verge of walking out of his present job, right in the middle of a demanding project. His Sun was conjunct Neptune, the planet we associate with serious mental illness, delusions, psychosis, disorganization. After speaking with him for an hour I was convinced Chris wasn't crazy at all. He presented as completely lucid mentally, but physically and emotionally unhealthy. He drank way too much (plenty of the hard stuff), had few friends, and was a hermit who stayed up all night and slept during the day. With Uranus and the south node squaring the Ascendant and widely conjunct his Sun, his whole pattern of existence was against the grain of the collective. Chris worked in the field of computer security systems programming and was much sought after, earning a six-figure income. Natal Sun in Sagittarius conjunct Jupiter and Uranus signified his advanced mind and prodigious intellectual capacities, conceptual sophistication and inventiveness with computer science and mathematics. He said, "The only thing I know about is mathematics and computers." When transiting Uranus squared his natal Sun-Uranus, Chris became recognized in his field as an innovator and genius, publishing numerous articles; he'd been invited to teach at several universities, though he had no graduate degree. He was wired and eccentric, but not, in my opinion, delusional. With his Sun-Uranus, he exuded a rebellious, disrespectful attitude that had gotten him fired from several jobs, and he was currently in trouble at work because of his erratic behaviors and work habits.

While transiting Uranus in Pisces formed its final square to his Sun and Neptune, Chris told me this dream: *There's a passenger in my vehicle. I killed him through accident, and I didn't know what to do. I left the body there. A cop drove past.* I asked about the passenger, who Chris said reminded him of "my best friend Morty from high school. He shaped me in various ways. Throughout high school he had a better defined sense of identity. He was a brilliant dude, he played in a punk-rock bar band. He was the most rotten alcoholic; for years I drank with him. He was troubled, got kicked out of school." This was the model for Chris's Sun-Uranus-Neptune. *He had to be that guy*, a defiant, alcoholic troublemaker. I said, "This dream represents a need to kill or sacrifice the attitude represented by Morty—heavy drinking, getting kicked out of schools and jobs, being a badass punker and troublemaker. This attitude of consciousness is ready to die. It has caused you trouble at work, and psychological trouble. You need to shed this part of you. I think the Cop signifies guarding, protecting, maintaining order, self-ordering. You need to watch over yourself more closely, to have an ordering principle watching out for you more closely so you don't do things that hurt you."

Chris took these comments to heart and made immediate changes. That's the optimal response to Uranus: immediate change. He quit drinking abruptly after his doctor told him that he was on the brink of cirrhosis of the liver, at age 27. He started going to bed at a reasonable hour (Uranus square Neptune: changing his sleeping patterns), eating more consciously, working out at a gym, and quickly shed 25 pounds. He tapered off all his medications under medical supervision, combed his hair, and started online dating. He also transformed the defiant, disrespectful attitude that was making him unemployable. He went to his boss and explained some technical issues that were preventing him from completing his work project and then made extra effort to set things right and to complete his contracted assignment. Chris made significant progress in turning his life around in four months. His dream brought freedom from drinking, chaos, and arrogance (Uranus square Sun-Neptune). He was also introduced to meditation, dreamwork, and astrology. It was the beginning of a new life. This is the nature of Uranus, the awakener who reveals the path of change.

Neptune

On the path of transformation we may experience unusual states of mind or feel the presence of mysteries and unseen worlds. From the planet Neptune emanates a vibrational incitement to merge and align one's being with a spiritual Reality or source, to access various expansive states of knowing—mystical, imaginal, intuitive, meditative, unitive, clairvoyant, telepathic. During transits or progressions involving Neptune, we're influenced by subtle, etheric realms beyond the visible, the physical, the temporal domains. We may become the mystic, the gnostic visionary. For those on a spiritual path, Neptune is the gateway to a world of meditation and inner space, and brings an urge for divine consciousness. We experience heightened vision, intuition, and creative imagination, and seek the state of Self-realization. At such times, typified by Sonia's experience during Saturn-Neptune square natal Neptune, we can open our awareness to a wider sphere of existence, becoming permeable and receptive to its subtle, transforming influence. To develop at the level of Neptune is to meet life with peace, detachment, and tranquility, feeling the enfoldment of the Whole. Neptune is a symbol of devotion to the inner light, listening to intuition, dreams, and the invisible spirit of guidance.(85) It's the disciple's inner surrender, openness, and transparency of being that invites the *maha shakti* of Pluto, the grace (or *baraka*) that initiates us.

Whatever practices and paths we pursue, with Neptune we feel a longing to achieve a spiritual state, to seek a higher realization. For example, between 1903 and 1909, the Sufi sage Hazrat Inayat Khan (see chart on page 148) experienced an extended transit of Neptune conjunct his Nadir and natal Sun. Inayat Khan had already achieved notoriety as a performing musician (Venus in Leo in the fifth house). But during this transit, he began to meditate deeply, became fascinated with Persian mystical poetry, and dreamed of uplifting Indian music and culture (Neptune in the fourth house). He experienced states of ecstasy and rapture while singing and playing the *veena* and felt that music and religious feeling were one and the same (natal Venus square Neptune). He realized that he didn't want worldly success, but rather to help humanity and to experience God through music. He began to have mystical experiences in meditation—visions of inner light and inner voices giving him direct spiritual guidance. Pisces Moon in the twelfth house, trine the Sun, showed an inclination toward mysticism. Inayat Khan found a spiritual master who taught him physical exercises for purification, meditation practices, and Sufi doctrine. He experienced telepathic communication with his teacher and with others. During this period he attained high stages

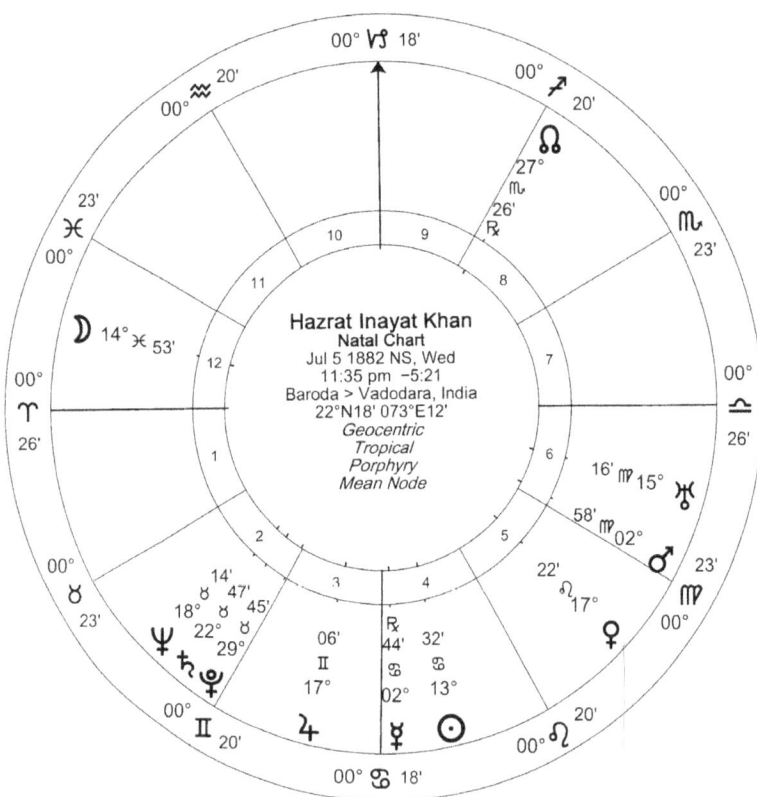

of mystical realization and spread his vision of the Sufi message, the upliftment of human consciousness through music, poetry, and teachings such as Al-Ghafur's "The Divine Quality of Forgiveness that Keeps the Knowledge of our Faults Even from the Angels." Inayat Khan's beautiful prayer *Khatum* reads:

> O Thou, who art the Perfection of Love, Harmony and Beauty, The Lord of heaven and earth, Open our hearts, that we may hear Thy Voice, which constantly cometh from within. Disclose to us Thy Divine Light, which is hidden in our souls, that we may know and understand life better. Most Merciful and Compassionate God, give us Thy great Goodness, Teach us Thy loving Forgiveness, Raise us above the distinctions and differences which divide men, Send us the Peace of Thy Divine Spirit, And unite us all in Thy Perfect Being. Amen.

Inayat Khan exemplifies a pure expression of Neptune's spiritual unifying urge.

For those pursuing a spiritual path, transits of Neptune and transits to natal Neptune correspond to periods of access to expanded consciousness, meaningful dreams, meditative states, and mystical experiences. At such times, a person's consciousness isn't focused primarily on the material world, the Saturnian realms of work and earthly responsibilities. We become aware that we're not separate, but interconnected, interwoven with everything.

Neptune and Holotropic Consciousness

A lucid conception of the perspective emerging at the Neptune level of consciousness is found in Stanislav Grof's distinction between *holotropic* and *hylotropic* states of consciousness.(90) *Hylotropic* consciousness is the experience of oneself as a solid physical entity with boundaries and a limited sensory range, living in three-dimensional space and linear time in the world of material objects. This is Saturnian consciousness. Basic assumptions of hylotropic consciousness are that matter is solid; past events are irretrievably lost; future events aren't experientially accessible; one can't be in more than one place at a time; one can exist only in a single time frame; and a whole is larger than a part. *Holotropic* consciousness refers to the experience of a field of consciousness with no definite boundaries that has experiential access to different aspects of reality without mediation of the senses. Here there are multiple viable alternatives to three-dimensional space and linear time. The solidity and continuity of matter is seen as an illusion; time and space are seen as ultimately arbitrary; being a part isn't incompatible with being the whole; form and emptiness are interchangeable. We can identify experientially with another person, another life form, animal or plant consciousness. According to Grof, living exclusively in the hylotropic mode, while denying the holotropic mode, is unfulfilling and fraught with lack of meaning. But an exclusive focus on the mystical, holotropic mode is incompatible with adequate functioning in the material world. Like the hylotropic mode, holotropic consciousness can be difficult or pleasant, but it presents no major problems as long as the external situation of the experiencer is protected. Ultimately, both modes must be integrated with each other into an experience of a higher order. Grof's model articulates the tension between the experience of separate existence as a material object and that of limitless existence as an undifferentiated field of consciousness. Hylotropic and holotropic modes of existence represent the polarity of form and emptiness, matter and spirit, linear time and eternity, Saturn and Neptune.

The Downside of Neptune

Neptune, this beautiful planet of spirituality and unity consciousness, can also pose challenges and create unsettled conditions. At times we pass through periods of disorientation and confusion, ordeals that test our faith in life and in ourselves. In some instances we experience the dysfunctional side of Neptune—in states of weakness and dependency, depression and depletion; or maladaptive responses to life, including denial, idle fantasy, slothfulness, sloppiness, remaining a helpless victim. Neptune holds the potential for a wide range of indiscriminate lifestyle choices. Addictions can be very disorganizing and sap our energy. With Neptune we may follow paths that are vague, impractical, unrealistic, grandiose, or self-deluding. At times we may be especially laden with *dukkha*, sorrow and suffering. It's important that we do some work to transform the weak, regressed, chaotic, and incompetent parts of ourselves.

Alicia, a woman with Taurus Sun in the eighth house (shared finances, taxes, credit, money owed to others) opposite Neptune in Scorpio in the second house, neglected to file her tax returns, ran up huge debts on credit cards, and was always late paying bills. When Saturn transited conjunct natal Neptune, her boyfriend insisted she come out of the clouds and stop avoiding these financial realities, which were adversely affecting their finances, exposing them to late payment fees and tax penalties. Sometimes Neptune, with its spaciness, fuzzy boundaries, and attentional lapses, seems to work at cross purposes with Saturn, the executive function. We have to work out the coordination of Saturn and Neptune, through appropriate responsiveness to both vibrational influences.

Delusion or the Dawning of Enlightenment

To understand the higher potentials of Neptune, Buddhism provides some helpful teachings. In Buddhist terms, Neptune represents our Buddha nature, the potential to experience clear, wakeful awareness. But Neptune also represents the principle of *ignorance* or *delusion*, mental states of confusion that lead to unwholesome actions and states of mind. Ignorance is caused by *kleshas*, which are *obscurations* clouding our awareness, such as anxiety, fear, anger, jealousy, and depression. The term kleshas refers to afflictions, defilements, disturbing emotions, mind poisons. I associate these with Pluto, which represents fixation and negativity. The kleshas create a mental fog that prevents clear perception of reality. In extreme cases, they can even give rise to states of disorganization, paranoia, or psychosis, some of the most confused manifestations of Neptune. In Theravadin Buddhism, the three kleshas of ignorance, attachment, and aversion (or lust, greed, and hatred) are called the *three poisons*; they're identified as the sources of suffering and cause us to create endless karma that keeps us bound in the world of *samsara* or illusion. Mahayana teachings added the kleshas of pride (or conceit) and jealousy.

Those seeking to wake up and become enlightened beings need to clear these obscurations or defilements of the clear mind, gaining freedom from the kleshas. Pluto, which also signifies the principle of purification, works in tandem with Neptune to uncover and eliminate these obscurations, liberating us from countless emotional, behavioral, mental, and energetic fixations. When we cleanse our minds, speech, and actions so our better nature radiates, when we clear the impurities of delusion, rage, craving, and slothfulness, what remains is our inborn sanity and clarity. This is *bodhi*—enlightenment, the state of being awakened. Chogyam Trungpa calls this *basic goodness*, our primordial purity. Meditation brings us in touch with "the sanity we're born with," and helps us realize the Neptunian truths of egolessness, emptiness, and interconnecteness, and evokes a widening compassion and friendliness (*maitri*). In Tibetan Buddhist doctrine, the seat of spirituality is the mind, and there are three levels of mind: *sem*, keeping track of things; *lodro*, the intellect and sense of thirst for knowledge; and *rigpa*, the all-pervading sense of wakefulness, wisdom.(86) Astrologically, these levels of mind are represented by Mercury, Jupiter, and Neptune.

Neptune can signify ignorance or enlightenment; it's up to us which path we choose. For those who are consciously responsive rather than passive victims, the influence of Neptune can awaken a desire to attain the advanced spiritual realizations articulated in various practice lineages, for example an urge to realize what Tibetan Dzogchen Buddhism calls rigpa—innate awareness, a state of mind in which we become "free from all mental constructions. . . without any distraction or grasping. . . . Rigpa [is] a primordial, pure, pristine awareness that is at once intelligent, cognizant, radiant, and always awake. It could be said to be the knowledge of knowledge itself."(87)

The path of Dzogchen, the Great Perfection, is also known as Atiyoga, the "Primordial Yoga," which refers to "the Primordial State of the individual, . . . the state of inherent Buddhahood, known as the Bodhichitta. . . . The inherent original nature of the individual is said to be like a diamond: unchanging, indestructible, translucent."(88) This realization was described by Buddhist yogi and translator John Reynolds:

> [T]he impure karmic vision that afflicts the ordinary ignorant sentient being is not only cleansed, but actually transformed into the pure vision and gnosis of an enlightened being. . . . Dzogchen has its own method, called self-liberation, where, within the individual's meditation practice, thoughts are allowed to self-liberate as soon as they arise. . . . [T]he original state of the individual, one's inherent enlightened nature, is seen as being primordially pure and spontaneously self-perfected. . . . In Dzogchen the essential point is the state of contemplation, that is, the state of immediate intrinsic awareness. . . . [O]nce the individual is introduced to this primal awareness (this knowledge or gnosis) which is self-existing and present within oneself (from the very beginning), it will no longer be something that must be sought after somewhere else (outside of oneself). . . . [Dzogchen is] a

> way of seeing with naked Awareness, where one's vision is unobstructed and unobscured by conceptual constructions fabricated by the mind.... [W]hat is absolutely prerequisite for Dzogchen practice is the direct introduction to the Primordial State.... [T]he proper procedure is to introduce the practitioner directly to the state of contemplation by way of first dissolving one's mental activities. If one observes the mind and searches for where a thought arises, where it remains, and where it goes, no matter how much one researches and investigates this, one will find nothing. It is this very "unfindability" of the arising, the abiding, and the passing away of thoughts which is the greatest of all finds. Thoughts do not arise from anywhere, they do not remain anywhere, and they do not go anywhere. They do not arise from inside the body, nor do they arise from outside the body. They are truly without any root or source. Like the clouds in the sky, they arise only to dissolve again. Thoughts arise out of the state of emptiness and return again into this state of emptiness, which represents pure potentiality. We have only to observe our mind to discover this for ourselves. And this shunyata, this state of emptiness, is in fact the very essence of the mind.... In the state of contemplation, we are freed from all conceptions and find ourselves in the state of the Dharmakya, that is, in a directly penetrating naked Awareness that remains just as it is, a knowledge or primal awareness that has transcended the mind.(89)

A teaching such as this helps us envision an enlightened state so we can strive to attain it. Astrology aids travelers on the transpersonal way who aspire to realize a pristine, diamondlike consciousness and to maintain this state of mind while going though innumerable challenges correlated with transits and progressions, especially those involving Neptune.

Methods for Expansion: Meditation, Yoga, Pranayama

Buddhist practices begin with awareness of the breath to generate tranquility and mindful and spacious awareness. Stan Grof teaches his own method of breathwork to access holotropic states and promote accelerated consciousness evolution, using rhythmic breathing, music, massage, and the support of a sitter who watches over the session.

Awareness of the breath is fundamental to nearly all spiritual practices, such as hatha yoga, Buddhist mindfulness meditation, Sufi Zhikr, Christian Hesychacean prayer, shamanic journeying, and rebirthing. Expanding the breath is the quickest way to expand your mind. Many people find it difficult to meditate, but it's easy if you approach it through gentle breath release, for example, through yogic *pranayama*. Any qualified yoga instructor can teach you how. The techniques of *ujjayi, nadi shodhana, kapalabhati, bhastrika,* and *sitali pranayamas* all flow easily into deep meditation, into the expansive awareness symbolized by Neptune.(91)

Meditation is the practice of stillness. It can involve concentration on the breath, contemplation of a sound, repetition of a prayer or mantra, focusing the mind on a candle flame, a *mandala* or *yantra* design, on chakras and internal energies. It can involve visualization and contemplation of a saint, guru, or spiritual master. Meditation involves focusing and quieting the mind, so we drop naturally into our true nature—Atman, the Self, rigpa, a state of unconditioned awareness. Meditation is a state of stillness, a return to the tranquil source.

Neptune represents the possibility of an expanded evolutionary state. Ultimately, Neptune is about non-clinging, realizations of impermanence, the cultivation of equanimity and detachment, and an inner release and letting go. Neptune represents the ability to gracefully transmute our states of suffering into joy, compassion, serenity, and contentment. Peace is in this moment, when we inwardly surrender to reality.

Neptune and Surrender

A fascinating example of a Neptune crisis occurred in the life of former U. S. Vice President Al Gore (see chart on page 154), who lost the disputed 2000 presidential election despite winning the popular vote, due to the decision of the Supreme Court awarding the election to George W. Bush. At the time, Gore had transiting Neptune conjunct his Descendant, as well as transiting Uranus opposite natal Mars in Leo—symbol of a dispute and heated circumstances. Under the influence of transiting Neptune, Gore had to surrender to events that were beyond his control. He met this challenge and never complained or griped publicly about what happened. He sustained his essential dignity and composure. With his Pluto, Saturn, and Mars in Leo, he exhibited a royal demeanor; he handled this letdown in a classy manner. From an astrological perspective, losing the election and the presidency could be seen as a spiritual initiation, a personal crucifixion, after which Gore accelerated his pioneering work on behalf of the environment, in the service of humanity and the Earth. With natal Sun opposite Neptune, Gore is vibrationally attuned to Neptune. He was able to rise above his personal ambitions and self-interest, yielding to a situation that was unprecedented and unfathomable. Gore transcended the loss of the Presidency and has gone on to become one of our clearest, most grounded and inspiring visionaries, doing essential work on global climate change and mapping the future. He is one of those rare individuals during this time of planetary chaos who can explain the world sensibly. It will be intriguing to note any changes in his public role that may occur after Uranus transits his MC in 2016-17.

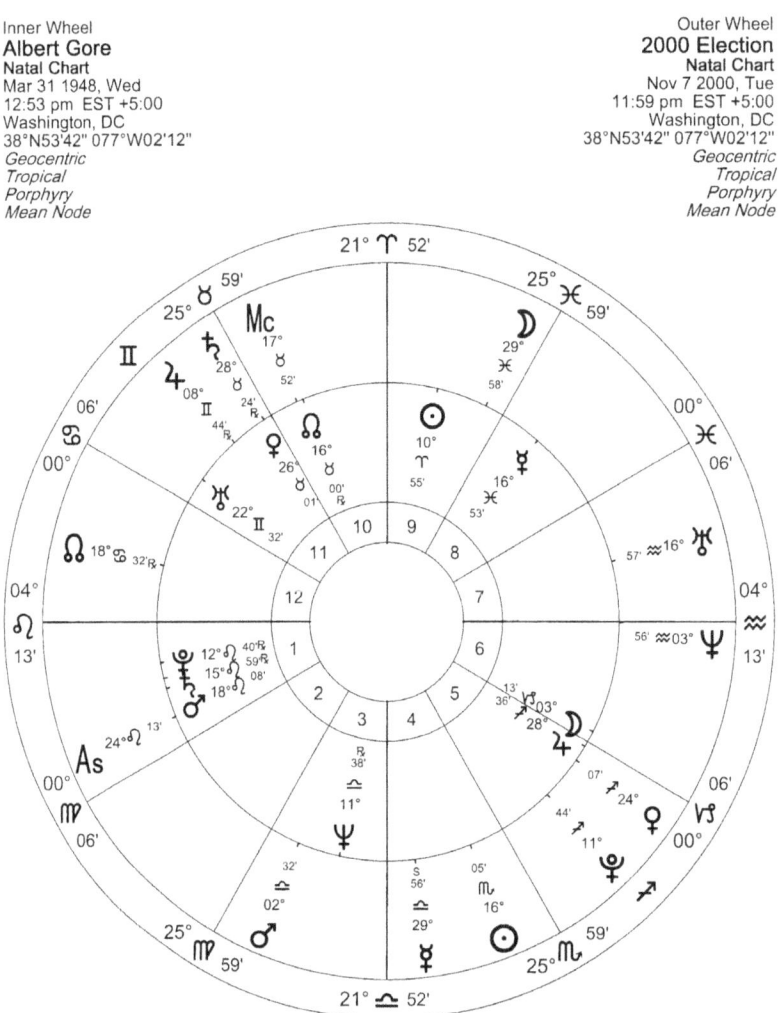

Although our experiences of Neptune's influence can transform our vision of life, we may feel at times as if we've lost our bearings and are walking on shaky ground. We saw this earlier in Sonia's confused condition during the transit of Saturn and Neptune to her natal Neptune. Rudhyar described the whole initiatory process as

> an unfamiliar mountainous path whose end always seems to recede beyond the horizon. . . . On that path of radical transformation, faith is required—a faith requiring humility, as well as the courage which can only be born of an inner realization of the irrevocable character of a decision whose source is more than purely mental. (92)

Recognizing "the irrevocable character of a decision whose source is more than purely mental" brings us to a threshold. This is the point of no return, beyond which we cease to look backward, longing for safer paths. Through an inward self-offering, the energies and priorities of the ego are reoriented. Something bigger than us can freely move through us. Neptune signifies receptivity to the spirit within and all around us, a state of openness and trust that invites an inpouring of transpersonal forces.

Pluto

Major thresholds in consciousness are crossed under the influence of Pluto, a planet that creates intensification of life and greater urgency of events, and, when all channels are clear, seeks to bestow the empowerment of the whole, the cosmos. In the astrobiography of Swami Muktananda (Chapter 9), we'll see an example of how Pluto can signify yogic transformation through awakening of an intense inner shakti. In many instances, Pluto operates as a catalyst for depth psychological work and necessary personality transformation. The energy of the universe is available and flows through us, but it also reveals the areas where that energy leaks out or is blocked by attachments and fixations, places where our personalities and attitudes need reconstruction. This might entail emotional crisis (Pluto-Moon), crisis in romance or friendships (Pluto-Venus), crisis involving anger, conflict, discord, or injury (Pluto-Mars), and crisis of identity (Pluto-Sun). Pluto can signify meetings with the difficult, shadow side of human nature, with mean, viperous, unscrupulous, or untrustworthy people. We encounter someone abusive, hostile, resentful, or manipulative, or we indulge our own most insufferable qualities. Under Pluto's influence we may need to make amends for various hurts and misunderstandings in our human relations.

Ravi, a man with Taurus Sun opposite Pluto in the fourth house, reported that his father was a cruel, abusive man with a volcanic temper who engaged in criminal activity and illegal business enterprises. When transiting Saturn in Scorpio was conjunct natal Pluto, and when his progressed Sun reached a quincunx to Pluto, Ravi's father died suddenly, which brought up strong surges of intense emotions and grief. For months, while transiting Saturn was retrograde, Ravi raged against his father (Pluto in fourth house of family and emotions). Over time he saw how his father had been traumatized and oppressed within his own family and turned to crime out of desperation. Ravi had enormous stores of resentment that he needed to cathartically express, and during this period he was very difficult and prickly for his wife to live with (Pluto in fourth). As Saturn made its third pass over natal Pluto, the emotional storm subsided and he felt that he could begin to forgive his father, and he apologized sincerely to his wife for behaving in an unpleasant, disagreeable manner.

Pluto has an innate intelligence for bringing things to the surface and precipitating character transformation, by clearing impurities in our feelings, behaviors, and attitudes. For example, we might become aware of the tendency to explosively discharge anger and lose self-control, harming our relationships and our bodies. We could let angry feelings fester and walk around under a dark cloud of negativity. By exposing these tendencies, we can transmute and transform them. Pluto is an impersonal intelligence that flushes out imperfections, but we have to consciously let go, seek closure and completion, and make determined effort to change our behaviors. Then it's possible to transform and become empowered to express our essential nature in alignment with the needs of a greater whole—our family, our community, our nation, our planet.

Amrit Desai (see chart on page 41), founder of Kripalu Community, has natal Pluto conjunct the Midheaven (using the speculative birthtime one of his students gave me), symbol of his being a shaktipat guru, a conduit of transmission. I experienced this in his presence in 1983; he's a powerful yogi. However, in 1994, when Uranus and Neptune in Capricorn opposed natal Pluto, Desai was expelled from his yoga community and publicly chastised by students and devotees after he had affairs with several female disciples. Various lies and duplicities were exposed; he was embroiled in scandal and engaged in denial and attempts at cover-up to save face. This is how Pluto sometimes works to uncover the hidden truth. Having his natal Sun configured with Pluto and Uranus empowers the soul, but these aspects also catalyzed astonishing events that stripped Desai of his position of respect (Sun square Saturn) and attracted "the wrong kind of attention" (Sun: being seen and known, being a center of attention). Desai experienced a fall from power, a period of retreat and purification, and eventually he reemerged as a spiritual teacher. My attitude is that everybody falls sometimes, and everybody deserves a chance for atonement and redemption.

During a Pluto transit we may experience how people try to dominate and bend other people to their will. Sometimes we have to submit and accept someone else's power over us, gracefully yielding. At the same time, we need to learn the ways of power and influence. Pluto occasionally signifies confrontations with abuses of power, controlling tendencies, self-destructive attitudes or behaviors. We could encounter some ruthless person who seems like an unstoppable, relentless force, a hardened adversary, or an impersonal, uncaring institution. Greta, a nurse with transiting Pluto conjunct Mars in Capricorn in her tenth house, experienced a professional crisis when she was verbally attacked and berated by a colleague who maligned her by spreading false rumors and questioning her professional competence. While under attack in the professional arena (Pluto conjunct Mars in the tenth house), Greta was strong and impeccable, never losing her temper. She eventually left to work for a different hospital; she took charge of the situation by finding a different job. The ruthless person who went after her was fired less than six months later. Pluto prepares us to live in a state of greater purity, but also with power, effectiveness, and indomitable mastery. Its transits correspond to periods when our motives and our singleness of purpose and commitment are tested:

> The aspirant to rebirth in spirit cannot become a safe and valuable member of a galactic type of community if there exists in him the slightest desire for acting as a Sun to a group of dark planets. This is the Plutonian test of total denudation, . . . of absolute humility. Only if the Plutonian catharsis is successfully met can an individual be trusted to be a true "companion."(93)

Pluto is an agent of purification and a catalyst to refine our character and expression of personal power. It teaches us to act without conceit, without the urge to dominate, injure, or exploit others. Pluto reorients our actions and intentions, to align my personal will and desires to the intention of a greater whole, the will of the universe. Pluto is the unfolding of the evolutionary serpent; the regenerative ouroboros is empowered and sealed. Pluto can be shamanic transformation through initiatory ordeals, fasting, journeys into the underworld, visionary encounters with elemental powers of nature. During a lengthy transit of Pluto to his natal Sun in Sagittarius, a man went on an extensive voyage through the Amazon where he experienced many *ayahuasca* journeys. Some of these sessions were very difficult, dredging up intensely charged feelings and memories. Some of the imagery of his visions were of dying and being reborn, ordeals of birth, physical and emotional purging. His experience was in accord with Dr. Grof's idea that transformation of consciousness is often shaped by themes of prenatal and perinatal life and imagery of the birth passage, as well as death and dying. Pluto is the rebirth from the ashes of the charred bird, the phoenix rising with renewed purpose and instinctual seed power. Pluto represents encountering, and merging with, a will greater than one's own, a power greater than oneself.

Two Meditations on Death

Sometimes that great power we encounter is the unfathomable mystery of death itself. Consider this story. A friend of mine, Jeffrey (see chart on page 158), passed away unexpectedly in a mountain climbing accident. He fell off a steep embankment, hit his head, and died instantly. Jeffrey's natal Moon and Mars were conjunct in Aries, which rules the head, and at the time of the accident, transiting Saturn at 23° Libra 40' was stationary direct in exact opposition to Moon and Mars, apt symbolism for an injury, a blow to the head. Six months earlier Jeffrey went to Mexico to have major dental work done, to save money. But one of the root canal operations was botched and he developed an infection in his face and jaw that had caused him headaches and intense discomfort (Mars in Aries). For months he talked about having fevers, a head cold,

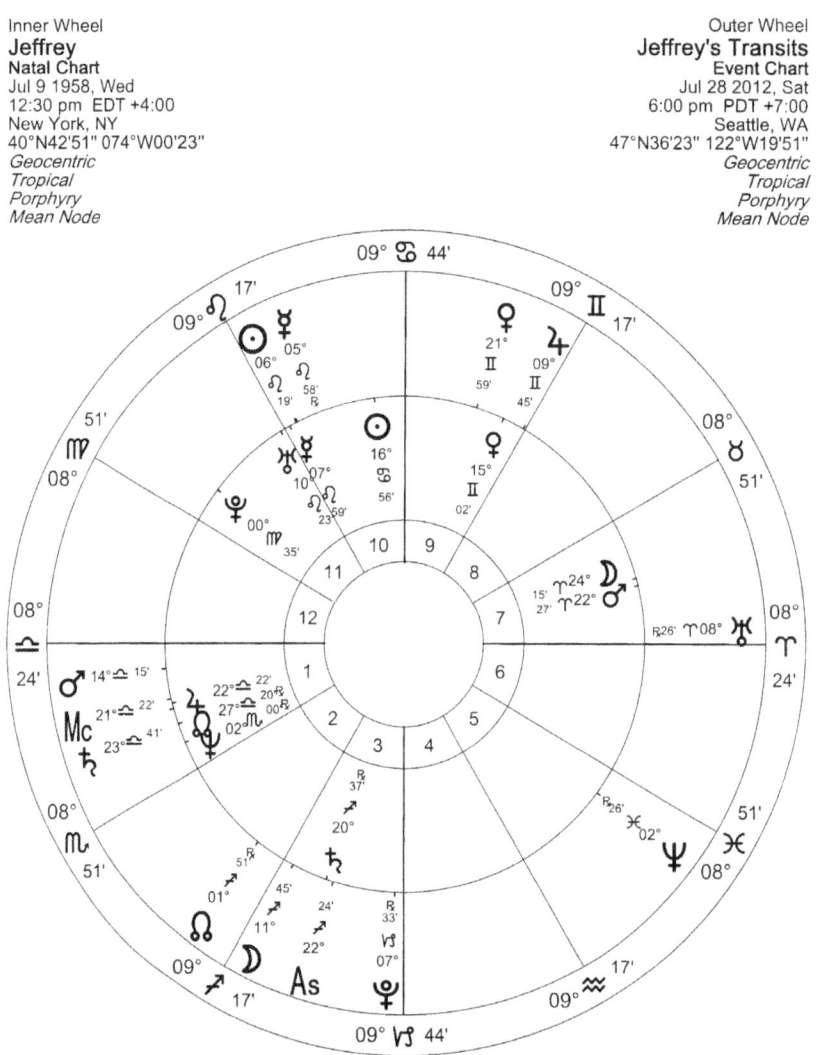

pain and congestion in his inner ears. The day of the accident was the first time he'd tried hiking since this dental fiasco, and some of his friends and family speculate that having a stuffy head may have affected his equilibrium at high altitude, contributing to his loss of balance and the fall that ended his life. Viewing Jeffrey's chart from a place beyond the ego, I glimpse the perfection that was woven into his final day on earth. Transiting Uranus was conjunct the Descendant, showing unexpected release from the body and this realm of existence. It goes without saying that the same transit can have completely different outcomes when it occurs in a different context. Simultaneously, transiting Pluto, lord of the underworld, was conjunct the IC (end of life),

The Transpersonal Level of Chart Interpretation

and square his Ascendant (the body). Thus, for me, Jeffrey's death has the meaning of a liberation. He died doing what he loved to do and he suffered only for an instant. At his date of death, solar arc Pluto was at 22′ Libra 25, in partile (exact) opposition to natal Mars (signifying an injury) and conjunct natal Jupiter. Solar arc Pluto aspecting Mars-Jupiter depicts him dying as the adventurer, hero, and noble athlete that he was. All of these meanings are eternally inscribed in his death moment. Pluto sometimes makes the visible form die and takes a pristine being such as Jeffrey down into the underworld in the prime of life as the instrument for some inscrutable intention, impersonal and ruthless, expressing the mandate of the universal will. As transiting Pluto squared Jeffrey's Ascendant, he was reabsorbed into the whole, reassimilated.

As an astrologer, I avoid predicting death, but sometimes we need to calmly discuss this issue with someone. This is illustrated in the next example, which shows the combined influences of Pluto, Neptune, and Saturn.

One of the most intense consultations I recall was with a woman named Renee (see chart on page 160) who had Saturn conjunct Neptune in the eighth house and was about to have her second Saturn Return. Her natal Sun was closely conjunct Pluto, in the sixth house of health. Transiting Uranus at 8° Aries and transiting Pluto at 8° Capricorn were both in 135° aspect to her natal Sun at 23° Leo 42′. I noted silently that natal Sun was conjunct Pluto, planet of the journey through the underworld, and that her Sun was now receiving a powerful 135° aspect from transiting Pluto. As I looked at Renee's chart I felt increasing concern about her health.

Renee informed me that recently, while receiving treatment for a broken arm, it was discovered that she actually had a tumor in her arm, which was swollen rock hard, all the way down to her hand. Further tests showed that tumors had spread throughout her body; biopsies showed that these were cancerous. She was in considerable pain. As I took this information in, I thought about what I could say that would be most helpful, and I inwardly asked for guidance. With these aspects of Uranus and Pluto to her sixth-house Sun-Pluto, it seemed that a health crisis was coming to a head, as life-threatening masses were spreading throughout her system.

I noted that transiting Saturn in Libra was turning retrograde and was going to go stationary direct for about 90 days exactly conjunct Renee's natal Neptune in the eighth house. Steering the conversation toward this upcoming transit, I suggested that she'd need to surrender to the treatment, radiation or chemotherapy, and she probably wouldn't be able to work; she needed time to rest and recuperate. I thought she should consider applying for disability, which she'd already set in motion (Neptune in the eighth house: money received from others or through government benefits). I said, "This Neptune transit signifies a period lasting several months when you'll need

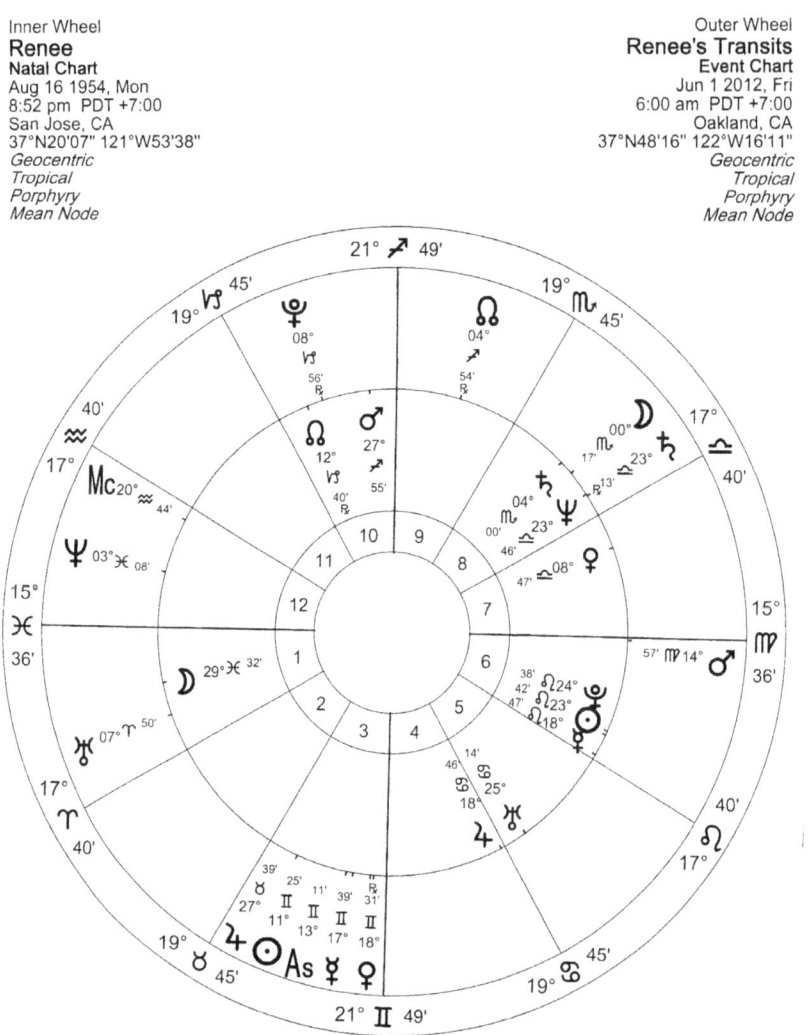

to surrender to the experience, submit to the treatment, to rest and recover, and also in some sense to rise up and transcend the situation." I spoke slowly to make sure every word was absorbed.

I wanted to say more about transiting Saturn turning stationary direct on the degree of her natal Neptune, in the eighth house. I explained that Saturn conjunct natal Neptune can have several meanings. It can be a time for spirituality, but it can also signify a spiritual or religious ordeal, a test of faith as we encounter some form of suffering, to which we can attribute spiritual or symbolic meaning. Neptune signifies Christ, the archetypal figure who represents redemption through suffering and then transcending, rising up into spiritual freedom. I told Renee that Saturn conjunct Neptune is a moment to raise our consciousness to a higher level, to experience a silent, expansive, witness consciousness, unidentified with the body, to abide in a state of tranquility, in deep meditation. Yogis call this the attainment of moksa, freedom. It's a time to turn toward God, to let go and assent to the divine will, to inwardly submit to whatever happens. Saturn conjunct Neptune provides a strong impetus to take a breath, release the mind, and plunge into deep meditation, finding the still point within. Here one experiences a vast awareness not limited to the body. I told Renee how the great sage Ramana Maharshi had a cancerous tumor in his arm. He refused medical treatment and remained constantly in the state of the Atman, the Self, in a state of peace and detachment. He was completely unafraid to shed the body. He was centered in the radiance of consciousness, in a state of spiritual transfiguration. From the perspective of the Self, the body's passage is moksha, a loss of density, evaporation into essence luminosity.

At this time Renee also had progressed Mars at 25° Capricorn 11', exactly opposite natal Uranus at 25° Cancer 14'. She had an acute inflammatory condition (Mars) while her arm was swollen with the tumor. For various reasons she was feeling fiery anger toward her boss and others at work. Also, transiting Pluto was sesquare natal Pluto, which I believed signified undergoing radiation, receiving a penetrating vibrational energy influence. In some instances, Pluto can be a planet of surgery, which was a likely course of treatment in her case. With progressed Mars opposite Uranus, it felt like things were going to happen fast, without delay, an immediate intervention. Renee passed away the day before her surgery was scheduled. To the best of my knowledge her last days were spent in a caring hospital environment. She certainly didn't linger on the earth as she was swiftly transported beyond this realm. I'd like to think that our conversation about her transits may have helped her prepare to disidentify from the body and abide in the state of a calm witness while making her final passage. Sometimes we need someone to tell us that this is what you're supposed to do at this juncture—to let go completely.

Here I must assume the reader's maturity. The fact that I discuss these examples of death doesn't mean I'm saying this is going to be the outcome every time we undergo a transit involving Pluto, or Neptune in the eighth house. Obviously that's not the case. But these are realities we're sometimes confronted with when we lose our loved ones or prepare for our final liberation. Astrology helped initiate Renee into the experience of death, just as it guides us so reliably throughout life. Finally, I want to note how the mind of the astrologer can be illuminated while spontaneously interpreting chart symbolism. I truly didn't know that I knew these things until I spoke to Renee at that moment.

Pluto: The Dynamic Ground and Regeneration in Spirit

Pluto is the symbol of the cosmic principle of death and birth, and represents a recycling and circulation of energy, an instinct to integrate and bring closure to prior experience. At the consciousness level of Pluto we experience an archetypal process that can transform the personality and activate dormant potentials.

For further insights into Pluto as an evolutionary intelligence, let's consider the transpersonal psychoanalytic mysticism taught by Michael Washburn, and his theory of the Ego and the Dynamic Ground, which describes the process of energy repression and regeneration. (94) Washburn uses the term "Dynamic Ground" to describe the spiritual energy source from which the sense of separate ego identity emerges, from which the ego becomes estranged, and to which we long to return. In pre-egoic development (infancy), the ego hasn't differentiated and feels the Dynamic Ground's influence in instinctual cycles of hunger and satiation, waking and sleeping, and during blissful states of primary process and symbiosis with the mother described by Freud, Margaret Mahler, and other psychoanalytic thinkers. In the egoic stages of life, during childhood, adolescence, and early adulthood, we experience primal repression of the Dynamic Ground, becoming self-contained, identified with thinking and mental life, and dissociated from physical, instinctual existence. The individual gets involved with Saturn socialization tasks and experiences ego independence and self-control, but also emptiness and alienation. *Primal repression* seals the Dynamic Ground, reducing it to a nearly dormant state where it's primarily expressed as sexual libido, and through our competitive and aggressive drives (Mars). In its deeper reality, the Dynamic Ground is *psychic energy*, a nonspecific amplifier of psychic processes. This is one way to conceptualize the energy that Pluto activates in us.

Awareness of the Dynamic Ground enlivens the body, perceptions, and feelings so that the outer world is imbued with intensity and a "sheen of numinosity." (95) However, primal repression closes off the Dynamic Ground, divesting experience of its magic and its power to astound. The power of the Ground remains unconscious, lying dormant or asleep, causing an experience of contraction and alienation. This is exactly the worldview of yoga psychology, with its description of the *kundalini* as a dormant evolutionary energy that can awaken with intense force, generating a feeling of expansiveness and union with a pervasive spiritual source. This is also the worldview of transpersonal astrologers responsive to the depth power signified by Pluto. Washburn writes:

> Primordial repression . . . submerges the Ground and supports the ego; it transforms the body from a supple and open vehicle for the free circulation of the power of the Ground into a rigid, impervious structure that caps the Ground. The transpersonal levels of the unconscious come into play

only after primordial repression has been lifted and the potentials of the non-egoic pole of the psyche have been liberated. The lifting of primordial Repression reawakens non-egoic potentials. . . . The ego experiences the upwelling of non-egoic life, which can be disturbing. The ego experiences the power of the Ground as a spiritual power that redemptively transforms the ego and enriches all dimensions of its experience.(96)

According to Washburn, in transegoic stages of development, there's a growing impetus toward self-transcendence, expansion, and liberation. Sometimes a person experiences *regression in the service of transcendence*, under the influence of the Dynamic Ground. Periods of difficulty can occur—stages of withdrawal, alienation, guilt, disillusionment.(97) As the ego comes into contact with the energetic potentials of the non-egoic sphere, one may experience catharsis, strange bodily sensations or movements, or emergence of difficult feelings. Sometimes this occurs during intense Pluto transits. When the Dynamic Ground awakens—spontaneously, or as a consequence of practicing yoga, breathwork, drumming, meditation, or entheogenic journeys—it breaks into the field of awareness as a presence that is numinous, awe-inspiring, ineffable, entrancing, and transporting. This reawakening of the Dynamic Ground challenges the ego's sovereignty. We encounter a power stronger than ourselves that's gravitationally and magnetically attractive. In a process Washburn calls *regeneration in spirit*, this autonomous evolutionary power is roused and begins to purge everything inhibiting its free movement and unfolding. This begins a process of transformation whereby the personality is spiritualized and becomes an unobstructed vehicle of spirit.(99)

What does this actually look like in real life? I look at Sonia, our distressed professor, as an example of someone undergoing a phase of regression that's ultimately in the service of transcendence and rebirth. In the next chapter I'll detail further stages of Sonia's spiritual awakening, referring to the yoga of Kashmir Shaivism, which describes the unfolding of dormant powers. I'll explain several yogic principles that can be useful in transpersonal chart interpretation and process work.

Planetary symbolism informs us about the challenges of evolution beyond the rings of Saturn toward the stations of consciousness represented by Uranus, Neptune, and Pluto. The clear light of astrological symbolism counteracts the fears and uncertainties inevitably faced on this path. As Rudhyar observed at the beginning of this chapter, inwardly-consecrated individuals allow spirit to become "the positive factor" directing the life and infusing the personality with the light of a supramental source. Transpersonal astrology is a guide through a multitude of transformations that prepare us to become refined instruments through whom the wholeness of life can act.

Chapter 5

The Six Shaktis

TO GUIDE A PERSON SUCH AS SONIA THROUGH A PERIOD OF TRANSFORMATION, I find it helpful to draw upon religious, philosophical, or mystical doctrines to inform the study of the birth chart. There are many maps of the process of spiritual awakening that could be suitable, such as the Ox-herding pictures of Zen Buddhism; teachings of Jewish, Christian, or Islamic (Sufi) mysticism; Native American teachings such as awareness of "All My Relations." I believe each practitioner can approach planetary symbolism in the light of whatever teachings give meaning and focus to their own spiritual journeys.

This chapter describes a model based on what Rudhyar called "the six *shaktis*." According to Rudhyar, the path of transformation may be conceptualized as a process of gaining mastery of six shaktis—six faculties that enable a person to respond as a stable center of consciousness, able to use power in alignment with a spiritual or transpersonal purpose.(100) The brief discussion of the six shaktis in his book, *An Astrological Mandala*, is highly evocative, however Rudhyar wasn't fully informed about the origins of these concepts, and his understanding was based solely on the writings of an early twentieth century Indian philosopher named Subba Row. In fact, the six shaktis are derived from the teachings of Kashmir Shaivism, a yogic philosophy and lineage in which I was initiated by Swami Muktananda. In this chapter, I combine astrology with Kashmir Shaivism as a framework for moving through a spiritual emergence crisis. I use these principles to delineate themes in development that reach beyond the level of psychological self-knowledge and social adaptation—in other words, post-conventional levels of development. What I'm proposing here is that to truly understand the instinctual evolutionary drives signified by the outer planets we need a different kind of psychology, a spiritual psychology of liberation. That's what I'll attempt to articulate in this chapter.

This discussion suggests one way of applying astrology at the transpersonal level. I can easily imagine other models, based on Zen or Tibetan Buddhist doctrines, Sufism, Theosophy, Kabbalah, Native American and other indigenous teachings, or any other map of spiritual awakening that can be applied to chart interpretation. I invite readers to use their own creativity in formulating new approaches to transpersonal astrology.

Kashmir Shaivism is a philosophy and set of practices developed by yogis in Kashmir and Northern India between the eighth and twelfth centuries, C.E.(101) Shaivism can be distinguished from the Vedanta philosophy that Brahman transcends the phenomenal world, which is unreal, an illusion, *maya*. Shaivism holds that all phenomena are manifestations of universal consciousness (Shiva), not an illusion. All creation—all of this that surrounds us at this moment—is the vibration and emanation of Shiva, the inbreath and outbreath of Shiva. Kashmir Shaivism envisions that the Supreme Source of all that is, *Shiva*, exists in a condition of eternal, self-existent consciousness, bliss, and tranquility. For sport and amusement, Shiva manifests countless forms and universes through the agency of his creative aspect—his shakti, also called *citi* or *cit* (consciousness). A subtle vibration or ripple appears in the divine stillness, giving rise to subsidiary powers (shaktis) and the stages of material evolution. This spontaneous movement within the divine Being is termed *parashakti*. It can be compared to a wave movement within the stillness of infinite waters. It is the cosmic creative principle. Parashakti brings about the concealment and cloaking of Shiva's eternal presence within the realms of visible manifestation. *Cit* contracts itself into material forms. The one becomes many. This is what Washburn calls primal repression. Instead of knowing ourselves to be infinite Shiva, we become identified with individuality, the limited mind and body, and thus we live our lives estranged from Shiva, the transcendent, dynamic ground of existence. The mind becomes occupied with perceiving, naming, imagining, remembering, and acting upon infinitely varied forms and objects within this manifest world of duality. But eventually we yearn for return to the primordial state of Shiva, which remains eternally present and available; and through *parashakti's* capacity for *bestowal of grace*, the concealed energy of supreme Consciousness (Shiva) eventually reawakens in an experience of spontaneous Self-recognition, called *pratyabhijna*. Pluto signifies the power of Shiva's resurgent evolutionary drive to unfold within us, to shed all limitations, to return to Self-awareness, a state of nonduality.

Parashakti refers to the subjectivity of Shiva, the feeling of *being all existence*, the all-pervading source. It expresses as the cosmic principle of *spanda*, expansion, the vibration or movement of an ecstatic, self-regenerating consciousness. Spanda is the internal-ization and externalization of consciousness, the eternal dance of waxing and waning cycles in all forms. Shiva is *anuttara*, the fundamental reality underneath the whole universe, present in all manifestation. Every object, act, and perception is filled with nondual being-consciousness-bliss. Everything is vibrating Shiva, Shiva's emanation, throbbing and pulsating. The term *spanda* describes the expansive quality of divine consciousness. At this very moment, in this very place, Shiva is blissfully expanding and contracting, breathing inward and outward, waxing and waning. Shaivism is a life-affirming yoga and doesn't require negating the senses or transcending the world. It involves tuning the senses to the presence of Shiva in all forms, sounds, tastes, smells, and sensations, as well as in imaginal, visionary, and mystical states of consciousness.

Shiva's parashakti creates material universes and also makes possible Shiva's reawakening as infinite consciousness. *Parashakti* operates through the mediation of five derivative shaktis: *maitrikashakti*, the power of letters and language, giving rise to myriad forms and objects; *ichchashakti*, the power of will through which creation occurs and through which a yogi's consciousness is reestablished in its own blissfulness and stillness; *jnanashakti*, the power of mind to transcend conceptual thought in true knowledge—the power of consciousness to detach from objects of perception and imagination, becoming aware of itself *as awareness*; and *kriyashakti*, the power of manifestation of forms. Finally, the concealed power of Shiva Consciousness manifests through unfolding the coiled energy of *kundalinishakti*.

My own understanding, combining the original meaning of these terms with interpretations given by Rudhyar,(102) is that *parashakti* represents spontaneous movement of the supreme Spirit, which initiates physical, emotional, and energetic purification and renewal. *Jnanashakti* is the power of knowledge and cyclical wisdom. *Ichchashakti* is the power of desire and focused will. *Maitrikashakti* is the power of language to facilitate communication, creative self-expression, and spiritual liberation through the subtle, vibrational language of *mantra*. *Kriyashakti* is the capacity to act in accordance with imagined goals or visualized images. And *kundalinishakti* is the evolutionary power that brings our individual consciousness into alignment with a transpersonal energy source and a transpersonal will. Now I'll explain how Sonia's transformation can be understood as an unfolding of the six shaktis, which initiate the process of regeneration in spirit.

Para Shakti: Physical and Emotional Purification

Psychospiritual transformations often begin with activation of *parashakti* as a result of intensive yoga practice, meditation, fasting, or through *shaktipat* initiation by a spiritual master (see Chapter 9). *Para-shakti-pata*, descent of the power of the divine, initiates purification of the physical, emotional, mental, and subtle energetic bodies, preparing the individual to become a radiant, unimpeded vehicle for expression of the power of the whole.

On the spiritual path it's important to cleanse the physical body and liberate it from obstructions through exercise, consistently healthy diet, and practices that increase strength, flexibility, and alignment, such as hatha yoga. This doesn't mean adhering to any particular practice or discipline or having extraordinary athletic capacities; it means doing what we can to exercise and liberate the body so it becomes an open channel for free flow of the life force. This facilitates strengthening of vital energy, awakening of *kundalinishakti*, the power of expansion of consciousness. *Parashakti* can activate spontaneous movements of the physical or subtle bodies—swaying, trembling, assuming yogic postures, or feeling energy pulsate and flow through the *chakras*. Let's more closely examine the manifestations of the six shaktis, using Sonia's story to illustrate.

Sonia needed to improve her physical condition to further her spiritual journey. She sought renewed physical health by taking hatha yoga classes and preparing more balanced meals (transiting Chiron in the sixth). With Pluto square natal Pluto she eliminated a lot of toxins through moderate fasting, colon cleanses, and blood purifying herbs prescribed by a naturopath. She discovered she had parasites and eradicated them with medications prescribed by her doctor. She felt her physical body becoming a more refined instrument of light (transiting Saturn-Neptune square Neptune).

Inner awakening typically stirs emotional catharsis, sometimes involving states of fear, resentment, and negativity. This often coincides with transits or progressions contacting natal Moon, the planet of emotional memory. The transit of Uranus to Sonia's natal Moon precipitated a remembrance of early traumas and upsets. That transit, combined with Pluto square natal Mars-Pluto, brought to the surface some highly charged memories of childhood abuse, the origin of lifelong conflicts. The conjunction of Mars, Saturn, and Pluto in her seventh house symbolized an emotional complex about power and injury in relationships. This contributed to her marital struggles because whenever her husband became angry it was very traumatic for her. I felt that she needed to change her experience of the fiery energies of Mars-Pluto, to increase her feeling of strength, power, and assertiveness so she wouldn't feel that she was always subjected to the aggression emanating from others (seventh-house planets). This could help her stay present in the midst of marital conflict without inwardly collapsing.

In addition, Saturn and Neptune were transiting in Sonia's twelfth house, a transit that often brings into focus the unresolved issues of an entire cycle of life that is now coming to a close—which for Sonia meant her tenure-track career. This was traditionally considered the house of endings, karma, and confinement. The period of Saturn's transit through the twelfth house can be a period of uncertainty, dissolution of identity, letting go of the past, as well as reaping the karmic results of our past actions. This can be a time of fascination with mysteries, mysticism, and meditation. It marks the end of a cycle and the gestation of a new cycle. Sometimes there's a crisis due to the falling away of outer goals and former ambitions. Intense material can surface from the unconscious in dream images and narratives, which vividly portray central themes, conflicts, and complexes and show paths to liberation of one's creative potentials. A wise person is prepared to receive this material, writing down any and all dreams and working them through as an integrative internal yoga. I explain this in abundant detail in *Dreamwork and Self-Healing*.

Saturn transiting in the twelfth house can illuminate karmic and archetypal forces shaping present life experience, and tasks that need to be accomplished during the upcoming cycle. This is the time to live a *symbolic life*, discovering the archetypal, mythic dimensions of one's present circumstances. At this time, Sonia had several dreams featuring violent imagery and unpleasant male characters who reminded Sonia of her father. These dream images were consistent with natal Mars-Saturn-Pluto in the seventh house. It became apparent that her present marital struggles tapped into the feelings of a difficult father complex (Mars and Pluto conjunct Saturn: anger at the father). It was important for Sonia to make space within herself to relate consciously with the powerful archetypal forces in her seventh house, including Mars, the feisty warrior, and also Pluto, representing uneasy power dynamics, but also her own untapped power. We talked about the mythic abduction of innocent Persephone by Pluto-Hades. Sonia expressed how all her life she'd suppressed fury stirred in response to experiences of physical and emotional domination (Pluto-Mars). Sonia became deeply involved in the process of clearing her body and psyche of these feelings and memories.

Jnana Shakti: The Power of Knowledge and Eonic Wisdom

Connecting the poles of the individual and the spiritual source results in monumental changes in the person's mind and cognitive state, giving rise to new ways of knowing. *Jnanashakti*, the power of mind and knowledge, represents the evolution of our cognitive faculties. First and foremost, Jnanashakti is the power of consciousness to apprehend its own nature and to experience Self-recognition. Jnanashakti is expressed through cognitive activities such as perception, memory, anticipation, and rational thought, and higher mental faculties such as telepathy, precognition, clairvoyance, and telekinesis. Jnanashakti takes the form of what we now call *multiple intelligences*, which flow through linguistic, mathematical, spatial, musical, emotional-interpersonal, bodily-kinesthetic, and intrapersonal forms of knowing, existential intelligence, as well as mythic-archetypal intelligence and mystical, nondual cognition. Jnanashakti also refers to a holistic, spiritual mode of knowing that Rudhyar calls the "mind of wholeness," which perceives every entity as part of larger wholes, and every event as a meaningful phase of a cycle. In a passage cited earlier, Rudhyar stated that the mind is a consecrated place in which spirit and matter can unite. He wrote, "A factor existing within the human psyche beside the mind has somehow to act directly upon the mind, or to serve as a hidden gate through which 'inspirations' of a spiritual nature may enter and gradually transform the mind." (103) In this chapter I'm attempting to describe the nature of this transpersonal factor operating within the psyche.

To move gracefully through this tumultuous period, Sonia needed to detach from the critical inner voice of her father, who condemned her path of interior search as misguided and irresponsible. Natal Mars and Pluto conjunct Saturn signified a harsh and aggressive internal father. She saw that some of her marital problems stemmed from directing her belligerent attacks against her husband; these were ways she'd learned to respond to her father. Becoming aware of these parental introjects and negative thoughts and beliefs, we set out to deliberately construct a more positive cognitive and attitudinal frame through the practice of affirmations: *I am finding my true Self. I am living in accord with my highest nature. I am beautiful and worthy. I deserve this time to find myself.* Sonia realized that one period of her life had to end before a new period could begin (Pluto square Pluto: closure and endings). Her identity and her role as a professor hadn't allowed full expression of her creative potentials. One evolutionary cycle was complete and a new cycle of activity was about to begin, when Saturn transited over her Ascendant, a transit that marks clarification of identity and objectives. The Ascendant is the point of self-awareness and self-determination; it's the cosmic Reset point in the horoscope, a fresh new beginning. During one session, Sonia's anxiety lifted and her face radiated peace as she recognized that this chaotic period was a meaningful phase of transformation.

Ichcha Shakti: The Power of the Will

Ichchashakti bestows the power of focused application of will. *Ichcha*, a term deriving from the Sanskrit verb *ichchh*, meaning to wish or desire, implies the capacity to mold our experience and our reality through the power of intention. There's a place for Neptunian surrender and yielding to a greater will, but it's easy to use this as an excuse for passivity and lack of motivation. Ichchashakti is conscious expression of our personal will, so we become vehicles for a multitude of energies to move through us. At this stage, we're in accord with the process that's unfolding in our lives in exquisite harmony with the celestial evolutionary tapestry.

Sonia realized she wasn't a helpless victim of circumstances in her career and marriage, and that her actions and choices were powerful forces shaping the course of her life. Cultivating a feeling of self-efficacy, I asked her to focus on crafting herself into the image of her personal ideals. One expression of this was that Sonia became determined to experience deep meditation, fulfilling the potential of transiting Saturn and Neptune in the twelfth house square natal Neptune.

In Shaivism, Jnana and iccha shaktis play a crucial role in inner yoga, as the basis of concentrating and absorbing the mind into pure consciousness. Knowledge of the ultimate reality comes through *shambovapaya*, the practice of emptying one's mind completely of all thoughts. It's also called *nirvikalpayoga* because no *vikalpa* (a mental idea with name and form) emerges in it. The mind is kept completely motionless and calm, yet awake. This experience materializes by one's strong will and thus is called *ichhopaya* or *ichha yoga* by the great Shaivite guru, Abhinavagupta.(104) The individual consciousness, by its free will, merges into universal consciousness so that one is in alignment with the source. Liberation is attained by concentration on the consciousness in between the inbreath and outbreath.

To reach this state, one silently intones mantras such as *Shivo'ham* (*I am Shiva*), or *So'ham*, which means *I am That. I am consciousness.* A method I was taught by Swami Muktananda is to mingle the mantra *So'Ham* with the inbreath and outbreath. Sometimes he taught us to reverse the sounds, forming the mantra *Hamsa*. They are one and the same, interchangeable. By this method the meditator's breath becomes shallow, refined, and barely wavers; the mind expands and is absorbed into *samadhi*.

Maitrika Shakti: The Modes of Creative Activity

According to Kashmir Shaivism (and Hindu Tantrism in general), creation occurs through the power of sound vibration rippling through the eternal silence and stillness of Shiva. This initial sound or movement of the creative force, *citshakti*, evolves into letters, syllables, and words that generate innumerable material forms and linguistically describe them. The creative, emanating power of language is *maitrikashakti*, which forms the basis of *mantra yoga*, the use of sound vibrations to induce meditation and the stillness of pure Shiva consciousness.(105)

Maitrikashakti is a means of vibrational attunement to the spiritual realms and a vehicle to turn the mind inward in meditation; it's also a vehicle for creative evolution. An individual in transformation who wields maitrikashakti (the power of letters and speech) through various artistic or literary expressions can exert a resonant impact on the world. Rudhyar taught that spirituality is more than inward enlightenment and peaceful meditation; it's a dynamic life of *transpersonal activity* and intentional creative acts.

Rudhyar distinguished several levels of creative activity, each with a distinct purpose: *aesthetic art*, which celebrates the traditions, symbols, and institutions of one's culture; *romantic art*, which celebrates the emotional expression of the individual artist; *catabolic art*, an expression of rebellion or protest against the established social order; and *hierophanic art*, which reveals new possibilities for the future of a culture or social group.(106) In Rudhyar's view, periods of historical crisis, such as our own, call forth *hierophanic creativity*—the "conscious release of power" through the personality. Hierophanic creativity reveals new myths, new conceptions, new visions of the future and of the way through planetary and social upheavals, as expressed through innovations in business, the arts, science, and education, or in any other field of life and work.

I told Sonia I thought creativity could be a key to her transformation. As a child she wrote sonnets and felt pleased with her mastery of this form. In her teens and young adulthood she was an aspiring bohemian poet who publicly read urgent, incendiary writings at cafes and political rallies (Moon-Uranus in Gemini in the fifth house: literary creativity). Having thus experienced the aesthetic, romantic, and catabolic levels of artistic expression, Sonia put aside poetry and returned to graduate school for her doctorate. Now, years later, she felt enlivened as her submerged creativity reawakened, as Uranus transited opposite her fifth-house Moon. She brought to my office some new tempestuous poetry featuring descriptions of betrayal and violation (Pluto square natal Pluto) and relating these personal experiences to humanity's mistreatment of the Earth. The poems were of more than personal significance.

While transiting Uranus was conjunct Venus (planet of art and beauty), Sonia also began painting and drawing mandalas depicting the changing state of her inner world and the renewal she envisioned. These paintings were an aid in mythologizing her current transition, transforming it into a sacred passage. Sonia used this artistic medium to communicate her story to others (Uranus opposite Moon in Gemini). The paintings conveyed images referring to current social issues, especially those concerning the rights, health, and dignity of women (Moon). These creative activities were essential in Sonia's emergence from a period of crisis.

Kriya Shakti: Action Transformed Through Visualization

Energized by the power of the will, mental images can exert a formative influence on our lives. According to Rudhyar, *kriya shakti* is the power to reorient and evolve our consciousness based on a visualized image or archetype to which we become committed with a deep "feeling-urge." The practice of shaping personal reality through conscious use of mental imagery has been utilized for millennia. Ancient shamans used images perceived in altered states of consciousness to bring about healing of individuals and communities, (107) and many mystical traditions emphasize visualization practices. It's also well known that hypnotic imagery can be utilized to bring about therapeutic changes in behavior, attitude, and personality (108). Modern athletes, actors, musicians, and public speakers use mental imagery for performance rehearsal, mentally walking through their performance movements and their quality of embodiment.(109)

Shakti Gawain outlined "four basic steps for effective creative visualization":

> 1. Set your goal. . . . 2. Create a clear idea or picture. . . of the object or situation exactly as you want it. You should think of it in the present tense as already existing the way you want it to be. . . . 3. Focus on it often. . . . 4. Give it positive energy. . . . Think about [your goal] in a positive, encouraging way. Make strong, positive statements to yourself that it exists, that it has come or is now coming to you. See yourself receiving or achieving it.(110)

Visualization is a process of envisioning goals and organizing our efforts around internal images. I first used mental imagery years ago when I was experiencing conflict and poor communication with my father. A counselor advised me to visualize his higher Self and to see us reconciled and expressing ourselves to each other with love and mutual understanding. After several weeks of doing this exercise, there was a noticeable improvement in our communication. These changes were sustained over time, becoming permanent features of our relationship, which became very close.

I find it useful to visualize being calm in front of an audience, which helps me when giving talks or performing music in public. My body remembers the feeling of groundedness and centeredness, which aids me while I talk or play music.

One client manifested a new job; he visualized it, made himself ready for it, and took steps to find it. I know people who have lost significant weight and sustained the weight loss after envisioning a slimmed-down form and taking consistent steps to manifest it.

Visualization is the basis of Tibetan Buddhist *guru yoga*, the invocation and meditation on the Guru, the embodiment of wholeness and perfection. We visualize our spiritual ideal and merge into this being's Consciousness. I describe this practice and its effects in my book, *In the Company of Sages*.(111)

At each stage of our life journey, astrological symbolism allows us to envision the next stage of evolution, so this ideal can become "an irrefutable reality for the consciousness and a steady, indestructible commitment."(112) I asked Sonia to envision a new identity emerging from her current crisis, a teacher illuminated by her voyage to the interior of the psyche, and now able to teach others from a deeper, wiser perspective.

At her core, Sonia was still a person with Sun-Jupiter conjunction in Sagittarius; there was little doubt she'd continue to be a scholar and educator. Sonia began to form images of herself as a creative individual working in several intellectual and artistic disciplines. She felt she'd benefit from more travel and adventure, so she asked her husband to accompany her on a group pilgrimage and tour of sacred sites (Venus in Sagittarius in the eleventh house: harmonious travel in a group). These enlivening mental images guided the next stage of her development, but there were still obstacles and internal impediments to work through; she needed to definitively confront her shadows.

Sonia began to recognize some of her limitations as a person—her anger, arrogance, and condescending attitude; her tendency to manipulate others through her sexual attractiveness, and her imposing intellect. She felt remorse for things she'd done that had been injurious to others (Pluto square natal Pluto in seventh house). Inspired by her studies of Buddhism, she actively cultivated compassion, lovingkindness, and *bodhicitta*, a desire to assist others and relieve suffering. This is the kind of person she now aspired to be. She asked friends and colleagues to forgive her for past actions and expressed her willingness to support them in their own transitions and changes. While at times she continued to argue with her husband, increasingly she forgave him, acknowledging her own mistakes and imperfections. In this way, she came to embody the ideal she visualized.

Sonia became immersed in studies of mythology, art, and anthropology, and made plans to teach again, with a different scholarly and spiritual focus. Sonia was transformed from a materialistic and almost entirely intellectual person into one who exuded a serene and loving presence. Eventually, a few years later when Saturn entered Pisces and squared her natal Sun-Jupiter, Sonia took a job at a smaller, less prestigious and less pressured college where she resumed her teaching career but also continued pursuing her artistic and spiritual interests.

Kundalini Shakti, Self-Consecration, and Transpersonal Activity

Seekers on the spiritual path advance through an internal transformation that Rudhyar calls *self-consecration to the whole*—self-offering to the universe, to a greater purpose or task. Self-consecration opens the individual to a larger field of existence, which can manifest as *kundalinishakti*. Kundalini, the "serpent power," is a powerful energy that emerges from a dormant state at the base of the spine and rises toward the crown of the head. An inner force catalyzes powerful bodily movements and streams of energy in the *chakras* (energy centers), removing blockages in the physical and subtle bodies. Kundalini is described in the yogic traditions of India and Tibet, and in Chinese Taoist mysticism. There are allusions to it in European alchemy, accounts of Christian and

Sufi contemplatives, among African !Kung tribesmen, and in descriptions of shamanic experience.(113)

Dr. Lee Sannella, founder of the Kundalini Clinic, hypothesized that kundalini is the manifestation of a physiological mechanism leading to a series of psycho-physical symptoms:

> Such physical sensations as itching, fluttering, tingling, intense heat and cold, photisms (perceptions of inner lights) and the perception of primary sounds, as well as the occurrence of spasms and contortions, seem to be "archetypal" features of the process. . . . It is this universality that leads me to postulate that all psychospiritual practices activate the same basic process, and this process has a definite physiological basis.(114)

Sannella contends that kundalini awakening is due to activation of an energy current in the brain that causes these symptoms. But, he says, the physiological mechanism by which it operates doesn't explain "the meaningfulness of the kundalini experience itself," especially its emotional components, which can range from confusion and depression to ecstasy and "superlucidity."(115)

Mary Scott explained the deeper significance of kundalini, describing it as a "cosmic force" that "guides evolution from within as well as from above" (116). She notes "kundalini's connection with terrestrial currents," viewing it as the microcosmic aspect of the same energy that flows through the geomagnetically sensitive "ley lines" along the earth's surface.(117) She calls kundalini "a force in nature which can connive at the evolution of the ego and then, in due time, facilitate its transcendence."(118)

Beyond the physiological and evolutionary significance that Sannella and Scott attribute to this phenomenon, the subjective experience of kundalini suggests yet another level of meaning: Experiences of kundalini are accompanied by a sense of confronting an autonomous power with its own intention. Once we make an internal shift beyond egoic motivations, offering up the instruments of personality in the service of a greater wholeness, then a spiritual force awakens and begins to guide our actions. This spiritual power, the serpent power, carries a transpersonal intention. Rudhyar called kundalini a principle of *coordination* between the individual and the universe.(119). The awakening of kundalini energies reorients our individual will, actions, and intentions so we achieve alignment with the will of a greater existence. The spiritual power of the whole reveals itself to us, seeks to be embodied through us, and becomes the "guiding field" of the personality. With the feeling and attitude of self-consecration, we offer ourselves as the conscious agent of a transpersonal purpose:

> When the individualized "mind of wholeness" apprehends the archetype which is his or her guiding field and begins to resonate to the spiritual Quality of his or her innermost beingness, then individual freedom can only mean choosing the best way to actualize this archetype. In this sense, the truly "liberated" person is consciously and willingly determined by his or her archetype. Freedom and determinism merge.(120)

While transiting Pluto was square her natal Mars and Pluto, as she meditated more intensely, Sonia became aware of a surging force streaming inside her body and she realized this was the same creative energy that existed in all dimensions of the universe. She longed for this energy to evolve within her. Sonia's inner work, guided by astrological symbolism, moved her through crucial stages of physical, emotional, and relational transformation. She strengthened her will, purified her body, and aligned herself with visualized ideals. She surrendered inwardly, becoming self-consecrated, willingly determined by her archetypal structure and increasingly dedicated to service and creativity. She was committed to becoming an instrument and conveyer of the Light. In some respects, she ended up in the same place where she began, as a university professor, but internally, atitudinally, and spiritually, Sonia was completely changed.

From Karma to Dharma

Rudhyar taught that the universe calls forth the birth of each person for a reason, as an answer to a need of humanity.(121) In transpersonal chart interpretation, we try to imagine the collective need to which our individual birth was a potential response. Studying the archetypal symbolism of the birth chart, we discern images of our *dharma* or life path, and achieve alignment with the needs of a larger whole, becoming agents through whom this greater whole can act:

> The human receiver acts as a focalizing agent for the need of his people and his culture. Though he or she may be unaware of it, the entire inner being of such an agent takes the form of a "prayer" of the Pleroma—the greater planetary whole operating at a higher level of the hierarchy of being. . . . The transpersonal action or communication answers not only a personal need, but, even more, the need of the community.(122)

Study of the birth chart reveals the purpose for which the individual's birth was called forth. It also illuminates the nature and timing of crises, which are occasions for *transmuting karma into dharma*. The transpersonal life is a sacred performance of the purpose with which we were invested at birth.(123) The next section of this book examines the lives of some exceptional individuals who transmuted karma into dharma, who transcended cultural conditioning and responded effectively to collective needs and the dictates of Spirit.

To sum up, Rudhyar taught that astrology can guide us into a life of hierophanic creative acts inspired by a more-than-personal purpose. Approached from a transpersonal perspective, astrology can help us proceed through the ordeals of physical, emotional, mental, and spiritual preparation for an awakened, self-consecrated life. Whereas the purpose of astrology at the humanistic level is to aid our fulfillment as individuals, the goal of transpersonal astrology is to transform personal problems by referring them to a new purpose: the opening to an infusion and descent of supramental forces.

Part III

Astrological Biographies of Spiritual Teachers

Now we'll study a series of astrological biographies of well known spiritual teachers. These are intended to demonstrate astrology in action through detailed chart interpretations. They also provide examples of the kinds of tests we're likely to face on the path of transformation. These studies vary in length and breadth. For example, the chapter on Rajneesh focuses on one brief but significant period of his life, while the analysis of Tagore's birth chart is very detailed and finely woven, allowing us to appreciate an extraordinary, multi-faceted life exemplifying the principles of transpersonal activity.

As we turn our attention to these famous lives I'm not suggesting that any of these individuals was spotless. Many of them are known to have shadows and character flaws. Eliade was accused of being politically aligned with fascism in his native Romania. Muktananda and Kriyananda had problems with sex scandals. Rajneesh was accused of financial misdeeds and was getting high on nitrous oxide and hoarding Rolex watches and a fleet of Rolls Royce sedans. Nobody is perfect. Here I choose to focus on their positive contributions to humanity, lessons from their lives that can inspire our own spiritual journeys.

A few words are necessary about my approach to chart interpretation. In these studies I emphasize the basics of astrology. I make occasional references to midpoints and to interplanetary cycles, for example the transiting conjunction, squares, and opposition of Jupiter and Saturn. However, I don't discuss minor aspects (such as quintile, septile, and novile), or the asteroids. Nor do I refer to the New Moon Before Birth, harmonics, solar arc directions, Uranian methods, or heliocentric charts. Some students of Rudhyar's work may note that my interpretations aren't based predominantly on techniques that he emphasized, such as the use of Sabian Symbols and the Progressed Lunation Cycle. I also don't examine elemental emphasis or triplicities because I personally don't find these useful.

Our understanding of these charts could undoubtedly be enhanced by utilizing any of these methods and perspectives. However I've intentionally chosen not to do so, for I believe that in our eagerness to learn and utilize as many techniques as possible, many students of astrology are unable to give coherent interpretations of the most basic factors in a birth chart. Thus, I focus on the fundamentals of astrology: zodiacal signs, house placements, dispositorships, and major aspects of natal planets, transits, and secondary progressions. These studies demonstrate how much depth of understanding is available when we dwell with basic horoscope symbols fully, interpreting them within the context of the transformational process.

Each astrologer follows an idiosyncratic method of interpreting a birth chart. Thus I emphasize certain features of these charts and have inevitably omitted features that others might find important. No astrologer can interpret all of the information contained in any horoscope. Noting those details I've neglected to mention, I hope you'll be inspired to fill in any gaps and develop your own understanding of each chart presented. And by all means, look up the Sabian Symbols for the Sun, Moon, and other important degrees of each chart, study midpoints, harmonic charts, and Solar Returns, or use whatever other method that works for you that supplements my analysis. Our goal here is to savor the beautiful connections between biographical events and planetary symbolism. This is how astrology comes alive.

Finally, while one may feel humbled when studying the biographies of great individuals, it's important not to judge oneself harshly in comparison to them. The key is to learn from their stories, to be inspired by them, and then to live one's own life fully. Each of us has to develop our own skills, our own spiritual qualities; we have our own tests to pass through. It's our consciousness of purpose in each stage that forms our character and shapes our becoming. Each of the individuals we're about to study had a singular *dharma* or path to Wholeness. Studying their lives can help us find our own path.

Chapter 6

An Astrological Biography of Meher Baba

THIS CHAPTER EXAMINES THE LIFE OF MEHER BABA, a great spiritual teacher of modern India, in relation to his birth chart. I consulted Hopkinson and Hopkinson's book, *Much Silence*, for biographical information.(124)

Meher Baba was born with a prominent Pluto-Neptune conjunction in the fifth house. The Aquarius Ascendant and Venus in Aquarius square Uranus on the Midheaven, suggesting someone striving to become a being of love (Venus in first house), and that he might be somewhat unusual or eccentric. Meher Baba did many things that surprised, baffled, and shocked the public. He also had a revolutionary quality that fits the Uranus-Aquarius emphasis. This was mainly expressed through a kind of social work project to which he became committed, as we'll see later. While he was mostly a mystical, Neptunian visionary, Uranus also gave him a commitment to social betterment. With Ascendant ruler Uranus elevated, culminating in the chart, this was the chart of a person who was quite unique and known for unpredictability, controversy, or for shaking things up in his environment. Later we'll note several examples of Meher Baba's tendency to suddenly and radically change everything in his life.

With Uranus squaring Venus in Aquarius, he wasn't drawn toward an ordinary social life. Venus retrograde often symbolizes an interiorization of social energies. It doesn't mean that the person doesn't get along well with others; but it suggests that one's fundamental social orientation goes against the conventional grain. A person with Venus retrograde has to define unique values or needs with respect to social interaction and personal tastes. In keeping with his Uranus square Venus, Meher Baba never married or had any interest in conventional social relationships.

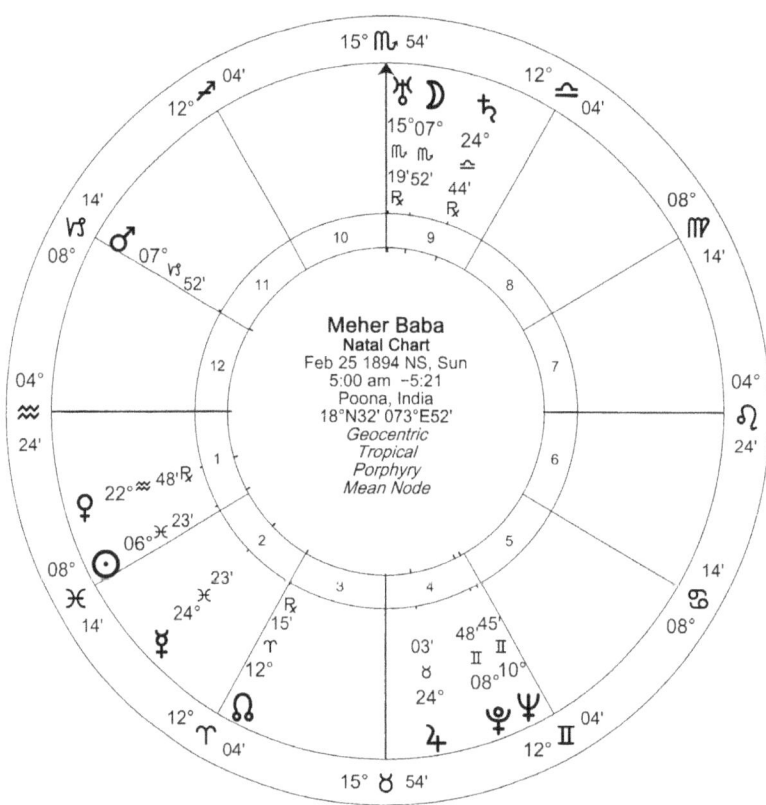

Note his Sun in Pisces at the second house cusp, square to its ruler, Neptune, which is conjunct Pluto. Also, Mars is in the twelfth house, the most interior zone of the chart, the area associated with Pisces and generically governed by Neptune. The second-house Pisces Sun is the symbol of someone who felt called to practical expression of his compassion. He took on responsibility for alleviating other people's suffering through very concrete, material forms of service. It also symbolized an attitude of nonattachment with regard to money. With the Sun square Neptune-Pluto in the fifth house, he projected himself as an embodiment of God, a mystic, a seer, a sage, or a holy man. Meher Baba openly proclaimed that he was the Avatar of the age, the "God-man."

Sun square Pluto and Neptune is a major aspect that needs further examination. Any close aspect of the Sun is significant, but it's especially important when the Sun is aspecting its own ruler, Neptune. Here there's an identification with the circuit of energies symbolized by the Pluto-Neptune conjunction, which coincided historically with breakthroughs in electronics, quantum physics, x-rays, new communication technologies, psychoanalysis, and the growth of an international, global kind of awareness. With Pluto-Neptune square his Sun, Meher Baba became a person who was a vehicle for the spread of a transformational social and spiritual vision.(125)

Sun square Neptune-Pluto signifies a dedication to higher ideals such as service and the relief of suffering. Pluto conjunct Neptune represented a powerful compassion and devotion to service of the greater whole, which Rudhyar and Sri Aurobindo called self-consecration. Having a Pisces Sun while Pluto is conjunct Neptune implies the potential for self-surrender, self-sacrifice, awakening of visionary capacities, and expansion of consciousness.

With Pluto-Neptune square his Sun, Meher Baba had a strong urge toward self-renewal, to undergo a transformation of awareness. This aspect generated charismatic energy, a concentrated intensity that he utilized in service of others. With Sun in Pisces square Pluto and Neptune, this was the chart of someone with the potential to become an illumined mystic, a servant of humanity, a spiritually awakened person, a man of power and influence. It could also mean that his consciousness was going to be infused with a higher force or presence, perhaps experiencing dissolution of ego boundaries and spiritual death and rebirth. Meher Baba lived out all these themes most dramatically.

In addition to having Pisces Sun squaring Neptune, Meher Baba also had natal Mars in the twelfth house, the realm of transcendence through introspection, meditation, solitude, retreat, or monasticism. In the twelfth house, self-transcendence is also lived through altruistic activity, which was important to Meher Baba. With Mars in the twelfth house, he focused a lot of energy toward solitude and meditation. Mars wasn't expressed outwardly through sexuality, and his vital energy was directed solely to the quest for spiritual life. This is an evolved expression of a twelfth-house placement of Mars.

Mars was square to the Moon's nodal axis and sextile to both the Sun and Moon. In fact, Mars was exactly conjunct the Sun-Moon midpoint. In addition, his Moon was in Scorpio. The strength of Mars in the chart and the Scorpio Moon symbolizes his great power and charisma. Scorpio can signify sexual energy, but it also represents shakti, the force of kundalini, and a vibrational magnetism that draws people to you and impacts them.

Natal Mercury in Pisces suggested that he'd speak softly or sensitively. Eventually Meher Baba took a vow of silence for many years. He relinquished the function of speech, and communicated through a mysterious, subtle inner language. He felt that by shutting off his words, his transforming influence could be more effectively conveyed to others. Communicating without words fits the symbolism of Mercury in Pisces perfectly.

A Sudden Awakening

In 1911, Meher Baba began college. He had many friends and was known for his love of poetry, especially the writings of Hafiz, a renowned Sufi devotional poet, a great mystic. At that time, transiting Saturn was conjunct natal Jupiter and square natal Venus, which fits his social popularity, his love of poetry, and his literary interests (Jupiter). His Venus was expressed less through personal love and more through love of God.

In May 1913, he met Hazrat Babajan, an elderly and extremely unusual guru, who lived by herself underneath a tree. A lot of people apparently thought that she was crazy, while many other people revered her as a mystic of the highest order. As transiting Uranus crossed his Ascendant, Meher Baba met her, and she kissed him on the forehead. This was the beginning of a long relationship with this woman, who was one of his two main teachers. She had a tremendous impact on him and after meeting her his whole life changed. He lost interest in everything except God and became deeply drawn into the spiritual life. In January 1914, she blessed him and he experienced electric shocks moving through his body, a sign of *kundalini* awakening. He soon entered a state of trance and complete disinterest from the world for nine months. My understanding is that he didn't eat at all during this period. I don't know whether or not other people fed him, as was the case with the young Ramana Maharshi, who was kept alive for months by devotees. Meher Baba had no impulse at all to eat. He was completely "out there." Several transits occurring at that time suggest that a profound reorientation of consciousness was occurring: Transiting Saturn was conjunct his natal Pluto-Neptune; his potential for an awakened state was tapped, his ego-centered awareness was eclipsed, and he was absorbed in the Light, in higher consciousness. He wasn't of this world during this period.

Transiting Uranus was square his Moon as well as conjunct his Ascendant. The square to his Scorpio Moon in the ninth house suggests the sudden, penetrating, electrifying contact with this female guru, who was also like a mother to him. With transiting Uranus on his Ascendant, he was acting strangely from the viewpoint of observers. His parents thought that he'd gone mad because he was acting in what seemed to be an irresponsible manner (Uranus), not working, just sitting in samadhi all the time. Transiting Neptune was forming a square to natal Saturn, which can symbolize loss of control, loss of focus, loss of identity, dissolution of ego boundaries, and acting in what appears to be a delusional fashion. In fact, he was having a mystical experience, in keeping with Neptune's influence. Throughout 1914, as Pluto was sesquiquadrate to natal Uranus in his tenth house, he developed a reputation as a somewhat unusual, strange person. Clearly he didn't seem suited for a conventional profession or career. Medical treatment had no effect on his condition, and it was said that he suffered acutely at this time.

Saturn was sesquiquadrate to natal Uranus, and transiting Uranus passed over his Ascendant for the final time. The coordinated activity of transiting Saturn, Uranus, Neptune, and Pluto combined to bring about a complete change in his personality, his state of consciousness, his life-orientation, and his position in the world. Such is the nature of those crisis periods when major transits of the outer planets coincide.

In December 1915, he visited another great sage named Upasni Maharaj, who greeted him by flinging a stone at his forehead. It's curious that the woman had kissed his forehead and that Upasni threw a stone at his forehead. Perhaps that was a manifestation of the natal square between Mars (which rules the head) and the Moon's Nodes. He began to visit Upasni, as well as Hazrat Babajan, and in 1916 he began to take some odd jobs. He was 22 years old and was starting to work a little bit, presumably getting out of his state of *samadhi*, and trying to figure out what to do.

He'd work, sit with Hazrat Babajan, and visit a temple called The Tower of Silence. At this time, transiting Uranus was conjunct natal Venus. His main relationship was with this odd woman, who was considered an outcast. Apparently she refused to move from underneath her tree and her devotees built an ashram right around where she sat. For him to have an unusual relationship with an eccentric, older woman was in accordance with his Venus in Aquarius square Uranus, then being activated by transiting Uranus. During his period of close contact with this mystic teacher, transiting Neptune was conjunct his Descendant.

In *Memories, Dreams, and Reflections*, Jung described his confrontation with the collective unconscious, during which he was flooded with prophetic dreams and symbolic material. This occurred while transiting Neptune was conjunct Jung's Descendant and near his natal Sun. Similarly, Meher Baba was experiencing divine consciousness, which was awakened in him by the blessing of Hazrat Babajan.

A Transmission of Power

In July 1921, he spent six months with Upasni Maharaj, undergoing training with this great sage. Upasni Maharaj proclaimed Meher Baba a Satguru and an Avatar—a guru with a special mission to assist humanity's evolution during a particular historical period—at the age of 27. At that time, transiting Neptune was square Uranus, transiting Uranus was conjunct his natal Sun and square to Pluto-Neptune, and there was a Jupiter-Saturn conjunction in his eighth house, opposite natal Mercury. According to Alexander Ruperti, the Jupiter-Saturn conjunction represents formation of a new sense of "social destiny."(126) Meher Baba's social destiny for the entire twenty-year period of that Jupiter-Saturn cycle centered around receiving spiritual energy from his teacher and having a great impact on others. This point deserves further explanation.

The eighth house refers to those circumstances in which two persons meet deeply and intimately through a close business association, sexual relationship, or, in this case, the mutual commitment of guru and disciple. Through the contact of their respective boundaries, a spark ignites that can transform both individuals involved. Traditionally this eighth-house process was conceptualized in terms of the confusing notion of "occult power"; whereas it can be more easily understood in terms of the conflicts of will and the purification of interpersonal motives—to control, dominate, or manipulate—that emerge whenever two people attempt to fuse their wills and energies for a common purpose.

The transiting Jupiter-Saturn conjunction in Meher Baba's eighth house may be a symbol of his being called to receive and to offer to others the transmission of spiritual energy known as *shaktipat*. He had a transforming influence on others through the inner power with which he'd been invested by his teacher. Upasni wasn't just proclaiming him a teacher; he was also passing on to him the power of his lineage. The eighth house is concerned with making relationships productive through a merging of wills and energies. Here it's experienced as a transmission of energy, consciousness, and authority from one awakened soul to another, the kindling of the flame of the heart. Upasni Maharaj set Meher Baba on fire and then sent him forth into the world as a living fire in his own right.

During a significant eighth house transit, we might experience a kindling through a sexual relationship. Or we might change our attitude or orientation through committment to a business partnership in which our tendencies toward dominance or manipulation are exposed and purified. In a myriad of ways, power is generated in the eighth house through interpersonal transaction. It will be experienced differently depending on the level of consciousness at which the person is operating. Here it's operating at quite an evolved level.

Because Uranus is both his Ascendant ruler and placed near his Midheaven in the tenth house, the transit of Uranus to his natal Sun had great importance. Meher Baba was blessed with this recognition, this spiritual investiture, this proclamation that he was a sanctified person with a unique mission, path, and destiny. All of this was proclaimed and acknowledged by Upasni Maharaj. As often occurs during Uranus transits, this event happened suddenly, unexpectedly, and was relatively unprecedented. It's not typical to be proclaimed a living Avatar by a great guru. As it contacted his Sun, Uranus also activated the Pluto-Neptune conjunction, so his identity as a great mystic, saint, and spiritual teacher was awakened and confirmed.

Austerities

Subsequently, in 1922, Meher Baba spent five months in retreat, living in a hut. He soon began to gather disciples around him, and in May 1922 he moved to Bombay to found an ashram. He underwent rigorous discipline and also imposed it on his followers. Transiting Pluto was sesquiquadrate Venus, signifying Meher Baba's magnetic influence, which drew people to him after the announcement of his avatorhood by Upasni. In May 1922 there was a Full Moon right across his Midheaven-Nadir axis. This kind of transit can affect a person's public standing or bring about some kind of notoriety, if there are other major transits operating at the same time. Transits occur in a hierarchy. A Full Moon across your Midheaven might not mean much unless other major transits are underway, for which the Full Moon acts as a trigger. That's how it operated here. This Full Moon changed his position in the world and allowed him to come more fully into public view. It also saw him establishing a new foundation or base (fourth house/Nadir) for his work.

Let's look at the rigorous discipline for a moment. To fulfill his potential for evolution into a higher state of consciousness Meher Baba had to strip himself completely bare. With natal Neptune-Pluto square the Sun, it wasn't difficult for him to relinquish worldly attachments, to eat very little, and to meditate a great deal. His natural orientation was to flow inward and upward toward the Source. He didn't want to be encumbered by worldly activities or by food. With Sun square Neptune-Pluto, he was drawn toward solitude and retreat, spending long periods alone in a hut.

In March 1923, he embarked upon a time of traveling and austerities for himself and his followers. Transiting Jupiter was conjunct the Midheaven, while transiting Pluto was conjunct his sixth house cusp and opposite natal Mars in the twelfth. This was the beginning of a long period of spiritual practices, fasting, little sleep, and intense meditation. The sixth house is a realm of self-purification through discipline, through following practices of any kind. Transiting Pluto opposite Mars in the twelfth symbolized energetic pursuit of the inner quest. With Pluto on the sixth house cusp, he changed his habits and his diet. He also began to lead others along a similar path right into the heart of spiritual life and the inner kingdom through these kinds of disciplines.

In March 1924, Meher Baba founded his second ashram in Meherabad. He ate once every week or two and lived the rest of the time on liquids. This was during his Saturn Return. With Saturn in the ninth house (education), he created a new teaching institution that solidified his stature as a teacher. During his Saturn Return, he felt compelled to create the form and structure of this new ashram. He also became aware of social realities in a new way and began to get involved with community service and education projects. This also occurred while transiting Jupiter was in his eleventh house of social awareness.

Silence

On July 10, 1925, Meher Baba went into silence, giving no indication that this silence would, in fact, last for the rest of his life. Uranus was conjunct natal Mercury, and Meher Baba became known for his odd practice of not speaking. Natal Mercury is in a Yod or Finger of God pattern with Saturn and Jupiter, suggesting a desire to communicate his wisdom through restraint of speech. Under the transit of Uranus to Mercury, Meher Baba did something one wouldn't expect from a great spiritual master who is supposed to give discourses and teach people: He stopped talking and began to write on a little blackboard. He'd put his hands to his lips as if to say, "Shh. Listen to the inner truth."

Another surprising event occurred on October 26, 1925 when he announced the closing of the ashram. Transiting Mars was on his Nadir that day and transiting Saturn was conjunct natal Uranus. He initiated changes and acted unpredictably in public, baffling everyone. He created a big upheaval around him and no one could figure out what he was doing.

Saturn was conjunct his Midheaven in late 1925 and into 1926. On his birthday in February 1926, twenty thousand people came for his *darshan*, literally to have a look at him. His stature as a spiritual master was evident at this point. He was proclaimed the Avatar in 1921. But in 1926, he was getting public recognition, and his reputation became firmly established while transiting Saturn was conjunct the Midheaven. At the same time, transiting Neptune was opposite natal Venus, which elicited an outpouring of the boundless love for which he was noted. In addition, Meher Baba's progressed Sun had moved from the natal square to Pluto-Neptune to sextile those same planets; this lasted from 1926 until 1929 and symbolized the culmination of his spiritual awakening and expansion of consciousness.

In 1930, he became ill while transiting Saturn was conjunct Mars in his twelfth house. Then, in 1931, he embarked upon several years of travel in the West, where he met many people and mingled with the masses. Transiting Neptune was opposite natal Sun, square natal Pluto-Neptune, signifying the widening of his circle of influence as a spiritual master, and being surrounded by an aura of holiness and mystery. This transit also symbolized his mystical, liberating influence on others.

Serving the Masts

In 1935 and 1936, Saturn was conjunct Meher Baba's natal Sun, a transit that corresponded to the beginning of his work in India with the *masts*, a class of socially marginal outcasts who seemed a little crazy, but whom he viewed as evolved beings. They're distinguished from *sadhus*, the wandering mendicants and yogis, because they're dissociated and withdrawn. Western psychologists would diagnose masts as schizoidal or schizophrenic as they're unable to communicate with others for the most part. Some of them are catatonic. They were considered insane, cast out of ordinary social affairs, and no one paid much attention to them. Most of them would wander around aimlessly, like some street people in American cities today. However in India they were also known as "God-intoxicated mad-men" (and probably mad-women, too). There were tens of thousands of these people in India at that time.

In 1936, with Saturn conjunct his second-house Sun, Meher Baba felt a commitment to working with and serving these people. The theme of self-sacrifice and dedication to the welfare of others was evident as Meher Baba now embodied some of the qualities associated with Pisces, Neptune, and the twelfth house. He spent years serving the masts, washing them, feeding them, communicating with them silently, honoring them, and giving them money. As transiting Saturn activated his Pisces Sun square Pluto-Neptune, all of his personal resources were directed toward service and healing. He became selfless.

The New Life

In 1949, an incredible series of events unfolded. First, Meher Baba went into what was called "The Great Seclusion," in which he gave away everything he owned. Then on October 16, 1949, he proclaimed "The New Life." This was perhaps the most astonishing event in his life. Meher Baba had thousands of followers and a huge ashram. No one had the slightest inkling of what was about to happen. He announced the closing of the ashram (again!) and the entire operation was to be shut down immediately. Everything was to be given away to the poor. Everyone would have to leave. Then he said, in effect: "Those of you who are my real disciples will henceforth enter the New Life with me. This means that we'll wander together as companions, depending only on God for our every need, for our food and our shelter. We will own nothing, and we'll travel without knowing where we're going or where we'll stay." Here we see his second-house Sun in Pisces manifesting. He gave everyone about one day to decide whether or not they'd leave the world with him. Within a few days, his thousands of followers had been reduced to about twenty people. He was challenging his followers to make a profound commitment that would transform their lives. He asked for complete surrender and renunciation without desire.

He and these twenty or so followers began to wander around with no possessions, begging for food. They underwent great sufferings, poverty, and deprivations. During this time, he didn't allow others to view him as a guru, but rather insisted upon being treated as a "companion." He didn't allow others to show him signs of respect, and he washed and served the poorest of the poor. The group members loved and served one another, living in a state of "complete hopelessness and helplessness." Hopelessness and helplessness relates to the symbolism of Pluto-Neptune square Sun in Pisces: letting go completely, dying for no reason. Meher Baba taught them to practice *manonash*, "the annihilation the mind into love." It was said that the ordeals that New Life participants underwent weren't tests, but were ends in themselves. This way of complete surrender, service, dependency on God, the Great Spirit, this was the New Life.

Saturn was just past the square to natal Pluto-Neptune and opposite natal Sun, again bringing into focus themes of selflessness, divine-consciousness, and self-consecration. Transiting Pluto was square natal Uranus and Meher Baba's Midheaven: he was disrupting the lives of many people and profoundly impacting them. He himself was also undergoing a death and rebirth and emerging in a completely new role. Transiting Uranus was opposite natal Mars in the twelfth house, showing a sudden intensity of yearning for God, renunciation, inner life, and complete surrender. Transiting Uranus in the sixth house led him to teach a new spiritual discipline: manonash, annihilating the mind into love, a sixth house discipline undertaken to achieve twelfth house liberation.

During that time, transiting Uranus was conjunct the Venus-Uranus midpoint, especially significant since the planets are square to each other natally. This symbolized the "companionship" and group living of the New Life. That transit activated love for his circle of companions, his community of love, an apt expression of Venus in Aquarius. Thus, when Uranus—an important planet in his natal chart, associated with so many unpredictable actions in his life—transited his twelfth-house Mars, he took this shocking new direction, which took everyone by surprise.

Skipping ahead to 1951, Meher Baba went into seclusion again while transiting Neptune was sesquiquadrate his Sun. On May 24, 1952, he had a car accident. Transiting Saturn was on his sixth house cusp, opposite Mars, a transit that manifested as a car crash and an injury (Mars), hospitalization (twelfth house), and health issues (sixth house). Neptune was still sesquiquadrate his natal Sun, which suggests themes of being convalescent, weak, and unable to move.

The Avatar

In September 1953, during his second Saturn Return, Meher Baba proclaimed himself the Avatar of the modern era. With natal Saturn in his ninth house, he felt compelled at this time to announce his mission as a teacher, with confidence and authority. This is just after Jupiter's transit conjunct natal Pluto-Neptune. Interestingly, the notable event didn't occur until after the exact aspect of Jupiter was over. One possible explanation is that his sense of divinity was reconfirmed to him during the exact transit of Jupiter over Pluto-Neptune and that only subsequently did he announce this publicly. The Jupiter transit awakened an awareness of his destiny, causing him to openly proclaim his avatarhood and his commitment to service of the masts, and ultimately all of humanity. According to Rudhyar, avataric beings reveal to others an emergent spiritual quality that becomes the model for action in a future cycle of a culture. I think Meher Baba's avatarhood can best be understood in terms of his demonstration of the spiritual quality of compassionate service.

Meher Baba had another car accident in December of 1956, after which he imposed a new suffering on himself by refusing medical treatment. Transiting Saturn was square his Pisces Sun, so he became a suffering servant or savior and underwent a form of self-imposed martyrdom. At this time, he demanded total love, obedience, and acceptance of himself as the Avatar from his followers. His demand that others acknowledge his divine identity corresponded to Saturn's transit square the natal Sun and opposite Pluto-Neptune. In addition, Uranus was conjunct the Descendant and square his Moon. He was acting in an unusual way, changing his relationships with others (no longer just acting like a "companion"), inviting others to perceive his unique manifestation of magnetic spiritual power (Uranus in Scorpio).

In May and June of 1960, he gave darshan to ten thousand people per day while Uranus squared his Midheaven. Transiting Neptune was conjunct his Moon, and he no doubt had a euphoric, uplifting sway over the masses. He may have been in a mystic mood of compassion and generosity of spirit. This transit symbolized a magical air in the life, an expanded emotional outpouring, and warm nurturance of others.

In 1961–1963, Meher Baba passed through a period of seclusion, solitude, disinterest in the world, and inner silence. He also underwent a great deal of physical suffering. Transiting Saturn was in his twelfth house, an apt symbol for a period of retreat, withdrawal, and inner detachment. Pluto was opposite natal Sun and square Pluto-Neptune, bringing out even more deeply his state of spiritual intoxication. This could be the essence of his life's work: to achieve and maintain this total absorption in the Source, to rest in that state where awareness of the self has passed away and only the fullness of God remains.

In 1969, Meher Baba's last major darshans were planned. Transiting Saturn was conjunct natal Venus, and he urged many people to visit him on a certain day that he promised would be an important occasion. Tens of thousands of people arrived, and that was the day he left his body.

Chapter 7

An Astrological Biography of Bhagwan Rajneesh (Osho)

IN THIS CHAPTER, WE EXAMINE THE BIRTH CHART OF BHAGWAN RAJNEESH, a controversial spiritual teacher who inspired devotion from some quarters and animosity from others. We'll focus on one critical period of his life, November 1985, when Rajneesh was suddenly expelled from the United States after pleading guilty to federal immigration law violations. In the aftermath of that deportation, the community of Rajneeshpuram in Antelope, Oregon disbanded. I was saddened by the demise of that community and by Rajneesh's death, for while I disagree with some of his actions and ideas, I'm sympathetic to aspects of his teaching and to the unique spiritual and cultural experiment that his communities represented.

Rajneesh's natal Sun is in Sagittarius on the Descendant, in a Grand Trine with Uranus and Jupiter. Sun trine Jupiter symbolizes his understanding of philosophical issues and the fact that he was a great teacher. Before becoming a guru, Rajneesh was a philosophy professor at the University of Jabalpur in India. The aspects of Uranus with Sun and Jupiter symbolize the originality of his philosophy and teachings, and his unusual vision of the future and of a new approach to spiritual life. Also note the T-Square between Moon-Saturn in the eighth house, Uranus in the eleventh house and Pluto in the second house. Attempting an initial synthesis of the planets and houses involved, this pattern seems to signify important issues regarding finances and concentrations of wealth (Pluto in the second house), feelings stirred by working relationships with others (Moon-Saturn in the eighth house), and his involvement in groups, communities, and living experiments (Uranus in eleventh house).

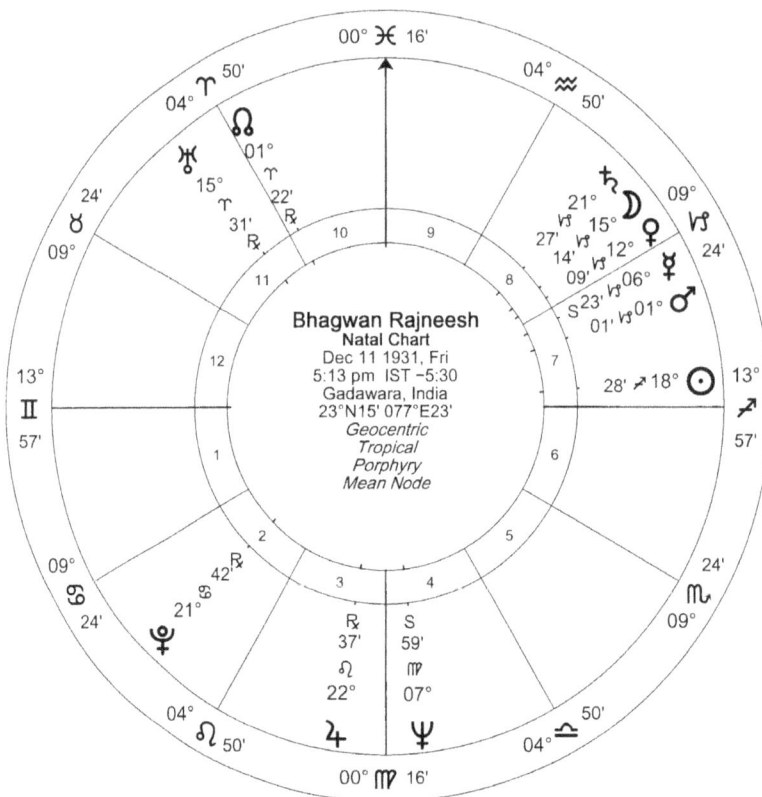

This combination also signifies that Rajneesh was a radical figure, an iconoclast, a breaker of traditions. With Uranus at the apex of his T-Square and square Saturn and Moon, Rajneesh often questioned and opposed authority and tradition. He was famous for outraging devout Hindus. The priests and established institutional, religious people in India disliked him because he challenged their authority, criticizing the anti-life and anti-sexual attitudes implicit in the teachings of most religions and spiritual teachers. He was a profoundly rebellious person with a passion for questioning old doctrines and attempting to create new ones, and with a penchant for confronting taboos and inhibitions. He challenged the repression of aggressive and sexual impulses, and his communities are famous for the space they give for free expression of these energies. He reinterpreted the teachings of world religions and articulated the nature of the spiritual path in a highly innovative way. Rajneesh was truly a revolutionary figure.

Rajneesh also had problems because of his tendency to confront authority, symbolized by Uranus square Saturn. This became particularly obvious with the establishment of the Rajneeshpuram community. Uranus is a strong planet in his chart as it's trine to the Sun and Jupiter and also the focus point for the dynamic tension of the Saturn-Pluto opposition. One of the other main themes in his life was that he always wanted to build a community (Uranus in the eleventh). He inspired his followers to try to create a new world at Rajneeshpuram. But his unwillingness to operate within the bounds of propriety backfired in Oregon. The neighbors of the community were very Saturnian, traditional people, many of them "born again" and not very receptive to New Age ideals or lifestyles. They felt that they were treated with disdain and disrespect by members of the Rajneesh community and they responded in kind. These neighbors were upset by the sudden influx of thousands of unusual, uranian, orange-clad people to their vicinity. And they were put off by Rajneesh's brash, confrontational style, especially as this was communicated by Anand Sheela, Rajneesh's lieutenant. Just as had occurred in India a few years earlier, the local people exerted great pressure on Rajneesh to leave Oregon.

At the time Rajneeshpuram was founded, in 1981 and 1982, Saturn was transiting through Libra along with Pluto. Saturn was opposite his natal Uranus and square both Pluto and natal Saturn. Thus Saturn was forming a Grand Cross with his natal T-Square, an important transit. During this time, all of the possibilities implicit in his T-Square came to fruition. The founding of the community was a major event in his life, and fulfilled his natal potential to generate wealth through soliciting financial contributions and the freely donated labor of others (Moon-Saturn in the eighth house) in order to sustain the growth of a progressive, controversial New Age community (Uranus in eleventh house). However, the experience at Rajneeshpuram was turbulent, and there were great tensions involved in constructing that community. Many of their neighbors mistrusted Rajneesh and his followers, and the antagonistic feelings were mutual.

Rajneesh had a Moon-Venus conjunction, trine Neptune, which gave him a capacity for compassion, warmth, and lovingness. The Mercury-Venus conjunction is the symbol of his melodious speaking style, as well as his skill in writing. But Rajneesh also had a strong Mars-Mercury conjunction in Capricorn, which gave him an acerbic tongue, sarcasm, a critical way of speaking, as well as a quick mind. He was very funny and often criticized other gurus in a vitriolic manner.

Note that Saturn is in its own sign, ruling the eighth house of his chart, and it's dispositor of Moon, Venus, Mercury, and Mars. This might indicate that he was an authoritative person who'd find it important to organize and manage things, to have a certain degree of control, and to provide leadership, especially in his eighth house working partnerships. However, in 1984-85, Neptune entered Capricorn and transited back and forth over Rajneesh's natal Mars. For a couple of years it appears that someone deceived him, particularly with respect to the movement's financial holdings and dealings (Moon and Saturn in the eighth house). In 1985, Uranus was also passing repeatedly over his Sun and Descendant: There were unexpected changes in his personal relationships and some of his followers rebelled against him, which took him largely by surprise.

Most importantly, his secretary, Anand Sheela, director of the community, his mouthpiece—one of the closest people in the world to him—betrayed him. If Rajneesh had been married, one might have expected some restructuring of his primary relationship, a breakup, or a divorce. In a sense that's exactly what happened. Rajneesh and Sheela got "divorced" from each other. She embezzled a bunch of his money, fled the United Staes, and denounced Rajneesh. This was very shocking and disruptive, especially since with his Sagittarius Sun in the seventh house he'd dedicated much of his teaching to demonstrating his wisdom about relationships.

With Neptune crossing over natal Mars, things got out of control. Perhaps he trusted other people too much, giving other people too much authority for dissemination of his work and administration of the community, instead of exercising it himself. When Neptune came along, Sheela appears to have used her authority in a deceitful manner. The disagreement between them involving the movement's financial holdings was murky and shrouded in lies.

Having two simultaneous transits of trans-Saturnian planets was enough to precipitate a major life crisis for Rajneesh. This can provide some perspective on the deep changes that we ourselves may have gone through or may be going through now during similar periods of multiple transits.

One would expect that, with all the negative publicity that Rajneesh received at this time, there would've been some important tenth house activity. Neptune, ruler of his tenth house, was associated with these difficult events as it transited over natal Mars. With this transit, he experienced dissolution of his community, his financial stability, and some of his charismatic aura. He lost much of his credibility in the eyes of the public. The community in Oregon disappeared practically overnight, eroded by Neptune like a sandcastle by the shore.

In the year or so before these events, Pluto was semi-square his Sun and conjunct his Vertex (an angle in the birth chart formed where the Prime Vertical intersects with the Ecliptic). This was a period of power struggles between Rajneesh and Sheela, as well as with his other associates. During the time of these Pluto transits, Rajneesh was faced with all sorts of animosities, as well as issues about control and the utilization of his power and influence.

An interesting point about Rajneesh's chart is that with natal Pluto in the second house, he was fascinated by (some might say obsessed with) possessions, wealth, Rolex watches, and expensive cars. Another reason why Rajneesh could never be a total ascetic, a celibate, or a renunciate, and why he initially became famous as the "sex guru," is that his chart featured Venus-Mars and Venus-Moon conjunctions. The conjunctions of Venus-Mars (despite its wide orb) and Moon-Venus make sensuality, love, Tantra, and sexuality central themes in his path and his teachings. With Venus and Mars trine Neptune, he was interested in the fusion of sex and spirituality, music, dance, and ecstasy.

Looking briefly at Rajneesh's progressed chart, two major aspects had formed during the turbulent period when his community disbanded and he was deported. First, Ascendant ruler Mercury had progressed to exact conjunction with progressed Saturn. This correlates with the fact that he'd been silent for several years, refraining from speaking. The progressed conjunction of Mercury and Saturn also heralded a change in Rajneesh's thinking. Imagine the circumstances: things were falling apart all around him. Perhaps he suddenly had to sober up and think realistically about the fact that he had to sell everything, leave the country, and pay the $500,000 fine that was levied against him. He needed to think seriously about the misappropriation of funds and criminal actions that some of his followers allegedly carried out—for example, attempting to poison the patrons of a restaurant or trying to illegally affect the outcome of local elections. Much of this may have happened without his awareness or consent. Now, however, he was faced with some very limiting, confining circumstances, and had to make concrete decisions about where to go from there. This couldn't have been an easy time. But this could be viewed as the beginning of a new evolutionary cycle for Rajneesh. For although he was an ecstatic mystic and philosopher, during this progressed Mercury-Saturn conjunction he now had to deal with planning and decision-making, because most of the people he'd depended upon in the past were gone.

This example has taught me to take more seriously the traditional astrological lore about the strength of the Ascendant ruler. Here the progressed conjunction of Rajneesh's Ascendant ruler, Mercury, with Saturn created a major change in his life, one requiring a more realistic, clear-minded perspective.

Rajneesh's progressed Sun was conjunct Mars in the ninth house at the time of these events. This might also relate to his numerous moves from country to country after he was deported from the United States (ninth house: foreign travel). Several other countries denied him asylum and pressured him to leave. The aspect was separating in 1985, so it had been developing for several years before his deportation. Note that Mars ruled his sixth house natally. Rajneesh was having a lot of health problems, and was in a wheelchair with back problems when he was deported; Mars sometimes manifests as pain, injuries, inflammation. Moreover, transiting Saturn was in the sixth house at the same time. Saturn in the sixth, plus the progressed Sun conjunct Mars, corresponded to considerable strain and difficulty regarding his health.

The progressed Sun conjunct Mars symbolizes the embattled climate of Rajneesh's world at that time. It was certainly a period of strife and discord. During this progressed aspect, things are generally not so calm, smooth, or loving in a person's life. One becomes more aggressive, volatile, impatient, and irritable, and one is faced with confrontational situations that evoke anger. Rajneesh encouraged his students to express their aggression in encounter groups. He didn't believe in trying to transcend our feelings and taught people to go deeply into anger and follow it to its source. The progressed Sun conjunct progressed Mars (which also ruled his eleventh house) symbolized the emergence of his own anger as a result of the problems and misunderstandings within his community. This progressed Sun-Mars conjunction was an incendiary aspect, symbolizing the hostility, friction, and battles that seemed to follow Rajneesh at every turn.

Between 1988 and the time of Rajneesh's death in 1990, Saturn, Uranus, and Neptune were all in Capricorn, transiting over his Capricorn planets. Because of the eighth house placement of these planets, he may have had much to learn about working with others to rebuild his community in India after his expulsion from the U.S. Rajneesh had complex financial dealings and in all likelihood he had to deal with creditors and seek out new sources of loans to revive his spiritual community, perhaps courting people of social position to help bankroll his operations (eighth house: money received from others). He may have also had to manage the resources solicited from others in a more disciplined way. And, in keeping with the traditional connection of the eighth house with death, when transiting Saturn came into conjunction with his eighth house natal Moon and the midpoints of Moon-Saturn and Moon-Pluto in early 1990, Rajneesh's health deteriorated until his death from a heart attack on January 19.

Chapter 8

An Astrological Biography of Mircea Eliade

MIRCEA ELIADE WAS A SPIRITUAL AND INTELLECTUAL GENIUS whose accomplishments in the fields of religion and philosophy rank among those of Jung, Rudhyar, and Aurobindo. In addition to being our foremost historian of religions, he was also a prolific novelist. His books on yoga, shamanism, alchemy, and myth are among the most profound scholarly studies of these subjects available. He also lived a most fascinating life. In this chapter I'll examine some events of his first twenty-six years described in volume one of his *Autobiography*(127). His birth data was published in a recent biography(128).

Eliade was born with Venus rising in Aquarius conjunct Chiron. Although it was several degrees above the Ascendant, using whole sign houses I interpret Venus as being placed in the first house. He was considered an attractive person, much sought after by others. He had a fairly exciting love life, featuring both wounding and healing experiences with women (Venus conjunct Chiron). Several of Eliade's relationships were unconventional, fitting Venus in Aquarius. Insofar as we view Venus as placed in the twelfth house, it signifies his love of solitude and contemplation as well as some secretive and mystical features of his relationships, including an experience of enlightenment through yogic sexual practices.

Like Meher Baba, Eliade had Sun in Pisces at the end of the first house, but also influencing the second house from the perspective of whole sign houses. Eliade's path wasn't to renounce physical attachments as Meher Baba did, but rather to earn his livelihood (second house) through involvement in the field of religious and mythic studies. With Sun conjunct Saturn, Eliade was a very serious person focused on professional achievements. By the age of thirty and his Saturn Return, Eliade had written

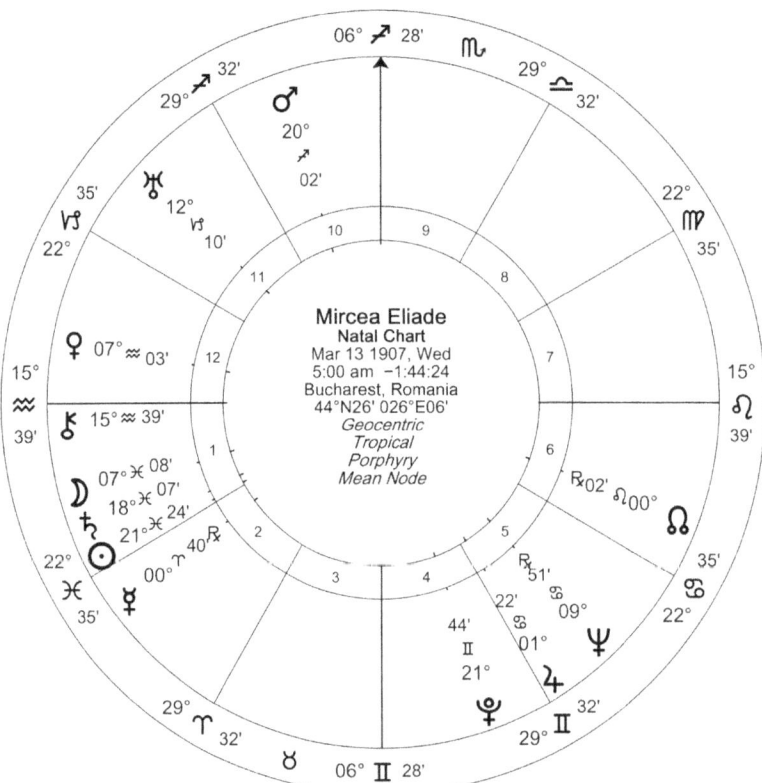

and published fifteen books, and had achieved widespread recognition in Europe as one of the foremost authorities in the study of myth, religion, and philosophy. The Sun-Saturn combination in Pisces symbolizes Eliade's methodical, disciplined exposition of mystical and religious doctrines and their deeper meaning. He studied all facets of world religions, utilizing a variety of historical, thematic, and cross-cultural methodologies. With Sun-Saturn in the second house along with Mercury, he supported himself as a professor of religions and established himself as an eminent researcher and professor in this field.

With natal Sun-Saturn square Pluto in Gemini, his inner life sought literary expression not only in scholarly writings but also in novels that seemed to erupt periodically from deep within himself. Somehow he found balance between his professional responsibilities as a scholar and professor of religions and the flow of his literary creativity (Sun-Saturn square fifth house Pluto in Gemini). Both endeavors were expressions of his piscean attunement to the worlds of myth, dreams, symbols, and religious mysteries.

An Astrological Biography of Mircea Eliade

Eliade spent most of his life reading and writing, and engaged in an active intellectual life. This is symbolized by the placement of Mercury, planet of writing and communication, in the second house closely square to Jupiter, Neptune, and Uranus. Jupiter gave his writings depth of philosophical understanding, Neptune attuned his thinking to religious concerns, and Uranus gave his ideas and writing style great originality.

Eliade's natal conjunction of Jupiter and Neptune (ruler of his Pisces Sun) symbolizes an interest in comprehending (Jupiter) spiritual or metaphysical (Neptune) truths and doctrines. Throughout his life, Eliade was focused on the Quest, the search for higher knowledge, liberatory wisdom, spiritual awakening, and direct spiritual experience. These planets placed in his fifth house signified his creative, intellectual output. He was a charismatic person who had many mysterious and seemingly other-worldly interests. Jupiter-Neptune in his fifth house signifies his identity as a mystic, one who wrote about esoteric knowledge, yoga, shamanism, and ancient religions, seeking to understand the mysteries of myth, symbols, and the human encounter with the sacred, an existence of a wholly other nature than the profane world. The fifth house emphasis suggests that creativity and expansive scholarship was his spiritual path. As Jupiter also ruled his Sagittarius Midheaven, the Jupiter-Neptune conjunction shows a person who embodies the archetype of the spiritual teacher or *pandit*. He wasn't exactly a guru, but he was a kind of spiritual teacher, sage, or wise man. Mars in Sagittarius in his tenth house also symbolized his identity as a scholar and intellectual, as well as an adventurous traveler.

In a revealing section in his autobiography, he says that he was often subject to fluctuations between an exalted opinion of himself and a megalomaniacal sense of failure. On the one hand he was full of a sense of his importance and great wisdom, and identified with the image of the Sage possessing all-encompassing knowledge. Eliade was a lucid scholar who reinterpreted world religions and developed a grand intellectual edifice. Jupiter-Neptune is an abundant fountain of ideas. Wisdom flowed through him. His books are brilliant and captivating. He also had unrealistic feelings of worthlessness and insignificance. These fluctuations in self-image were expressions of Jupiter-Neptune in the fifth house. Jupiter expands Neptune's tendency to make an individual feel exalted, expansive, uniquely illumined, even a bit inflated; it can also expand Neptune's tendency to erode or weaken a person's self-confidence. This combination signifies Eliade's desire to express himself in an inspired manner using the language of myth, symbols, and archetypes. Eliade spent his time absorbed in writing novels and books about myth, religion, and mysticism, and often seemed to others as if he were lost in another world altogether. Eliade utilized these Jupiter-Neptune energies productively, transforming his own personal experiences into interpretation of the deep structures of religious experience.

Early Years

In his autobiography Eliade states that from his youth he was engaged in prolific reading and writing. He read all the great novelists, poets, and philosophers of Europe during his teens and early twenties. He especially loved Dante, Goethe, Kant, and East European folk literature. He explored his cultural heritage and made it a part of himself. He was in love with learning, including natural sciences, anthropology, botany, and hermeneutics—the interpretation of religious and literary texts.

Eliade suffered from severe myopia as a youth, was extremely shy and awkward with girls, and frequently experienced melancholy moods. These traits relate directly to his Sun-Saturn conjunction: feeling shy, sad, socially inept, and very serious. With these two planets in Pisces he was quite withdrawn, absorbed in his studies of world religions. He was a sensitive young man, totally focused on his interior world of fantasy, fiction, imagination, mythology, and philosophy.

From his mid teens he began to systematically deprive himself of sleep. He periodically set his alarm back a few minutes earlier and slept progressively less and less so he could read through most of the night. Eventually he slept no more than four hours per night. This was an intense, Saturnian discipline. With Saturn in Pisces, it was an effort to structure and gain mastery over sleep.

Eliade had tremendous will power (Mars square Sun-Saturn) and his intellect was insatiable. He began to write and publish articles in his teens. At the age of 12 he started to do well in school and collected information on all kinds of subjects, such as plant morphology, entomology, evolution, chemistry, physics, the Orient, occult sciences, and philosophy. In the spring of 1921, he wrote and published his first article on entomology in "The Newspaper of Popular Sciences." Subsequently he entered a contest the publication was sponsoring, submitting a story called "How I found the Philosopher's Stone," about a chemist who falls asleep in his laboratory and has a dream about a chemist who shows him the philosopher's stone. This is fascinating because at the time he hadn't even heard of alchemy. However, later on he became fascinated by this subject and wrote many books about the alchemical symbols and practices of many cultures, most famously *The Forge and the Crucible*. Eliade's story won first prize in the contest and was published in the fall of 1921. He won some money and was asked to contribute regular articles to the magazine. For some time he wrote articles about entomology, until his interests changed. He was just fourteen years old at this time.

At the time of this event, there was a progressed Mercury-Saturn conjunction, signifying a period of serious study of mysterious, esoteric subjects (Mercury-Saturn in

Pisces). In addition, transiting Neptune was conjunct his Descendant and transiting Pluto was conjunct natal Neptune, apt transits for a dream revealing deep religious and symbolic insight. From the deep unconscious, Eliade was discovering new vision. There was also a Jupiter-Saturn conjunction in Virgo directly opposite Eliade's natal Sun, in his eighth house. This transit represented his immersion in piscean religious mysteries and the living symbolism of alchemy—an eighth-house process involving magic, power, and transformation. His interests would soon broaden to include the transformative practices of yoga and shamanism, archaic techniques of ecstasy.

Voyage to India

During his teens he became obsessed with India. This was back in the 1920s before the fascination with oriental cultures and religions was popular among westerners. Eliade read all the early studies of Indian mythology and philosophy that were being written by scholars such as Max Muller and he started to study Indian languages. In 1925, when Eliade was 18, his progressed Sun was square Neptune and progressed Neptune. This progressed aspect was within orb for most of the time he was in college; thus the whole period was tinged with the undercurrents of Sun-Neptune. The progressed Sun square Neptune represents a time when a person can experience opening to another level of perception, to a world of mystery, magic, mysticism, Spirit. It signifies an interest in spiritual, religious, or metaphysical realms. Eliade was a seeker of enlightenment and sacred knowledge and was absorbed in studies of religion, mysticism, and mythology. Neptune seeks expansion, spiritual liberation, moksa, nirvana. These subjects became Eliade's passion during this period of internal alignment with Neptune. Progressed Sun square Neptune symbolized a powerful spiritual awakening during this period of his life.

Eliade's exploration of the wisdom of the East began at the time of the progressed Full Moon at 7° Aries/Libra 58′, which closely squared natal Neptune. He experienced illumination of the purpose and direction of his life, focusing upon religious studies, the spiritual quest, sacred knowledge, and liberation. Progressed Moon aspecting the Sun-Neptune square acted as a trigger that brought these developments into vivid focus. The inner tide of his life was culminating through this Full Moon square Neptune.

Soon Eliade had exhausted all of the resources available to him in Romania for continuing his studies of Indian languages, philosophy, and culture. Then he got the idea of writing a letter to an Indian *maharajah* whom he'd heard was a philanthropist who'd helped other scholars pursue their work. Eliade asked for assistance in coming to India to study philosophy and Sanskrit. To his great surprise, the maharajah wrote back offering him a scholarship and introductions to some prominent people. He also received a scholarship from the government of Romania.

This was the beginning of one of the most important phases of Eliade's life, his sojourn in India, which lasted three years. He set sail on November 28, 1928. Nowadays such journeys aren't such a big deal. We simply get on an airplane and fly to India for a few months to study with our favorite guru, then fly back. In the 1920s, however, it was unheard of for a young man in Romania to leave home and go to live in the Far East. This is in keeping with the fact that at this time Eliade's progressed Sun was at 12° Aries 55', square to natal and progressed Uranus, an electrifying aspect. This progression symbolizes Eliade's individuation and his freedom from social convention and the opinions of others. He created his own archetype, the spiritual religious scholar pursuing the hermeneutics of the Sacred. Because Uranus was ruler of the Ascendant and Venus and placed in the natal twelfth house, the progressed Sun's contact to Uranus caused him to seek freedom from social norms and expectations regarding his personal identity (Ascendant), his unusual spiritual quest (Uranus in the twelfth house), and (as we'll soon see) romantic relationships (Venus in Aquarius). This progressed Sun-Uranus aspect manifested as a life path that was unusual, original, innovative, shocking, and unprecedented, according to the standards of his time. Going on this voyage was an act of destiny and individuation. By leaving Romania to go to India, Eliade sought the freedom to discover himself and develop his unique ideas on religion, spirituality, and yoga.

This illustrates what Rudhyar called the test of severance from the mindset of the collective. Eliade's commitment to an unusual, self-created life-project emphasizing religious studies came into focus while progressed Sun squared Neptune, then squared Uranus. Sun-Uranus signifies a reinvention of self and identity. Simultaneously, transiting Uranus was in Aries, squaring his natal opposition of Uranus and Neptune, between 1929 and 1931, corresponding to the period of Eliade's sojourn in India. This transit signified pursuing unusual religious and spiritual interests, and the potential for Eliade to have significant personal experience of yogic practices and higher states of consciousness.

Progressed Mercury was at 19° Pisces 04', near natal Sun-Saturn, an appropriate symbol for a period when Eliade was about to undertake a prodigious scholarly endeavor requiring incredibly strenuous and focused mental effort, described below. This significant progressed aspect of Mercury lasted for many years.

On the day he left Romania for India, transiting Mars was conjunct his Jupiter-Neptune, so he was in an ecstatic, euphoric mood, in a state of great excitement about his wondrous journey to this mysterious, magical country. Transiting Jupiter was square his nodal axis and Venus, and transiting Saturn was conjunct his Mars in Sagittarius, both symbolizing traveling across the world, one of the ultimate Sagittarian experiences. The progressed Moon was at 19° Sagittarius 10', also in his tenth house conjunct natal Mars, symbolizing a period of study and heroic adventure in a foreign culture. Transiting Saturn was also square natal Sun-Saturn and opposite Pluto. The activation of his natal T-square involving Sun, Saturn, Mars, and Pluto corresponds to a period of learning and becoming a great writer and scholar.

Transiting Uranus was conjunct Mercury at this time. This was an unconventional voyage involving unusual learning and studies. He was considered quite strange for going on this voyage, as his friends and family didn't understand what he was doing. Uranus was also square natal Jupiter, which gave the trip the quality of foreign travel as well as the emphasis on reading (Mercury) philosophical material (Jupiter). Uranus awakening his natal Mercury square Jupiter led to new kinds of reading and learning during this period.

When Eliade arrived in India he settled in at the home of the teacher whom the maharajah had arranged for him to meet. This teacher was Surendranath Dasgupta, the most esteemed scholar of religion and philosophy in modern India. He was a great pundit, author of a classic five volume history of Indian philosophy. He was an imposing figure, an intellectual giant. Eliade began a program of study with him that involved twelve to sixteen hours a day of learning Sanskrit and translating primary sources from the Hindu and Buddhist scriptures. Practically all he did was read and study Sanskrit. His progressed Mercury was stationary direct, conjunct natal Sun-Saturn. During this period, Eliade became mentally sharp, focused, disciplined, and productive, bringing out the best potentials of his Sun-Saturn conjunction. He was engaged in reading, learning, foreign languages, and translating, all focused on the piscean realms of Indian religion, philosophy, and mythology—an enormous task.

Then came a dramatic interlude. In 1929, Eliade fell in love with Dasgupta's daughter, Maitreyi, who was apparently both brilliant and quite beautiful, a poetess. They were attracted to each other but were rarely allowed to be alone. But at one point they were assigned the task of working on the index for Dasgupta's *History of Indian Philosophy*. As Eliade recounts the story, "One day our hands met over the little box of cards and we could not unclasp them."(129)

On September 18, however, Maitreyi sent Eliade a note saying that her father had found out about their love and that she'd confessed everything to him. The following day Dasgupta kicked Eliade out of his house and banished him forever. Think of what a blow this must have been, to be rejected by his guru and mentor! Apparently this was a pretty serious matter and Dasgupta took it as a matter of honor to punish Eliade for acting inappropriately.

At this time, there was a progressed trine between Venus and Jupiter, signifying an experience of falling in love. However, transiting Uranus was square natal Neptune, perhaps symbolizing a lapse in his judgment, but also a strange euphoria and the surfacing of their secretive, indescribable feelings for each other. He was romantically smitten with the young beauty, and she became the focus of his famous novel, *Maitreyi*. The relationship between them was also socially unacceptable, at least to Dasgupta, whether it was because of the differences in their nationality and cultural background or because Eliade didn't court her in a discrete manner. Uranus square Neptune also symbolizes a feeling of confusion Eliade may have felt, precipitated by his banishment from Dasgupta's home. He probably didn't know what had hit him. During Uranus square to Neptune, this romance ended up a complete mess, a calamity for the young scholar.

A Tantric Interlude

Eliade's natal Venus was conjunct the Ascendant and Moon's south node, semisquare Sun (showing popularity and attractive appearance). Venus in Aquarius was a symbol of relationships that were unconventional and a focus of some social controversy. Venus was quincunx Neptune, a symbol of exalted love and devotion, but it's also suggests that Eliade's love life could be somehow unsettling or subject to illusions, disappointments, and also transcendent urges. That brings us to the next remarkable episode.

After Eliade left Dasgupta's home in Calcutta, he traveled to Hardwar and Rishikesh in the Himalayas, seeking a hermitage where he could dedicate himself to yoga practices. He met Swami Shivananda and stayed in his ashram for some time. Then, around Christmas of 1929, a woman named Jenny arrived from South Africa to visit the ashram. Jenny was quite dedicated to the disciplined yogic lifestyle being practiced in the ashram, and often came to Eliade seeking spiritual guidance.

At one point, Shivananda left town for a while and Jenny came to see Eliade. They got involved in a discussion of Tantric Yoga, about which Eliade had been reading. He tried to avoid the subject, but she was insistent on finding out whatever he knew. Soon they began their own explorations of the practices of sexual yoga. This was strictly forbidden according to yogic tradition, for a guru was thought to be necessary to pursue these practices safely and fruitfully. For several weeks Eliade visited her frequently and they would make love through most of the night. He wrote:

> From then on I came late, after midnight, and returned to my kuitar an hour before dawn. I succeeded in preserving my lucidity and my self-control, not only in the "preliminary rituals," but also in all that followed.

> Jenny was astonished, but I sensed that I was on the road to becoming another man. Sometimes I only slept two or three hours a night, yet I was never tired. I worked all the time, and I worked better than ever before. I understood then the basis of all that vainglorious beatitude that some ascetics, masters of Hatha-yoga proclaim. I understood, too, the reason why certain yogis considered themselves to be like the gods, if not even superior to them, and why they talk about the transmutation and even the immortality of the body.(130)

Then the following incident occurred. Eliade lived in a hut next to another hut inhabited by a naga, an ascetic with matted hair.

> Upon returning to my hut one morning in March, I found my naga neighbor waiting for me in the doorway. "I know where you've been," he said as soon as we had entered the kuitar. "I believe you could be compared with Maha Bhairava! But do you have enough virya (energy) to proceed on this path? People of today are impure and weak. Very soon you will feel a strong fever in the crown of your head. You will know then that you do not have much time. It is better that you stop before this happens."
>
> He had spoken as clearly as he could, using whole clauses of Sanskrit so that I could understand him. I understood him.
>
> "But what if I find a Guru?" I asked.
>
> "You already have a Guru," he said smiling. Then he saluted me, bringing his palms together in front of his face and returned to his hut.(131)

In January 1930, when Eliade began his relationship with Jenny, there was a transiting Saturn-Mars-Venus conjunction between 2–5° of Capricorn, near the cusp of his twelfth house, and opposite his natal Jupiter-Neptune—symbolizing a secret (twelfth house) love affair and a sexual relationship (Venus-Mars) oriented toward mystical experiences and altered states of consciousness. Saturn conjunct Venus and Mars represented the self-control involved in their tantric lovemaking. Moreover, progressed Venus and Jupiter were still in an exact trine and progressed Mars was opposite natal Jupiter, symbolizing Eliade's experience of adventure, strength, and sexual prowess. This intense relationship, although it only lasted a short time, was a major event in Eliade's life; for this represented his most profound and direct personal experience of the ancient yogic teachings he had been studying.

Soon Eliade left the ashram and continued to travel throughout India gathering material for his doctoral thesis. He began to feel that he'd been mistaken in attempting to leave behind his own cultural heritage and retire to the life of an ascetic yogi:

> What I had tried to do—renounce my Western culture and seek a "home" or a "world" in an exotic spiritual universe—was equivalent in a sense to a premature renunciation of all my creative potentialities. I could not have been creative except by remaining in my world—which in the first place was the world of Romanian language and culture. And I had no right to renounce it until I had done my duty to it; that is, until I had exhausted my creative potential. . . . To believe that I could, at twenty-three, sacrifice history and culture for "the Absolute" was further proof that I had not understood India. My vocation was culture, not sainthood. I ought to have known that I had no right to "skip steps" and renounce cultural creativity except in the case of a special vocation—which I did not have. But of course I understood all this only later (132).

Return to Romania

Eliade's travels and studies were cut short suddenly by the notice that he was being recalled to Romania for military service. On Christmas Eve 1931 he arrived back in Romania after three years abroad. Let's think carefully for a moment about what had just happened to him. While transiting Uranus was square natal Uranus and Neptune, Eliade went on this incredible journey to the exotic land of India to study esoteric, mystical subjects.

The influence of trans-Saturnian planets like Neptune and Uranus can draw some people more or less permanently beyond the boundaries of Saturn into a transcendent realm or an unconventional lifestyle. But Eliade had natal Sun conjunct Saturn, so his dharma, his path, was to be a man of prominence and stature in the world. The force of gravity pulled him back to earth, deeper into his career and role as an academician, enjoying advancement at the socio-cultural level, signified by Saturn.

On the day Eliade arrived back in Romania (Christmas Eve 1931) there was a Full Moon at 2° Capricorn/Cancer 13', across his natal sixth and twelfth houses. Moreover, progressed Venus at 5° Pisces 40' was nearing conjunction to natal Moon, symbolizing a warm return to his family, friends, and homeland.

Upon his return home a number of things happened. First, he began to enjoy considerable professional success and notoriety. He wrote and published *Maitreyi*, which won him first prize in a major literary contest, and also caused a scandal; for it was a scarcely veiled description of his love affair with Dasgupta's daughter, written almost directly from his journal notes. This book made Eliade a famous writer. Transiting Neptune was opposite natal Moon in late 1931 and throughout 1932 when the book—one of his most imaginative, emotional, and inspired works—was conceived and written. Neptune opposite Moon stirred public feeling and controversy. In addition, transiting Pluto had moved from its natal square to the Sun to trine Eliade's Sun between 1931 and 1933, corresponding to growth in his public influence and prominence in the fields of literary fiction and religious studies (Sun in Pisces), and to his increased income (Sun in second house) upon returning to Romania. In April 1933 he won the literary prize for *Maitreyi*, which appeared in May and made him instantly famous. In June he also received his doctorate. Progressed Mars at 3° Capricorn 01' was opposite progressed Jupiter (3° Capricorn 38'), especially important because Jupiter ruled his tenth house (career). Moreover, as progressed Venus reached exact conjunction to natal Moon, Eliade soon became involved in another romantic adventure.

Two Women

In the spring of 1932, while transiting Saturn was nearing conjunction to his natal Venus and while transiting Jupiter was conjunct his Descendant, he met a woman named Sorana, with whom he soon became involved. She seemed an appropriate partner for him, as she was bright, beautiful, and from a family of high standing. However, Eliade soon became uncomfortable with her. He wrote:

> Sorana Topa was always with us. Accompanying her home, I would have to listen once again to her criticisms of the symposium—her criticisms of me in particular, if I had happened to have spoken that evening. Sometimes her observations were just and invaluable, but at other times they seemed irrelevant and pretentious. On the first of December, 1922, I concluded my military service and received my discharge papers. Now Sorana and I could spend more time together. This concentrated and prolonged intimacy was not always to my liking. For one thing, Sorana's presence was exhausting. With her it was always necessary to be unceasingly intelligent, profound, original—and above all, "spontaneous." Love, for her, was a constant "burning at white heat," as she liked to say.(133)

Transiting Saturn was conjunct Venus throughout the year, corresponding to their challenging relationship, which was marked by her criticism of him, his annoyance with her, and, perhaps, his desire to free himself from her. Then, around Christmas 1932, he met another woman, Nina, who captured his interest. This occurred while Saturn was passing for the second time over his natal Venus in Aquarius, the sign of freedom, experimentation, and non-normative behavior. In keeping with his aquarian Venus, he was involved with both women for many months. He tried to keep the secret from both of them, but eventually they found out, as did a number of his friends. This, too, became something of a scandal.

Today we may take polyamorous arrangements for granted, but the 1930s was a different era. This situation caused considerable tension for Eliade, for he knew things couldn't continue as they were; but he couldn't decide between Sorana and Nina. The following passage reveals his internal struggle, as well as the meaning he attributed to this experience:

> I sensed that the trials through which I was passing were pursuing an end that was for the time being indecipherable, but one that I did not despair of deciphering some day.... I had to acknowledge that... there was something I wanted very much: namely to be able to love—simultaneously and with the same intensity—two women.... I tried to make sense out of it by saying that I wanted to live a paradoxical experience... because I wished to attain to another mode of being than the one we are fated to live.... Even in adolescence I had tried to suppress normal behavior, had dreamed of radical transmutation of my mode of being.... Perhaps my yearning to love two women at the same time was none other than an episode in a long secret history.... In my way, I was trying to compensate for my fundamental incapacity of becoming a "saint" by resorting to a paradoxical, non-human experience.... (134)

His effort to conduct two relationships at once became a quest to attain a sacred, non-ordinary mode of existence.

Nina was considered quite unacceptable for a man of Eliade's stature by his friends and his family. They considered her to be beneath him, socially and intellectually. Her first marriage had ended in tragedy and divorce. No one could understand why someone so highly esteemed and successful as Eliade would be attracted to a poor, divorced woman. She was considered unworthy, especially when compared with someone like Sorana, a woman of high social standing. Yet Sorana aggravated him constantly, and he cared deeply about Nina. Between April and September, 1933, Eliade was tortured by this dilemma, vacillating between his affections for the two women, trying to deceive them, then filled with shame and remorse as the facts became known to both Nina and Sorana. His guilt was so great that he considered leaving the country forever to escape the situation.

Finally, after agonizing all summer, he broke off his relationship with Sorana and made a commitment to Nina in September 1933. He married Nina, to the consternation of his family. At the time of this crucial decision, progressed Venus was at 7°

Pisces 12', opposite the vertex. Transiting Saturn was conjunct natal Venus during this whole episode. Since Venus was in Aquarius, an energy that's at times shocking to mainstream social values, it's not surprising that Eliade was drawn to some relational experimentation and attracted to a woman of a different social class and background.

In going to India, Eliade made a crucial choice that involved defiance of the wishes of his family and the norms of society for the purpose of establishing a unique identity. While Saturn passed over Venus in Aquarius and stationed conjunct his Aquarius Ascendant (in September and October 1933), Eliade made another crucial choice. Eliade's decision to marry Nina was an act of courage, enabling him to break free of binding social conventions and follow a path that led to fulfillment of his individual path. He married the woman he truly loved, despite facing social disapproval and estrangement from his family.

Saturn's passage over Eliade's Aquarian Ascendant marked a moment of self-definition and autonomy. During Saturn's transit over his Venus and Ascendant in Aquarius, Eliade's choice of a marital partner was an occasion to will his own destiny. Thus, this event carries great spiritual significance.

Chapter 9

An Astrological Biography of Swami Muktananda

SWAMI MUKTANANDA WAS A BEING OF POWER AND WISDOM who inspired and guided countless seekers, kindling in them the longing for truth and illuminating the path to liberation. Thousands of people experienced spiritual awakenings through hearing his words, receiving his gaze, his touch, being in his presence. Many people reported having profound meditations while in his company. Others felt waves of joy, currents of kundalini energy in their bodies, or intense pressure at the top of their heads. My book *In the Company of Sages* recounts many stories of my experiences in his presence.

Muktananda's Birth Chart

Swami Muktananda was born with a Full Moon straddling the horizon of his birth chart, with Sun in Taurus on the Ascendant, and Moon in Scorpio on the Descendant. Taurus is the zodiacal phase of developing an appropriate relationship with the material world, whether this means enjoyment of money and physical comforts or the attitude of detachment from the Taurean realm prescribed by many spiritual traditions. His Taurus Sun suggests that there might be an emphasis in the life either on the physical plane, material concerns, and money, or their renunciation. He was born into a well-to-do family, and his father was a wealthy landowner. This fits with his Jupiter in the fourth house, which often indicates that the native comes from a family of prominence, noble standing, and means. However, from a young age, Muktananda gravitated toward the monastic path, which encourages the renunciation of wealth and possessions, control of the senses, turning of awareness inward away from objects that cause craving. If he hadn't become a renunciate, Muktananda would have inherited land from his father.

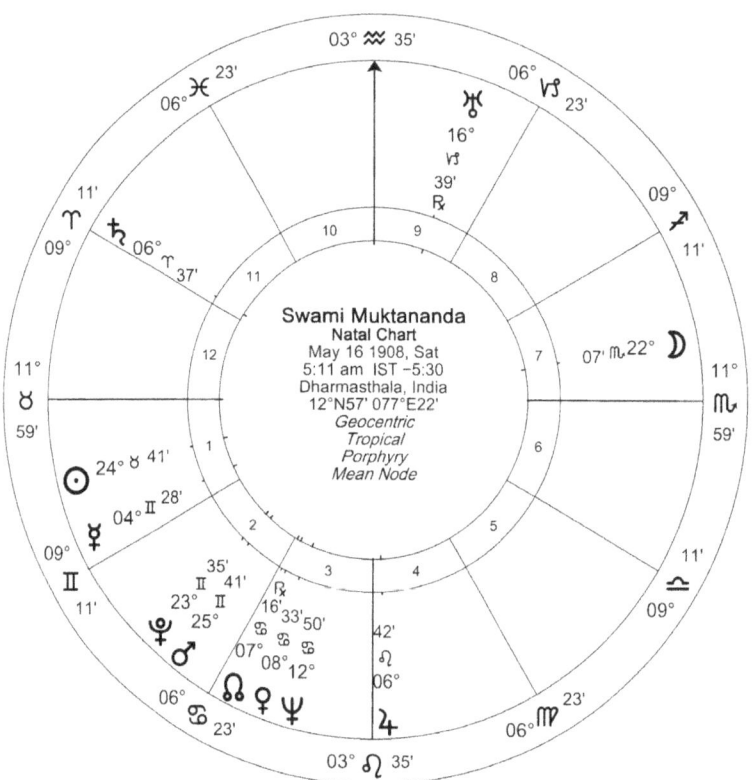

He possessed many of the qualities typically associated with Taurus: stubbornness, determination, perseverance, practicality. He loved nature, and was a master gardener and cook. His physical appearance was also in keeping with his Taurus Sun and Ascendant. His physique was bullish; he was short, stocky, and muscular. Later in life, he established a large organization and was quite involved in its administration and finances. He approached the spiritual quest pragmatically, trying every available method to alter his consciousness and to find a path to liberation.

The Sun and Moon in his chart were in their strongest configuration, the opposition. The Scorpio Moon was reflecting the Sun fully. Scorpio is the phase of the zodiac that concerns transmission of energy from one person to another, and the powerful impact such an interchange has on both persons. In the most mundane sense Scorpio concerns one's use of financial power in business, investment, and partnerships of all kinds. In a deeper sense it concerns the transformation of sexuality, generating energy through yogic practices and through shaktipat—the transmission of power from an illumined guru to a spiritual seeker.

This Full Moon is a key symbol in his chart, signifying one of the most significant themes of his life. His Moon in Scorpio in the seventh house suggests a longing for transformative experience through interactions with others, for intense interpersonal transmission of energy. It implies a need to be deeply affected by some significant other person in his life (Scorpio Moon in the seventh), but also to powerfully impact and transform others. Much of Muktananda's life was spent searching for a teacher who would transmit the liberating divine shakti to him that would awaken the dormant kundalini energy, which yogis believe dwells coiled up at the base of our spines. The fulfillment of his spiritual journey was initiated by a relationship with a guru who awakened kundalini through shaktipat, greatly accelerating his evolution. Subsequently Muktananda himself became the holder of a vast wealth of energy or shakti, which he transmitted to others, and which profoundly affected everyone he met; he embodied a tremendous spiritual force. His powerful impact on others can be directly correlated with the symbolism of Scorpio Moon in the seventh house. He spent years searching for the gaze of the Master that would transform him. And he bestowed that same gaze on others and had an intense, liberating, and catalytic effect on many people.

Venus, ruler of his Taurus Sun and Ascendant, is conjunct the north node and Neptune, symbolizing an inclination toward an unconditional, all-encompassing, spiritual love, a love of God (bhakti). Muktananda was drawn from his early youth to devotional music, plays, and chanting and enjoyed these throughout his life.

Note also that Venus rules the sixth house, where we pursue self-improvement and purification through methods, techniques, apprenticeship, or discipleship. Muktananda ultimately found that for him the most important facet of the spiritual path was discipleship. He concluded that self-effort in spiritual practice must be accompanied by a receptivity to a higher force—the guru's grace-bestowing power. In his own case, that force was received through being in the presence of his guru, Bhagwan Nityananda. He used to say, "I attained nothing on the path until I became a disciple." This refers back to the fact that the dispositor of his Sun and Ascendant is also dispositor of the sixth house. With Venus conjunct Neptune, Muktananda's sixth house apprenticeship was with a highly evolved, God-conscious, and completely ecstatic being: Nityananda.

Uranus is the most elevated planet in the chart and is in a T-Square, opposite Venus-Neptune and square Saturn in the twelfth house. Uranus is in the ninth house, the realm of the teacher or guru; thus we might expect Muktananda's teacher to be unusual. Nityananda was an unpredictable character who hardly spoke and walked around practically naked. He was fully liberated, completely free, an *avadhut* who moved in the world according to his own inner law. Moreover, in the ninth house, we define a belief system, a cosmology or doctrine that gives meaning to life. With Uranus there, we'd expect that Muktananda's worldview was in some way radical or unusual. He was a follower of Kashmir Shaivism, a philosophy and initiatic tradition that affirms the physical world as an emanation of the divine. Muktananda was impatient with philosophies, always restless for direct experience of the truths they proclaimed. Also, he passed through periods of rejecting philosophy and religion because they hadn't led him to any significant inner realization. He longed to experience a higher consciousness beyond all conceptualization. The placement of Uranus in the ninth house also relates to the fact that he walked all over India; the ninth house rules long distance travel, and he went on many pilgrimages to sacred sites.

Let's look now at the opposition of Uranus to Venus-Neptune. Uranus in the ninth accounts for the restless checking out of various teachers that we'll see later on and his experimentation with many philosophical ideas. Venus and Neptune are placed in the third house of language, words, and the narrative faculty. With Venus and Neptune in the third house square Saturn, Muktananda believed that control of the faculty of speech was important for meditators and recommended that seekers remain silent as much as possible, purify their minds and thoughts, avoid small talk, and repeat mantras inwardly. With Venus-Neptune in the house of words and speech, he was an enrapturing lecturer, a great teacher of the scriptures. He'd go into an ecstatic state talking about his love of God, his guru, and the visions and realizations he had in meditation. Also, in yogic philosophy and science, sound is considered the purest material manifestation of Spirit, thus Muktananda's preferred spiritual practice was to chant mantras, the names of God. Venus-Neptune in the third house symbolized devotional love and his desire to give voice to it through inspired lectures and chanting.

The natal Uranus-Neptune opposition is quite significant. Uranus-Neptune aspects can signify sudden mystical experiences, visions, or expansions of consciousness. Muktananda experienced many alterations of consciousness that revolutionized his awareness. Moreover, he broke with the precedent of secrecy in esoteric traditions by writing a unique book (Uranus in the ninth house), *Play of Consciousness*, openly describing the process of kundalini awakening he experienced over the course of nine years after receiving shaktipat initiation from Nityananda. (135) This awakening process included periods when he feared he was going crazy, as well as meditation experiences that were mystical, mysterious, numinous, and awe-inspiring. Natal Uranus opposite Neptune manifested in unusual mystical experiences that haven't been written about by many other people. He experienced spiritual guidance coming to him suddenly and from unexpected sources, another manifestation of Uranus in the ninth house.

His natal Sun is widely trine Uranus and semisquare Venus-Neptune. The latter aspect suggests that Muktananda's spiritual aspiration was central to his life-purpose. Through the stability and solidity of his Taurean personality, he was to transmit to others the fullness of spiritual energy that he generated through meditation and devotion. His Sun contacted the Saturn-Neptune midpoint, perhaps symbolizing a transformation in which the subtle spiritualizing influence of Neptune would refine the physical structure (Saturn), creating what Tibetan Buddhists call the Diamond Body, the body of light and power.

Muktananda's natal Venus was opposite Uranus. Like Meher Baba, who had Venus square Uranus, he wasn't interested in marriage and a conventional expression of Venus. His relationships with people for many years were those of a monk and his few close friends. His friends tended to be strange or unusual people like Zipruanna, a sage who used to sit around on dung heaps, and Hari Giri Baba, a mysterious teacher who wore five or six layers of clothing, spoke cryptically, and was viewed by many people as a madman. Also, at times when Muktananda was deeply involved with his meditation practice, he was known to sometimes tell people to go away so he could be alone to meditate. He had a very expansive, loving side; but he was also somewhat detached from others.

Venus square Saturn was a symbol of his monastic lifestyle and austere values, and his renunciation of attachments to others. He consciously chose not to expend a great deal of energy relating to people during the period of his sadhana (spiritual discipline). He was serious about his inner quest (Saturn in the twelfth house) and chose his interpersonal associations carefully. It's possible that he experienced some conflict between the friendly, congenial, open-hearted qualities shown by Venus-Neptune opposite Uranus and the way his twelfth-house Saturn was calling for solitude and inwardness. A recurring theme in the story of his spiritual awakening is the tension he felt between letting himself be sociable and outgoing, and keeping his vow to remain in solitude, to meditate.

The Mars-Pluto conjunction signifies that he was quite forceful, willful, powerful, magnetic. The native with this aspect may feel impelled to transmute or sublimate sexual energy. With the Sun in Taurus along with Mars-Pluto in the second house, the essence of Muktananda's wealth or personal resources was spiritual energy or shakti. He was a kundalini guru who taught primarily not through philosophizing and techniques (although he did teach methods and philosophies) but through the energy he transmitted. He was a man of power, a shaman, a magician, who transformed people through contagious influence. With Mars-Pluto in the second house, he was sizzling with shakti, and people who were in his presence would often experience intense heat, visions, emotional catharsis, movements of energy through the chakras, and expansive feelings of love.

Natal Saturn is in the twelfth house, the domain of solitude, retreat, or, in some cases, monasticism. It's the house associated with spirituality and mysticism, visions, altered states, kundalini awakening, superconscious or transcendent states, meditative and ecstatic experiences. Many of us think of these types of phenomena as the essence of spirituality. However, altered states and mystical experiences are only one facet of the process of transformation.

Here we're looking at the chart of someone whose life involved a major focus on mystical experiences. But this doesn't necessarily mean that they should be the major focus of everybody's life, since we each have different life-tasks that are reflected in our birth charts. In my personal contact with him, Swami Muktananda repeatedly discouraged me from being overly preoccupied with dramatic mystical experiences and led me to understand that they'd unfold in a natural way after I'd completed other kinds of personal development, especially in the realms of work and relationships. It's important to broaden our conception of spirituality and of the activities conducive to its unfoldment. The key is to understand the symbolism of our own birth charts clearly, so we discern what kinds of tasks we're supposed to accomplish. Hazrat Inayat Khan once said, "The perfect life is following one's own ideal... and each one should ... travel along the path that is suited to his temperament." (136) While it's important to emulate saints and sages, each of us also has to find our own path in life.

With Saturn in the twelfth house, Swami Muktananda made a determined effort to experience higher stages of consciousness and the deepest realizations of meditation. But it didn't come easily, and there were many obstacles and fears to overcome before his inner vision fully awakened. The twelfth house is the realm that Jung called the collective unconscious, from which contents emerge that aren't merely one's own, and that can overwhelm or disturb the stability of ego consciousness. The material that arises from this realm can be frightening because the entire ancestral memory of the species is contained here, including images of violence, catastrophe, and suffering. In the course of his meditative journey Muktananda passed through a confrontation with the unconscious, experiencing some intense and frightening visions. Gradually, however, he became fearlessly stabilized in states of expanded consciousness.

Saturn refers to processes that occur over long periods of time, with determination and patience. Muktananda's enlightenment through yogic meditation didn't happen all at once. Prior to receiving shaktipat, he spent many years trying to alter his consciousness through yogic techniques, penances, fasts, and prayers; and he would've been the first to say that not a whole lot happened.

Once Muktananda received initiation from Nityananda, his inner experience deepened, and he embarked on nine years of concentrated Saturnian effort in meditation practice. His monastic discipline was severe. He followed strict vows and spent most of his time in solitude, staying in his hut in a small village. In *Play of Consciousness*, he repeatedly mentions his need to strictly limit social contact with others, as their presence disturbed his meditation. The only thing that concerned him was to be able to meditate deeply three times a day. He spent all of his time meditating, reading about meditation, and thinking about his meditative experiences. All of this was the manifestation of Saturn in the twelfth house. Nothing else mattered to him.

Early Interest in Spiritual Life

Let's examine the details of his life more closely. When he was around 12 or 13 years old, he became interested in spirituality, chanting, and learning about the lives of sages and spiritual masters. This was about 1920–1921. Between 1920 and 1925 transiting Pluto passed over his Venus-Neptune, corresponding to the time when the young seeker began to yearn for God realization. Between 1920–1922, progressed Sun in Gemini sextiled natal and progressed Jupiter, which signified a search for understanding of life's meaning. A progressed New Moon also occurred in 1922. Because the progressed New Moon was sextile to Jupiter, Muktananda became interested in philosophy and in meeting people of learning and wisdom. This progressed aspect to Jupiter also signified his emerging love of travel and adventure.

A crucial event occurred in 1923. One day while he was near his school, he met a wandering naked *sadhu* (holy man), who walked over to him and patted him on the head. Muktananda was deeply moved by the man's presence, but soon the sadhu walked away and disappeared into the jungle. This encounter made a great impression on Muktananda. Within six months he left home in search of Truth. He set forth without telling anybody and traveled a thousand miles across India before he wrote a letter home to his parents. Although his Sun was in Taurus, he preferred a life of poverty to the considerable wealth he would've inherited from his father. Remember that a Taurus emphasis in a chart doesn't necessarily mean the individual will be "materialistic," "sensual," or "avaricious." It means that the person must define an appropriate attitude toward money, possessions, and the material world. In some cases that means following the path of renunciation.

In 1923, transiting Jupiter crossed his Descendant. In Indian astrology, Jupiter is called "Guru." When it crossed his Descendant, he had this significant encounter with a sadhu, which had a continuing impact upon him. Also, transiting Saturn was passing through his sixth house, square to natal Uranus and Neptune. During that time he experienced a sudden awakening of higher consciousness and of love. He was suddenly captivated by the possibility of attaining a higher mode of existence, and this led to actions that were uranian, rebellious, unconventional: breaking away, running away from home. When Saturn activated his Venus-Neptune opposite Uranus, he was struck by a longing for divine love and, perhaps, a desire to meet this man again. His encounter with the sadhu lured him beyond the point where he could remain a conventional youth. He had to get away to seek enlightenment.

In the period after he left home, he wandered all over the vast reaches of India. There's a gap in our knowledge of Muktananda's life between the early 1920s when he left home, and the mid 1940s. A biography written by Swami Prajnananda mentions some anecdotes about that period but few dates are given. It's known that around 1925, at the age of 17, Muktananda settled in a Vedantic ashram and took *sannyas* initiation, meaning that he became a monk, a Swami, taking vows of poverty, homelessness, and celibacy. He also studied Vedanta philosophy and other scriptures. At this time, transiting Jupiter was in his ninth house conjunct Uranus and opposite Venus-Neptune. Advaita Vedanta isn't a conventional worldly philosophy, but rather a system of radical non-dualism, which posits that *Brahman* (God, the Absolute) is the only reality; and that the physical world as we perceive it is a deceptive illusion (*maya*) created by our limited perceptual frames. Thus, while Jupiter was in his ninth house, he was studying philosophy and religion. Transiting Saturn was conjunct his Descendant at the same time; he had an important relationship with his Vedanta teacher, whom he revered until the end of his life. This crucial association with a teacher occurred with transiting Jupiter in the ninth house of the teacher and with transiting Saturn entering the realm of primary relationship, the seventh house.

Transiting Pluto was conjunct natal Neptune and opposite Uranus. His longing for God-consciousness was fully awakened during this transit. The transit of Pluto conjunct Neptune often corresponds to a deepening involvement in a spiritual path. During this transit it became clear to Muktananda that the spiritual path was the direction for him. He developed a passionate desire to experience the highest states of consciousness.

Finding the Guru

Between 1923 and 1947, Muktananda wandered all over India. During that time, he met over sixty of India's greatest living spiritual teachers, but he felt that none of them was his Guru. With Uranus in the ninth house, he was restless and didn't stay with any one teacher. The fact that he hadn't met anyone he could accept as his spiritual master was very discouraging to him. He himself was known by many as a great yogi, very powerful, learned, and wise. He was a practitioner of hatha yoga postures, pranayama (breathing practices), and different sorts of meditation; but as he'd often say later on, he hadn't experienced the higher states of awareness he was seeking. Finally one of his favorite friends and teachers, Zipruanna, advised him to stop wandering around and to go to Bhagwan Nityananda in Ganeshpuri. Nityananda turned out to be the same holy man he'd encountered so many years earlier as a youth.

In 1947, at the age of 39, after wandering around India since he was 15, he went to Nityananda. There are different accounts of what happened next. Apparently Nityananda tested Muktananda for several months, giving him a hard time and ignoring him for long periods. It's customary for teachers to test students who approach them for initiation, to check whether the student is a worthy recipient of the teacher's knowledge. They create trials to test the student's one-pointedness, faith, and maturity.

Muktananda was determined to stay, for he perceived the greatness of Nityananda. He visited the guru's ashram often and began to practice a form of meditation described in the *Yoga Sutras* involving meditation on an enlightened person, worship of the guru. He sat with Nityananda, gazing at him, inwardly merging with him, mentally installing Nityananda inside his own body. He became absorbed in this practice. Nityananda indicated that this was the correct meditation for him to practice and encouraged him to continue. Gradually Nityananda began to show his favor toward Swami Muktananda.

Shaktipat Initiation

Then a significant event occurred, described in his book *Play of Consciousness*, which I'll explore in some detail.(137) One evening he stayed late near Nityananda, who didn't give his characteristic indication that Muktananda should leave. He sat up all night watching his guru and meditating. At dawn on the fifteenth of August 1947—during a remarkable conjunction of Sun, Venus, Saturn, Pluto, Mercury, and Moon in Leo, all squaring Jupiter in Scorpio—Nityananda lovingly offered him food, a shawl, and a pair of sandals he'd been wearing. He then looked directly into Muktananda's eyes and the awestruck disciple saw rays of dazzling, radiant, multicolored light emanating from the guru's eyes.

Muktananda was overwhelmed with gratitude for this powerful transmission. After Muktananda prostrated at his teacher's feet, Nityananda sent him away, telling him to go to a small village named Yeola to practice meditation. While leaving Ganeshpuri, Muktananda entered an altered state of consciousness, perceiving all things as filled with divine light. He was in an ecstatic, high state.

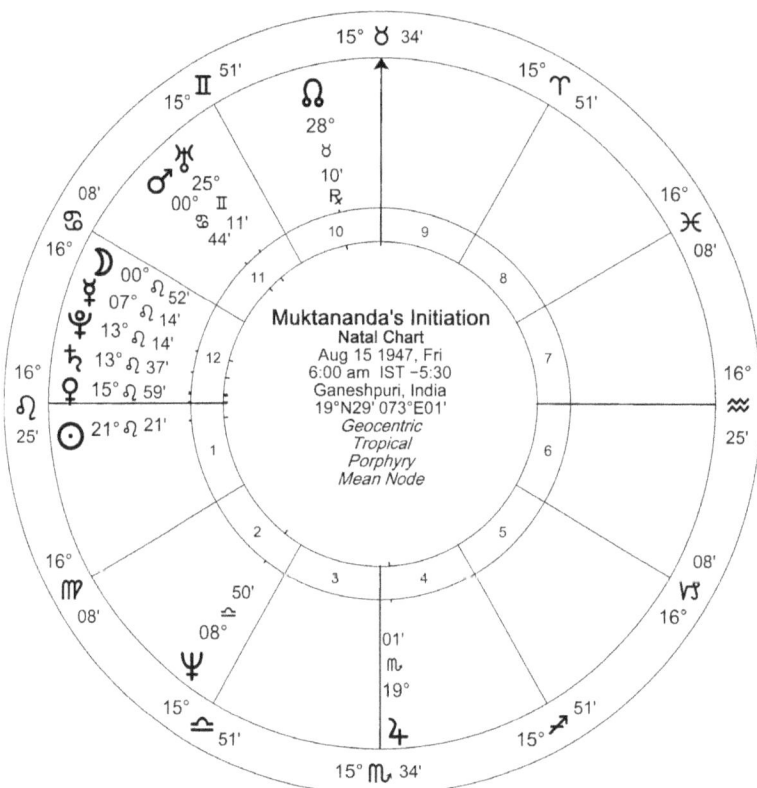

When he arrived in Yeola, however, problems emerged. He began to experience vague fears and devotes a chapter of his book to describing what he called "My Confused Condition." (138) He didn't know why but he began to grow very anxious, troubled by bad dreams, aches and pains, feeling as if every cell in his body was being pierced with needles. His previous ecstasy vanished and he was filled with fear and remorse. He became filled with a sense of panic, a desire to jump around and scream that he couldn't explain. "The whole earth was spinning. The sky was twirling and so were the trees." (139) His body was very hot. He became frenzied and feared that he was going completely crazy. He had visions of a universal conflagration, dissolution, and apocalypse, and of strange, terrifying creatures dancing naked with their mouths agape. In his own words, "I was fully conscious, objectively witnessing a state of madness."(140)

This extraordinary account shows an interior crisis and eruption of intense apocalyptic imagery comparable to visions Carl Jung had during his encounter with the collective unconscious as described in his book, *Memories, Dreams, and Reflections*. On the path of transformation we sometimes have to navigate confusing upsurges of disturbing imagery and feelings, which these days might be called a *spiritual emergency*.(141)

Let's examine what was going on astrologically when he received this powerful initiation and experienced these dramatic alterations of consciousness, encompassing both a unitive, mystical state and a state of temporary madness. In 1946–1947, around the time that Muktananda returned to Nityananda, transiting Jupiter was again conjunct the Descendant, the same transit that occurred during his first meeting with the sadhu as a boy. Jupiter conjunct the Descendant brought further development of this important relationship.

Also, he had a progressed Venus-Mars conjunction. For most people such a progressed aspect would suggest marriage, sexual desire, or falling in love. However, we always refer back to the natal chart to understand how an individual will respond to such a progressed combination. Muktananda had natal Venus conjunct Neptune, suggesting a longing for bhakti, or divine love. Thus, Muktananda channeled the energy of Venus-Mars into a devotional relationship focused on the transmission of shakti (spiritual energy) from guru to disciple. In this transmission we see the operation of a principle similar to, but distinct from, what we ordinarily experience through sexuality: interpenetration, psychic merger, changing of boundaries of both individuals, who are separate and yet deeply connected by a force that changes them forever. Expressing the energy of the Venus-Mars conjunction, Muktananda was enraptured with Nityananda and became his devotee.

This progressed Venus-Mars aspect lasted several years and had a lasting impact. It also relates to the fact that, even though he was a very austere monk, committed to celibacy, he still actively struggled with sexual energies. In *Play of Consciousness*, he reported that for a brief period he became inflamed with desire, which disturbed his meditation greatly. He described this as an energetic piercing of the second chakra by the kundalini, bringing about a transmutation of sexual energy. The whole episode seems to directly relate to the symbolism of the progressed Venus-Mars conjunction.

Transiting Jupiter activated the natal Full Moon between January to October 1947. During this time Muktananda formed a strong connection with Nityananda. Transiting Saturn reached the Nadir about the time he settled in Ganeshpuri, ceasing his wandering and deciding to stay around for a while and become a disciple of Nityananda. He settled down when Saturn entered his fourth house and passed over natal Jupiter. He established a new residence and organized his life around his deepening commitment to the great Bhagwan.

In addition, transiting Uranus was conjunct natal Mars-Pluto between July 1947 and the spring of 1948. Uranus was exactly conjunct Mars on August 15, 1947, the day of his initiation, which he described as "the most remarkable day of my life—the most significant day not only of this lifetime, but of many lifetimes!"(142) Uranus conjunct Mars symbolizes this remarkable, sudden, powerful transmission of energy and the awakening that ensued. His kundalini was quaking through Nityananda's initiation, and he began to undergo extraordinary experiences: He had numerous visions, spontaneously assumed difficult yoga postures, and began to roar like a lion or hop around like a frog while he was meditating. He had innumerable *kriyas*, purificatory movements of energy unfolding the powers and intelligence of the awakened kundalini, which removes blockages and impurities as it unfolds. Uranus conjoining natal Mars-Pluto symbolized the powerfully charged circuit of energy that was activated within him.

Uranus is known as the Great Awakener, which works suddenly and irrevocably to awaken us to the existence of a greater whole, to new possibilities. Transiting Uranus conjunct natal Mars-Pluto manifested as the awakening of power, shakti. Many images Muktananda used seem quite appropriate for this transit. He said his body felt as if it were burning hot, on fire, and as if pins and needles were penetrating every cell. Mircea Eliade has noted that one of humankind's primordial religious experiences was the mastery of fire and that ancient shamans were masters of fire. (143) Part of the process in becoming a shaman is to experience the body as filled with fire and to allow it to purify and divinize the body. Bodily heat was considered a sign that one had entered a sacred condition.

When Muktananda received shaktipat initiation, transiting Neptune was square natal Venus and his nodal axis, symbolizing an awakening of devotion. This is a very important transit since the two planets are conjunct at birth. Neptune had moved from the natal conjunction to the square to Venus. Transits involving two planets are especially important if these planets were aspected at birth.

Right after Muktananda received initiation, in the last two weeks of August 1947, transiting Mars was conjunct transiting Neptune, triggering mysterious, wondrous, expanded states of consciousness, but also his "confused condition." The process felt out of his control, which we can sometimes expect during a major Neptune transit. The Neptune transit combined with transiting Uranus conjunct Mars-Pluto formed the potential for mysterious, mystical forces and energies to awaken. The kundalini shakti was moving inside him. The activation of natal Mars-Pluto also relates to the somewhat violent, cataclysmic imagery of some of his visions.

In addition, when all of this happened transiting Neptune was opposite natal Saturn, activating the natal T-square and forming a Grand Cross with it. Neptune contacting Saturn can disturb one's sense of personal focus and will. Neptune temporarily weakened Muktananda's psychic equilibrium and evoked visions and strange energetic experiences. Neptune dissolved his previous structure, his normal state of consciousness and sense of identity, so his awareness could expand. This major Neptune transit opened up Muktananda's consciousness, making him open and receptive for deep transformation. And Neptune's disintegrative action was complemented by the internal awakening precipitated by Uranus conjunct Mars-Pluto.

Intensive Meditation

During to the nine year period when Muktananda was doing intensive meditation practice and experiencing many visions and transformational events, the progressed Sun was square to Saturn and progressed Saturn. The discipline with which he pursued his twelfth house solitude, retreat, monasticism, and meditation practice was intense and unshakable. He devoted himself completely to the quest for enlightenment, meditating three times a day for several hours each time. Meditation was his job, his leisure, his passion. Saturn is a symbol of austerity, and his natal Sun in Taurus semi-square to Saturn signified his renunciation of desire and attachment. With progressed Sun square Saturn (1952–1955), he was focused on strenuous ascetic activity, retreat, and contemplation.

Between 1954 and 1958, progressed Mercury and Neptune were in conjunction, suggesting Muktananda's constant reflection on spiritual truths, scriptures, and doctrines. His mind was becoming subtle and expanded, his intelligence refined.

Between 1958 and 1960, progressed Sun was conjunct natal and progressed Neptune. Progressed Sun had been crossing over the natal North Node-Venus-Neptune conjunction since 1952, when a Progressed New Moon occurred conjunct his north node, and 1953, when progressed Sun conjoined natal Venus. Throughout this time (1952–1960) his mind and consciousness became filled with love and established in an expanded state. When progressed Sun contacted Neptune, he reached the culmination of his visionary awakening, his quest for enlightenment.

He also concluded that the attitude of renunciation of the world he'd maintained for most of his life was no longer appropriate, because he now perceived that the whole world is vibrating with consciousness. He understood that the material world isn't separate from God, and that what needs to be renounced is the dualistic attitude, the false separation of self from world. The realization that the world of substance and forms is the embodiment or play of Spirit was the ultimate outcome of the spiritual journey of this man who had started out by turning away from the world. The physical plane, he discovered, is filled with the divine presence, the throbbing consciousness of Shiva. He was later known for his great love of food, plants, flowers, and animals, aptly expressing his Taurus Sun.

When the progressed Sun contacts a natal planet, the individual absorbs the essence of that planet. When progressed Sun conjoined Neptune, Muktananda attained an expanded state of all-inclusive awareness, culminating in his final enlightenment in 1956. He lost awareness of himself, and his boundaries were dissolved in the highest stages of samadhi in meditation. In *Play of Consciousness* he describes how he experienced a continuous vision of divine blue light throbbing in all directions as bliss.

> I was conscious of the world no longer. . . . Muktananda was bereft of consciousness and memory. The distinction of the 'inner' and 'outer' evaporated. He was no longer aware of himself.(144)

This is the kind of experience that's possible when the progressed Sun aspects Neptune, for a person who is consciously working to expand consciousness and evolve spiritually.

A similar thing happened to Sri Aurobindo, whose natal Sun was trine Neptune. When his progressed Sun moved into the quincuncx to Neptune, Aurobindo was temporarily thrown off balance. Previously he'd been a journalist and political activist. However when progressed Sun was quincunx Neptune he developed an interest in spirituality for the first time. Soon thereafter he was arrested on charges of sedition and imprisoned for a year, much of it in solitary confinement. There he heard an inner voice tell him, "The bonds you had not the strength to break, I have broken for you." His crisis of imprisonment was purposeful, extricating him from his involvement in politics and social issues and bringing him to the threshold of the divine adventure. He experienced many profound meditations and visions of other worlds. Neptune wiped out his previous identity and work in the world and uplifted his consciousness to a different plane altogether. The mysterious events that occurred at that time seemed to ruin his outer life as a journalist and activist, but ultimately allowed him to pursue a higher destiny.

Similarly, while progressed Sun was conjunct Neptune, Muktananda completed his spiritual journey and achieved yogic liberation (moksa). He understood the universal truths of the world's religious traditions, confirming the findings of great mystics. He had visions of other planets, past lives, and his future. He became enlightened, God-conscious, fully awakened. Such a progression can symbolize becoming highly sensitized, even to the extent that, as in Muktananda's case, it's possible to reach *nirvikalpa samadhi*, the condition of fully expanded consciousness.

Transiting Uranus was conjunct natal Venus-Neptune in 1950–1952, during which time his state of wisdom and illumination and enlightenment was awakened. This transit was significant since natal Uranus opposed natal Venus-Neptune. Uranus now activated his potential to experience divine love and mystical states of awareness.

In 1956, transiting Saturn was conjunct his Moon and opposite natal Sun. Remember that when the same transit occurred for the first time thirty years earlier, he stayed in the Vedantic ashram, absorbing spiritual teachings from a great teacher, from whom he took *sannyas* initiation. The difference with the second transit is that the activation of the natal Full Moon refers both to a transformational relationship with his guru Nityananda and the growth of a personal, devotional relationship with the Supreme Being. Because natal Venus is conjunct Neptune, his primary relationship was always with God. In his description of his final realization he recounts his visions of numerous deities, beings from other planes of existence. Thus, at this time most of his interaction was with beings in the inner world.

After 1956, it began to be apparent to other people that something profound had happened to him, that he was fully enlightened, and he began to be known and recognized as the chosen disciple of Nityananda, between about 1956 and 1961 when Nityananda died. In 1959, progressed Sun and Venus reached an exact conjunction exactly along the Uranus-Neptune midpoint. His Uranus-Neptune-Venus axis was activated by the progressed Sun throughout the 1950s, corresponding to the culmination of his inner journey.

Progressions show processes of growth and maturation through which the potentials of the birth chart are actualized. When progressions make the time ripe, then transits can have maximum impact. Many transits to Muktananda's natal Venus-Neptune during his lifetime symbolized major events in his quest for God, truth, divine love, and higher consciousness. Recall that he left home as a youth to seek enlightenment when transiting Saturn was square Venus-Neptune. But the process didn't reach fruition until his late forties when the progressed Sun was conjunct Venus-Neptune and opposite Uranus, activating the Venus-Neptune-Uranus circuitry of higher consciousness that was latent in his birth chart.

Understanding Muktananda's life astrologically can inspire us to study our own charts carefully, looking for the factors that correspond to our own spiritual aspirations. Somewhere in the chart of each person reading this text is a symbol of your interest in astrology, mysticism, spirituality, and enlightenment. We study the chart of people like Swami Muktananda in order to reflect upon what our birth charts might teach us about our own spiritual paths, so we can gain some understanding of our own evolution. Hazrat Inayat Khan said, "For everything there's a time, so there comes a time for the unfoldment of the soul."(145) This ripening of the soul has many phases, including periods of discipline, suffering, joy, testing of our courage and patience, and refinement of our aesthetic and spiritual sensitivity. Astrological study has the power to foster in us the knowledge that we're ripening perfectly, in our own way and in our proper time.

Muktananda's Career as a Guru

During 1958, transiting Saturn was opposite natal Mars-Pluto. At this time Nityananda began to let people know that Muktananda was a teacher in his own right and began sending students to him. Subsequently, in 1961, Nityananda died and public focus began to move toward Muktananda, who was now recognized by others as an illumined being. Before Nityananda died, he told Muktananda to move down the road to Ganeshpuri to a piece of land. Muktananda lived there, planted gardens and orchards, and continued to meditate. A remarkable ashram, Shree Gurudev Siddha Peeth, now stands there and continues to operate under the direction of Swami Chidvilasananda, current head of the Siddha Yoga lineage.

In 1961 there was a transiting Jupiter-Saturn conjunction which fell exactly on Muktananda's Midheaven, coinciding with his rise to public prominence. His spiritual father (tenth house) died, and his own stature began to be seen and appreciated. His public identity as a spiritual master began to grow. As noted earlier, the Jupiter-Saturn cycle concerns the formation of one's sense of "social destiny." At the Midheaven and in the tenth house one's social and spiritual accomplishments begin to be recognized. Having this conjunction fall on his Midheaven heralded a twenty-year cycle of public activity, notoriety, and broad social influence. Previously he'd lived mostly as a monk in solitude. Now, during the Jupiter-Saturn conjunction on his Midheaven, his career as a guru began. Over the next twenty years, he became one of the world's most famous and influential spiritual teachers.

Transiting Uranus squared natal Sun and semisquared Venus-Neptune between August 1960 and May 1962, around the time Nityananda died. There was a major change in how he projected his identity, and, true to his Taurus Sun, suddenly he had lots of fertile soil in which to plant gardens and orchards. Transiting Neptune was conjunct his Descendant at this time, a transit that was also significant in the lives of Jung and Meher Baba. Neptune signifies surrender, and Muktananda had surrendered his existence to God and to Nityananda, making him ready to assume the role of a guru for others.

In 1962–63, progressed Mars was conjunct the Nadir; Muktananda was busy building up his new ashram, which would later be visited by thousands of seekers from around the world. Around 1964, there were some initial contacts with people from the West. During 1969, while progressed Venus and Mercury were in conjunction, he wrote *Play of Consciousness*, his most important book. The Mercury-Venus combination enabled him to experience an easy, harmonious, graceful flow of writing. The first major influx of Western disciples occurred between 1968–1970, and he took his first world tour in 1970. In 1970–1971, progressed Venus Retrograde went back over its natal position and the North Node, and he made contacts with many people who became important disciples. Swami Rudrananda (Rudi) invited him to America where he formed many new friendships and connections.

In 1970, progressed Mars was conjunct natal Jupiter in the fourth house. Jupiter is the symbol of travel, contact with foreign nations and cultures. He traveled all over the U.S. and wherever he went he was treated like a king. With Jupiter in Leo the fourth house, he enjoyed regal circumstances. In fact, he'd always had good fortune with finding places to stay even when he was a wandering mendicant. While progressed Mars was conjunct Jupiter, he traveled far and wide, came in contact with all sorts of people, cultures, and places of importance, and lectured extensively.

One progression aptly symbolized his growing reputation as a shaktipat guru: Progressed Pluto conjoined natal Mars from 1969 until the end of his life. At birth, Pluto was only two degrees away from Mars, but Pluto moves very slowly by progression. When it came to the conjunction to Mars, his tremendous power became evident. He had an intense impact on others, shaking them up, awakening kundalini. These phenomena fit the symbolism of Pluto and Mars. He initiated thousands of people into Siddha Yoga—the yoga that unfolds spontaneously as a result of receiving the grace of an awakened being, a *siddha*. This path had previously been revealed only to the most prepared, seasoned aspirants. No one had ever spoken so openly before about the way a guru can awaken the dormant kundalini energy in others through shaktipat initiation. And it was unprecedented for a guru to initiate people on such a large scale.

In 1970, the Jupiter-Saturn cycle, which began with the conjunction on his Midheaven in 1960, reached its culminating phase as these planets came into opposition. At this time, Saturn was conjunct natal Sun, and Jupiter was conjunct his Moon, both falling across his natal Ascendant and Descendant. Jupiter and Saturn activated the heart of his birth chart—the natal Full Moon—and his destiny began to unfold. He made all kinds of contacts with people and turned on the Western world to a new approach to yoga and meditation. He transmitted to the public the shakti with which he'd been entrusted by his guru, establishing transformative relationships with many people, thereby fulfilling an essential life-purpose (Saturn conjunct natal Sun, opposite Scorpio Moon in the seventh house).

His second world tour began in 1974. Saturn was conjunct Venus-Neptune in his third house, and he traveled a lot, speaking on spiritual topics, and chanting with large crowds. Progressed Mars and Pluto were in semisquare in 1974–1975; these two factors that were conjunct natally were now in another important aspect, manifesting as a potent expression of his heightened energy and magnetism.

In August 1975, Muktananda underwent a health crisis, a series of major heart attacks. The doctors didn't know what was happening to him, and many people feared that he might die. He sat in his hospital bed, gazed at Nityananda's picture, and chanted. When it was all over, he said it had been a test of his faith in God and the result of some past karma. In July 1975, there was a transiting Full Moon right across his Midheaven/Nadir, indicating some developments that might involve increased public attention. In August, transiting Mars was conjunct his Sun and opposite the Moon, a transit that could precipitate fevers or heart attacks (Sun rules the heart), as well as intensifying other transits occurring at that time. During the attacks transiting Pluto was conjunct the sixth house cusp, exactly opposite natal Saturn, precipitating a major health crisis, hospitalization, a near-death experience, and a test of faith and surrender (Saturn in twelfth house). Because of the natal Sun-Saturn semisquare, transiting Pluto was also sesquiquadrate to natal Sun in 1975 and 1976 from the sixth house. In keeping with the Pluto symbolism, this transit precipitated a death-rebirth experience.

During the heart attacks there was a potent aspect pattern between Jupiter, Saturn, Uranus, and Neptune: Jupiter was at 25° Aries, square Saturn at 26–27° Cancer; Uranus was at 29° Libra, square Saturn and opposite Jupiter; and Neptune, at 10° Sagittarius, was in a sesquiquadrate to Saturn and Jupiter, and semi-square to Uranus. Having such an intense configuration form while transiting Pluto was opposite natal Saturn indicates the possibility of a crisis that affected many people who cared about him and feared he wouldn't live through it.

At around the same time as this health crisis, Muktananda established his U.S. residence in Oakland, California. Transiting Saturn was conjunct his Nadir in the fall of 1975. He stayed put for a while after these heart attacks and established the SYDA Foundation to promote his work.

In 1977 and 1978, his progressed Moon was in its balsamic phase, which feels internally like an ending, the closing of a period in one's life. Muktananda went back to India and stayed at home in the ashram, where a new wing was being built. There was considerable growth in the Siddha Yoga movement during this time, which corresponded to the progressed Sun reaching the Nadir. There was an initiation of some of his western disciples into *sannyas*, with a series of ancient fire ceremonies called Yajnas. This refers back to the progressed Sun conjunct the Nadir—tapping into the ancient roots of his yogic lineage and establishing a new foundation for the future, both through expansion of the physical ashram, and through continuing the lineage of transmission, preparing a small group of qualified disciples for a deeper level of commitment to the path. Progressed Moon was conjunct natal Mars-Pluto at the time, an apt symbol for the purificatory fire ceremonies that were conducted as part of these sannyas initiations.

On the day when he departed from the earth, October 2–3, 1982, there was a Full Moon at 9° Aries 30' conjunct natal Saturn and square natal Venus-Neptune-Uranus. Transiting Mars was conjunct the eighth house cusp and transiting Jupiter was near the Descendant in Scorpio. Transiting Neptune was at 24° Sagittarius 28', quincunx natal Sun from the eighth house, while transiting Saturn and Pluto in Libra were also quincunx the Sun from the sixth house. Thus, his natal Sun was the focus of a Finger of God pattern involving transiting Saturn, Neptune, and Pluto.

The progressed Moon was in his fourth house, often associated with the end of life, conjunct Jupiter and progressed Mars. He left his body in a state of peace, after saying goodbye to many people during the preceding days. His sudden passing was mourned by thousands throughout the world.

Chapter 10

An Astrological Biography of Sri Kriyananda

SRI KRIYANANDA (BORN DONALD WALTERS), founder of the Ananda Expanding Light Community, was born with Sun in Taurus, the sign of pragmatic intelligence and constructive, productive activity. His Sun is involved in a Grand Cross with Jupiter in the ninth house, Saturn in the fifth house, and a Moon-Neptune conjunction in Leo in the third house. With Sun square Jupiter in the ninth house, Kriyananda was interested from his youth in philosophy, religion, and the search for wisdom and truth. In college he was very thoughtful about philosophical matters and eventually wrote a book entitled *Crises in Modern Thought*. Jupiter in the ninth house square the Sun symbolizes a search for truth and the urge to seek a teacher and become a teacher. The fact that Jupiter is in Aquarius suggests developing an unusual or innovative world view, deriving new perspectives from foreign cultures, and adhering to progressive beliefs or doctrines.

From a young age, Kriyananda yearned for expansion of consciousness, as symbolized by Sun square Neptune and Moon conjunct Neptune. The Sun is the point of release for the Jupiter-Neptune opposition, signifying the potential for achieving an expanded state of consciousness. With Jupiter and Neptune square his Sun, Kriyananda was very sensitive, experienced dissatisfaction with worldly life, was a seeker of meaning, and eagerly pursued a spiritual quest for enlightenment and God consciousness.

His Sun is placed in the eleventh house of groups and communities, conjunct Mercury in Taurus. In Aquarius and the eleventh house, one moves from the tenth house and Capricorn focus on one's own ambitions and achievements to a concern with society as a whole and the future of humanity. In the tenth house you want to achieve things,

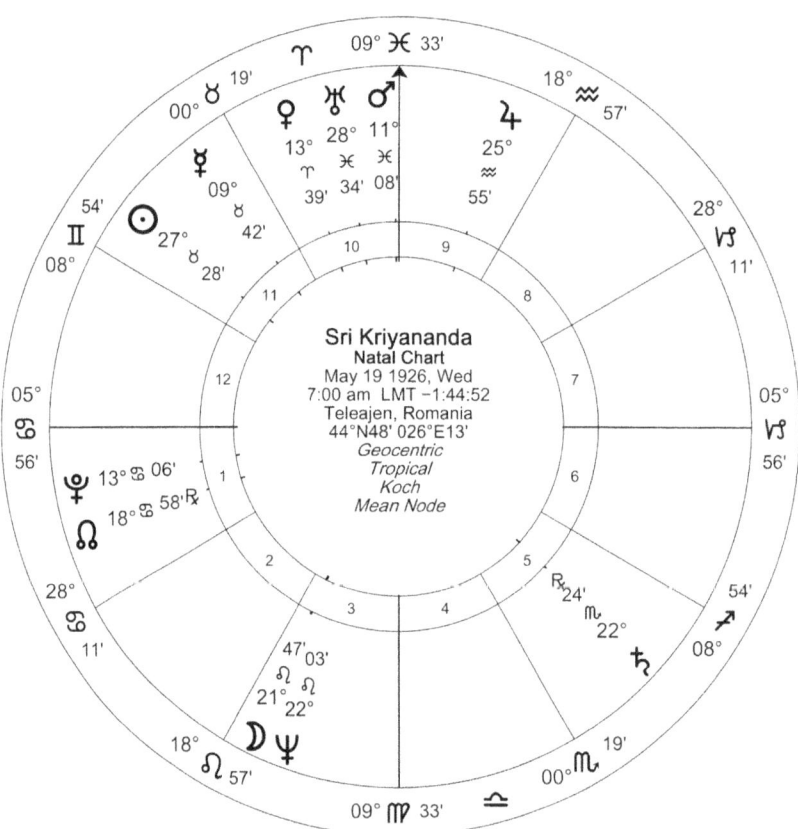

to become someone, to assume your rightful place in the social hierarchy. In the eleventh house and Aquarius you become concerned with how you fit into the community and how your efforts will contribute to a better future for humanity as a whole. This is the realm of *sangha*, belonging, group activity, and building community with like-minded people who share common goals and ideals. Kriyananda's eleventh-house Sun, square Jupiter in Aquarius, gave him these kinds of concerns. Moreover, with Sun in Taurus since his early twenties he was interested in the economics and practical details of forming and sustaining intentional communities.

His Grand Cross includes the opposition of Jupiter-Neptune, two important planets for anyone on the Path. Jupiter, ruler of Sagittarius, signifies philosophical understanding, while Neptune (ruler of Pisces) symbolizes the urge to attain higher consciousness or transcendental experiences beyond philosophy, intellect, and doctrine. Strong aspects of Jupiter and Neptune often indicate interests in religion and spirituality. Such a person approaches the spiritual quest philosophically, with refined intellectual understanding. Mircea Eliade, the great historian of religions, had a Jupiter-Neptune conjunction. David Spangler, the noted mystic and spiritual teacher, also has a Jupiter-Neptune conjunction, and so does professor Stanley Krippner, who has written more than five hundred articles and books on parapsychology, dreams, shamanism, psychedelics, and psychic phenomena. With Jupiter and Neptune in opposition from the third and ninth houses, Kriyananda was interested from youth in learning and reading (third house) about religion, yoga, meditation, the lives of saints, and eventually became a spiritual teacher and writer himself.

With Sun opposite Saturn, Kriyananda was a very serious and responsible person who sought out involvement in a group. With Saturn in the fifth house, Kriyananda became highly creative as a musician, singer, and poet.

The Jupiter-Saturn square signifies a desire for social accomplishment. Strong aspects between Jupiter and Saturn suggest a desire to achieve and to attain social stature. With Sun in a Grand Cross with Jupiter, Saturn, and Neptune, he possessed a deep spiritual devotion, but he also had a task to accomplish in the world—to found a community. The Grand Cross symbolism suggests a need to achieve integration between spiritual and material accomplishments (Saturn and Neptune), to ground his quest for spiritual knowledge and realization (Sun square Jupiter and Neptune) in a practical, Taurean way by raising money to buy land and forming the Ananda community.

When Kriyananda was 22, he read Paramahamsa Yogananda's *Autobiography of a Yogi*. He devoured the book quickly and was so taken by its stories of saints and Kriya Yoga (an ancient system of meditation) that he immediately knew what he wanted: to find a teacher and follow the spiritual path. Then he did something courageous: He bought a bus ticket, left everything, traveled across country to California, and knocked on the door of Yogananda's community, asking to be admitted. He literally walked into his first meeting with Yogananda and said I want to be your disciple. Yogananda accepted him right away, which was very unusual, as most people had to wait months just for an interview.

Let's look at the transits and progressions for these events. This was the time of a progressed New Moon. Thus, a new cycle of life was beginning. The progressed lunation cycle shows the cyclical development of the personality over a thirty-year period. The New Moon begins a cycle of activity that climaxes about 15 years later at the progressed Full Moon. Kriyananda's progressed New Moon was at 19° Gemini in his natal twelfth house. In the twelfth house we transcend attachment to our personal identities, open ourselves to Spirit, and engage in service. The progressed New Moon in the twelfth house initiated a new cycle in Kriyananda's life devoted to spiritual life, meditation, retreat, and monasticism. He let go of his worldly ambitions and became a monk, aspiring only to God-realization. He wanted to meditate, to pray, and to follow the spiritual path above all else.

At this time, transiting Uranus, planet of freedom, had moved from its elevated position in his tenth house into conjunction with the Ascendant. He broke free from his old life and established a new identity. When Uranus transits the Ascendant, your sense of identity changes profoundly and you feel compelled to do unconventional things; you're not the same person thereafter. Events often unfold quite suddenly, and one's actions can be very surprising to others. Kriyananda's parents and friends thought he was crazy and didn't know what to make of the new lifestyle he adopted.

A crisis of severance is often required on the spiritual path, when we feel compelled to break free of social conditioning and pursue unconventional goals and ambitions. Uranus arouses boldness and a willingness to experiment. Kriyananda's life took a completely new turn during the transit over his Ascendant of Uranus, the planet associated with social experimentation and communities. He now became a member of an unusual religious community.

At this time, progressed Jupiter (planet of the teacher or guru) moved into an exact square with natal Sun, symbolizing a quest for knowledge and the potential for him to connect with a great sage like Yogananda.

In addition, transiting Neptune in Libra was opposite natal Venus, and one could say he fell in love with Yogananda. From the very first meeting they were devoted to one another. With Neptune opposite Venus he experienced an unconditional, spiritual love, as embodied by his beloved guru.

Kriyananda soon became a central organizer and teacher in Yogananda's community, the Self Realization Fellowship (SRF). When he left home to seek out Yogananda, transiting Saturn was conjunct natal Moon-Neptune, activating his natal Grand Cross and all of its potentials for spiritual growth and awakening. When Saturn passed over his Moon-Neptune he traveled across the country (the third house governs travel, driving, taking a bus trip) and began reading, writing, and absorbing knowledge from his teacher (Jupiter in the ninth, opposite Moon-Neptune in the third). Saturn clarified the realization that his aspiration was to be a spiritual seeker and member of a spiritual community. These life changes were precipitated when Saturn activated his natal grand cross, along with Uranus crossing his Ascendant. He now knew the path to which he wanted to commit himself. Saturn can lead us to choices and commitments that have long-lasting impact. He never wavered from his decision, and from then on he was devoted to spiritual life and the project of building community.

With Sun in the eleventh house square Jupiter in the ninth, his path was to become a teacher within a community. When Saturn went three quarters of the way around his chart by transit he changed his life dramatically to align with his true nature, in accordance with his birth chart symbolism. Then, when Saturn crossed over his Nadir, he settled down and found a new home and a new family. He had difficulties with his own parents, as they didn't understand his new pursuits (fourth house: family of origin). Kriyananda then settled into a new cycle of activity as a teacher and writer, and was given the job of transcribing Yogananda's lectures and written lessons, commentaries on various scriptures, and the SRF newsletter. With Saturn transiting through his fourth house opposite Mars in Pisces, he was also involved with construction projects on the SRF property (fourth house), doing physical work (Mars) in a spirit of service (Pisces). This community was now his home.

Kriyananda stood out because of his youthfulness and enthusiastic devotion to Yogananda. While Saturn opposed natal Mars and Uranus in his tenth house, he became a great organizer and had a spirited manner that marked him as unique. Progressed Venus had moved into conjunction with natal Mercury and he easily grew into the roles of an editor, writer, and lecturer.

Around 1950, he began to lecture and travel a lot for the SRF churches, while transiting Jupiter was passing over his Midheaven. Jupiter's transit through the tenth house often brings some expansion in your career and public stature. Also, during the time he was undergoing his training with Yogananda, Neptune was opposite Venus, a transit that lasted three years. In this period, his heart opened, and he learned to love in a transpersonal way, a non-grasping expression of Venus. He enjoyed a close, devotional relationship with his teacher during that period. However, Yogananda died on March 7, 1952, when Saturn transited opposite natal Venus. In the ensuing period he met many people and his friendshps and alliances were tested.

Soon, Kriyananda began to travel all over the country conducting services and teaching Kriya Yoga at various SRF centers. Transiting Pluto moved into the third house, the realm of traveling, mobility, driving, and speaking. The Moon-Neptune conjunction brings a longing for the infinite; Moon symbolizes our longings and Neptune symbolizes meditation and the expansion of awareness. From the time when Saturn crossed these two planets he became hungry for enlightenment, the transcendent experience of divine consciousness. Now when Pluto began to pass over natal Moon-Neptune that hunger intensified and his commitment to the spiritual path deepened. Pluto activated Kriyananda's natal grand cross again, signifying this new phase of writing, teaching, and lecturing. With natal Jupiter square Sun and opposite Moon-Neptune, he was well suited for the role of a minister, exercising a priestly function (Jupiter), organizing the Neptunian religious experience through ceremony and doctrine. He was a central figure within the SRF community.

Just before his Saturn Return Kriyananda took vows of renunciation and was given the monastic name, Swami Kriyananda. Many years later, in the 1980s, he decided to marry, dropping the appelation "swami" and became known as Sri Kriyananda.

While Saturn was in Sagittarius and in his seventh house from 1958 to 1962, Kriyananda traveled extensively in India and began meeting many saints and yogis. Since he wasn't involved in romantic relationships or marriage his interest was in meeting sages, spiritual friends. Transiting Uranus was also in the third house, approaching his Moon-Neptune conjunction. A new phase of his spiritual journey was beginning, which he experienced as an intensification of his longing for meditation and realization. While he traveled in India, Pluto passed back and forth across his Nadir—the foundation of one's sense of roots, family, national or ancestral heritage, and connection to a cultural tradition. With Pluto conjunct his Nadir, Kriyananda discovered the mysteries of Indian civilization, connecting with his lineage as a yogi by going to the source. But this transit was also about to throw his personal foundations into some disarray.

Transiting Uranus was close to transiting Pluto at that time, nearing the conjunction that symbolized the cultural revolution of the 1960s. These planets were conjunct throughout the sixties, corresponding to the psychedelic revolution, political upheaval, and volatile forces of social unrest that were unleashed at that time. We're going to see these planets operating dramatically in Kriyananda's chart, altering the direction of his life.

Under their influence of outer planet transits we may feel transforming forces whose intention may not always be in accord with the ego's intentions, plans, and desires. Sometimes changes occur that are unsettling, destabilizing our certainties and life structures. Astrology is the path of intelligence in change; and sometimes that means allowing change to occur, setting aside our resistance and flowing with it. Uranus, Neptune, and Pluto are agents of transformation that act in a series of tests, crises, or rites of passage, which are sometimes turbulent and chaotic. The key is to cooperate with the process; even when our life is apparently falling apart, we may understand intuitively that a transformative process is operative. It's important to go through such a process with the maturity and practicality bred by attunement to Saturn. With this Saturnian sensibility, when our life structures are disrupted by an outer planet crisis, we can allow it to happen with equanimity and faith, striving to discern the spiritual intention of the process. We're about to witness Kriyananda going through a major crisis, very gracefully.

About the time that his travels in the East came to an end, transiting Uranus formed a square to his natal Sun in the eleventh house. Earlier, he'd been named Vice President of the SRF, and was fairly powerful in the organization. However, when he arrived home from India, he was suddenly and unexpectedly ousted from SRF in July 1962. He was expelled from the group whose work he'd spent years promoting. He was fully committed to the SRF's mission and teachings. But during this transit there was a rupture in his connection with this group. Uranus can bring about disruptions and disturbances, stirring change, movement, and the freedom to pursue new directions.

The progressed Sun was exactly conjunct Kriyananda's Ascendant in July 1962. The progressed Sun crossing an angle is usually momentous, signifying a milestone in life. The progressed Sun crossing the Ascendant marks a time of destiny in defining one's identity. Also, his progressed Ascendant was trine natal Uranus, suggesting that this was a time for him to discover his individuality.

Transiting Mars was going through his twelfth house and square his Midheaven and natal Mars when he was ousted from SRF. Although it's usually brief, Mars's transit through the twelfth house can be a period when feels one feels misunderstood or isolated, or one can't control the course of events. This transit may have corresponded to momentarily feeling sorry for himself, and that his former friends and colleagues had abandoned him. To Kriyananda's credit, he demonstrated strength of character and eventually overcame the painful sense of betrayal this experience caused. With natal Mars in Pisces, the disruption of his involvement with the group that was the center of his life for fourteen years led, at first, to confusion about what to do with himself or how to direct his personal energies.

Kriyananda's ouster from SRF appears to have been a purely political matter. The eleventh house is where you deal with group politics. When Uranus squared his Sun there was a sudden divorce from this community. At the same time, after he was thrown out of this group he awakened to a new sense of futurity, a new vision, a new ideal that wouldn't have been possible for him to actualize within the SRF. Uranus transits often correspond to developments that we're ready to have happen, even if we're not consciously aware of it. Kriyananda was ready to become the leader of a new, more revolutionary kind of community. Even though he was quite attached to SRF, Uranus's transit to his Sun uprooted him from it, as if to say, "You've got something very different on your agenda; something else is being called forth by the universe."

At the time he was ousted, transiting Jupiter was conjunct his Midheaven and natal Mars. This, too, was a sign that this event was a manifestation of grace, even though he couldn't see this at the time. During life crises we're often unable to perceive the divine intention at work, as we feel that our lives are being torn apart.

In addition, transiting Saturn was in the eighth house of divorce, endings of relationships, and the hostilities and resentments that can result. This was clearly a period of interpersonal conflict, crisis, and the symbolic death of some important relationships. Also, transiting Pluto was opposite natal Mars, signifying a phase when there was bound to be some interpersonal tensions and discord. There was no getting around this difficult transit. Even an evolved, enlightened person has to live through, and exhaust, some difficult karma. The question is, how do we meet the challenge of the outer planet transits—with bitterness, despair, and defeat, or with courage, faith, and resilience?

At this time, Neptune was transiting opposite his Mercury, symbolizing the confusion he experienced after his split from SRF, his difficulty focusing his mind, and his inability to decide what he should do with himself. As Mercury rules his fourth house, Neptune opposite Mercury corresponded to a period when he didn't know where to go.

Uranus was square his Sun and Pluto was still conjunct his Nadir, the backbone of the chart. Thus, it's no surprise he experienced a crisis at this time. This transit initiated a period of several years of struggle, during which the central difficulty was that he couldn't find a place to live. With Pluto and Uranus in conjunction and moving into his fourth house, Kriyananda went through a period of not knowing where he belonged and what to devote his energies to. Uranus transiting through the fourth house often marks changes in location. He wandered around for several years without a clear sense of where he was supposed to be. He tried living in monasteries of various religious orders because he was a monk. Kriyananda was a renunciate who made a commitment to spiritual life. To find himself put out on the street by his religious order must have presented him with a great test of his faith and equanimity. His expulsion from SRF, and the conniving politics and skullduggery that may have led to it, were manifestations of the potent Pluto transit.

Jupiter was transiting back and forth over his Midheaven and conjunct natal Mars in Pisces. Although he felt abandoned and victimized a bit, he soon began to receive lecture invitations. Jupiter's transit through the tenth house often corresponds with some professional improvement, or emergence of new goals and aspirations. At this time, he met Haridas Chaudhuri, a disciple of Sri Aurobindo and president of the Institute of Asian Studies (later known as California Institute of Integral Studies), who invited him to speak. His lecturing expanded. At first, he didn't want to do it, feeling he was unfit for teaching. But in his book, *The Path* (on which this present account of his life is based), he noted that when he became willing to serve others as a teacher many doors opened up for him. (146) With Mars in Pisces in the tenth house, his calling in life was to be a mystic, a servant, motivated by generosity and altruism.

Soon things began to go his way again. In the mid 1960s, around 1966–1967, progressed Venus came into conjunction with his Sun, leading to harmonious expression of his identity as the leader of a community. He began to write books about the economics of communities and community life (Taurus Sun in the eleventh house). Taurus is concerned with economics, money, tangible concerns. From his youth, Kriyananda had been fascinated with the idea of forming spiritual communities, and his teacher, Yogananda, spoke extensively about the importance of forming "world brotherhood colonies." When progressed Venus came to conjunction with natal Sun, everything in this area came to fruition. He began to connect with people around whom the Ananda community formed. Transiting Jupiter crossed over the Ascendant. The transiting north node passed over his natal Sun, bringing a network of connections that enabled him to fulfill his natal potentials.

Transiting Uranus was opposite natal Uranus, a transit that occurs at around age 40–42 and signifies an urge for freedom and individuation. When Uranus and Pluto transited together in his fourth house, Kriyananda pursued a new vision of community, family, and the right use of land, purchasing property in the Sierra mountains of northern California, where he established the Ananda community. Kriyananda's life is an example of how to make the transition from self-interest and egoic striving to a life of service and sustainable community living, a path that many people may find increasingly attractive and compelling in coming decades.

Chapter 11

An Astrological Biography of Rabindranath Tagore

The incense wants to be one with the scent,
the scent to wrap itself round the incense.
Melody wants to take shape in rhythm,
rhythm turns to melody instead.
Feeling looks for a body in form,
form can only find itself in feeling.
The infinite seeks the intimate presence of the finite,
the finite to disappear in the infinite.
I do not know whose scheme this is
in the eternal cycle of beginning and end
that between feeling and form should be this interchange,
that the bound should be on a search after freedom,
freedom asking to be housed in the bound.

Introduction

These beautiful words were written by Rabindranath Tagore, one of the spiritual and literary giants of modern India, a poet, critic, statesman, playwrite, nature mystic, and educational reformer. Let's look at the general structure of his birth chart before examining his life in detail. I've made extensive use of a chronology of Tagore's life found in Radhakrishnan (147). I've also been assisted in my understanding of Tagore by my friend Dan Johnson, an authority on Tagore's life and work.

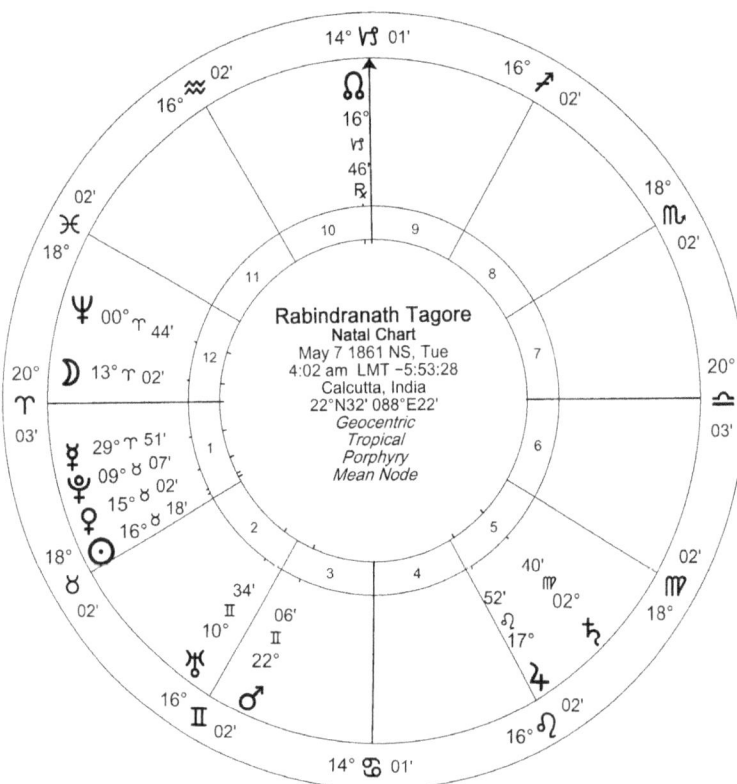

Notice the Moon rising over Tagore's Ascendant, exactly square the Midheaven and Nadir. This is a symbol of Tagore's patriotism, his love of his homeland, Mother India, and the importance of his family.

Mercury is also rising over the Ascendant of the birth chart, while Uranus and Mars are in Gemini and in the third house. Immediately we notice the horoscope's emphasis on communication, language, and narrative, suggesting that the native might become a speaker or a writer, someone with a calling to tell stories, to express his ideas.

Tagore's Sun is conjunct Venus and Pluto in Taurus. Sun-Venus conjunction in Taurus signifies a person who appreciates beauty, nature, and the material world. It could be a symbol of potential for wealth, even if that wealth derived from the family, as in Tagore's case.

Because natal Sun is conjunct Venus, we surmise that Tagore would be an amiable, outgoing person who loves people and wants to be loved, and also someone interested in the arts. Because Sun and Venus square Jupiter, Tagore enjoyed the things of this world. He wasn't an ascetic, by any means. This is illustrated in one of his poems, where he writes:

I shan't become an ascetic, I shan't...
I tell you, I shan't become one, unless
I find a lady to renounce with me.
I have taken a vow. I shall not relent —
if I do not find a bakul grove to sit in,
do not find a mind after my heart and win it,
I shan't become a renouncer, I shan't
unless there be a lady beside me,
sitting in penance as an ascetic.
I shan't leave home and wander around,
indifferent as a mendicant,
if nobody smiles a charming smile
that makes you forget the world...
I shan't become an ascetic, I tell you, I shan't
unless there be a lady with me doing her penance....

Tagore embraced the world. He was a lover, an artist, a poet, and a singer.

Tagore's artistic nature expressed itself through dramatic and literary works, writing plays and poetry. This is symbolized by the square of Venus-Sun to Jupiter, which is placed in the fifth house along with Saturn. Jupiter and Saturn aren't in conjunction by sign, but they seem to work together as a unit. Because the fifth house is associated with creativity and self-expression, transits contacting Tagore's Jupiter and Saturn corresponded to periods of artistic activities such as writing poetry and plays.

Sun square Jupiter is the symbol of someone with intellectual and cultural interests and a yearning to comprehend the truths of religion, philosophy, and morality. Tagore was involved not just in Indian cultural affairs, but in international politics as well. This aspect also symbolizes his frequent travels abroad. Sun-Venus square Jupiter in the fifth house gave him the ability to create beautiful and dramatic works.

Uranus and Mars are widely conjunct in Gemini. Although Uranus is a few degrees from the third house cusp, I interpret Uranus and Mars as a unit placed in the third house. Some astrologers might disagree with me, but I don't interpret house cusps strictly. I look at the shape of the chart as a whole to determine the house placement of certain planets. For example, I may interpret a planet two or three degrees to the left of the Nadir as being placed in the fourth house. Planets near a cusp often affect the following house very strongly. Tagore's Moon is a few degrees above the Ascendant, but I place it in the first house because it's close to the horizon. If the Moon was seven degrees above the Ascendant but in a different sign, then I'd place it in the twelfth house. Tagore's Uranus and Mars are both in Gemini and in the third "zone" of the chart, especially if looked at from the perspective of whole sign houses. We'll repeatedly see evidence of Uranus expressing itself, with Mars, through third house activities of writing and speaking. Uranus in the third also denotes sudden reversals in travel plans, a repeated theme in Tagore's life, where he'd plan trips but would unexpectedly turn around and go back. Uranus and Mars were also expressed through fierce criticism of other people's ideas and of governmental policies. Tagore's polemical writing and political activities were almost always associated with transits to natal Uranus-Mars in the third house.

Neptune is the most elevated planet in the chart, placed in the twelfth house, the house with which Neptune has the greatest affinity, and semi-square to Sun-Venus. This strong placement of Neptune signifies the central place of spirituality in Tagore's life and the connection of his artistic expression (Sun-Venus) and his mystical orientation (Neptune). His identity and essential life-purpose (Sun) was to create beautiful forms that were expressions of his expanded consciousness, his sense of beauty and wonder (Venus and Neptune). These aspects also gave him philanthropic interests, a concern with appropriate use of his money and how to help others through charitable activities. With Sun conjunct Venus in Taurus, Tagore was a wealthy aristocrat, but the aspect to Neptune gave him sensitivity to the plight of those less fortunate.

With Neptune placed in the twelfth house, Tagore had a strong yearning for God, for the experience of the infinite. With Neptune aspecting Venus-Sun in Taurus, Tagore connected to the sacred though the beauty of the earth and nature. With those two Taurus planets, his spirituality involved nature mysticism, an appreciation and worship of the divinity of creation. The Venus-Neptune contact also gave him a devotional nature, and an inclination toward romantic and spiritual love poetry. He wasn't into structured disciplines such as zazen or complex philosophical systems. He followed a path of the heart, with an emphasis on music, art, nature, and poetry. His favorite spiritual practice was to watch the sun rise and set every day.

Tagore's Youth

Tagore made his first attempts at writing poetry and translation when he was seven and eight years old. The boy was described as romantic (Venus-Neptune). In his ninth year he went to private tutors from whom he learned science, geometry, arithmetic, history, geology, physiology, anatomy, Sanskrit, Bengali, English, drawing, music, wrestling, and gymnastics. Progressed Mercury was conjunct his Sun-Venus conjunction, showing an early awakening of mental faculties.

In addition, at about the ages of 8 and 9, transiting Pluto and Jupiter simultaneously crossed over natal Sun-Venus, a major transit. At this time Tagore was absorbing all kinds of knowledge, including several foreign languages (Jupiter), and the principles of drawing (Venus). Pluto and Jupiter were bringing his identity into focus. He learned many aspects of culture and the arts that he'd later draw upon for creative activity and expression (Jupiter in the fifth house). With transiting Jupiter square Sun-Venus, and progressed Mercury also conjunct Venus-Sun, from an early age Tagore demonstrated intelligence, versatility of mind, artistic skill, and hunger for knowledge.

The natal Sun-Jupiter aspect symbolizes his early contact with pandits, learned people, and private tutors. But with Jupiter and Saturn placed in his fifth house (which rules recreational sports, athletics, and other fun activities) he was also practicing wrestling and gymnastics. Tagore's love of play and recreation manifested from his early youth.

Also, transiting Uranus was conjunct the south node in Cancer, in the fourth house. The Moon's south node is considered one of the primary indicators of past karma, inherited influences, areas of life with which we have much experience in previous incarnations. These become familiar behaviors, traits, or skills that need to be balanced through new growth in the area of life indicated by the north node's position. Transiting Uranus conjunct his south node in Cancer in 1869 symbolized his visceral affiliation with Mother India, the traditions of the past, and a sudden awakening to his cultural inheritance.

Transiting Saturn was moving into the ninth house, opposing natal Uranus and Mars during this period when Tagore was immersed in a wide ranging education. Even though Tagore was only a young boy he was engaged in higher learning. With the Mars-Uranus conjunction in Gemini, he had a sharp, brilliant mind, and developed an original style with words, a unique literary voice.

In his tenth year, he was admitted to the Bengal academy, an Anglo-Indian school, but soon became a truant. He began to cut school while transiting Uranus squared natal Mercury. With Mercury on his Ascendant, he was probably a restless and lively child. Transiting Uranus aspecting Mercury made the young boy discontented with formal education. During this transit of Uranus, Tagore became active and curious, but also very rebellious and unstable in school.

At age 11, due to an epidemic in Calcutta, he was removed to a garden house and became acquainted with the countryside of Bengal, giving him a new awareness of the beauty of the land. Transiting Saturn was square his Moon and conjunct the Midheaven. In an older person this would relate to professional achievements or a period of focus on career. But in his youth, Saturn's transit over his Midheaven brought a recognition of qualities or tasks that would be achieved later. The realizations he had now about the sacredness of his country foreshadowed his lifelong commitment to the nation of India. Subsequent transits to the Midheaven, during which he received honors and traveled around the world, all, in a way, referred back to that moment when Saturn was conjunct his MC in 1879.

At the time of his Brahmanical initiation at age 12, he visited the family retreat, Shantiniketan, for the first time. He then accompanied his father on an extensive tour of North India, including three months of travel in the Himalayas. His father was reclusive and was widely regarded as a holy man, thus the fact that he singled out Rabindranath to accompany him was significant (148). At this time he received lessons from his father in Sanskrit, English and astronomy. During this voyage in North India and the Himalayas, transiting Mars was in the ninth house, opposite natal Mars and Uranus. The ninth house often involves voyages to places of learning or holiness, such as this pilgrimage.

Transiting Saturn and Neptune were in a square, with Neptune in Aries and Saturn in Capricorn. Saturn was square natal Mercury, and Neptune was conjunct Mercury; he was engaged in learning, developing his mind, and accumulating knowledge. Neptune transiting natal Mercury corresponds to his contact with sages of the Himalayas and the instruction he received there from his father. It also symbolizes an exhilarating, magical experience of travel, meeting spiritually oriented people, reading and conversing about spiritual and religious topics, and having his father teach him Sanskrit. Neptune began to awaken in him a yearning for the Absolute through contact with his father and his father's yogi friends.

At age 13 his poem "Desire" appeared anonymously in a publication; the poem's title referred to spiritual desire, the longing for God. He went to a school in Calcutta and came in contact with Father Penerenda, a saintly Jesuit teacher. Transiting Neptune was still conjunct natal Mercury. He conversed with a holy man, a person consecrated to a spiritual life.

In 1875, at age 14, Tagore made his first public appearance, reciting a patriotic poem at the Kumbh Mela (a religious festival). Also, his mother died in March of 1876. At that time, there was an alignment of Uranus in Leo and Saturn in Aquarius. Both planets were square Venus and Sun. Uranus hadn't quite reached conjunction to Jupiter, but it was, along with Saturn, directly aspecting Sun-Venus, across the fifth and eleventh houses.

We see here a fifth house activity: displaying himself in public, a performance (Uranus conjunct Jupiter in Leo). While transiting Saturn aspected his Venus-Sun, Tagore began to express himself as an artist, creating beauty. The transiting North Node was also conjunct the Midheaven at this time, and the nodal axis was square to the Moon; he read a patriotic poem, and his mother died. Perhaps there was some connection between his feelings about his mother, and his expression of love for Mother India. According to Dan Johnson (149), the loss of his mother at an early age was a catastrophic event; for she'd inspired in him a love for the humanities and throughout his life he was trying to compensate for that loss.

When the north node crossed his Midheaven, he made contacts that enabled him to show his talents and to receive acclaim. But it was focused through the Moon, through expression of his feeling for his country, his motherland. And he did this in an artistic manner, while Saturn and Uranus contacted natal Sun-Venus-Jupiter.

Turning to the death of his mother, transiting Saturn was square natal Sun and Venus, symbolizing a confrontation with the realities of time, aging, and death. Also, progressed Venus was square to natal Saturn, and he experienced sadness of the heart over the loss of his beloved mother. Simultaneously, the progressed Sun was sextile Neptune, the beginning of a deeper attunement to this expansive planet. At this time he publicly recited a poem entitled Nature's Lament, in which he mourned the sad plight of Mother India. He then composed a song for a patriotic play, Sarojini, and a long narrative poem. He also left school without getting advanced to the next grade.

A lot was happening to him at age 14. With his progressed Venus-Saturn square and the nodal axis squaring the Moon, he lamented the loss of his mother and his nation's challenges. While transiting Saturn and Uranus activated natal Sun-Venus-Jupiter, he wrote many poems, expressing himself as an artist, even though inwardly it was a time of emotional loss and sorrow.

Because progressed Sun was sextile Neptune, Tagore was also expanding and becoming more sensitive. Compassion is born from suffering. The twelfth house, where Neptune is placed, is often associated with situations where you're powerless and may feel self-pity because of circumstances beyond your control. But because of the intense transits of Saturn to Sun, Venus, and Jupiter, he used his intellectual and artistic resources to channel his suffering into creative activity.

A Young Social Critic

In 1876, Tagore joined a secret society, and published his first literary criticism. Transiting Saturn was opposite natal Saturn and had moved into the eleventh house (group affiliations). Transiting Jupiter was in the ninth house (publishing), opposite Uranus and Mars in the third house (writing). With Mercury in Aries, and Mars conjunct Uranus in the third house, Tagore was a passionate, dynamic speaker and a revolutionary thinker and writer—whether it was through poetry, statesmanship, drama, or literary criticism.

At age 16, he composed and publicly recited a poem satirizing the Queen of England, the Empress of India. The poem was a severe indictment of the princely rulers of India who "hugged the golden chain" while the country was ravaged by famine. He also made a stage appearance in a comedy and contributed to a journal several poems and a scathing review of a novel. Then he wrote and published a long story, The Beggar's Maid, and his first novel, *Karuna*. This was right before his progressed Full Moon in Sagittarius opposite Sun in Gemini, which fell across his third and the ninth houses—indicating his capacity for writing, literary expression, and moral conviction.

In 1877, Tagore's progressed Sun squared natal and progressed Saturn, symbolizing the serious effort to accomplish things and to gain recognition for his ideas. The progressed Sun-Saturn square can promote hard work and discipline to cope with life's pressures and to attain excellence. Here the professional focus of Tagore's effort was intensified because Saturn ruled his tenth house, the house of career, public life, and social status.

Tagore's growth in maturity (progressed Sun square Saturn) meant becoming aware of the oppressive power of the State, and how it was impinging upon people's lives. He was becoming aware of difficult social realities and directly challenged the Queen of England, Empress of India, who, in his view, was exploiting his nation. His confrontation with Saturn manifested in opposition to existing governing authorities as well as in efforts to assert his own authority.

Simultaneously, transiting Saturn was in his eleventh house, which kept his attention focused on political activity, humanity's future, and working with others to promote social and political change. Saturn also formed a square to Mars and Uranus in Gemini, especially in the summer of 1877, symbolizing an activation of Tagore's mind, which was on fire with revolutionary ideas. His poetic indictment of the British was a direct confrontation of the rulers of India. Note that with progressed Sun square Saturn, which natally was in the fifth house, he gained recognition through his performances.

Also, with transiting Saturn square Mars-Uranus in Gemini, the variety of his writing was remarkable. Gemini is the sign of versatility and diversity. Tagore's plays, literary criticism, and poetry were all expressions of his Mars-Uranus conjunction, symbol of a unique literary talent.

Artistic Development

In 1878, Tagore was sent to Ahmedabad to study English. Here he set some of his lyrics to music. He traveled to Bombay, took English lessons, and composed articles on English life and letters and on the romantic love poetry of Dante, Petrarch and Goethe. At this time, transiting Jupiter crossed the Midheaven, again foreshadowing his future literary achievements. The musical, romantic, and dramatic elements of his creative work are symbolized by natal Jupiter in the fifth house, square to Sun-Venus. Jupiter symbolizes the desire to travel abroad and encounter places and people that expand our horizons. Thus, when Jupiter was conjunct his Midheaven, Tagore went to Bombay, stayed with an anglicized family and studied English. The transiting nodes were square Sun-Venus and conjunct Jupiter, corresponding to this outpouring of music, poetry, and songs.

Also, transiting Saturn was in the twelfth house, conjunct Neptune. Natal Neptune aspects Venus and Sun, which gave Tagore the desire to implant his spiritual vision and yearning into music, to blend devotion and music. Venus-Neptune combinations often signify the kind of awareness to which William Blake referred when he wrote, "Eternity is in love with the productions of time." Neptune represents eternity, an all-encompassing, timeless perspective, while Venus represents the creations of time. When they're in close aspect, as in Tagore's chart, a person may seek to cast a vision of perfection or the eternal into beautiful musical or artistic form. Transiting Uranus was conjunct his fifth house natal Jupiter, squaring Sun-Venus, during this period of creative activity.

At this time Tagore went to London and entered the University College, where he began to get some praise from Professor Henry Morley, a well-known figure in British letters. Tagore attended a session of the House of Commons and began to get more sophisticated politically. Transiting Jupiter was in Aquarius and in the eleventh house (social awareness), expanding his political consciousness. Jupiter isn't in itself a mystical planet but represents the desire to give meaning to life through learning and philosophical doctrines. Also, with Jupiter squaring natal Sun-Venus and opposite natal Jupiter, he was learning Irish and English melodies and songs, exploring a foreign culture's (Jupiter) musical structure and popular styles (Venus).

Impatience with Schooling

Tagore returned to India in 1880 without completing any course of study. Transiting Jupiter was now squaring Mars-Uranus in the third house; he was unable to stay focused on any one field of learning, and left England without a college degree. Also, transiting Uranus was conjunct natal Saturn. Uranus and Saturn are antagonists in the planetary drama, Uranus representing an urge for freedom and experimentation that's often disruptive to Saturn's concern with stability and convention. Uranus-Saturn transits often bring deviations from socially sanctioned pathways such as attending college. In Tagore's case this transit may be viewed as one that liberated him to unfold his own genius. He later wrote that, "At this time the fountain of my song was unloosed at age nineteen." Tagore began to compose melodies and words while his brother played piano. The transiting North Node was conjunct the Midheaven; he was following the path in life that was truly intended for him. Tagore was a free thinking person who was impatient with schools and unsuited for traditional, structured education. It was more important for him to develop his own voice without limitations.

Illumination of Identity

The transit of Saturn over his Ascendant and Moon was crucial. The Ascendant symbolizes the dawning of self-awareness. When Saturn comes to the Ascendant, a person's identity begins to come into focus more clearly. In Tagore's case, getting praise and approval from his literature teacher may have been an important affirmation of his gifts as a writer. This major Saturn transit also correlates with Tagore's increasingly sober assessment of intercultural and international affairs, and his appraisal of English society. This was the period, he said, when "the fountain of my song was unloosed." All of these developments mark a strengthening of his identity at age 19.

At age 20, Tagore composed his first set of devotional songs and his first musical play was staged, with the poet himself appearing in the title role. Some polemical writing condemning the opium trade appeared. He also gave a public lecture on music and healing with vocal demonstration. On the day after the lecture he sailed for England, but on the way he changed his mind and returned home to Madras.

Transiting Neptune was conjunct natal Sun-Venus in Taurus, which rules the throat and singing, a beautiful symbol for his public lecture on music and healing. This transit awakened an outpouring of love and spirituality that got cast into artistic form.

Transiting Uranus was square to natal Uranus. During this transit he expressed his individuality, his uniqueness, his radical views. In addition, transiting Jupiter and Saturn were in conjunction, in his first house and exactly conjunct natal Mercury. The house in which the conjunctions of Jupiter-Saturn fall and the planets Jupiter and Saturn aspect indicate the direction, and the kinds of social activity, to which a person is called for a twenty-year period. With Jupiter-Saturn in his first house conjunct Mercury, Tagore awakened to his identity as a writer and began to publish his ideas. He was absorbed in his writing. After turning back from his voyage to England, he started working on a series of essays and a novel, *The Young Queen's Market*. Although he'd planned a voyage, with Saturn and Jupiter conjunct Mercury he didn't want to travel around. He wanted to stay home and do some constructive work as a writer. In addition, Mars was transiting through Gemini, conjunct natal Uranus and Mars. We'll see repeatedly that during major transits to Mars-Uranus in Gemini Tagore wrote with great intensity.

A Mystical Experience

In 1882, Tagore established Sarasvat Samaj, an organization that was a precursor of the Academy of Bengali Letters. He also had his first glimpse of cosmic unity, a mystical experience he described in a poem entitled The Awakening of the Fountain. Then a musical play, The Fatal Hound, was performed and he appeared as a blind hermit. Transiting Neptune was still conjunct his Sun and Venus, an apt symbol for a religious experience. Tagore's innate urge toward spiritual awakening and love of God was symbolized by the natal semi-square aspect of Neptune to Sun-Venus. Note that this mystical experience occurred when transiting Neptune was conjunct Sun-Venus.

Transiting Saturn and Jupiter were both conjunct Sun and Venus within three months of one another. During January, February, and March of 1882, transiting Saturn and Jupiter joined Neptune. The Neptune transit over Sun-Venus took about two years, but when Saturn and Jupiter linked up with Neptune, they intensified it. Lengthy transits of the outer planets represent significant developmental processes that get triggered by faster moving planets. Tagore experienced a major period of spiritual awakening during the combined transits of Neptune, Jupiter, and Saturn over natal Sun-Venus.

When Saturn conjoined Sun-Venus, Tagore expressed himself with great clarity. Despite the adversity or difficulties we may face when Saturn transits the Sun, it becomes clearer what we must do to express our true nature. During this transit Tagore came to realize that he must create beautiful art, music, and literature (Sun-Venus square Jupiter in fifth). Thus his plays were performed and he played the part of a blind hermit, a Neptunian, spiritual kind of role.

During the period when The Awakening of the Fountain was written, transiting Mars, Mercury, Venus and Mars were conjunct in his ninth house, opposite natal Mars in Gemini. Although his important mystical experience occurred while Neptune passed over his Sun, only during the ninth house transits did he come to understand the meaning of that experience. Only then could he cast it into a form that could be published and disseminated.

Marriage and Maturation

Tagore married in 1883 while progressed Venus was sextile his natal Moon, indicating a pleasant, harmonious time, a period of emotional happiness. His wife was born in 1873, so she was only ten years old at the time of their prearranged marriage.

In 1884 he was saddened by the death of his sister-in-law, to whom he was deeply attached. This was just after transiting Saturn's third quarter square to its natal position, a transit that often signifies a period of maturation through facing the responsibilities and disappointments of adulthood.

In 1995, Tagore was placed in charge of a new Bengali magazine for young people. Over the course of the year he contributed numerous poems, essays, and letters. He also had several books of his songs and serious essays published. This was during his Jupiter Return, which intensified his aspiration to become a creative writer and dramatist (Jupiter in fifth).

Note that the conjunction of Jupiter and Saturn had fallen exactly on his natal Mercury. The entire subsequent twenty-year cycle of Jupiter and Saturn was an outgrowth of all the writing he began at that time. This process continued now, as Jupiter and Saturn formed their first quarter square. Saturn was in the third house conjunct natal Mars, while Jupiter passed through the sixth house, square to natal Mars. With both Jupiter and Saturn transiting his third-house Mars, it's not surprising that he did so much writing in this period, publishing essays, translations, and songs.

In 1886, he engaged in controversies over social and religious subjects, and composed and sang the inaugural song for the Indian National Congress. Transiting Saturn was conjunct the Nadir and square natal Moon and Ascendant. During this Saturnian period, he was quite concerned about the affairs of the nation. The fourth house governs not only the family of origins but also our connection to our people, our heritage, and our ancestral roots. As Saturn crossed the Nadir into his fourth house and squared natal Moon, Tagore composed a song entitled Gathered Are We Today at the Mother's Call. He was organizing his existence around his love for Mother India. The progressed Sun was conjunct Uranus in 1886, signifying his involvement in social issues, becoming more politicized, radical, and outspoken.

In addition, while Saturn was square his Moon and conjunct the Nadir, Tagore's first child was born, a daughter. He may have felt a great pressure to get his home organized for his family. He faced new responsibilities, perhaps a certain degree of anxiety. He had to grow up and get organized as he established a family.

Soon thereafter Tagore received a literary prize in the form of a large check from his father in appreciation of the devotional songs he'd composed. With Saturn square Moon-Ascendant and conjunct the Nadir, his father was an important figure in his life. Perhaps his father's approval gave him a feeling of stability, a sense of getting his life together. This is what the Nadir and fourth house are all about. The Saturn-father gave him financial assistance and helped him prepare for the arrival of his daughter.

A collection of his literary criticism appeared in 1888, and his first son was born in November. Transiting Saturn had entered Leo and was conjunct natal Jupiter. This wasn't quite his Saturn Return, but Saturn conjunct Jupiter in the fifth house in Leo signified enthusiasm for children, enjoying being playful with them, and feeling very proud. While Saturn was conjunct natal Jupiter, Tagore also wrote The King and The Queen, considered one of his most important plays.

Transiting Pluto and Neptune were beginning to form the great conjunction of the early 1890s and both planets were square to Tagore's fifth-house Saturn. He assumed the responsibilities of fatherhood, and felt the need to achieve, to be recognized and respected professionally. But his Saturn Return would have a very distinctive quality, due to the concurrent transit of Neptune and Pluto square to natal Saturn during 1889 and 1890. He may have had great dreams of glorious accomplishments in the fifth house realm of drama and creative activity, as well as grand dreams for his children. Moreover, because his fifth-house Saturn was activated by two transpersonal planets, his personal self-expression addressed developments and changes in the collective consciousness.

As noted in Chapter 5, Dane Rudhyar described a transpersonal form of creativity that reveals a vision of the future and has a transformative influence upon the audience, reader, listener, or witness. Transiting Neptune and Pluto square to Saturn evoked in Tagore the urge to create such evocative, transformational art.

Tagore's Saturn Return

Tagore's Saturn Return occurred in 1890. A play called The Visarjan was staged, and he read a paper at a public meeting in Calcutta protesting the reactionary, anti-Indian policy of the British. He advocated appointment of elected representatives of the people as members of the Viceroy's Executive Council. He then spent the summer months at Shantiniketan, took charge of management of the Tagore family estates, and attempted to read Goethe's *Faust* in the original German. Thus, during his Saturn Return he was involved with politics, he took a vacation, he took charge of his family, and he read classics.

With natal Saturn in the fifth house, he was working constantly, possibly making it difficult for him to relax and enjoy recreation. Nevertheless, with Saturn here, he needed to take a good rest periodically. On the other hand, the time had come for him to take over the management of the Tagore estates, a big responsibility. He was becoming the head of his family during his Saturn Return.

He also confronted the State again, protesting against British policy in India and proposing appointment of elected representatives—while transiting Mars was in Sagittarius and the ninth house (March through August), opposing natal Mars and Uranus. Transiting Jupiter was in the eleventh house, focusing him on political issues. There was also a performance of one of his plays while Jupiter opposed natal Jupiter, square Sun-Venus.

Transiting Neptune and Pluto were squaring both transiting Saturn and natal Saturn. The Neptune-Pluto conjunction was the symbol of the coming of the twentieth century and of new scientific discoveries that revolutionized the consciousness of humanity. Rudhyar wrote, "The rhythm of the cycle of relationship between Neptune and Pluto establishes the pattern of development in man's unceasing effort at emerging from the lesser to the greater social units" (150). This conjunction augured new possibilities for the achievement of freedom, social betterment, and humanitarian goals on a global scale. New collective ideals were emerging; and because these planets squared his fifth-house Saturn, Tagore attempted to focus this new social vision through his own creative expression. He was becoming a mouthpiece for emergent collective trends.

A Fusion of Politics and Spirituality

Tagore sailed for England while transiting Uranus was opposite his Mercury in late August 1890. In 1891, his second daughter was born and a book of short stories was published. He also started a new Bengali monthly magazine, *Sadhana*, to which he contributed poems, short stories, essays, reviews, and political and scientific articles.

At this time, Jupiter and Saturn were in opposition, the climactic Full Moon phase of their cycle, and both were square to Mars. The last conjunction of these two planets had contacted his Mercury, corresponding to one of his most significant periods of literary activity. At their first quarter square, while Saturn was conjunct Mars, Tagore had engaged in intensive political activity, debates, lecturing, and writing. Now with Jupiter and Saturn opposing one another, squaring natal Mars, the cycle that received its initial impulse at the conjunction reached its culmination: the founding of *Sadhana*, a journal that was both political and spiritual in orientation, and which acted as a vehicle for both his romantic, mystical poetry and his critical, polemical essays. It was the means for Tagore to define an all-inclusive, encompassing form of spirituality that included politics and literature.

Educational Reform

In 1892, Tagore toured North Bengal and came into contact with the life of the local inhabitants. Transiting Jupiter was conjunct the Moon, and he became concerned with the welfare of the people, trying to gauge their needs and responding empathically to them. With transiting Neptune and Pluto now in exact conjunction, closely conjunct natal Uranus, Tagore engaged in a great deal of radical writing and anti-authoritarian social activism.

At this time, he wrote a major criticism of the education system introduced by the British. The third house governs early education, the acquisition of basic skills and knowledge about the world. Tagore had predominantly negative experiences in schools, being a feisty, rebellious truant, and not graduating. Now he wanted to reform the educational system, and wrote an essay called Tortuosities of Education, a plea for acceptance of the Mother Tongue as the medium of instruction. This occurred as Jupiter was conjunct his Moon: "Mother Tongue." He wrote and published this essay while transiting Mars was passing through the ninth house. While Jupiter was conjunct his Moon and Ascendant, his second daughter was born and he was probably in a joyful, enthusiastic mood.

Change of Heart

In 1894, Tagore composed the poem Turn Me Away Now, which was a call to his own self to turn away from a life of ease to a strenuous life of struggle dedicated to the service of humanity. Tagore's dedication to service is symbolized in his chart by the natal Sun semi-square aspect to Neptune. He was becoming a self-consecrated individual. At the time he wrote this poem, Uranus opposed natal Venus in Taurus, symbolizing reevaluation of his materialistic values and desires. With transiting Saturn opposite natal Mercury, he was thinking and writing in a somber, renunciatory vein.

At this time, Tagore also collected folk rhymes and nursery songs. His interest in folk and folk culture, which remained strong throughout his life, was an expression of the prominence of his natal Moon conjunct the Ascendant. Later, he became fascinated with the folk cultures of Eastern Europe and other nations.

In the mid 1980s, while Tagore was managing the family estate, he sailed along the Padma river, a tributary of the Ganges. This brought him into contact with impoverished people and the middle classes of India. Many people viewed Tagore as an esoteric intellectual. But most people didn't know that he was very interested in the common people and folk cultures. According to Dan Johnson, nature now began to take on a new, symbolic significance for Tagore (Sun-Venus in Taurus). (151) Whereas in his youth nature had been like a playmate to him, during this period nature became

Tagore's teacher, revealing philosophical truths. For example, the river represented the passage of time, as well as the principle of continuity within change. Tagore began to view his own life as being like a river, with many sudden changes of direction, color, and speed, yet maintaining an underlying constancy. This awareness was expressed in a long poem entitled The River.

A Period of Social Activism

In 1896, Tagore began expressing indignation at the insolence of British officers and the cowardly submission of the Indian people to it. With transiting Jupiter and Pluto conjunct natal Uranus in the third house, he wrote critical reviews of contemporary publications, and he'd soon initiate a variety of innovative social projects, focusing especially on educational reform. This was also the time of the third quarter square of the Jupiter-Saturn cycle. Saturn was opposite natal Jupiter in the fifth house, square natal Sun and Venus, while he was also experiencing his third Jupiter Return. Thus he was inspired again to express himself in poetry and other creative works.

In 1898, Tagore took over editorial charge of *Sadhana*, and contributed many poems, short stories, and essays on political, literature, philosophical, and educational subjects. He initiated agricultural experiments and wrote articles protesting reactionary government policies. Transiting Uranus and Saturn were conjunct in his eighth house (business ventures) in the early degrees of Sagittarius (publishing). Tagore responded to the turbulent political developments often associated with Uranus-Saturn conjunctions by taking charge of a radical, revolutionary publishing business.

During this period when Tagore was actively criticizing the government, and fighting reactionary political trends, he had the opportunity to sing the Indian national anthem before a government conference. Neptune and Pluto were in Gemini near natal Uranus, while transiting Saturn was moving into the ninth house, opposite transiting Neptune-Pluto and natal Uranus. On the dates of this conference, May 31 through June 2, the transiting Sun was conjunct Neptune and Pluto, acting as a trigger for the slower moving transit of the outer planets. During this transit of Pluto and Neptune conjunct his Uranus, Tagore was radicalized, becoming much more politically active. He participated in efforts to create a more humane and free society, and contributed to this process of social transformation through literary expression of his progressive ideas (third-house Uranus).

When Neptune was conjunct natal Mars, Tagore became involved in organizing a relief effort for plague victims in Calcutta. The Pluto-Neptune conjunction was manifesting in India in the form of mass death and the eruption of panic and hysteria, feelings of helplessness and victimization by conditions that were brutal, mysterious, and unfathomable. This mass calamity unleashed in Tagore a feeling of compassion, a desire to serve and relieve suffering.

With transiting Saturn in his ninth house, the house of meaning and wisdom, Tagore's understanding was deepening. And because of Saturn's opposition to Pluto and Neptune, he envisioned new evolutionary possibilities for humanity and became committed to the creation of a social order based on humanitarian principles and ideals. Thus, during a period in which all three outer planets, Pluto, Neptune, and Uranus were influencing Tagore simultaneously, he worked toward the goal of transforming entrenched, aristocratic and reactionary attitudes and social institutions.

In 1900, Tagore wrote an inspiring exposition of the spiritual values of the Indian way of life. He read this work to his father, who gave him his blessing and some money for its publication. Increasingly Tagore affirmed the historical foundations of Indian culture and deplored the prevailing tendency toward blind imitation of the West. This was during the next Jupiter-Saturn conjunction, which fell exactly on his Midheaven and conjunct his north node, between March and December of 1901. Appropriately enough, he received his father's (tenth house) blessing. During this period, Tagore gained recognition for his contributions to society as a patriot, poet, dramatist, and activist political writer (Mars-Uranus in Gemini). Moreover, Tagore now founded a school based on the model of the ancient forest schools, teaching the boys himself and living with them. He must have felt a great sense of pride and accomplishment in being able to translate ancient values and knowledge into a meaningful form of contemporary social activity. In line with this conjunction in his tenth house, Tagore was concerned with upholding the laws and values of the social order and restoring the historic foundations of Indian culture.

Because the transiting Saturn-Jupiter conjunction fell on his Midheaven, it was likely that Tagore would enter a cycle of great professional influence and success. He now began to gain recognition for founding this remarkable school, implementing the deepest spiritual values of the Indian way of life in the modern world. With Jupiter and Saturn conjunct his Midheaven, Tagore's accomplishments were bringing him stature and acclaim. Later, Tagore would go into retreat, but for the moment he was out in the world, making his mark. This culminated with his father's recognition of his work.

A Period of Sorrows

In 1902, Tagore faced severe financial difficulties. To cover the expenses of the school, he liquidated an unsuccessful business and had to sell his house, property, even his personal library. His wife was forced to sell jewelry to tide him over the crisis. He also had many problems with teachers at the school. Transiting Saturn was square the Moon and Ascendant during this difficult time. Transiting Neptune was square natal Neptune and aspecting natal Sun and Venus. All certainty and security in life was undermined (Neptune), and he experienced confusion and tenuousness in his financial situation (Sun-Venus in Taurus). Because Saturn was conjunct the North Node and square the Moon and Ascendant, it was a rough period of struggle, sadness, and austerity.

Added to this, Tagore's wife became seriously ill and died at the end of 1902, another manifestation of Saturn squaring the Moon and Ascendant. Also, transiting Neptune was square Neptune and semisquare to natal Sun and Venus—the symbol of the wife in a man's chart, and the ruler of Tagore's seventh house. Tagore's wife died while Neptune aspected Venus, mysteriously undermining her health. During this transit, Tagore may have experienced a tremendous devotion to his wife and a sense of spiritual connection with her, a love that would endure even after her passing.

Subsequently, while transiting Uranus was exactly opposite natal Mars and transiting Pluto was conjunct the midpoint of Mars and Uranus, Tagore began to throw all of his energies into political and literary activities. This transit, a conjunction of Neptune and Pluto in Gemini opposite Uranus in Sagittarius, was a very rare and historically significant one. As it closely contacted Tagore's natal Mars, the transformational energies of these planets were focused through him in powerful expressions of his ideas. He wrote an article in which he referred to the synthesizing genius of India and declared that India's mission was to establish unity in the midst of diversity. He also got involved in an agitation protesting a racist remark by a prominent British aristocrat, writing a bitter retort.

Tagore seemed to be very angry, and experienced many heated circumstances and hostilities during this period. For example, three teachers resigned suddenly from his school, leading to arguments, animosities, and sudden explosions of anger that got channeled through radical writing aimed against the British. Because transiting Uranus was opposite the Pluto-Neptune conjunction, he seems to have sensed the incredible possibilities for social reform, yet he experienced upset because these possibilities were not being realized. Nevertheless, he was working toward the eventual restructuring of social institutions, and for a rebellion against the racism and propaganda of the British aristocracy.

Transiting Pluto and Uranus were in exact opposition throughout 1902, especially in the summer when transiting Mars passed through Gemini along with Pluto, corresponding to this period of political struggle and personal crisis. The opposition of transiting Pluto and Uranus directly activated the volatile, explosive Mars-Uranus midpoint. As Mars symbolizes outbursts, fevers, and accidents, and Uranus represents sudden, unexpected developments, this too may relate to the sudden illness and death of Tagore's wife. His daughter also got sick suddenly, deteriorated rapidly, and died when Uranus exactly opposed natal Mars. Mars rules Tagore's eighth house, the house in which we sometimes confront the inevitability of death. Thus, when Uranus contacted Mars, there were two unexpected deaths in Tagore's family.

During 1904, Tagore's growing interest in the political problems of India found expression in a series of essays in which he stressed the need for rural reconstruction based on mutual aid, and proposed a scheme for reorganization of village life. Saturn was moving into the eleventh house, again focusing him on social dynamics and the need to respond to historical and collective conditions. He was preoccupied with politics, even in the midst of the chaos of his personal life caused by the sudden deaths of his wife and daughter.

Later in 1904, he wrote his first autobiographical article, interpreting his life as a poet. During this period of self-reflection and introspection, transiting Jupiter crossed the Ascendant (awareness of self) and conjoined natal Mercury (writing). In 1905, while Jupiter was still conjunct Mercury, Tagore took up editorial charge of a new publication, creating a forum for discussion of important current topics. He also addressed a meeting of students, exhorting them to engage in first hand study of villages to be able to better serve the people.

This was while transiting Uranus in early Capricorn was square natal Neptune, awakening a desire to consecrate his life for the benefit of others. Neptune represents transcendence of our own suffering. Because Uranus is involved here, his focus was political, oriented towards social conditions. Tagore's passionate patriotism was expressed in a large number of nationalist songs that he wrote when transiting Jupiter went through Gemini, conjunct Uranus and Mars. He also began advocating a policy of noncooperation toward the British. This was several decades before the emergence of Mohandas Gandhi.

Dissatisfaction and Retreat

Tagore began to grow increasingly dissatisfied with the character of the political agitation in India, especially its narrow political aims and its disregard for the wider perspective of social and economic regeneration. He established another school and an agricultural cooperative bank, and initiated various rural reconstruction projects. This period of political activism occurred while transiting Uranus was still squaring Neptune and while transiting Pluto was conjunct Mars. Tagore was troubled by prevailing conditions, and he acted vigorously to promote social change.

In 1907, perturbed by the growing alienation between Hindus and Moslems and a sense of the utter futility of the resistance movement, Tagore withdrew from active politics. From his retreat at Shantiniketan, he wrote an article called, The Disease and Its Cure, advocating acceptance of a radical social program for the attainment of freedom. However, he was severely criticized by many of his contemporaries for his withdrawal from political activities (transiting Pluto conjunct Mars: under attack). Transiting Jupiter and Neptune were in conjunction and Jupiter soon crossed the Nadir, again focusing him on national concerns (fourth house), filling him with social idealism. But the reality in India at this time was pervaded by divisiveness and animosity between different religious groups. Jupiter and Neptune awakened in him an expansive and idealistic vision of his nation and its potentials. During this period of disillusionment and retreat, transiting Saturn was in the twelfth house, conjunct natal Neptune. It was an appropriate time for interiorization, solitude, turning to God in prayer (twelfth house).

At this time Tagore relinquished editorship of *Sadhana* and other publications, letting go of some of the responsibilities of his outer life. It's similar to the story of how Sri Aurobindo was put in jail and held in solitary confinement, letting go of his whole political life and embarking on his inward adventure of consciousness and meditation. When Neptune came into conjunction with Tagore's Nadir in August 1907, he became disillusioned and longed for retreat and meditation. Neptune also further undermined the stability of the family, as his younger son died suddenly from cholera when transiting Jupiter and Pluto were conjunct natal Mars—another rude shock. With Neptune conjunct the Nadir and transiting Saturn in the twelfth house (which, by derived house analysis, is the death/eighth house from the fifth house of children), there was nothing to do at such a time of personal tragedy but to relinquish control, to surrender. This illustrates that every life, even an exalted one, has its low points and changes of fortune. Tagore's life had changed greatly since the period a few years earlier when Jupiter and Saturn were conjunct his Midheaven and he was at the peak of his public stature.

Service to Humanity

In 1908, Tagore delivered his first presidential address, reiterating his call to the young men of Bengal to dedicate themselves to constructive projects in villages with Hindus and Moslems working together. At this time, Uranus was conjunct his Midheaven and once again he came into the public eye for his political activism. With Neptune still conjunct the Nadir, Tagore had an idealistic vision of India's future. Both Neptune and Uranus were square to the natal Moon, signifying his patriotism and commitment to the betterment of the nation and its people. With Neptune and Uranus in exact opposition, with Uranus on the Midheaven and Neptune conjunct the Nadir, Tagore was again focused on issues of social concern. Neptune bestows an all-inclusive perspective, for example, a vision of universal freedom, regardless of caste or religion. Uranus symbolizes the process of societal restructuring driven by new political movements. During this transit, Tagore was dedicated to the implementation of programs for social betterment, even while he himself was in deep sorrow and mourning stemming from his personal tragedies.

This is the kind of crisis that Dane Rudhyar taught could lead to a transpersonal metamorphosis. Tagore's personal life was in shambles, yet the call to service only grew stronger. He didn't dwell in self-pity, but rather responded courageously to the pressing needs of his community and nation. He became an agent of collective transformation, even though his own personal happiness was eclipsed at this time. Tagore transcended his own suffering, dedicating his life to a higher cause, in a state of self-consecration to humanity.

It's important to understand his actions in the context of the chaotic events in India at the time of this Uranus-Neptune opposition. The repressive policy of the government was so severe that idealistic young patriots were driven to desperation, setting off bombs in the middle of cities. People were going berserk and rioting, and an atmosphere of hysteria prevailed. It was in this context that Tagore defined a program of social change, and a concept of non-violent non-cooperation as a political weapon. He was thus a predecessor of Gandhi and his tactics of nonviolent resistance.

In December of 1908, Tagore started delivering a series of daily sermons in which he upheld the ideals of universal religion, the synthesis of cultures, and the oneness of humanity. At this time, a T-square had formed across the angles of his chart: transiting Saturn was conjunct natal Moon, and squared transiting Uranus on the Midheaven and Neptune on the Nadir. This represented a moment of destiny and dedication to social ideals, in which his humanitarianism and spirituality (Neptune) were translated into concrete plans (Saturn) for social transformation (Uranus).

Financial troubles plagued Tagore in 1911, when transiting Saturn was conjunct natal Sun and Venus in Taurus. Tagore had always lived off his family's money, but at this point in his life he was forced to confront some difficult economic realities. Also, plans for visiting abroad in October 1911 didn't materialize as intended; transiting Mars was stationary retrograde exactly conjunct natal Uranus, leading to another reversal of his travel plans.

Acclaim

At the beginning of 1912, with Saturn still conjunct his Sun and Venus, Tagore received an unparalleled ovation at the town hall in Calcutta, the first time such an honor had been given to a literary figure in India. Saturn ruled his tenth house, thus its transit over natal Sun-Venus brought recognition for his achievements in drama, poetry, and music, as well for his social and political contributions.

Then, on November 13, 1913, Tagore received the news that he'd been awarded the Nobel Prize for literature. A large number of people from Calcutta went to Shantiniketan to honor and congratulate the poet on November 23, the day that transiting Jupiter went stationary direct in exact conjunction with his Midheaven. Subsequently, Tagore received tremendous public recognition and numerous awards, including honorary doctorates from universities, and traveled all over the world—showing the power of this contact to the Midheaven.

Finally, between 1913 and 1916—especially in 1915 and 1916 while transiting Pluto semisquared Sun-Venus and Jupiter and squared Neptune—Tagore gave many performances and lectures. For the remainder of his life, although the demands of being a public figure reduced the time he had available for writing and reflection, Tagore continued to travel throughout the world and to express his devotion to God, nature, and nation, as well as his vision of intercultural unity and world peace.

With transiting Pluto aspecting natal Sun, Venus, Jupiter, and Neptune, Tagore became a beloved spiritual leader in India, a world renowned writer and a prophet of a unified humanity. In his life he achieved a synthesis of mysticism, poetry, theatre, journalism, and social activism. Torrents of creative energy poured through him in a variety of media. With his ascending natal Moon trine Jupiter in Leo, his artistic and political activities were expressions of deep feeling and caring for his world, his family, and his nation. I consider Tagore one of the most inspiring examples of a transpersonal individual and a transformational artist. His many refined expressive acts convey awareness of life's delicate beauty and mystery, a feeling of peace and contentment in the Taurean realm of nature, and a deep knowing that we are part of the body of the earth.

Chapter 12

An Astrological Biography of Ram Dass

IN THIS CHAPTER WE'LL EXAMINE THE BIRTH CHART OF RAM DASS (born Richard Alpert), famous American psychedelic researcher and popular guru of service and compassion. Ram Dass was born with a conjunction of Sun-Uranus in the tenth house, suggesting that he was born with the potential to become a unique personage with an unusual career, perhaps a revolutionary figure of some kind. Sun-Uranus suggests that he might become an agent of cultural change, an individual embodiment of progressive social trends. With his tenth-house Sun, Ram Dass has been a prominent public figure for most of his life, bringing his unique and humorous spiritual wisdom to appreciative audiences. With Sun square Jupiter in his first house, Ram Dass became a man of learning with a prominent position (tenth-house Sun) as a professor (Jupiter) at Harvard. The Sun-Uranus conjunction suggests that in his career he would stir controversy.

Jupiter and Pluto are conjunct in Cancer on his Ascendant, a symbol that has multiple meanings. On the physical level, Jupiter on the Ascendant signifies the fact that Ram Dass is quite tall; moreover, in his childhood he was somewhat overweight and very emotionally sensitive (Cancer) about this as a youngster. With Pluto in Cancer, it's fitting that his career began as a psychoanalytic therapist trained to delve into unconscious memories and personality dynamics. Later he became a leader in the movement to provide more compassionate care (Cancer) for the dying (Pluto). The Jupiter-Pluto conjunction suggests power and influence, having a great impact on others, being a person of benevolent magnetism. With Jupiter amplifying Pluto's influence, Ram Dass has *shakti* and charisma. With Mars in Leo, trine the Moon in the fifth house, Ram Dass has the demeanor of a performer, a "stand-up comedian for God," as he was once called. He's a regal personality (Mars in Leo) who shines in the limelight, on stage

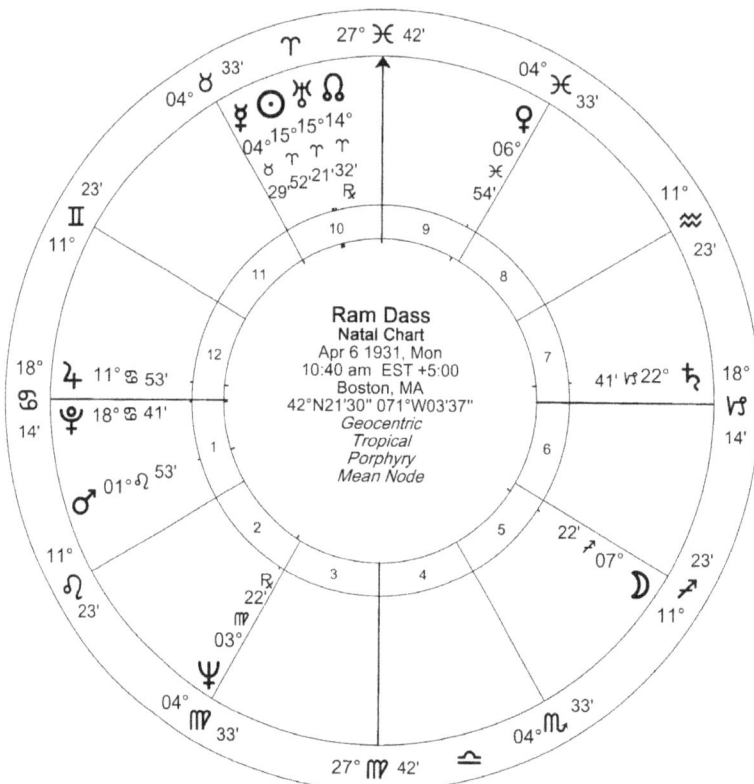

(Moon in fifth house). With Mars in the first house, sexuality is likely to be a central evolutionary issue, and personal assertiveness would be marked. He also has Mars and Sun in mutual reception, a symbol of fiery will and strength of character, and Jupiter and Moon in mutual reception, a symbol of emotional warmth and generosity.

Saturn is placed in his seventh house, suggesting that relationships might be a major priority. Ram Dass's teachings emphasize honoring our relationships and serving our fellow human beings. He seems to have maintained stable, loyal, long-term connections with a wide circle of spiritual friends. Ram Dass has never been married, and remaining single has been a matter of choice for him. He has described himself as bisexual but predominantly gay. Ram Dass has described how relationships often become so complicated that they get in the way of his inner spiritual work, thus he has chosen to remain whole within himself. He has spoken quite a bit publicly about relationship issues he has faced and he has used his challenging experiences as a basis for some lucid teachings.

Saturn's opposition to Pluto in the first house could refer to problems that arise with other people due to his charismatic, commanding personality—for example, negative projections that might be directed at him. It could symbolize the fact that at times other people (including older colleagues and teachers) have confronted him with his shadows.

Natal Venus is in Pisces opposite its ruler, Neptune, indicating a potential for devotional, unconditional love. Ram Dass' spiritual path is *bhakti*, loving God, and awakening through love and service. Venus is exalted in Pisces; its placement here shows a capacity to love freely, with a heart that's open to the suffering of others. With Venus in his ninth house opposite Neptune, love and service are the focus of Ram Dass's teaching.

With his Sagittarius Moon in the fifth house, trine Sun-Uranus, Ram Dass is constantly refining his understanding of the Dharma and expressing it through his unique teaching style. Neptune in the third house symbolizes ecstatic, inspired speaking. Mercury is trine to Neptune, symbolizing abilities as an inspiring, captivating speaker. Neptune's placement in Mercury's house symbolizes the fact that he speaks about spirituality, consciousness change, enlightenment, and meditation.

The Harvard Years

With Sun in the tenth house square Saturn, career and ambitions were quite important to him. During his twenties, Richard Alpert was appointed to a position at Harvard, one of the most prestigious universities in the world. Saturn opposed natal Jupiter-Pluto in 1960, a period when he was enjoying prominence and success as a professor, a powerful man in the world, an influential teacher and intellectual (Jupiter-Pluto).

At the time of his Saturn Return in 1961, he met Timothy Leary and took his first psilocybin trip. His Saturn Return coincided with a Jupiter-Saturn conjunction exactly conjunct his Descendant. A new Jupiter-Saturn cycle was beginning with both planets entering his seventh house. It was quite significant to connect at that time with Tim Leary, who became his friend, associate, and teacher. This friendship had a significant effect on his career (natal and transiting Saturn in the seventh house, square Sun in the tenth) as they began conducting research and publishing papers together. Progressed Moon was also entering his seventh house, symbolizing his inner focus on friendships. With transiting Jupiter-Saturn and the progressed Moon in the seventh house, his alliance with Leary represented a lifelong bonding of their destinies. Leary and Alpert's research into psychedelic drugs and their subsequent dismissal from Harvard were historic, epochal events. During the Saturn Return important structures are built; in his case, enduring friendship were formed. They had their disagreements, but they always remained friends. The careers of Alpert and Leary are wedded in history.

When transiting Pluto came into contact with his natal T-square of Neptune-Venus-Moon, Alpert's life took a dramatic turn. When Pluto conjoined natal Neptune, he took psilocybin mushrooms and LSD and experienced a powerful expansion of consciousness. His mind was opened to new realms of perception. With Pluto opposite natal Venus, he had the experience of falling in love with everybody. Pluto's square to his fifth-house Moon reflects a period of intense emotional experience as well as some heavy partying (Moon in fifth). Someone with a different natal chart or different current transits might take acid and have a total bummer. But with transiting Pluto conjunct Neptune, opposite Venus, and square his Moon, Alpert was in ecstasy. This period was characterized by travel, lecturing, publishing articles on psychedelic experience, and boldly expressing new theories (Moon in Sagittarius) awakened by psychedelics (Neptune). Alpert and Leary didn't shut themselves up in libraries and laboratories. They were making wild pronouncements in their classes and articles, voicing idealistic, Neptunian ideas about psychedelic research and their implications for understanding the mind.

On the day of his first psilocybin trip in early 1961, transiting Venus was in Aries, exactly conjunct Sun-Uranus. Venus represents pleasant events, in this case, a nice experience that illuminated his purpose (Sun). That first trip showed him that his life was going to change. He reported standing outside of himself, seeing all of his identities as a professor, pilot, psychologist, and cellist all disappear until he experienced the witness consciousness that exists behind those roles and identities. He began to undergo a transformation of identity (Sun-Uranus).

At the time of his first mushroom trip, transiting Mars was in Cancer in the twelfth house of altered states; thus, this period awakened his interests in psychedelics, meditation, enlightenment, and experiences of transcending the ego.

Transiting Uranus was in Leo, quincunx natal Saturn. I'd speculate that this stressful transit might have stressed his relationships with some of the stodgy professors in the Harvard Psychology department. Uranus-Saturn aspects are often struggles with authority and structure. With Saturn squaring Uranus natally, Alpert experienced conflict between the traditional, conservative, professorial part of himself and the revolutionary, psychedelic side of his personality that wasn't bound by social norms. The transit of Uranus to Saturn symbolized a disturbance of the stability of his relationships with the Saturnian authority figures that occurred when he started promoting use of LSD. Neptune was also trine natal Jupiter, showing a potential for higher consciousness and psychedelic vision.

Two years later, in 1963, Alpert and Leary were fired from Harvard. A big press conference was held regarding the dismissal of these controversial professors. One would expect that the astrological symbolism of this event would portray the loss of his Harvard position as a great tragedy, the early end of a promising academic career. Surprisingly, transiting Jupiter, the traditional benefic planet of grace and opportunity, was conjunct his Midheaven, near Sun and Uranus. We'd expect this transit to bring expansion and growth in his career. In this case Jupiter brought him into public prominence, but his notoriety was in alignment with the Sun-Uranus symbolism; he was viewed as a rebel, a radical, a renegade who broke the rules by giving drugs to students.

Alpert and Leary conducted research projects in which they administered LSD and psilocybin to people from many walks of life, including alcoholics, prison inmates, creative individuals, to study the effects of these drugs. They did the research seriously, as part of a scientific effort to understand human consciousness. But the changes of values, lifestyle, and behavior that often resulted from psychedelic use made their work a clear threat to the authorities. Jupiter brought Alpert public visibility as a pioneer in psychedelic research, but also as a pariah in the eyes of the academic establishment. He was saddened that the people at Harvard couldn't understand the exciting potentials of psychedelic research. He was probably quite shaken up about being fired but it didn't seem to faze him much. The fact that Alpert was taking LSD fairly often helped him maintain a somewhat bemused perspective on the whole situation. His progressed Venus was conjunct natal Sun-Uranus, symbolizing his many unusual friends and associations within the 1960s counter-culture.

The progressed Sun was exactly conjunct natal Chiron, the planet of the wounded healer. Chiron initiates you into new levels of consciousness, but some pain is usually involved in the initiatory ordeal. Being fired from Harvard was a rite of passage stripping away his personal and social identity; feeling ostracized and cast out by society must have been difficult for him. He was embodying the wounded healer—wounded because he'd been fired from Harvard, but also wise and sharing knowledge freely with others.

Psychedelic Explorations

At this time Pluto and Uranus were coming into conjunction, signaling the cultural revolution of the 1960s. Uranus and Pluto aligned in the early degrees of Virgo, and came into conjunction with Alpert's natal Neptune. A lot of the people who were enlightened in the 1960s experienced this transit. For example, Da Avabhasa's enlightenment occurred during similar transits over his ninth-house Neptune. The same transit brought about a major awakening for Grateful Dead guitarist-sage Jerry Garcia. Alpert moved to the Millbrook, New York estate with Leary and other psychedelic associates and embarked on a program of public programs, meditation, high dose LSD sessions, and studying mystical texts like the Tibetan Book of the Dead (third-house Neptune).

Transiting Uranus was opposite Venus and he continued to fall in love with everybody. Alpert describes wandering around at the Millbrook mansion and seeing that there were lovers everywhere. With his natal Venus-Neptune opposition being activated by transiting Uranus, he was stoned on love.

In the spring of 1963 transiting Uranus and Pluto turned stationary direct equidistant from Neptune—the midpoint of transiting Uranus and Pluto was exactly conjunct his natal Neptune. He was getting really high during this period, experiencing states of higher consciousness. He may have also been confused, wondering what to do with himself now that he'd been thrown out of Harvard. Neptune also governs fantasy and imagination. Alpert and his friends at Millbrook were reading Herman Hesse's novels, especially *The Glass Bead Game*, and trying to recreate Hesse's mystical land of Castalia in their psychedelic mansion.

For the next several years (1964–1965), while transiting Saturn was in Pisces in his ninth house, conjunct natal Venus and opposite Neptune, Alpert used psychedelics extensively and lectured widely on their use. Transiting Saturn in Pisces was opposite transiting Uranus and Pluto; all three transiting planets were contacting his Venus-Neptune axis, across his third and ninth houses. He became a leader of the burgeoning consciousness movement and was widely loved (Venus-Neptune). Between 1964–1966, while transiting Jupiter was in his twelfth house, he was at Millbrook, sometimes staying high on LSD for days at a time.

In 1966, while transiting Saturn crossed his Midheaven, Alpert was a prominent spokesperson for the psychedelic movement, involved in publishing the *Psychedelic Review*. Saturn's transit over the Midheaven was important, but not as momentous as its passage over natal Sun and Uranus was about to be.

Meeting Maharaji

After the Millbrook psychedelic community was busted and shut down by the police, Alpert went on a trip to India with some of his friends. Having been forced to leave the Millbrook Estate, they were on a spiritual quest, a pilgrimage. Eventually Alpert met his guru, Maharaji, as described in his book, *Be Here Now*. The ex-Harvard professor was quite suspicious upon first meeting Maharaji, who appeared to be just an old man lying on a blanket. But his attitude soon changed one day when Maharaji read his mind, recounting how Alpert had been thinking about his mother the night before, and how she'd died of spleen failure the previous year. Alpert's mind was totally blown, because Maharaji had no apparent way of knowing these facts. It seemed that

Maharaji knew everything about him. Soon he was crying at the guru's feet. Shortly thereafter Maharaji gave him the name Ram Dass, which means servant of God.

At this important time, transiting Saturn was still in his tenth house (career). Even though he was going into retreat for a while, Alpert was still a public figure and was quite identified with his professional identity and social status. Also, transiting Uranus was crossing his Nadir, symbolizing the dramatic changes he was about to experience. Transiting Jupiter in Virgo was conjunct Neptune, opposite Venus: He experienced a spiritual expansion and awakening of love for Maharaji. His ninth-house Venus symbolizes both his love for his spiritual teacher, and meeting a teacher who was a being of love and who taught the path of love.

Ram Dass had a progressed Sun-Chiron conjunction at this time. He was fired from Harvard when progressed Sun was conjunct natal Chiron; when he met Maharaji his progressed Sun was conjunct *progressed* Chiron. During this whole period he was initiated by Chiron and met the embodiment of Chiron, which, according to Richard Nolle, is the planetary symbol of the guru, the mentor, the spiritual master. (152) At the same time, progressed Mars was trine his natal Sun-Uranus conjunction, symbolizing intensified expression of his individuality. Ram Dass wasn't just going to stay in India, meditate, and disappear into the void. He was entering a period when he'd become a leader and agent of cultural change (Uranus in the tenth).

Transformation of Identity

In the spring of 1968 Ram Dass returned to the U.S. with bare feet and long hair. At the airport, his father told him to get in the car quickly before anyone saw him. Transiting Mars and Saturn were conjunct Sun-Uranus near the time his father was shocked to see him and became upset about Ram Dass's appearance and lifestyle. With transiting Mars and Saturn conjunct his Sun, it was a bit of a harsh return, with his father (Saturn) openly expressing disapproval.

Upon his return from India, Ram Dass began talking publicly about his transformation and about the existence of a path beyond psychedelics, a path of yoga and purification, of gurus and mysticism. He began lecturing widely and attracted a great deal of public attention. He was a changed man, with a new, unusual identity (Sun-Uranus in Aries). He was no longer Richard Alpert, Ph.D., clinical psychologist; now he was Ram Dass, the servant of God. With transiting Saturn conjunct natal Sun-Uranus, he now embarked on a socially unconventional path, using a Hindu name, wearing white robes, long hair, and prayer beads, and chanting in Sanskrit.

Also, the transiting north node was conjunct Sun-Uranus; transiting nodal contacts to the Sun are always moments of destiny. Transiting Uranus was conjunct the IC; he was changing his lifestyle, diet, and personal habits, becoming more of a nomad, getting up early to meditate, doing all of these unusual things. This transit corresponds to his changed appearance (Uranus) in the garb of a *sadhu*, and the disturbance this caused in his family (IC, fourth house).

Natally, Ram Dass has Uranus square Saturn, showing implicit tension between the saturnine part of him that's conventional, that wants to fit in and be respected in the world, and his uranian solar identity (Sun-Uranus), which is unusual or somewhat radical. During his Saturn Return he became a prominent Harvard professor, embodying Saturn respectability. However, when Saturn conjoined his Midheaven and Sun-Uranus he transformed into a yogi and mystic. He needed to evolve beyond his identity as a Harvard professor. The Saturn transit activated the natal tension between Sun-Uranus and Saturn, thus he experienced a conflict about abandoning his prior pursuits and career goals. Only when liberated from narrow Saturnian institutions, conventions, and norms was he free to be Ram Dass.

His progressed Moon was conjunct natal Sun-Uranus at the same time. He had a new career as a spiritual teacher, a new identity. There was also a progressed Mercury-Midheaven conjunction, showing his constant travel, movement, and talking.

His progressed Ascendant was trine natal Sun-Uranus, illuminating his sense of purpose. This aspect signifies that this was the stage of life when he could actualize his true nature and his calling to the spiritual path.

In 1970, he returned to India to look for Maharaji, feeling lost in the world and in his desires, seeking more training. He spent time with Maharaji over the next year or so, doing meditation retreats and yoga. With transiting Saturn in the eleventh house he also led groups, and was looked to as a leader by many young Westerners who had followed him to India. A spiritual community (eleventh house) was forming around Maharaji, and Ram Dass had a central role in this group as a teacher.

With transiting Pluto conjunct his IC, Ram Dass was confronted more directly with his desires and attachments. Pluto brought to the surface some hidden power motives and sexual seductiveness. With natal Pluto on the Ascendant, Ram Dass freely admitted that he had to face his shadow, his hidden attachments and drives for power and control. When Pluto transited over his IC, Maharaji exposed his desires, his anger, and his pride (natal Pluto conjunct Ascendant, square Sun). Pluto's passage over the Nadir also signified connection with his ancient roots (fourth house) in the yogic traditions of India, especially his specific lineage of devotional yoga. He was in the balsamic progressed Moon phase. A cycle was coming to a close, and a new cycle was about to begin.

Struggles With Trungpa and Joya

In fall of 1973, after Ram Dass returned to the U. S. and began teaching again, Maharaji left his body. With transiting Saturn going through his twelfth house, Ram Dass went into retreat and meditated, trying to contact his guru on inner planes. Then his progressed New Moon occurred, at 26° Taurus, in his eleventh house. A new period of personal evolution began, focusing on his involvement in groups and spiritual communities, and being a leader of a social movement. With progressed Mars and progressed Ascendant in conjunction, Ram Dass had some difficulty reconciling his efforts to be a pure, holy man with his desires for power, adulation, and sexual gratification. He was also about to have some unpleasant, abrasive interactions with others (progressed Mars-Ascendant conjunction).

In the summer of 1974, Ram Dass taught a course at Naropa Institute on the *Bhagavad Gita*. Chogyam Trungpa was reigning over Naropa and he and Ram Dass played out a not-too-subtle power struggle. Transiting Jupiter was in his ninth house and conjunct his Venus at that time; he was doing a magnificent series of lectures on the *Gita*, on *bhakti* and *karma yoga*. Jupiter was very strongly placed natally, close to the Ascendant, squaring his Sun. When Jupiter passed through his ninth house and contacted Venus, he was lecturing and teaching, often about the path of love.

However, with transiting Saturn conjunct his natal Ascendant, Jupiter, and Pluto, Ram Dass experienced interpersonal conflict (Pluto opposite Saturn in seventh house). He and Trungpa got iinto a kind of competition with one another and the Naropa community became divided in its allegiances toward the two teachers. Trungpa took it upon himself to expose Ram Dass's limitations as a spiritual teacher and engaged in some put-downs and one-upsmanship. Moreover, with Saturn conjunct his Ascendant, Ram Dass himself sometimes felt that he fell short of his own ideal. Saturn's transit over the Ascendant requires a clear evaluation of identity, and questioning whether or not you're embodying the ideal you have defined for yourself. Ram Dass recognized that he still had much inner work to do. He became discouraged because of his continuing entanglement in worldly desires and considered returning to India again for an extended retreat.

Before he could do so, however, Ram Dass had a vision in which Maharaji told him not to go back to India because he'd soon be guided to his next teacher in America. Soon thereafter he met a woman named Joya, who seemed to be the teacher Maharaji had told him would appear. She was very powerful, seemed to have psychic or telepathic communication with Maharaji, and channeled information from various other spiritual guides. Ram Dass moved to New York City to become Joya's student and proclaimed that she was enlightened. Many of Ram Dass's students followed him to New York to study with Joya. Transiting Neptune was conjunct his Moon; he was idealizing (Neptune) Joya as the Great Mother (Moon). He was experiencing expanded consciousness through meditation and worship of the divine Mother. Because his Moon squares Venus and Neptune natally, this transit opened his heart and his capacity for devotion. He was doing high spiritual practices and often spoke about various gurus and ancient masters being present in the room during his lectures. But with Saturn still conjunct his Ascendant, Jupiter, and Pluto and opposite natal Saturn, more interpersonal power struggles were soon to emerge.

In 1975 he studied intensely with Joya and was at the center of a spiritual community that gathered around himself, Joya, and another teacher, Hilda Charlton. Transiting Jupiter was conjunct the Midheaven and his Sun-Uranus. Just like when he was fired from Harvard, this was a very public period in which Ram Dass conducted large classes in New York, and acted as a spiritual guide for many students.

October 1975 through July 1976 was the most intense period of his training under Joya, who began initiating him into Tantra through devotional and sexual practices. Transiting Saturn was conjunct Ram Dass's Mars (sexuality). Joya's spiritual awakening occurred suddenly but seems to have had an inadequate foundation, for eventually she became psychologically imbalanced and appeared to burn out. But at that time she did wield a great deal of spiritual power. She also created alot of difficulty for Ram Dass, waking him up at all hours of the night with repeated phone calls, not letting him sleep, hassling him, keeping him off balance, all in the name of loosening his attachments.

Ram Dass tried to view this fierce teacher as the embodiment of Goddess Kali and honored the fire of purification he was experiencing under Joya's guidance. But as he became more deeply involved with Joya, Ram Dass began to perceive that she wasn't above attachments and lust, and thus wasn't as enlightened as he'd thought. The reality was that Joya had some very human problems and was quite manipulative. Ram Dass then began a painful process of severing this relationship, which was complicated by their public visibility and his prior endorsement of Joya. As Ram Dass struggled to free himself from Joya he unraveled a web of lies she'd woven around herself and he began to question her motives and purity. This required some unpleasant confrontations with Joya and her followers, and assertion of his own will to address the situation (transiting Saturn conjunct Mars in the first). Ram Dass had been wielding a lot of shakti, drawing spiritual energy from his meditation and tantric practices. Now he was also expressing anger and confronting people who were angry with him. While Saturn passed over natal Mars he evolved greatly through intensive work in the areas of power, anger, and sexuality. Transiting Neptune was quincunx natal Jupiter during this period: receiving distorted teachings, and feeling deceived by a teacher.

Finally, in September 1976, Ram Dass published an article in which he admitted that he'd been wrong about Joya, that she wasn't in fact an enlightened being, and he took responsibility for leading other people to her. This period featured conflict with Joya and her followers, some of whom made life quite unpleasant for him. Transiting Uranus was conjunct the south node, leading to unexpected problems. But Ram Dass' progressed MC was sextile Jupiter, while progressed Jupiter was exactly conjunct the natal Ascendant, symbolizing his moral courage (Jupiter) in confronting this situation honestly, despite the embarrassment this caused him. Uranus was also trine Jupiter, perhaps signifying the way that Ram Dass was acting as a spokesperson for the truth (Jupiter) above all else. He cited Gandhi, who, after changing his mind on an important decision, stated that his commitment was to truth, not consistency.

Ram Dass and the Yoga of Service

Ram Dass emerged from this period more independent and more able to serve others without glamor or desire to be worshipped as a spiritual teacher. From this metamorphosis was born his later involvement with the SEVA Foundation, a non-profit organization that carries out a variety of human service projects. SEVA has implemented programs to fight disease and preventible blindness. Ram Dass has also worked extensively with prisoners and with Cancer and AIDS patients, and supported various progressive political causes. Through his tireless efforts, Ram Dass has embodied love in action, contributed significantly to the eradication of human suffering, and taught and exemplified the yoga of service. His lucid teachings continue to influence thousands of people. He has been a model of candor, and of socially engaged spirituality. He has also never rested in his search for liberation, continuing to study and practice meditation. Ram Dass's life vividly demonstrates the positive social impact that can result from one person's commitment to the path of spiritual awakening.

In February 1997, Ram Dass suffered a stroke that altered his life thereafter. He had been writing a book about conscious aging, and this event would abruptly initiate him into the aging process. The stroke left him with expressive aphasia, making speech much more difficult. At this time, transiting Saturn was in Aries, approaching conjunction with his natal Sun-Uranus. Uranus is an unexpected event, and Aries refers to the head and brain. He was forever changed. Just as thirty years earlier during Saturn's transit over Sun-Uranus he metamorphosized into Ram Dass, now he underwent another major change in his identity and public role (tenth-house Sun). His progressed Moon was also in Aries conjunct Uranus when he experienced this unexpected crisis and storm surge through his brain. Ram Dass's progressed Mars had just entered Virgo and was approaching a long conjunction with Neptune during this time of disability when he had to use a wheelchair and could no longer drive his own car but was dependent on others to drive him from place to place. Mars conjunct Neptune in the third house signifies the difficulties with speech and transportation. Transiting Pluto in Sagittarius was conjunct Ram Dass's Moon and semisquare to natal Saturn for the next several years, representing the way he faced adversity and emotional upheaval at this time, but also found refuge in the assistance of friends (Saturn in seventh house) who provided much support during his long process of rehabilitation. With Pluto conjunct his Sagittarian Moon, Ram Dass found meaning in his personal crisis and gave beautiful, much more slowly articulated but profound teachings, demonstrating a peaceful, enlightened, and humorous attitude toward change and impermanence. Through the many stages of his personal odyssey, Ram Dass has inspired others to follow the path of spiritual awakening that leads to the realization of our divine potentials.

Conclusion

Writing Your Astrobiography

Each of the lives we've studied demonstrates intelligent unfoldment and manifestation of the birth pattern. Now I invite you, the reader, to apply all you've learned in this book to your own life. Meditate on your natal planetary placements and aspects to determine which of the twelve zodiacal yogas are highlighted by your natal chart and your current and upcoming transits.

You may find it helpful to write your own astrological biography by recalling the most important events of your life, the dates of these occurrences, and investigating the transits and progressions operative at those times. Planetary symbolism illuminates the significance of events and the implicit meaning in every stage of the life-cycle. Record and organize your discoveries. This is the astrologer's path. Even during the turbulent changes, we feel that our lives have a discernible order, which is aesthetically pleasing to contemplate.

Note what transits and progressions lie ahead and reflect on the kinds of tasks and challenges they herald for your near and distant future. Imagine who you'll be in one year, five years, and ten years by meditating on transits, and contemplate how your own actions will help shape the outcome. Consider and choose the optimum ways to use these transits and progressions to develop different facets of yourself. Determine what actions need to be taken to fulfill the potentials of your birth chart. Remember that to make your studies truly fruitful you need to go beyond astrology by taking the concrete steps needed to transform your life.

Reflection on the birth chart generates faith, the awareness that our lives are unfolding according to a celestial pattern, which expresses and reveals divine intention. This realization brings wave after wave of inner peace, the ultimate reward of our work. Through the wisdom ray of astrology, the spirit of guidance will always illuminate our path.

"The god Heh represents 'unending Time.' He holds two measuring staves, which were the hieroglyphic signs for 'millions of years'. On his arms hangs the Ankh, symbol of life."—M. L. Von Franz.(153) Cedar chair back from the Tutankhamen treasure. Egypt, 14th century B.C., Cairo Museum.

References

1. L. Rodden, *Profiles of Women: A Collection of Astrological Biographies* (Tempe, AZ: American Federation of Astrologers, 1979).
2. D. Rudhyar, *The Astrology of Transformation* (Wheaton, IL: Quest Books, 1980), 121.
3. D. Rudhyar, *Person-Centered Astrology* (Santa Fe, NM: Aurora Press, 1976).
4. For example, see S. Arroyo, *Astrology, Karma, and Transformation* (Sebastopol, CA: CRCS Publications, 1978); S. Forrest, *The Inner Sky* (New York: Bantam Books, 1984); and A. Oken, *Alan Oken's Complete Astrology* (Lake Worth, FL: Nicolas Hays, 2006).
5. B. Tierney, *Dynamics of Aspect Analysis* (Sebastopol, CA: CRCS Publications, 1983).
6. M. Harding, & C. Harvey, *Working with Astrology: The Psychology of Harmonics, Midpoints, and Astrocartography* (London: Penguin, 1990); also see R. Ebertin, *The Combination of Stellar Influences* (Aalen, Germany: Ebertin Verlag, 1972), 198.
7. K. Wilber, *A Theory of Everything: An Integral Vision for Business, Politics, Science and Spirituality* (Boston: Shambhala, 2001).
8. See "Venus and Mars: The Rhythms and Vitality of Relationships." In G. Bogart, *Planets in Therapy* (Lake Worth, FL: Ibis Press, 2012), 200–205.
9. A. Ruperti, *Cycles of Becoming* (Sebastopol, CA: CRCS Publications, 1978).
10. G. Bogart, *Astrology and Meditation: The Fearless Contemplation of Change* (Bournemouth, U. K.: Wessex Astrologer, 2002), 125-34.
11. N. Tyl, *Prediction in Astrology* (St. Paul, MN: Llewellyn, 1991).
12. L. Greene, *The Astrology of Fate* (York Beach, ME: Samuel Weiser, 1984), 151, 153.
13. C. G. Jung cited in M. Hyde, *Jung and Astrology* (London: Aquarian Press, 1992), 55.
14. M. Hyde, *Jung and Astrology*, 55.
15. C. G. Jung, Letter to Andres Barbault. *Letters* (London: Routledge Kegan Paul, 1954), 177.
16. M. Hyde, *Jung and Astrology*.
17. M. L. Von Franz, *Time: Rhythm and Repose* (London: Thames and Hudson, 1978), 5–7, 20.
18. D. Rudhyar, *Astrology and the Modern Psyche* (Sebastopol, CA: CRCS, 1976), 31.

19. H. Inayat Khan, *The Complete Sayings of Hazrat Inayat Khan* (New Lebanon, NY: Omega Press, 1978), 152, 202, 39.

20. J. Braha, *Ancient Hindu Astrology for the Modern Western Astrologer* (North Miami, FL: Hermetician Press, 1986); D. Frawley, *The Astrology of the Seers* (Salt Lake City, UT: Passage Press, 1990).

21. B. V. Raman, *Three Hundred Planetary Combinations* (Bangalore, India: IBH Prakashana, 1972).

22. Z. Dobyns & N. Roof, *The Astrologer's Casebook* (Los Angeles: TIA Publications, 1973).

23. See "Rudhyar's Astrology in Plain Language" in G. Bogart, *Planets in Therapy*, 81–116.

24. D. Spangler, *The Laws of Manifestation* (York Beach, ME: Weiser, 2009).

25. See P. E. Muller-Ortega, *The Triadic Heart of Siva: Kaula Tantricism of Abhinavagupta in the Non-Dual Shaivism of Kashmir* (Albany, NY: State University of New York Press, 1989).

26. H. Inayat Khan, *The Complete Sayings of Hazrat Inayat Khan*, p. 22.

27. A. Arrien, *The Four Fold Way* (San Francisco: HarperSanFrancisco, 1993), 66.

28. A. Arrien, *The Four Fold Way*, 69.

29. B. Vissell & J. Vissell, *The Shared Heart: Relationship Initiations and Celebrations* (Aptos, CA: Ramira Publishing 1984); J. Wellwood, *Love and Awakening: Discovering the Sacred Path of Intimate Relationship* (San Francisco: Harper Perennial, 1997).

30. L. Rodden, *Profiles of Women*, 111.

31. These passages are cited from Byron Katie's website, www.thework.com.

32. Satprem, *Sri Aurobindo, Or The Adventure of Consciousness* (Pondicherry, India: Sri Aurobindo Trust, 1968), 160–161.

33. For more on this topic, see G. Bogart, *Astrology and Meditation*.

34. I explore this point in G. Bogart, *Planets in Therapy*.

35. J. Reynolds, *Self-Liberation Through Seeing with Naked Awareness* (Barrytown, NY: Station Hill Press, 1989), 12–13.

36. *Metta Sutra*, translated in A. Buddharakkhita, *Metta: The Philosophy and Practice of Universal Love* (Kandy, Sri Lanka: Buddhist Publication Society, 2000).

37. A. Buddharakkhita, *Metta*, 26.

38. D. Rudhyar, *The Astrology of Transformation*, 112–113.

39. D. Rudhyar, *The Astrology of Transformation*.
40. L. Lehman, *Traditional Medical Astrology* (Atglen, PA: Schiffer Publications, 2011).
41. H. I. Khan, *Mastery Through Accomplishment* (New Lebanon, NY: Omega, 2000).
42. C. Luntz, *Vocational Guidance by Astrology* (St. Paul, MN: Llewellyn, 1942); N. Tyl (Ed.), *Vocational Astrology for Success in the Workplace* (St. Paul, MN: Llewellyn, 1992); N. Tyl, *Vocations: The New Midheaven Extension Process* (St. Paul, MN: Llewellyn, 2006); J. Wickenburg, *How to Find a Fulfilling Career* (Seattle, WA: Search, 1977); F. Cossar, *Using Astrology to Create a Vocational Profile* (London: Flare, 2012).
43. C. Luntz, *Vocational Guidance by Astrology*, 231.
44. D. Rudhyar, *Beyond Individualism* (Wheaton, IL: Quest Books, 1979).
45. N. Tyl, *Prediction in Astrology*.
46. E. Pagels, *The Gnostic Gospels* (New York: Vintage, 1989).
47. H. Jonas, *The Gnostic Religion* (Boston: Beacon Press, 1958), 250.
48. H. Jonas, *The Gnostic Religion*, 42–43.
49. H. Jonas, *The Gnostic Religion*, 253.
50. D. Rudhyar, *Astrology and the Modern Psyche*.
51. D. Rudhyar, *Astrology and the Modern Psyche*, 42.
52. M. Meyer, *A Handbook for the Humanistic Astrologer* (New York: Anchor Doubleday, 1974), 13–14, 21.
53. M. Meyer, *A Handbook for the Humanistic Astrologer*, 7.
54. D. Rudhyar, *Astrology and the Modern Psyche*, 111–12.
55. D. Rudhyar, *From Humanistic to Transpersonal Astrology* (Palo Alto, CA: Seed Center, 1975).
56. D. Rudhyar, *My Stand on Astrology* (Palo Alto, CA: Seed Center, 1972), 27–8. The booklet *My Stand on Astrology* was later incorporated into the online edition of Rudhyar's book, *From Humanistic to Transpersonal Astrology*.
57. Ibid, 30–1.
58. S. Jourard, *The Transparent Self* (New York: Van Nostrand Reinhold, 1972).
59. D. Rudhyar, *Person-Centered Astrology*, 78, 81, 95, 100, 102.
60. D. Rudhyar, *The Astrology of Transformation*.
61. D. Rudhyar, *The Astrology of Transformation*, 39.
62. D. Rudhyar, *An Astrological Mandala* (New York: Vintage, 1973), 378.

63. D. Rudhyar, *An Astrological Mandala*, 384.

64. D. Rudhyar, *The Astrology of Transformation*, xv, 50, 97, 99–101, 103.

65. D. Rudhyar, *The Practice of Astrology as a Technique of Human Understanding* (Baltimore, MD: Penguin, 1968), 21.

66. D. Rudhyar, *Astrology and the Modern Psyche*, 102.

67. D. Rudhyar, *Astrology and the Modern Psyche*, 33.

68. R. Walsh, "The Transpersonal Movement: A History and State of the Art." *Journal of Transpersonal Psychology*, 25 (1) (1993).

69. G. Hartelius, M. Caplan, & M. A. Rardin, "Transpersonal Psychology: Defining the Past, Divining the Future." *Humanistic Psychologist*, 35 (2) (1997), 1–26.

70. H. Chaudhuri, *Integral Yoga: A Concept of Harmonious and Creative Living* (Wheaton, IL: Quest, 1999).

71. G. Bogart, *Astrology and Meditation*.

72. D. Rudhyar, *Astrology and the Modern Psyche*, 81, 83.

73. R. Assagioli, *The Act of Will* (Amherst, MA: Synthesis Center, 2010).

74. R. Assagioli, *The Act of Will*, 21–2.

75. D. Rudhyar, *The Astrology of Transformation*, 118.

76. D. Rudhyar, *The Astrology of Transformation*, 118–19.

77. D. Rudhyar, *The Astrology of Transformation*, 151.

78. D. Rudhyar, *The Astrology of Transformation*, 151–52.

79. G. Bogart, *Astrology and Meditation*.

80. R. V. Dawis & L. H. Lofquist, *A Psychological Theory of Work Adjustment* (Minneapolis, MN: University of Minnesota Press, 1984).

81. D. Rudhyar, *The Sun is Also a Star: The Galactic Dimension of Astrology* (Santa Fe, NM: Aurora Press, 1975), 169–70.

82. M. Anthony, *Jung's Circle of Women: The Valkyries* (York Beach, ME: Red Wheel Weiser, 1999).

83. Bob Marley's Sun-Venus midpoint at 9° Aquarius is directly opposite the Uranus-Pluto midpoint, which Reinhold Ebertin describes as representing "revolution, restlessness, activity, creative energy, the fight for the establishment of innovations and reforms, a strong awareness of purpose and of objective, mobility, creative power, untiring effort; impatience, . . . fanaticism . . . ; pioneers, reformers, explorers, people who are very much out of the ordinary or who are endowed

with universal genius." R. Ebertin, *The Combination of Stellar Influences*, 198.

84. See "Better Than Prozac: Astrology and Mental Health." In G. Bogart, *Planets in Therapy*. Also see G. Bogart, *Dreamwork and Self-Healing* (London: Karnac, 2009).

85. I discuss this idea in G. Bogart, *In the Company of Sages* (Rochester, VT: Inner Traditions, 2015).

86. C. Trungpa, *The Sanity We Are Born With* (Boston: Shambhala, 2005).

87. S. Rinpoche, *The Tibetan Book of Living and Dying* (New York: HarperOne, 1994), 159, 47.

88. J. R. Reynolds, *The Golden Letters: The Three Statements of Garab Dorje* (Ithaca, NY: Snow Lion, 1996), 21, 26.

89. J. Reynolds, *The Golden Letters*, 31, 32–3, 35, 50, 68, 74, 75, 82, 85.

90. S. Grof, *The Adventure of Self-Discovery* (Albany, NY: SUNY Press, 1988).

91. I have described these breathing practices in my book, *In the Company of Sages*.

92. D. Rudhyar, *The Astrology of Transformation*, 113.

93. D. Rudhyar, *The Sun is Also a Star*, 170.

94. M. Washburn, *The Ego and the Dynamic Ground* (Albany, NY: State University of New York Press, 1998).

95. M. Washburn, *The Ego and the Dynamic Ground*, 136.

96. M. Washburn, *The Ego and the Dynamic Ground*, 138.

97. M. Washburn, *The Ego and the Dynamic Ground*, 123.

98. M. Washburn, *The Ego and the Dynamic Ground*, 171–72.

99. M. Washburn, *The Ego and the Dynamic Ground*, 127–28.

100. D. Rudhyar, *An Astrological Mandala* (New York: Vintage, 1973), 300, 310.

101. P. E. Muller-Ortega, *The Triadic Heart of Siva: Kaula Tantricism of Abhinavagupta in the Non-Dual Shaivism of Kashmir*.

102. See S. Muktananda, *Secret of the Siddhas* (South Fallsburg, NY: SYDA Foundation, 1980); and D. Rudhyar, *An Astrological Mandala*, 300–10.

103. Rudhyar, *The Astrology of Transformation*, 103.

104. M. L. Kokiloo, "Salient Features of Kashmir Monistic Shaivism." In *Glimpses of Kashmiri Culture*, volume 5 (Srinagar, Kashmir: Shri Parmananda Research Institute, 1982).

105. M. Dyczkowski, *The Doctrine of Vibration: An Analysis of the Doctrines and Practices of Kashmir Shaivism* (Albany, NY: State University of New York Press, 1987).

106. D. Rudhyar, *Culture, Crisis, and Creativity* (Wheaton, IL: Quest Books, 1987).

107. J. Achterberg, *Imagery in Healing* (Boston: Shambhala, 2002); M. Eliade, *Shamanism: Archaic Techniques of Ecstasy* (Princeton, NJ: Princeton University Press, 1964).

108. M. Erickson & E. Rossi, *Experiencing Hypnosis: Therapeutic Approaches to Altered States* (New York: Irvington, 1980).

109. M. Murphy, *The Future of the Body* (Los Angeles: Tarcher, 1992).

110. S. Gawain, *Creative Visualization* (Tiburon, CA: Whatever Publications, 1978), 29–30.

111. G. Bogart, *In the Company of Sages*.

112. D. Rudhyar, *An Astrological Mandala*, 308.

113. L. Sannella, *The Kundalini Experience* (Lower Lake, CA: Integral Publishing 1987), 37–56.

114. L. Sannella, *The Kundalini Experience*, 24.

115. Ibid.

116. M. Scott, *Kundalini in the Physical World* (London: Routledge & Kegan Paul, 1983), 77.

117. M. Scott, *Kundalini in the Physical World*, 108.

118. M. Scott, *Kundalini in the Physical World*, 109.

119. D. Rudhyar, *An Astrological Mandala*, 308–9.

120. D. Rudhyar, *Beyond Personhood* (Palo Alto, CA: Rudhyar Institute for Transpersonal Activity, 1982), 33.

121. D. Rudhyar, *Person-Centered Astrology*.

122. D. Rudhyar, *The Rhythm of Wholeness* (Wheaton, IL: Quest Books, 1983), 227.

123. D. Rudhyar, *The Astrology of Transformation*, 131.

124. T. Hopkinson & D. Hopkinson, *Much Silence: The Life and Work of Meher Baba* (Woombye, Australia: Sheriar Press, 1982).

125. See D. Rudhyar, *Astrological Timing: The Transition to the New Age* (New York: Harper & Row, 1969); and M. Baigent, C. Harvey, & N. Campion, *Mundane Astrology* (Wellingborough, Great Britain: Aquarian Press, 1984).

126. A. Ruperti, *Cycles of Becoming* (Sebastopol, CA: CRCS Publications, 1978).

127. M. Eliade, *Autobiography* (New York: Harper & Row, 1981).

128. M. Ricketts, *Mircea Eliade: The Romanian Roots* (New York: Columbia University Press, 1988).

129. M. Eliade, *Autobiography*, 185.

130. M. Eliade, *Autobiography*, 198.

131. M. Eliade, *Autobiography*, 198–99.

132. M. Eliade, *Autobiography*, 200.

133. M. Eliade, *Autobiography*, 237.

134. M. Eliade, *Autobiography*, 255–56.

135. S. Muktananda, *Play of Consciousness* (New York: Harper & Row, 1974).

136. H. Inayat Khan, *The Complete Sayings of Hazrat Inayat Khan*, 241-42.

137. S. Muktananda, *Play of Consciousness*, 58 ff.

138. S. Muktananda, *Play of Consciousness*, 66 ff.

139. S. Muktananda, *Play of Consciousness*, 70.

140. S. Muktananda, *Play of Consciousness*, 70–1.

141. S. Grof & C. Grof (Eds.), *Spiritual Emergency: When Personal Transformation Becomes a Crisis* (Los Angeles: Tarcher, 1989).

142. S. Muktananda, *Play of Consciousness*, 58.

143. M. Eliade, *The Forge and the Crucible* (Chicago: University of Chicago Press, 1979).

144. S. Muktananda, *Play of Consciousness*, 162.

145. H. Inayat Khan, *The Complete Sayings of Hazrat Inayat Khan*, 42.

146. S. Kriyananda, *The Path: Autobiography of a Western Yogi* (Nevada City, CA: Crystal Clarity Publishing, 1988).

147. S. Radhakrishnan (Ed.), *Rabindranath Tagore: A Centenary Volume* (New Delhi: Sahitya Akademi, 1961).

148. D. Johnson, *The Role of the River in the Life and Work of Rabindranath Tagore* (Ann Arbor, MI: University Microfilms International, 1989).

149. Dan Johnson, personal communication.

150. D. Rudhyar, *Astrological Timing*, 73.

151. D. Johnson, *The Role of the River*.

152. R. Nolle, *Chiron: The New Planet in Your Horoscope* (Tempe, AZ: American Federation of Astrologers, 1983).

153. M. L. Von Franz, *Time: Rhythm and Repose*, 70. Image reproduced with permission of Hirmer Fotoarchiv, Munich.

About the Author

Greg Bogart, Ph.D, MFT is a psychotherapist and astrologer practicing in the San Francisco Bay Area. He is a licensed Marriage and Family Therapist and a board certified professional counselor. He is also certified as an astrological counselor by ISAR and NCGR. Greg is currently a lecturer in the department of psychology at Sonoma State University. He also teaches at the California Institute of Integral Studies. His many books include *In the Company of Sages and Dreamwork* and *Self-Healing: Unfolding the Symbols of the Unconscious*.

www.ingramcontent.com/pod-product-compliance
Lightning Source LLC
Chambersburg PA
CBHW082059230426
43670CB00017B/2889